Preface

머리말

TOEFL iBT의 네 가지 평가 영역인 독해, 청취, 말하기, 쓰기 중에서 읽기는 가장 기본적으로 갖추어야 할 능력이지만, 탄탄한 기초가 없으면 고득점을 받기 힘든 영역이다. 더욱이 독해는 겉에 드러난 사실적인 내용을 이해하는 능력뿐 아니라, 글에 내포된 내용을 추론하는 능력, 글 전체에 대한 종합적인 이해능력 등 고차원적인 사고력이 필요한 영역이다. 그렇기에 기초를 더욱 탄탄하게 쌓아야 TOEFL iBT 독해에서 고득점을 받을 수 있다.

이번에 새롭게 개정한 본 교재는 새로운 디자인과 구성을 통해 보다 충실한 TOEFL iBT 시험 기본 준비서가 될 수 있도록 히었디. 본 교제는 iBT TOEFL 시험을 본격적으로 준비히기 시작히는 중급 영어 수준의 학습자들이 최상의 효과를 낼 수 있도록 설계되었다. 이를 위해 TOEFL iBT 독해에 출제되는 문제 유형을 철저히 분석하여 본 책을 구성하였으며, 학습자들이 개념 정리에서 실전 연습까지 체계적이고 단계적으로 접근할 수 있는, 맛보기 식 학습이 아닌 구체적이고 효율적인 TOEFL iBT 시험 대비서가 되도록 하는 데 중점을 두었다.

이 책이 부디 막연하기만 한 TOEFL iBT 시험 준비에 스마트한 가이드 역할을 할 수 있기를 조심스레 바래 본다.

LinguaForum Research Center

독해 연구팀

Structure

각 장의 구성

Overview

TOEFL *i*BT 독해에 출제되는 각각의 문제 유형과 접근 방법을 알아보고, 그 장에서 중점적으로 학습할 방향과 목표를 파악한다.

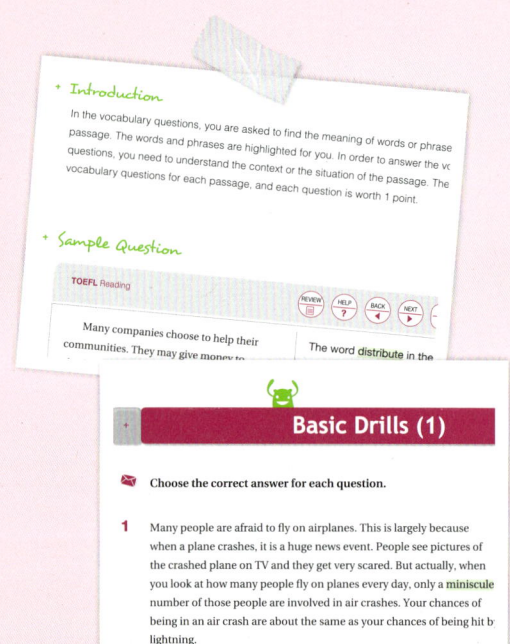

Basic Drills

본격적인 독해 연습에 앞서 비교적 간단한 지문과 함께 다양한 형태의 연습 문제를 풀어보면서, 단계적으로 글을 파악하며 문제를 풀 수 있는 감각을 익힌다.

Reading Practice

실제로 토플 시험에 출제되는 주제로 쓰인 다양한 지문을 읽으며 각 문제 유형을 집중적으로 학습한다. 또한 각 지문에서 사용된 어휘를 확인하고 익혀, 어휘 실력을 쌓는다.

NEW EDITION

M
TOEFL
READING

*i*BT

R

LinguaForum

TOEFL READING New Edition

기획	링구아포럼 기획편집팀		
지은이	링구아포럼 리서치센터 연구팀		
디자인	링구아포럼 디자인팀		
편집인	장기용		
발행인	이길호		
발행처	링구아포럼		
교재문의	02) 3480-6613	대표전화 02) 590-6900	
등록번호	제2000-000335호	등록일자 2000. 5. 17	ISBN 978-89-5563-681-9 (14740)	가격 16,000원

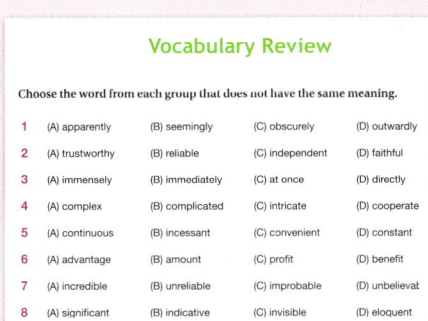

*i*BT Practice

실제 토플 화면과 비슷한 지면에서 여러 유형의 TOEFL 독해 문제를 종합적으로 접해본다. 문제를 풀고 자신의 실력을 테스트해보고 부족한 부분은 보충 학습한다.

Vocabulary Review

각 장에 등장한 어휘를 동의어와 문맥을 통해 복습하며 폭넓은 어휘 실력을 다져본다.

Actual Test

Actual Test 3회분을 실전에 임하는 마음으로 풀어보면서 실전 적응력을 높인다.

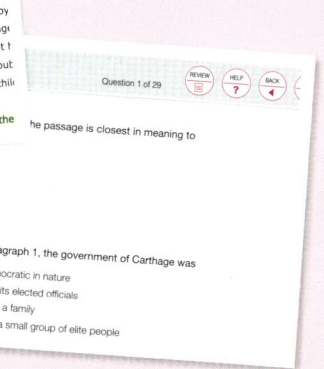

Contents

Basic
Comprehension

This part of the test examines your basic reading comprehension skills. You will be tested on your knowledge of vocabulary, ability to find corresponding ideas, and ability to judge whether statements about the passage are true or false.

PART A

Part **A** +

Vocabulary & Reference

Sentence Simplification

Factual Information & Negative Fact

Part B

Prose Summary

Schematic Table

Part C

Inference

Rhetorical Purpose

Sentence Insertion

Vocabulary

+ **Introduction**

In the vocabulary questions, you are asked to find the meaning of words or phrases in the passage. The words and phrases are highlighted for you. In order to answer the vocabulary questions, you need to understand the context or the situation of the passage. There are 3–5 vocabulary questions for each passage, and each question is worth 1 point.

+ **Sample Question**

TOEFL Reading

    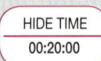

REVIEW   HELP   BACK   NEXT   HIDE TIME 00:20:00

Many companies choose to help their communities. They may give money to charities, or they may **distribute** food to hungry people. There are a number of reasons companies do this. Of course, some companies simply wish to help their community, but in addition to this, it is good advertising for the company.

The word **distribute** in the paragraph is closest in meaning to

(A) prepare

(B) give out

(C) sell

(D) locate

Answer & Explanation

The answer is (B). In the sentence "They may give money to charities or they may distribute food ...," based on its context we can predict that "distribute" has a similar meaning to "give."

+ Strategies

❶ Think about the context.

The meaning of a word or a phrase varies depending on the situation where it is used. Therefore, consider what the passage talks about and what happens in the passage.

e.g. I'm not in the mood for company.

"Company" has a meaning of "firm," but it means "accompanying someone" in this context.

❷ Find the clues hidden in the passage.

- Definition and restatement clues

e.g. US towns spend millions of dollars to repair potholes, *those deep holes in the road*.

- Synonym and antonym clues

e.g. The scientist could transform, *or change*, water into gasoline.

- Example clues

e.g. Natural catastrophes *such as floods, earthquakes, and hurricanes* are causing serious damage around the world.

- Word part (prefix, stem or suffix) clues

e.g. From the words "*pre*pare," "*pre*vent," and "*pre*view," we can predict that "*pre*" means "before."

+ Recognizing the Questions

- The word/phrase _____ in the passage is closest in meaning to
- Based on the information in the passage, the term _____ can best be explained as

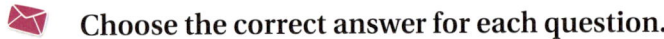
✉ **Choose the correct answer for each question.**

1 Many people are afraid to fly on airplanes. This is largely because when a plane crashes, it is a huge news event. People see pictures of the crashed plane on TV and they get very scared. But actually, when you look at how many people fly on planes every day, only a miniscule number of those people are involved in air crashes. Your chances of being in an air crash are about the same as your chances of being hit by lightning.

☐ be involved in: to experience

Q. The word miniscule in the paragraph is closest in meaning to

(A) frightening
(B) serious
(C) small
(D) unknown

2 Many people tell white lies. A white lie is a lie that is often told to keep from hurting a person's feelings. For example, if a friend buys a new outfit that you think is very ugly, you might tell your friend that you like the outfit rather than hurt your friend's feelings. This would be a white lie. Many people feel it is perfectly acceptable to tell white lies, but I favor honesty in almost every situation.

☐ keep from: to avoid

☐ acceptable: to be morally or socially good enough

Q. In stating favor honesty, the author means that he

(A) dislikes people who tell white lies
(B) does not wish to hurt people's feelings
(C) prefers to tell the truth
(D) does not trust most people

3 As cars get older they cause more air pollution. This is generally because they burn more oil than newer cars, especially if an older car is not kept in good condition. In fact, a car that is five years old can often produce ten times as much air pollution as a new car if it is not kept in good condition. For this reason, most governments require that owners of older cars have an emission test every year. If their car is producing too much pollution and they fail the emission test, the car owner must have his or her car repaired so that it does not burn as much oil.

☐ **produce:** to cause a particular result or effect

☐ **require:** to need someone to do something by law or rule

Q. Based on the information in the paragraph, the term emission test can best be explained as

(A) a test to see if drivers know how to repair their cars
(B) a test to determine the age of a car
(C) a test to make sure a car is not producing too much pollution
(D) a test to determine the skill of a driver

4 One of the most important parts of any prison system is the parole board. Most parole boards are made up of five to seven people, and they have a very tough job. They have to review the behavior of each prisoner and decide whether that prisoner should stay in prison or be released from prison. It is an important decision. The parole board can't let dangerous criminals out of jail because this would put regular citizens at risk.

☐ **be made up of:** to consist of

☐ **release:** to set someone free

Q. Based on the information in the paragraph, the term parole board can best be explained as

(A) prisoners who can safely be released from jail
(B) a group of people who must solve problems with prison overcrowding
(C) prison guards who make sure that dangerous criminals do not escape
(D) a group of people who decide which prisoners may safely be released

5   Do you know anyone who is extremely shy? Is it hard to get them to engage in a conversation? Do they only give short answers, or do they try to end the conversation quickly? Then maybe you know someone with social anxiety disorder. Social anxiety disorder is a mental problem in which a person gets very uncomfortable around other people. It is generally not a serious problem and can usually be treated easily by a psychologist.

□ **extremely:** to a very great degree

□ **social anxiety disorder:** serious fear in social situations

□ **mental:** related to emotions

□ **psychologist:** a medical specialist in mental diseases

Q.   The word engage in the paragraph is closest in meaning to

(A)   avoid
(B)   take part
(C)   enjoy
(D)   listen

6   Many companies these days have several offices in different cities, or even in different countries. This causes problems when the company needs to have a meeting. They may need to have people from their different offices at the meeting, but buying plane tickets to fly all of those people to the meeting would be very expensive. Instead, they hold a conference call. A conference call requires a special telephone line from the phone company. It is much less expensive than buying plane tickets, and it allows the people from different offices to talk as a group without actually being in the same room.

□ **allow:** to make it possible for someone to do something

Q.   Based on the information in the paragraph, the term conference call can best be explained as

(A)   a meeting for an international company
(B)   a telephone call in which more than two people can talk
(C)   a meeting organized by the telephone company
(D)   an inexpensive way to travel to a meeting

1-2 ▶ Reference

+ Introduction

In English, instead of repeating the same nouns or noun phrases, we use reference words. This helps the passage to read better and to flow more smoothly. Pronouns such as *it*, *they*, and *those* are among the most often used reference words.

Reference questions test your ability to figure out what the pronouns, noun phrases, or other reference words refer to in the passage. There are 0–2 reference questions for each passage. Each question is worth 1 point.

+ Sample Question

TOEFL Reading   REVIEW   HELP   BACK   NEXT   HIDE TIME 00:20:00

One of the big improvements in home stereos in the last ten years has been the development of surround sound systems. While a normal stereo has two speakers, a surround sound system has at least four: two in front and two in back. By using a special computer processor, the stereo sends different sounds to the different speakers. People find this most useful when they are watching movies. When they watch a horror movie, they can hear a murderer as **he** walks up behind the victim, and the sound will actually come from behind the listener!

The word **he** in the paragraph refers to

- (A) people
- (B) victim
- (C) murderer
- (D) listener

Answer & Explanation

The answer is (C). "**he**" is a third person subject pronoun used for males, and from the context we can also know that he is someone who follows the victim.

+ Strategies

❶ Understand the different usage of reference words.

When answering this type of question, check to see if the reference words include any features of:

- persons or objects
- gender (male, female, or neutral)
- singular or plural

List of Pronouns

Subjective	he	she	it	they
Objective	him	her	it	them
Possessive	his	her	its	their
Demonstrative	this	that	these	those
Relative	who	whom	which	whose
Other	all another any both	most a few many either	none one some neither	the first the last the other each

❷ Remember referents can be located anywhere.

Referents are the words that references refer to. Check the surroundings of the reference words. Referents can be close, far, before, or behind the reference words.

e.g. In his closet, Calvin found the diary he used to keep.

❸ Note the reference words may refer to parts of a sentence or a whole sentence.

e.g. You eat greasy food too much. That's why you are so fat.

❹ Double-check to see if the sentence still makes sense.

+ Recognizing the Questions

- The word _____ in the passage refers to

- The phrase _____ in the passage refers to

Basic Drills (2)

 Choose the correct answer for each question.

1 In Norway, there are only about three hours of darkness during the summer and only about three hours of daylight during the winter. (1) **This** is because of the way the Earth tilts. During the summer the northern part of the world is closest to the sun, and during the winter (2) **it** is the farthest away. That means that the amount of light that reaches there changes greatly during different times of the year.

☐ **tilt:** to move something into a position where one side is higher than the other

☐ **reach:** to arrive at

Q. Underline the parts these words refer to

(1) This
(2) it

2 In Pakistan and Afghanistan, people play an interesting sport. (1) **They** have kite battles. In a kite battle, people fly kites with a special kind of string which has tiny pieces of broken glass glued to it. The pieces of glass are about as small as pieces of sand, but (2) **they** are quite sharp. During the battle, the objective is to cut the string of the other person's kite. (3) **This** is done by flying your kite around the other person's in a circle. Once your string is wrapped around theirs, the glass on it will cut their string. The winner of the kite battle is the last person whose kite is still in the air.

☐ **battle:** a fight or a competition

☐ **objective:** a goal, a target

☐ **string:** a strong thread

Q. Underline the parts these words refer to

(1) They
(2) they
(3) This

Basic Drills (3)

✉ **Choose the correct answer for each question.**

1   Before the invention of the air conditioner, which was invented in 1901, people had to find other ways to deal with the heat during the summer. One such way was to simply do less during the summer. In fact, this is the reason that schools have summer vacation. Back in those days, it was simply too hot to have school in the summer.

☐ **invention:** making a new type of things

☐ **deal with:** to handle

Q. The phrase those days in the paragraph refers to

(A) 1901
(B) the time before the invention of the air conditioner
(C) the time when schools went on break
(D) the hottest part of the summer

2   Over the last twenty years, security cameras have become a part of daily life. They are in elevators, in parking garages, even on the streets. Of course, a security camera is only useful if there is a guard watching it, and there are definitely more cameras in our world than there are guards. That is why many of the security cameras you see are not actually real. They look like cameras, but they do not actually work. They are only there to make people think that they are being watched. Since criminals don't know which cameras are real and which ones are not, the fake cameras work just as well as the real ones!

☐ **security cameras:** cameras to monitor any illegal activities

☐ **criminal:** someone who is involved in illegal activities

☐ **fake:** not real

Q. The word ones in the paragraph refers to

(A) criminals
(B) security guards
(C) security cameras
(D) people

3 Almost everyone I know likes Tony a great deal, despite the fact that he is always late. I suppose the reason for this is that he always has such amusing reasons for why he's late. I've heard a great number of them because I've been friends with Tony since we were kids. I almost used to look forward to him being late just so I could hear what his excuse would be. I heard the best of these reasons from him last year. We were going to a Christmas party and he was late, of course. He said that he was really sorry but that he had been trying to get his father out of the chimney! Apparently his father had dressed up as Santa to surprise Tony's little brother and gotten stuck as he came down the fireplace!

☐ **despite:** in spite of

☐ **chimney:** a long, standing pipe that allows smoke from a fire to pass out

☐ **apparently:** seemingly

Q. The phrase **these reasons** in the paragraph refers to the reasons why

(A) most people like Tony

(B) Tony was late for the Christmas party

(C) Tony is late

(D) the author looks forward to Tony being late

4 When Jack was arrested for stealing, we were shocked. Jack had been our friend for years, and he had always been reliable and trustworthy. I immediately thought of the time we had found a wallet on the ground and Jack had insisted that we find the owner and return it. The police said that they had good evidence against him, but we still believed he was innocent. We simply did not believe he could be such a person.

☐ **reliable:** dependable

☐ **trustworthy:** can be trusted or depended on

☐ **immediately:** very soon, without delay

Q. The phrase **such a person** in the paragraph refers to a person who

(A) is reliable and trustworthy

(B) would become a police officer

(C) would return a wallet

(D) would steal

The Berlin Wall

After Germany surrendered at the end of World War II, the allied nations (Britain, France, the United States, and the Soviet Union) took control of the capital city of Berlin. At first, they agreed to run the city
5 • in **partnership**, but as the Cold War started to unfold, that agreement quickly broke down. The Soviet Union took control of the eastern side of the city and the US, France, and Britain took control of the western side.

Many Germans living in East Berlin left, preferring to live in West Berlin, which had a democratic
10 • government rather than a communist one. In response, the government of East Germany built a wall separating the two sides of the city.

This wall, known as the Berlin wall, had a **significant** impact on the lives of the people of Berlin. The wall made travel between the two sides of Berlin almost impossible. No one was allowed through the wall unless they had a permit from the governments of both sides of the
15 • wall. Anyone crossing without **these papers** was likely to be shot by the soldiers who guarded the wall at all times. The wall separated many families, and people who had held jobs on the other side of the city lost their jobs and had to find new work. Despite the hardships that it created for Germans on both sides of the wall, the Berlin wall stood for almost thirty years. For many people, the Berlin wall became the most visible symbol of the Cold War and the distrust between the US
20 • and the Soviet Union. When the wall was taken down in 1989, it seemed that the Cold War was finally at an end as well.

1 The word **partnership** in the passage is closest in meaning to

(A) cooperation

(B) peace

(C) democracy

(D) responsibility

2 The word **significant** in the passage is closest in meaning to

(A) terrible

(B) sad

(C) important

(D) immediate

3 The phrase **these papers** in the passage refers to

(A) papers separating the families

(B) permits allowing people to cross the wall

(C) orders instructing the soldiers to guard the wall

(D) the design plans of the wall

Find the right word from the passage!

❶ _____ countries, troops, or political parties are united by a political or military agreement.

❷ Socialist, Marxist: _____

❸ Sudden and powerful effect on a situation, process, or person: _____

❹ A situation in which your life is difficult or unpleasant: _____

Conflict Diamonds

Africa is home to some of the poorest nations in the world. Ironically, many of the poorest nations in Africa hold some of the world's greatest natural resources. Sierra Leone, Liberia, Angola, and Congo are all rich in diamonds, but most of the citizens in these nations live lives of poverty and fear. This is true because in each case, the nation's wealth of natural resources has helped to
5 • fuel conflicts which are both brutal and bloody. Both rebel groups and the governments in these nations use the profits from diamond sales to buy weapons and supply their armies, and the conflicts are now essentially fought over the control of the diamond trade. In such situations, the citizens of these nations are the victims. Not only are many innocent people killed in the fighting, the conflict also prevents the country from developing. Schools are destroyed and not rebuilt,
10 • and clean water and electricity are often lacking. Without such basic services, disease and hunger spread throughout the country.

While the governments and the rebels who actually do the fighting hold much of the responsibility for the suffering of their citizens, developed countries are also to blame. The diamonds
15 • from these countries, often called conflict diamonds, are sold in jewelry shops across Europe and the United States. The money from these diamond sales simply ensures that the wars will continue. In an effort to stop this, the United Nations has passed agreements under which advanced nations agree not to
20 • buy diamonds from conflict areas. This way, these terrible wars will perhaps come to an end.

1 In stating that natural resources **fuel conflicts**, the author means that natural resources

(A) start arguments
(B) support wars
(C) add to suffering
(D) help governments

2 The phrase **such basic services** in the passage refers to services like

(A) hospitals
(B) energy and public health
(C) the operation of diamond mines
(D) supplying the army

3 The word **ensures** in the passage is closest in meaning to

(A) guarantees
(B) requests
(C) provides
(D) continues

Find the right word from the passage!

❶ The state of being extremely poor: _____

❷ People who oppose some of their own country's policies: _____

❸ Cruel and violent: _____

❹ Serious disagreement or argument about something important: _____

The Caste System

Most modern societies believe that all men and women deserve equal rights, but this has not always been the case. For much of the history of mankind, societies have separated themselves into

5 • different groups, some of which have more power and privileges than others. In the most extreme form, these groups become castes. A caste is a social group that a person is born into. Once in a certain

social caste, a person usually cannot move into a different one. Many ancient societies had caste

10 • systems. The Greeks and the Romans had simple caste systems. In Rome, the higher caste was called the Patricians* and the lower class was the Plebeians*. Only Patricians could serve in the army or work in government. Plebeians were basically servants and worked for the Patricians.

Perhaps the most complex caste system in history existed in ancient India. The caste system in India consisted of five separate castes. Each caste had certain jobs that only they were

15 • allowed to do. They even had separate diets. In fact, one's caste controlled almost every part of a person's life, from where you could live to whom you could marry. Members of the highest caste in India were the priests and scholars. Members of the lowest caste were called the untouchables. Untouchables held the lowest jobs in Indian society, such as cleaning the streets and sewers. Because their jobs were considered dirty, they were not allowed to come into contact with people

20 • of other castes. Untouchables could not even drink out of the village well. The caste system still exists in some parts of India, especially in the countryside where traditional beliefs are still strong. In most parts of modern India, however, the caste system is growing less and less important.

☐ Patricians: elite Roman citizens with special status
☐ Plebeians: ordinary people

1 The word privileges in the passage is closest in meaning to

(A) rights

(B) money

(C) respect

(D) duties

2 The word scholars in the passage is closest in meaning to

(A) kings

(B) monks

(C) doctors

(D) academics

3 The word their in the passage refers to

(A) lowest jobs

(B) Indian society

(C) untouchables

(D) castes

Find the right word from the passage!

❶ Very great or unusual in degree:_____

❷ Belonging to the distant past:_____

❸ A religious leader:_____

❹ A large underground channel that carries waste matter and rain water away:_____

The Olmec Mother Culture

The best-known Native American civilizations are probably those of the Aztecs and the Mayans, who lived in Mexico and Central America about 1,500 to 1,000 years ago. But the mother culture for both of these kingdoms was the Olmec society, which occupied the same land nearly 1,000 years before either kingdom. The Olmecs were similar to the Aztecs and the Mayans in many ways. Like these later cultures, the Olmecs were excellent builders and artisans. They created the first pyramids in the Americas and probably the first large cities as well.

Olmec society was tightly structured. It was ruled by a small class of priests and nobles, while the other members of society were little more than slaves for this upper class, and were cruelly oppressed. The Olmecs had three large cities, each of which was placed in a location designed to take advantage of a different group of natural resources. Each one was centered around a pyramid, which was the focus of religious and social life in the city. We know that the Olmecs practiced human sacrifice at these pyramids because researchers have discovered the skeletons of the sacrificial victims. Unlike the Aztecs, however, who generally sacrificed warriors to their gods, most of the sacrificial victims of the Olmecs seem to have been the elderly or young children. It is unknown why the Olmecs chose these people as their sacrificial victims, but it is known that most of them were sacrificed as an offering to their main god, a half-human, half-jaguar spirit.

Although their society was cruel and oppressive, the Olmecs brought many inventions to the Americas. Not only did they build the first pyramids in the Western Hemisphere, but they also introduced the first writing systems and the first calendars. All of these inventions were later copied by the Mayans and the Aztecs. While the Olmecs are not as well-known as the Aztecs or the Mayans, theirs was truly one of the great civilizations of the ancient Americas.

1 Based on the information in paragraph 1, the term mother culture can best be explained as

(A) a very ancient culture

(B) a Central American culture

(C) a culture on which later cultures are based

(D) a culture which is similar to other cultures

2 The word artisans in the passage is closest in meaning to

(A) craftsmen

(B) politicians

(C) warriors

(D) scientists

3 The word one in the passage refers to

(A) city

(B) location

(C) natural resource

(D) Olmec

4 The word focus in the passage is closest in meaning to

(A) place

(B) center

(C) importance

(D) requirement

5 The phrase practiced human sacrifice in the passage refers that the Olmecs

(A) held dangerous jobs

(B) suffered from deadly diseases

(C) killed people as offerings to their gods

(D) worshiped their dead ancestors

6 The phrase these people in the passage refers to

(A) warriors

(B) the Olmecs

(C) the elderly and young children

(D) the Aztecs

iBT Practice 2

Language Families

Historians have always faced one particular difficulty. The earliest societies to read and write seem to have surfaced around 5,000 years ago. How could historians learn about earlier ones that had no written records? To make the problem even more difficult, most of the physical evidence which scientists normally use to learn about a society, such as the remains of houses and tools, no longer exists for these early societies. And yet scientists have managed to learn a great deal about these early societies. What has made this possible is the study of languages.

As you probably know, many languages have words that appear to be quite similar. For example, "police" in English is the same as "policia" in Spanish. By studying these similarities, we know that some languages are related; that is, they all come from an earlier common language. One example of this would be Spanish, French, and Italian, which all came from an earlier language, Latin. If different groups of people have a common ancestral language, we can guess that they also had a common group of ancestors. By tracing these language families back thousands of years, we can trace back to our earliest ancestors.

One of the largest language families is the Indo-European language family. Today the Indo-European language family consists of 431 languages. Over three billion people speak those languages, and they are spread all over the world. But 7,000 years ago, they all had a common group of ancestors who spoke the same language and lived together in a single society. Over many years, that society separated and moved into new areas, and that single Indo-European language slowly changed into the hundreds of different languages they speak today.

Studying languages can tell us much more than simply what groups of people have common ancestors. It can also tell us what the lives of those common ancestors were like. By studying what kinds of words the languages in a language family have in common, we can learn a great deal about our early ancestors. For example, we know that the Indo-Europeans rode horses, were herders and shepherds (they raised cows and sheep), wrote poems about the battles they fought, and worshiped a sky deity. And we know all of this just by studying the words we speak every day!

1 The author uses the word particular to indicate that the difficulty was

   (A) impossible to solve
   (B) specific
   (C) important
   (D) unique

2 The word surfaced in the passage is closest in meaning to

   (A) communicated
   (B) existed
   (C) appeared
   (D) invented

3 The word ones in the passage refers to

   (A) historians
   (B) societies
   (C) languages
   (D) difficulties

4 Based on the information in paragraphs 3 and 4, the term language families can best be explained as

   (A) the groups of people who speak a language
   (B) languages that came from Latin
   (C) languages that all developed from a common ancestral language
   (D) the common ancestors who spoke our languages

5 The word they in the passage refers to

   (A) people who speak different languages
   (B) common ancestors
   (C) speakers of languages in the Indo-European language family
   (D) scientists researching languages

6 The phrase worshiped a sky deity in the passage refers that the Indo-Europeans

   (A) studied the weather
   (B) respected the sky and the stars
   (C) prayed to a sky god
   (D) took care of their environment

Vocabulary Review

Choose the word from each group that does not have the same meaning.

1   (A) apparently   (B) seemingly   (C) obscurely   (D) outwardly

2   (A) trustworthy   (B) reliable   (C) independent   (D) faithful

3   (A) immensely   (B) immediately   (C) at once   (D) directly

4   (A) complex   (B) complicated   (C) intricate   (D) cooperate

5   (A) continuous   (B) incessant   (C) convenient   (D) constant

6   (A) advantage   (B) amount   (C) profit   (D) benefit

7   (A) incredible   (B) unreliable   (C) improbable   (D) unbelievable

8   (A) significant   (B) indicative   (C) invisible   (D) eloquent

Fill in the blank with the correct word from the box.

objective	visible	trustworthy	extreme
conflict	acceptable	innocent	outfit

9   It has become a lot more _____ for women to be lawyers and doctors.

10   I like your _____ today. Where did you buy that sweater and pants?

11   I don't think what you are talking about is generally true. It is just a(n) _____ case.

12   The neon signs were clearly _____ even in the far distance.

13   The main _____ of this exercise is to improve your vocabulary.

14   He is a real good friend of mine, and he is always reliable and _____.

15   The _____ between my two close friends lasted for a long time and made me very uncomfortable.

16   They all thought he was guilty, but I believed he was _____ and was just trapped by the situation.

Part **A** +

Vocabulary & Reference

Sentence Simplification

Factual Information & Negative Fact

Part B

Prose Summary

Schematic Table

Part C

Inference

Rhetorical Purpose

Sentence Insertion

Sentence Simplification

+ Introduction

Sentence simplification questions ask you to find the best restatement of key information from long and complex sentences. To answer this type of question, a broad knowledge of English grammar and a high level of paraphrasing skills are needed. There is usually 1 sentence simplification question for each passage. This question is worth 1 point.

+ Sample Question

TOEFL Reading

REVIEW | HELP | BACK | NEXT | HIDE TIME 00:20:00

For 160,000 years the Neanderthals, a species of early human, hunted and moved across Europe and Central Asia. Then, about 40,000 years ago, a new kind of man appeared. This new kind of man, modern man, was smaller than the Neanderthals, but being a bit smarter, made better tools and hunted more effectively. The new humans slowly pushed the Neanderthals out of their hunting territories and took over.

Which of the sentences below best expresses the essential information in the highlighted sentence in the passage? *Incorrect* choices change the meaning in important ways or leave out essential information.

(A) Although they were smaller, by being smarter, modern men were able to make better tools and hunt more effectively than Neanderthals.

(B) By being smaller and smarter than the Neanderthals, modern men were able to make better tools and hunt more effectively.

(C) Modern men were smaller than the Neanderthals, so they had to be smarter in order to make tools and hunt effectively.

(D) This new kind of man, modern man, was smaller than the Neanderthals but made better tools and hunted more effectively.

Answer & Explanation

The answer is (A). The highlighted sentence can be broken into three meaningful parts. "This new kind of man, modern man, was smaller than the Neanderthals, / but being a bit smarter, / made better tools and hunted more effectively." Only (A) contains all three of them.

+ Strategies

❶ Understand the exact meaning of the highlighted sentence.

- Divide the sentence based on the unit of meaning.

  e.g. He is quite good-looking, / but he's not very kind.

- Check what the reference words refer to. (If any)

  e.g. Culture consists of the language and values that define a society. These can be spread from one society to another through cultural contact.

❷ Eliminate the answer choices which:

- include only part of key information

- contain details that are not mentioned in the sentence

- mistate the relationship between the ideas

❸ Remember that paraphrasing is generally done by:

- changing the grammatical structure

  e.g. Unlike concrete and asphalt, which reflect a great deal of the sun's heat, natural surfaces such as grass and water absorb that heat, making these areas much cooler.

  → Grass and water, which are natural surfaces, are cooler because they absorb much of the sun's heat, while concrete and asphalt reflect that heat.

OR

- using synonyms or restatements.

  e.g. Every great jazz player knows that the unexpected is a key ingredient of jazz.

  → Every great jazz musician knows that surprise is an essential element of jazz.

+ Recognizing the Questions

> Which of the following best expresses the essential information in the highlighted sentence? *Incorrect* answer choices change the meaning in important ways or leave out essential information.

Basic Drills (1)

✉ **Read the sentences below and select the answer choice that correctly paraphrases each sentence.**

1 Although the weatherman called for clear skies and comfortable temperatures, I took an umbrella just to be sure.

(A) Although the weatherman requested good weather, I took an umbrella anyway.
(B) Although the weatherman called and said the weather would be good, I took an umbrella just in case.
(C) I took an umbrella just in case the weatherman called for good weather.
(D) I took an umbrella just in case, although the weatherman had predicted good weather.

☐ **call for** (=predict): to say something will happen

☐ **request:** to ask for politely

☐ **just in case:** in case something might happen

2 Spanglish, primarily spoken along the border of the US and Mexico, is a mixture of both the English and Spanish languages.

(A) Mainly used along the border of the US and Mexico, Spanglish is a combination of English and Spanish.
(B) Along the border of the US and Mexico, the English and Spanish languages are mixed with Spanglish.
(C) The Spanglish, who primarily live along the border of the US and Mexico, speak a mixture of English and Spanish.
(D) Spanglish mixes languages primarily along the border of the US and Mexico.

☐ **primarily:** mainly

☐ **border:** the official line between two countries

☐ **mixture:** a combination of two or more things

3 Bob Marley's music was highly political and critical of the Jamaican government, which made him their number-one target.

(A) Bob Marley was highly critical of the Jamaican government in his music because they had made him their number-one target.
(B) Bob Marley was number one in the Jamaican government, which made his music highly political.
(C) Bob Marley spoke out against the Jamaican government in his music, and was their number-one target as a result.
(D) The Jamaican government targeted Bob Marley's music because he was highly critical of them.

☐ **critical:** to be doubtful about other's ideas or opinions

Basic Drills (2)

 Which of the sentences below best expresses the essential information in the highlighted sentences in the paragraph? *Incorrect* **choices change the meaning in important ways or leave out essential information.**

Animals have all kinds of ways to defend themselves. ❶ Some animals can change their color instantly, an ability they use to hide from their enemies. The most famous example is the chameleon. The chameleon has special chemicals in its skin that let it change the color of its body. When sitting on a tree limb, a chameleon might be a dark brown. But when standing on a leaf, it might be a bright green color. Many deep sea fish also have this ability, and can change their color to match their surroundings. ❷ These animals also use their color changes as a form of communication, showing fear or anger through a series of quick color changes.

☐ **instantly:** quickly, immediately

☐ **limb:** a large branch of a tree

☐ **surroundings:** background

☐ **as a form of:** as a way of

1   (A)   Animals with the ability to hide from their enemies can change their color instantly.

      (B)   Some animals have special abilities, like changing their color or hiding from their enemies.

      (C)   By changing their color instantly, some animals instantly hide from their enemies.

      (D)   Some animals have the ability to change color instantly, which they use to hide from their enemies.

2   (A)   When these animals are afraid or angry, they can go through a series of quick color changes.

      (B)   These animals use their color changes to communicate, and express fear and anger through rapid shifts in color.

      (C)   These animals can use their color changes to communicate, but quick changes in color make them angry and afraid.

      (D)   Quick changes in color help communicate with animals that are feeling angry or afraid.

❸ During the Cold War, the CIA had a number of people in Russia and East Germany working as spies whose job was to get information on the militaries of these countries. Getting the information was hard enough, but getting it out of the country and back to the CIA was even harder. To do this, they used a special type of film called a microdot. A microdot is very small, as small as the period at the end of this sentence. The spy would take pictures of whatever information he or she had to send back to the CIA. ❹ Having hidden the microdot in a letter as one of the periods, they would send the letter to another CIA worker in the US. This ingenious invention helped countless spies complete their missions.

□ **the military:** the army, the armed forces

□ **microdot:** a very small photograph which carries secret information

□ **period:** a dot

□ **ingenious:** clever, smart, creative

□ **countless:** a lot of

3 (A) The CIA spied on the Russians and East Germans whose job was to get information on the military.

(B) The CIA employed many spies to get information on the militaries of Russia and East Germany during the Cold War.

(C) Russia and East Germany's militaries had a number of spies to get information on the CIA during the Cold War.

(D) Getting information on Russia and East Germany was the job of the CIA and the military during the Cold War.

4 (A) If they had a microdot, they would hide it in a letter and send it to another CIA employee in the US.

(B) CIA workers in the US regularly hide microdots in their letters as periods.

(C) They would send letters with a microdot hidden as one of the periods to other CIA workers in the US.

(D) CIA workers in the US knew to look for microdots at the ends of the letters they received.

❺ The first attempt to measure how smart a person was came with the Intelligence Quotient, or IQ test, which determines a person's intelligence level by testing his or her ability to recognize patterns and solve problems. In an IQ test, there are no questions about history or science; no special information is needed. Therefore, a person who has not gone to school should be able to take the test just as easily as a college graduate. ❻ But over the last two decades, more and more scientists have become dissatisfied with the IQ test, and have started looking for a new way to test intelligence. The most common complaint about the IQ test is that it only tests for certain abilities. For example, a person who is good at math may do very well on the IQ test. But is this the only way a person can be intelligent? Many scientists no longer think so.

□ **attempt:** a try

□ **measure:** to judge or to calculate

□ **graduate:** someone who has completed a course at a college, school, etc.

□ **decade:** a period of 10 years

□ **dissatisfied with~:** not pleased with

□ **complaint:** expression of dissatisfaction

5 (A) The IQ test was the first attempt to test the ability of intelligent people to solve problems.

(B) Measuring the intelligence of a person was first attempted by testing the ability to solve problems and recognize patterns.

(C) The IQ test, which tests problem solving and the recognition of patterns, was the first attempt to measure intelligence.

(D) The IQ test determines a person's intelligence by testing his or her ability to solve problems and recognize patterns.

6 (A) Scientists who are dissatisfied with the IQ test have been looking for a new way to test intelligence for over two decades.

(B) However, some scientists have grown unhappy with the IQ test over the last twenty years and have started looking for alternatives to the test.

(C) Scientists have developed new ways to test intelligence because they have been dissatisfied with the IQ test for two decades.

(D) The dissatisfaction of scientists with the IQ test lasted two decades, until they found new ways to test intelligence.

Slaves for Plantations

From the late 1500s to the early 1800s, European nations ran a huge number of plantations, farms that relied on slave labor, in the New World. While this took place in almost every European colony, it was most common in Caribbean islands like the Bahamas. It was on these islands that the Europeans ran their sugar cane plantations. Highly profitable for the plantation owners, sugar cane was the backbone of the slave economy, but it took a terrible toll on the African slaves who actually did the work. For a slave, being sent to a sugar plantation was practically a death sentence.

To make up for the high death rate among their slaves, the Europeans had to constantly bring new slaves from Africa. This led to one of the most horrible aspects of slavery in the Americas, the Middle Passage. After slaves were bought or captured in Africa, they had to be transported by ship to the Americas. This trip was known as the Middle Passage.

Packed side by side on a slave ship, the slaves were kept in chains for the entire duration of the trip, which could last anywhere from one to six months depending on the weather. They were fed just enough food to keep them alive. This served two purposes. Not only did it allow slave  traders to keep their costs down, the near starvation of the slaves also kept them so weak that they had little chance of resisting during the Middle Passage. Under such horrible conditions, it is not surprising that the death rate on the Middle Passage was often higher than the death rate on the plantations themselves. It is estimated that of the 20 million slaves taken from Africa, nearly half of them died before they ever reached the Americas.

✉ **The sentences below are from the passage you just read. Which answer choice expresses the same basic idea?**

1 Highly profitable for the plantation owners, sugar cane was the backbone of the slave economy, but it took a terrible toll on the African slaves who actually did the work.

(A) Although they were highly profitable and formed the basis of the slave economy, sugar cane plantations killed many slaves.

(B) In order to make sugar cane plantations profitable, plantation owners took heavy tolls from their slaves.

(C) Although it formed the backbone of the slave economy, sugar cane was only profitable when it took a high toll on African slaves.

(D) Working on sugar plantations took a high toll on the backbones of slaves because it was highly profitable for slave owners.

2 Not only did it allow slave traders to keep their costs down, the near starvation of the slaves also kept them so weak that they had little chance of resisting during the Middle Passage.

(A) Not only did slave traders try to keep their costs down, they also starved any slaves who tried to resist during the Middle Passage.

(B) By starving the slaves during the Middle Passage, slave owners were able to reduce their expenses and prevent rebellion on the ship.

(C) To keep their costs down, slave traders only took slaves who were near starvation and had little chance of resisting during the Middle Passage.

(D) Weaker slaves had little chance to resist the near-starvation that the slave traders used to keep their costs down.

Find the right word from the passage! ✏

❶ Almost, but not completely or exactly: _____

❷ To take something from one place to another in a vehicle: _____

❸ To make an approximate judgment or calculation of a quantity: _____

❹ The time during which something happens or exists: _____

❺ Extreme hunger, caused by lack of food: _____

Potential Dangers at Old Homes

For a number of reasons, many people choose to buy an older home rather than a new home. They may be attracted to the lower cost of an older home, or perhaps they enjoy the history associated with owning
5 • an older home. When buying an older home, however, people must be aware of the potential dangers they are exposing themselves to.

The main danger is the possible presence of asbestos in the home. Asbestos is material which is highly resistant to fire. Because of this property, asbestos was commonly used as a
10 • construction material. The problem is that over time, asbestos breaks apart into tiny airborne dust particles, which then can enter our lungs. Once in the lungs, asbestos is known to cause many serious diseases, most notably cancer. While the use of asbestos in building construction is now banned in most countries, the material is present in almost any building that was built before the 1980s. Asbestos can be removed from older buildings, but it is a costly procedure. In
15 • most cases, if asbestos is present in a building, it is covered with another material to prevent it from entering the air, although this is only effective as long as the building remains in one piece. When the building is demolished, or when serious work is done on the building, asbestos can once again be a danger.

Another common health danger in older homes is the presence of lead. Lead was an
20 • ingredient in many paints until 1978 in the US, and even later in some countries. Lead becomes a danger when paint containing lead breaks off the walls and is eaten. This is primarily a danger to small children, who do not know any better than to eat paint chips. Once it has been eaten, lead causes severe learning disabilities. As with asbestos, lead paint can be removed from a building, but again it can be costly to do so.

The sentences below are from the passage you just read. Which answer choice expresses the same basic idea?

1 The problem is that over time asbestos breaks apart into tiny airborne dust particles, which then can enter our lungs.

(A) Asbestos breaks apart if it becomes dusty, and can then enter our lungs, where it causes problems.

(B) Over time, dust particles in the air become a problem when they enter our lungs.

(C) Asbestos becomes a problem when it breaks apart, enters the air, and then enters our lungs.

(D) Tiny dust particles are problems because they can break up asbestos and then enter our lungs.

2 In most cases, if asbestos is present in a building, it is covered with another material to prevent it from entering the air, although this is only effective as long as the building remains in one piece.

(A) When asbestos is present in a building, keeping the building in one piece is the only effective method of preventing it from entering the air.

(B) If asbestos is present in a building, covering it with another material is effective in preventing it from entering the air in most cases.

(C) In most cases, asbestos is prevented from entering the air by covering it with another material and keeping the building in one piece.

(D) If a building contains asbestos, it is usually covered with another material to prevent it from entering the air, but this only works if the building remains in one piece.

Find the right word from the passage!

❶ To cause you to like or admire someone or something: _____

❷ Having the possibility to cause a particular effect: _____

❸ If you are _____ of something, you know about it.

❹ To destroy something completely: _____

The Moors in Spain

During the 16th and 17th centuries, Spain was widely known as the most Catholic of countries. It was in Spain that there was the strongest resistance to the Protestant Reformation. In the New World, it was again Spain that was the most active in converting native peoples to Christianity. This is in some sense ironic, because Spain was under Muslim control for much of its early history.

In 711, the Moors, Muslims from Northwestern Africa, invaded Europe. They quickly swept through the territory of Spain, which was ruled by a number of small, disorganized kingdoms, and pushed all the way into France before they were stopped by the Christian armies of northern Europe. The Moors were firmly in control of most of southern Spain, and remained so for hundreds of years. Under the Moors, Spain was controlled by the Umayyad Dynasty, a line of kings with loose connections to the Islamic kingdoms of the Middle East.

Under the Umayyad Dynasty, Spain made great advances, as the Moors preserved much of the knowledge of ancient Greece and Rome, which had been lost in the rest of Europe. Thus, it was easily the most culturally and artistically advanced part of Europe. The Moors built beautiful mosques and palaces in Spain, many of which still stand. Their art from this period is highly valued as well. The Moorish culture in Spain reached its height in the 11th century. After that, the Umayyad Dynasty broke up into smaller kingdoms, which were eventually defeated by the Christian kingdoms of the North. Their influence, however, can still be seen in Spain. One only has to look at the architecture in any major city in southern Spain.

✉ **The sentences below are from the passage you just read. Which answer choice expresses the same basic idea?**

1 They quickly swept through the territory of Spain, which was ruled by a number of small, disorganized kingdoms, and pushed all the way into France before they were stopped by the Christian armies of northern Europe.

(A) Ruled by a number of small disorganized kingdoms, the Moors quickly swept through Spain and were stopped by the Christian armies of northern Europe after having pushed all the way into France.

(B) The Moors quickly swept through Spain's territory, but the Christian armies of northern Europe stopped them before they pushed into France.

(C) The Moors easily conquered all of Spain, which had no large, unified government, and advanced as far as France before being stopped by the Christian armies of northern Europe.

(D) After being stopped in France by the Christian armies of northern Europe, the Moors quickly swept through Spain, which was smaller and more disorganized.

2 Under the Umayyad Dynasty, Spain made great advances, as the Moors preserved much of the knowledge of ancient Greece and Rome, which had been lost in the rest of Europe.

(A) With the Umayyad Dynasty (which kept alive much of the learning of ancient Greece and Rome that had been lost in the West) in control, Spain prospered.

(B) The Moors preserved much of the knowledge of ancient Greece and Rome, so Spain made greater advances than the Umayyad Dynasty.

(C) The knowledge of ancient Greece and Rome, which had been lost in Europe, made great advances under the Umayyad Dynasty.

(D) Spain made great advances under the Umayyad Dynasty and helped the Moors to preserve much of the knowledge of ancient Greece and Rome before it was lost in Europe.

Find the right word from the passage! ✏

❶ To change religious or political beliefs: _____

❷ Not arranged or planned in a clear order: _____

❸ Progress in understanding or in doing something well: _____

❹ At the end of a situation or process: _____

 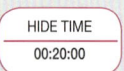
Climate Changes and Human Evolution

Scientists have long known that temperature helps control the body size and shape of animals, including humans. This can be stated in three simple laws. Allen's Law states that, within a species, animals living closer to the equator will have longer arms and legs. Bergman's Law states that animals within the same species living in northern climates will generally have

5 • larger, heavier bodies. Finally, Gloger's Law states that animals within the same species living closer to the equator will have darker skin coloration than those living in far northern or far southern climates.

All three of these laws seem relatively logical because all three physical characteristics directly relate to the conservation or loss of body heat. Animals with long arms and legs lose

10 • body heat more quickly than animals with shorter arms and legs. Larger, heavier animals generate more heat than smaller ones. And darker skin adds extra protection from the sun's rays, which are stronger near the equator. While these laws have been accepted as fact for a great while, scientists are now beginning to suspect that climate and climate change have a far greater impact on evolution, particularly human evolution, than previously thought.

15 • Scientists now believe that rapid changes in climate played an essential role in the evolution of early humans, and specifically in the evolution of more complex brains. The most compelling evidence for this comes from Africa, where our earliest ancestors began to evolve over 2 million years ago. Scientists found that from 3 million to 1 million years ago, Africa's climate underwent rapid and serious changes, especially in the amount of rainfall received.

20 • The timing of these changes closely matches important steps in human evolution, suggesting that it was these climate changes that prompted these steps.

Specifically, scientists believe that the climate changes were so rapid and serious that only the smartest of our ancestors could adapt and survive. According to this theory, the need to find new ways to live in a new climate pushed the brains of early humans to grow larger and

25 • more complex. There is a lot of evidence for this. These periods of rapid climate change were when early humans began making stone tools and when they started organized group hunts for large animals, both of which are signs of the growing intelligence which defines modern man.

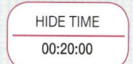
1 The phrase **three physical characteristics** in the passage refers to the characteristics of

Ⓐ climates in different locations
Ⓑ the three evolutionary laws
Ⓒ the bodies of animal species
Ⓓ the equator of the Earth

2 The word **conservation** in the passage is closest in meaning to

Ⓐ addition
Ⓑ production
Ⓒ reduction
Ⓓ saving

3 Which of the sentences below best expresses the essential information in the highlighted sentence in paragraph 2? *Incorrect* choices change the meaning in important ways or leave out essential information.

Ⓐ While these laws have been accepted as fact for a long time, scientists now think that climate is as important in evolution as these three laws.

Ⓑ For a long time, these laws have been accepted as fact, but scientists are now beginning to believe that changes in weather patterns play a larger part in evolution than they thought.

Ⓒ While these laws used to be accepted as fact, scientists now believe that the impact of evolution on climate change is greater than they previously thought.

Ⓓ Human evolution is thought to be controlled by these three laws, although scientists suspect that climate change plays a role as well.

4 The phrase **most compelling** in the passage is closest in meaning to

Ⓐ strongest
Ⓑ most interesting
Ⓒ easiest to understand
Ⓓ most recent

TOEFL Reading

REVIEW
HELP ?
BACK ◀
NEXT ▶
HIDE TIME 00:20:00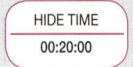

5 The phrase **these steps** in the passage refers to

   Ⓐ important steps in climate change
   Ⓑ important steps in human evolution
   Ⓒ important steps in receiving rainfall
   Ⓓ important steps in scientific theories

6 Which of the sentences below best expresses the essential information in the highlighted sentence in paragraph 4? *Incorrect* choices change the meaning in important ways or leave out essential information.

   Ⓐ These periods of climate change only occurred when humans used their growing intelligence to make stone tools and hunt in groups.
   Ⓑ The production of stone tools and hunting in teams, both of which are indications of the higher intelligence that characterizes modern man, began during these periods of climate change.
   Ⓒ When the climate began to change, humans used their growing intelligence to make stone tools and organize group hunts.
   Ⓓ During periods of rapid climate change, early humans began to make stone tools and hunt in groups, which shows that they had a high level of intelligence.

*i*BT Practice 2

Chernobyl

During the 1980s, there was strong, worldwide opposition to nuclear power. This opposition increased in 1986 after an explosion at the Chernobyl nuclear power plant in the former Soviet Union, which, to date, still stands as the worst nuclear accident in history. Over 135,000 people had to leave their homes because of the accident, and the areas around the power plant still remain highly contaminated.

The accident was largely due to the bad design of the nuclear reactor in the power plant and the failure of workers at the plant to follow proper safety procedures. On April 25th workers at the power plant were testing on how it operated at low power. In order to run these tests, they removed all but eight control rods, which control the rate of the nuclear reaction in the reactor and prevent an uncontrolled reaction. Safety procedures called for a minimum of thirty control rods to be used at any one time, but these were ignored. During the tests, the reactor became unstable and started producing far too much power. Without enough control rods, the workers were unable to slow down the reaction, and the reactor exploded.

The explosion spread radioactive gas and other harmful materials into the air. The resulting radioactive cloud spread over Russia, Ukraine, and Belarus. The most serious radiation contamination was limited to the ten miles around the plant, which is still too contaminated for humans to live in. A total of 56 people died immediately after the accident, but because the effects of radiation poisoning often only surface after many years, the true death toll may never be known. Studies have shown that areas affected by the accident have cancer rates that are up to ten times higher than normal.

In addition to these serious health problems, the accident had significant political consequences, both in the Soviet Union and worldwide. Within the Soviet Union, the accident forced the government to become less secretive and helped quicken the collapse of the communist government. Worldwide, it all but stopped the construction of nuclear power plants and caused many existing power plants to be shut down out of safety concerns. Now, however, high oil prices and a need for energy are pushing many countries to turn once again to nuclear power. China, for example, has plans to build at least two new nuclear power plants each year for the next ten years. With nuclear power growing once again, one can only hope Chernobyl remains an isolated incident.

1 The word opposition in the passage is closest in meaning to

    Ⓐ concern

    Ⓑ distrust

    Ⓒ resistance

    Ⓓ awareness

2 Which of the sentences below best expresses the essential information in the highlighted sentence in paragraph 1? *Incorrect* choices change the meaning in important ways or leave out essential information.

    Ⓐ The explosion at the Chernobyl nuclear power plant, which still stands today, was the worst nuclear accident in history, and increased opposition to nuclear power.

    Ⓑ The opposition to the nuclear power plant at Chernobyl increased after the plant exploded in the worst nuclear accident in history.

    Ⓒ The opposition to the former Soviet Union increased after the explosion at the Chernobyl power plant, which was the worst nuclear accident in history.

    Ⓓ The opposition to nuclear power increased after the explosion of the Chernobyl nuclear power plant, which remains the worst nuclear accident in history.

3 The word contaminated in the passage is closest in meaning to

    Ⓐ damaged

    Ⓑ polluted

    Ⓒ dangerous

    Ⓓ unpopulated

4 The word it in the passage refers to

    Ⓐ test

    Ⓑ power plant

    Ⓒ safety procedure

    Ⓓ reactor design

5 The word these in the passage refers to

    Ⓐ control rods

    Ⓑ workers

    Ⓒ tests

    Ⓓ safety procedures

6 Which of the sentences below best expresses the essential information in the highlighted sentence in paragraph 3? *Incorrect* choices change the meaning in important ways or leave out essential information.

(A) 56 people died after the accident, but the death toll from radiation is not yet known because the effects of radiation poisoning take a long time to surface.

(B) While 56 people were known to have died immediately after the accident, the real death toll may remain unknown because the effects of radiation poisoning can take years to appear.

(C) 56 people died immediately after the accident because the effects of radiation poisoning only surface after many years and remain unknown.

(D) It may never be known whether 56 people died because of the accident because the effects of radiation poisoning take a long time to surface.

7 Which of the sentences below best expresses the essential information in the highlighted sentence in paragraph 4? *Incorrect* choices change the meaning in important ways or leave out essential information.

(A) It completely stopped the construction of nuclear power plants worldwide and caused many other plants to shut down because of safety concerns.

(B) Worldwide, the disaster stopped nearly all construction of new nuclear plants, and many existing plants shut down due to worries over their safety.

(C) Worldwide, the disaster stopped the construction of new power plants, but existing power plants shut down their safety concerns.

(D) Many existing power plants shut down construction of new plants out of safety concerns

8 The word isolated in the passage is closest in meaning to

(A) deadly
(B) unfortunate
(C) unintended
(D) unique

Vocabulary Review

Choose the word from each group that does not have the same meaning.

1 (A) probable   (B) promising   (C) practical   (D) potential

2 (A) moment   (B) period   (C) length   (D) duration

3 (A) deal with   (B) demolish   (C) destroy   (D) knock down

4 (A) quickly   (B) instantly   (C) immediately   (D) quietly

5 (A) estimate   (B) keep up   (C) maintain   (D) preserve

6 (A) in the end   (B) finally   (C) step by step   (D) eventually

7 (A) convert   (B) change   (C) transform   (D) transport

8 (A) ask for   (B) review   (C) demand   (D) request

Fill in the blank with the correct word from the box.

aware	eventually	attempt	demolished
estimate	countless	dissatisfied with	duration

9 He read the books in a(n) _____ to make his son sleep.

10 I _____ that the total living cost will be up to $2,000 a month.

11 The hotel clerk asked us what the _____ of our stay would be.

12 You hate me now, but I'm sure that _____ you will like me.

13 Travelers should be _____ of the possible dangers they can meet during the trip.

14 I am _____ the information they are giving us. It's too little and sometimes not even correct.

15 They will check _____ applications in order to choose the best people for the company.

16 The construction workers _____ the old houses to build new ones.

Part **A** +

Vocabulary & Reference

Sentence Simplification

Factual Information & Negative Fact

Part B

Prose Summary

Schematic Table

Part C

Inference

Rhetorical Purpose

Sentence Insertion

Factual Information

+ Introduction

Factual information questions are based on the specific information in a passage. This type of question asks you to choose a statement that is correct according to the passage. Each passage has 3 - 6 factual information questions, and each is worth 1 point.

+ Sample Question

TOEFL Reading

 REVIEW HELP BACK NEXT  HIDE TIME 00:20:00

As a city grows, it is important for city planners to leave some areas undeveloped. There are a number of reasons for this. First of all, undeveloped areas contain trees, grass, and plants, which help clean the air in the city. Another reason is that undeveloped areas help keep the temperature of the city down.

According to the paragraph, why do city planners leave wooded areas in their plans for the city?

(A) Citizens enjoy undeveloped areas of the city.

(B) Wooded areas help keep the city's air fresh.

(C) Wooded areas make the city more beautiful.

(D) Wooded areas prevent the city from becoming too crowded.

Answer & Explanation

The answer is (B). The paragraph says that the underdeveloped areas "help clean the air in the city" and "help keep the temperature of the city down."

+ Strategies

❶ Identify the keywords in a question.

Keywords are normally nouns which are repeated in a passage.

    e.g. In a question "According to the passage, Picasso's late works are considered to be examples of synthetic cubism because," the keywords are "Picasso's late works" and "synthetic cubism."

❷ Scan a passage for the keywords.

To scan is to read quickly to find certain information. Scan the passage, locate the parts where the key information is mentioned, and check their surroundings for details.

❸ Note that the answers are paraphrased.

The answers may be worded in a different way, using other vocabulary choices or grammatical structures.

❹ Eliminate the answer choices which:

- contain incorrect information
- have correct information but are not closely related to the question
- are not mentioned in the passage

+ Recognizing the Questions

- According to the paragraph, which of the following is true of ...?
- The author's description of ... mentions which of the following?
- According to the paragraph, ... because ...

Basic Drills (1)

 Are the following statements true or false? Write "T" for true or "F" for false.

1 The Olympics were created in the city-states of ancient Greece in honor of the god Zeus. The first games were held in 776 B.C. and had only one competition, a foot race at the bottom of Mt. Olympus, where the Greeks believed that Zeus lived. By the 5th century B.C. the Olympics were the most important of all Greek festivals and there were many more games. The Greeks held their games every four years on the hottest days of summer and they had special rules. The most important rule was that any wars between the Greek cities had to stop during the games.

☐ **in honor of:** respectful of

☐ **annual:** once every year

(1) The Olympics were created in order to promote peace between Greek cities. _____

(2) The number of games held in the Olympics increased over time. _____

(3) The Greeks held the Olympics at an annual festival. _____

2 Many of the English names for the planets in the solar system come from Roman mythology. Jupiter, the fifth planet from the sun, is named after the Roman god of the sky. The ancient Romans would not have been able to see the planet Jupiter, but scientists later named the planet after this god because the Jupiter is the largest planet in our solar system. The ancient Romans could see the planet Mars, and named it after their god of war because of its blood – red color. Likewise, Venus, who was their goddess of love, was also visible to them.

☐ **mythology:** ancient stories about gods or natural events

☐ **visible:** can be seen, noticeable

(1) The Romans named all the planets after their gods and goddesses. _____

(2) The fifth planet was named after the Roman sky god because of its size. _____

(3) Mars was named after the Roman god of war because of its color. _____

Basic Drills (2)

 Choose the correct answer for each question.

1 One of the worst spiders to be bitten by would be the brown recluse. These spiders do not build webs. They are about half an inch in size, and are found only in North America. They prefer small, dark areas, like shoes and boxes, so most bites occur on the hands and feet. The brown recluse's poison is not fatal, but it can cause serious health problems. The bite of the brown recluse is extremely painful. A more serious effect is that its venom kills the skin around the bite. This will continue for up to two weeks, leaving an area of black, dead skin that can be several inches in size. The bite also takes a long time to heal, about six to eight weeks, and in some cases requires surgery.

☐ **recluse:** an outcast

☐ **fatal:** deadly

☐ **venom:** a liquid poison

Q. According to the paragraph, what is the most severe effect of a brown recluse's bite?

(A) The area bitten by the spider will be extremely painful.

(B) It will cause serious problems in your hands and feet.

(C) It will leave an area of dead tissue that often requires surgery.

2 The greatest enemy of early man was the great cave bear. This bear was truly frightening. A great cave bear could be up to 20 feet tall when it stood on its back legs. This is about twice as tall as the largest bears today. In addition, these bears were pack animals. That means that like dogs, they traveled in groups. So when humans attacked, they had to fight up to six of these giants at one time. How did the humans ever beat such powerful creatures? By studying the bones of the cave bears, we can find the answer to this question. Most of the bones of the cave bears are found inside caves. This would suggest that the humans waited until the bears went to sleep for the winter, and then went into the caves and killed them in their sleep.

☐ **frightening:** scary, terrifying

☐ **pack animals:** wild animals that hunt together

Q. According to the paragraph, why were cave bears so difficult to kill?

(A) Cave bears were much larger than modern bears and traveled in groups.

(B) Early humans only had very simple weapons to fight them with.

(C) They attacked the early humans from several different directions.

3   Great white sharks hunt mostly by sense of smell and by a special electrical sense in their noses. These sharks can smell blood in the water from miles away. They also can feel the electricity that all living animals have. Once a great white has found its prey, it usually attacks from below, tearing a large piece out of its victim. This first bite is usually enough to kill the unlucky animal. Great whites have been called "eating machines," and this is basically true. While their favorite food is seal, great whites will eat almost anything. Whale parts, turtles, and even car batteries have been found in the stomachs of great whites.

□ **prey:** an animal or bird that is hunted and eaten by another animal
‹ › predator

Q. According to the paragraph, great whites are called eating machines because

(A)   their victims usually die after the first huge bite
(B)   they will basically eat anything in large quantities
(C)   they can smell the blood of their prey from miles away

4   Before the 1800s, most European nations were ruled by kings who had total control of their governments. Many of them were cruel and uncaring rulers. While the citizens of these nations did not like this situation, there was little they could do about it. In the 16th and 17th centuries, however, a rising class of merchants and businessmen began to gain power. Because the monarchs needed the taxes that these rich businessmen paid, they could not entirely ignore them and began to lose some of their power.

□ **allow:** to make it possible for someone to do something

Q. According to the paragraph, the monarchs were unable to hold on to absolute power because

(A)   their citizens knew the monarchs did not care about them
(B)   they came to rely on the money generated by the taxes of the merchants
(C)   they tried to ignore the merchants and businessmen

Negative Fact

+ Introduction

Negative fact questions ask you to decide which of the four statements is not true according to the passage. It could be either opposite to the information in a passage or something not mentioned in a passage. Each passage has 0 – 2 negative fact questions. Each is worth 1 point.

+ Sample Question

TOEFL Reading   REVIEW   HELP   BACK   NEXT   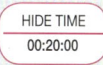 HIDE TIME 00:20:00

Deep on the ocean floor, miles from sunlight, you can find some of the strangest creatures ever found. Scientists used to think that the ocean floor was like a vast desert, totally lacking in life. That is because the environment on the ocean floor is the harshest environment anywhere on the planet. Deep in the ocean, there is no light and the temperature is only slightly above freezing. In addition, there is the crushing weight of all that water above the ocean floor. Scientists always thought that life was impossible under these conditions.

According to the paragraph, all of the following are true of the ocean floor EXCEPT

(A) It is impossible for life to exist there.

(B) It is a completely dark environment.

(C) Objects on the ocean floor are under incredible weight.

(D) The ocean floor is extremely cold.

Answer & Explanation

The answer is (A). Some scientists once thought that living creatures cannot survive on the ocean floor, but the words "used to" imply that this opinion has been proved wrong. At the beginning of the paragraph, it is also stated that some creatures are found on the ocean floor.

+ Strategies

❶ Identify the keywords in a question.

As we do with factual information questions, find the keywords in a question. Remember that keywords can appear in the form of synonyms.

e.g. According to the passage, what effect did his experiment have on art history?

The keyword "experiment" may appear as "test," "trial," "research," or "observation" in the passage.

❷ Scan the passage for the keywords.

Read the passage quickly for the keywords and then check their surroundings for details.

❸ Eliminate the correct statements one by one.

All answer choices are paraphrased. Identify their meaning carefully, and eliminate the statements which contain correct information.

+ Recognizing the Questions

- According to the passage, which of the following is NOT true of ...?
- The author's description of ... mentions all of the following EXCEPT...

Basic Drills (3)

✉ **Choose 2 statements which correctly state about each paragraph.**

1 The Golden Gate Bridge crosses the San Francisco Bay, a dangerous body of water. In the early days of San Francisco, the bay was only crossed by boat, but as the city grew larger, a faster way to cross the bay was needed. In 1929, President Hoover and California Governor Young started making plans for the Golden Gate Bridge. Construction of the bridge began in 1933, and the bridge was finally completed in 1937. Since then, the bridge has become one of the main tourist attractions in San Francisco.

☐ **construction:** the process of building

☐ **tourist attractions:** popular places among tourists

(1) The Golden Gate Bridge was built in order to deal with the growth of the city. ☐

(2) The Golden Gate Bridge was planned by both state and federal governments. ☐

(3) The Golden Gate Bridge was built to attract more tourists to San Francisco. ☐

2 In Indonesia, scientists have found an amazing discovery. On the island of Flores, scientists have found fossils of what appears to be a race of tiny humans. The find has started a controversy among scientists. Some scientists believe that these fossils represent an entirely different species from the humans we know today, just as the Neanderthals of Europe were a distinct species from modern humans. But another possible explanation is something called island dwarfing. If a group of people live on an isolated island for thousands of years, they can begin to grow smaller because there is not enough food for larger humans. Some scientists suggest that the fossils on Flores simply represent an extreme example of island dwarfing.

☐ **appear:** to seem

☐ **controversy:** a serious argument or issue

☐ **distinct:** clearly different

☐ **isolated:** to be completely away from

(1) Many scientists believe that the fossils found in Flores may be related to the Neanderthals of Europe. ☐

(2) Some scientists believe their isolation was the reason for the size of the fossils on Flores. ☐

(3) Some scientists believe that the fossils on Flores may represent a separate and distinct species of humans. ☐

3　The Americans first landed on the moon on July 20, 1969. Over the next three years, the Apollo program returned to the moon five more times and brought back 800 lbs. of rocks, but the American citizens were quickly losing interest. They had beaten the Russians to the moon and won a valuable stage in the space race, but the Apollo missions were very expensive and dangerous. In addition to the three astronauts who died in the Apollo 1 fire, three more astronauts almost died in Apollo 13. So in 1972 the Apollo program was cancelled, but it still remains one of the greatest achievements in American space history.

☐ **lose interest:** to be less and less interested

(1)　For the Americans, landing first on the moon was an important victory over the Russians. ☐

(2)　The Apollo missions were cancelled because Americans no longer felt they were worth the risks or the cost. ☐

(3)　Three more astronauts died on Apollo 13 during a fire after the Apollo 1 accident. ☐

4　While forest fires can be very destructive, they are also necessary. Forest fires perform several important functions. First of all, forest fires get rid of old and diseased trees in the forest. They also allow for the growth of new trees in a number of ways. The ash from the trees that burn in a forest fire is rich in nutrients and makes the ground better for new trees. In addition, some trees actually need fire before their seeds can grow. So while forest fires that grow too large or spread into populated areas are bad, some forest fires are actually necessary.

☐ **destructive:** causing damage to people or things

☐ **enrich:** to make something richer

(1)　Forest fires allow the spread of new seeds by making the wind blow. ☐

(2)　Forest fires allow the growth of new trees by enriching the soil in the forest. ☐

(3)　Forest fires help the forest grow by preventing the spread of disease in the forest. ☐

Basic Drills (4)

✉ **Choose the correct answer for each question.**

1 Off-road races are important for car companies. These races are used by car companies to test new technology in their vehicles. For example, a new engine or brake system that is successful in an off-road race may soon be placed in the cars that a company sells to the public. Off-road races are also an important form of advertising for car companies. If their car wins the race, it helps to increase the sales of their cars. One of the most famous off-road races is the Paris-Dakar Rally. This race stretches all the way from France to Africa, and crosses every type of terrain imaginable, from mountains to deserts. The race is extremely tough on the cars, and many cars don't even make it to the finish line. Because of its extreme difficulty, the company whose car wins the race gets to claim that they truly have some of the best cars in the world.

☐ **stretch:** to cover
☐ **terrain:** land
☐ **advance:** a change, discovery, or invention
☐ **typically:** normally, generally

Q. According to the paragraph, all of the following are true of the Paris-Dakar Rally EXCEPT

(A) it is used to test new advances in car design
(B) it helps the winners of the race promote their cars
(C) it is typically completed by all drivers

2 There are three types of volcanoes: cinder cone volcanoes, shield volcanoes, and composite volcanoes. Cinder cones are the most common volcanoes and also the smallest. They have steep sides and wide, round openings, called craters, at their tops. Cinder cone volcanoes are fairly predictable. When they erupt, the flow of lava is generally slow and constant. Shield volcanoes are made from eruptions over many years. Composite volcanoes are the tallest and most dangerous volcanoes. They are made from many different kinds of rock and can collapse very easily. Composite volcano eruptions are usually the ones that are associated with large losses of life.

☐ **erupt:** to explode
☐ **constant:** continuous
☐ **collapse:** to fall down suddenly
☐ **be associated with:** to be connected with, be involved with

Q. According to the paragraph, all of the following are characteristics of cinder cone volcanoes EXCEPT

(A) deadly eruptions   (B) steep slopes   (C) predictable lava flow

Barrier Islands

In the past few years, countries around the world have suffered increasingly severe damage from hurricanes and typhoons. At first glance, it might appear as if these storms are getting stronger every year. This, however, is not an entirely accurate statement. It would be more accurate to say that the natural protections against such storms have been disappearing, and as a result, they
5 • have been causing more damage.

The most important natural protections against these storms are barrier islands. Barrier islands are long narrow islands that are usually only a few miles offshore from the coastline. Barrier islands can be
10 • found off most coasts around the world, but the largest and most noticeable ones sit off the east coast of the United States. Barrier islands form an important protection against storms because they weaken the

waves of a storm before they reach the coast. This is important because the majority of the damage
15 • caused by a hurricane comes from the flooding that these large waves create. As barrier islands disappear, there is nothing to lessen the force of the waves and reduce flooding before they reach the coast.

There are two main reasons why barrier islands are disappearing. The first is the development of these islands. Barrier islands often make popular vacation spots. As hotels are
20 • built on the islands, the sand dunes that break the force of the waves are destroyed. Without these sand dunes, much of the island simply washes away in the next large storm. The other reason is the damming of rivers on the mainland. These dams block the dirt that would normally wash down the river and out to the barrier islands, naturally rebuilding the island. Without this dirt, the islands slowly disappear.

1 According to the passage, hurricanes are now more destructive because

(A) they have been growing stronger

(B) they have been growing more frequent

(C) small offshore islands are being destroyed

(D) more people are living in hotels near hurricane areas

2 All of the following are true of barrier islands EXCEPT

(A) they are unique to the east coast of the United States

(B) they are relatively close to the coast

(C) they are thin and long

(D) they are built by dirt deposits from rivers

3 According to paragraph 3, how does the development of barrier islands damage them?

(A) It prevents dirt from rebuilding the island.

(B) It allows larger waves to reach the island.

(C) It destroys the protective sand dunes.

(D) It attracts too many vacationers.

Find the right word from the passage!

❶ Correct or having no mistakes: _____

❷ Very obvious so that it is easy to see, hear or recognize: _____

❸ To make something smaller in size or amount, or less in degree: _____ ,

_____

❹ A hill of sand near the sea or in a sand desert: _____

Pickpocket

Every vacationer's nightmare is to reach into their pocket to pay for a purchase only to realize that their wallet has been stolen. In such a case, the unlucky vacationer has probably been the victim of a pickpocket. Pickpockets are thieves that take your wallet out of your pocket or purse without you knowing it.

The basic skill of every good pickpocket is distraction. A pickpocket needs to distract their victim, so that the victim doesn't notice that the pickpocket is reaching into their pocket. The most basic form of distraction is an accidental bump. A pickpocket will pretend to accidentally bump into a person on the subway or in the street. While they are bumping into the person, they reach into their victim's pocket. Because the feeling of the bump is stronger than the feeling of the hand in their pocket, the victims never notice that they are being robbed. Sometimes pickpockets will work in teams. One pickpocket will bump into a person while the other one takes their wallet. Most pickpockets are quite skilled, and it is very difficult to catch them.

There are, however, a few things you can do to protect yourself from pickpockets. The first is not to carry all of your money in one pocket. Even the best pickpockets can only pick one pocket at a time. Another thing you can do is to carry your wallet in your front pocket. This is typically the hardest pocket to pick, and most pickpockets don't even bother trying. Finally, try not to look like a tourist. Pickpockets know that people usually carry more money with them on vacation than they do on a normal day, so tourists make tempting targets for these thieves.

1   According to the passage, how do pickpockets distract their victims?

(A)   They use accidental contact to hide the feeling of taking the wallet.

(B)   They pretend to be tourists in the city.

(C)   They only take wallets from their victims' back pocket, which can't be seen.

(D)   They only work in crowded subways and streets where they can hide easily.

2   All of the following are mentioned as ways to protect yourself from pickpockets EXCEPT

(A)   keeping your wallet in your front pocket

(B)   not allowing others to touch you on the subway

(C)   keeping your money in several different locations

(D)   looking like a local resident rather than a visitor in a city

3   According to paragraph 3, pickpockets target tourists because

(A)   tourists can't protect themselves from pickpockets

(B)   tourists often ride the subways where pickpockets work

(C)   robbing tourists is generally more profitable for pickpockets

(D)   tourists can't speak the language and can't call the police

Find the right word from the passage!

❶ To take your attention away from something: _____

❷ If you _____ _____ into someone, you make physical contact with the person unexpectedly.

❸ In a way that shows the usual or expected features of someone or something:

_____

❹ Making you want to do something or have it: _____

Fire Walking

Ancient cultures and religions had many practices that were supposed to test a person's courage and faith. The idea was that the person would try a dangerous or seemingly impossible act, and if their faith was strong enough, they would be able to do it. One such practice is fire walking. In fire walking, a person walks across a bed of hot coals, without burning their feet or injuring themselves in any way!

Fire walking is an ancient and widespread ceremony. No one knows exactly when or where fire walking started, but the earliest written record of fire walking comes from almost 4,000 years ago in India, which still has a strong tradition of fire walking. That, however, is no guarantee that the practice started there. Fire walking has been recorded in almost every culture, from the Native Americans to the Japanese.

Ancient cultures believed that the ability to fire walk came from a person's faith and spiritual purity. Today, however, fire walking can easily be explained by science and the way that heat travels from one object to another. The first thing to know about fire walkers is that they do not actually walk across fire. They walk across coals. Coals are what remains of a log after it has burned. While coals are very hot, they put out their heat very slowly. In addition, the coals that firewalkers walk over are covered with a layer of ash. Heat does not travel through ash very easily. As a result of these two facts, a fire walker may walk across the coals with no injury. As long as the fire walker does not stand in one place for too long, the heat cannot travel quickly enough through the coals and the ash to burn his or her feet.

1 According to the passage, all of the following are true of fire walking EXCEPT

(A) it is an ancient ceremony

(B) it has been practiced worldwide

(C) it originated in India

(D) it can be explained through science

2 According to the passage, ancient cultures used fire walking to

(A) purify themselves spiritually

(B) test the strength of their religious beliefs

(C) test their ideas about science

(D) cure their injuries and diseases

3 According to paragraph 3, it is important for fire walkers not to stand in one place for too long because

(A) the coals will become hotter over time

(B) the heat will have time to move through the ash and coals

(C) the fire walker may begin to lose his or her faith

(D) the fire will eventually go out

Find the right word from the passage!

❶ Repeated or customary action: _____

❷ Appearing to be true, even though it may not really be so: _____

❸ Relating to people's thoughts and beliefs, rather than to their bodies and physical surroundings: _____

❹ Existing or happening over a large area, or to a great extent: _____

*i*BT Practice 1

Mass Extinctions

Almost everyone knows that around 65 million years ago there was a mass extinction that killed the dinosaurs. (Actually, it killed not only the dinosaurs, but also 85% of all other species on Earth.) Most people also generally accept that this was the result of a huge asteroid crashing into the Earth. What many people do not realize is that this was simply the most recent mass
5• extinction in the Earth's history. There have been other mass extinctions in the Earth's history, some of which were much worse than the one that killed the dinosaurs.

"Mass extinction" is the term scientists use when a significant portion of the Earth's species die out in a relatively short period of time (within a few million years). As far as we know, there have been at least six of these in the last 600 million years. The earliest one that we know
10• about occurred around 570 million years ago. We have very little information about this mass extinction because most of the animals at this time were very primitive. They were creatures like jellyfish and slugs*, which did not have bones, and therefore did not leave fossils for us to study. Later mass extinctions are better understood. The one thing that is not understood, however, is the causes of these mass extinctions. While scientists are fairly sure that the last
15• one was caused by an asteroid, it seems unlikely that all mass extinctions were caused in this manner.

Most of the other possible causes for mass extinctions involve some form of climate change. For example, scientists suspect that a sudden, significant change in sea levels around the world may have been responsible for one or more of the mass extinctions. Such a rise in sea
20• level would have most likely been started by the melting of large amounts of ice at the North and South Poles. Other possibilities include widespread droughts or significant changes in the average world temperature. What could have caused such changes in the first place, however, is not understood. Scientists know that severe climate changes can lead to extinction, but what initiates these changes is unknown. It is, however, an important question to answer if we are to
25• survive the next extinction.

☐ slug: a small slow-moving terrestrial mollusk without shell

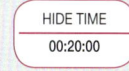
Part A

3

1 The phrase **most recent** in the passage is closest in meaning to

(A) most serious
(B) best understood
(C) latest
(D) best-known

2 Which of the sentences below best expresses the essential information in the highlighted sentence in the passage? *Incorrect* choices change the meaning in important ways or leave out essential information.

(A) Mass extinction is used by scientists to kill off significant portions of the Earth's species in a relatively short amount of time.
(B) When the Earth's species die out in a relatively short period of time, scientists use the term mass extinction.
(C) Within a few million years, scientists will use the term mass extinction for when the Earth's species die out.
(D) Mass extinction is a scientific term for when a large percentage of the Earth's species disappear relatively quickly.

3 The word **these** in the passage refers to

(A) periods of time
(B) mass extinctions
(C) species
(D) scientists

4 According to paragraph 2, why is little known about the earliest mass extinction?

(A) The animals' bodies were not advanced enough to leave behind evidence.
(B) The animals alive at this time were too different from modern animals for us to study.
(C) This mass extinction killed too many of the animals for us to study the survivors.
(D) Scientists are unable to study this far back in the Earth's history.

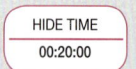
5 The author mentions all of the following as possible causes of mass extinctions EXCEPT

(A) collisions with asteroids

(B) significant periods without rain

(C) widespread disease

(D) increases in water levels

6 According to paragraph 3, what remains unknown regarding climate change?

(A) The role climate change plays in causing mass extinctions

(B) What effects climate change can have on world sea levels

(C) If severe climate changes are likely to take place in the future

(D) The reasons why severe climate changes occur

7 The word initiates in the passage is closest in meaning to

(A) results from

(B) sets off

(C) influences

(D) prevents

*i*BT Practice 2

The Mexican-American War

Much of the history of the United States has involved the expansion of its borders. In fact, many early Americans believed that it was the destiny of the United States to spread across all of North America. This idea was called "manifest destiny," and many Americans believed in it strongly. Some of the nation's expansion happened peacefully through the purchase of land from other nations. A good example of this would be when the United States bought the territory of Louisiana from the French in 1803. Many other expansions, however, involved the use of force.

In the early 1800s, Texas was actually part of Mexico. The Americans, however, had their eye on the territory and settlers began moving in. At first, those settlers lived as citizens of Mexico. However, as time passed they began to push for independence from Mexico. In 1836, those settlers, called Tejanos, revolted against the Mexican government and won their independence. At this point, Texas was still not part of the United States. It was an independent republic. In 1845, however, the United States annexed the territory of Texas. This meant that the Republic of Texas agreed to become part of the United States. There were problems with Mexico, however. The American government thought that the southern border of Texas should be the Rio Grande River. The Mexicans thought it should be the Neuces River, farther north.

In 1846, this disagreement grew into war. The Americans had decided to send troops to the Rio Grande to enforce their claim on the territory, and this only increased the tension between the two nations. In response, Mexican troops captured a small American guard post, and America quickly declared war. It proved to be a costly mistake for the Mexican government, as the Americans not only sent troops into Texas, but also invaded California, which was Mexican land at the time. The war was relatively short, and in 1848 Mexico signed a peace treaty with the United States. The peace treaty gave huge amounts of territory to the Americans, including California, New Mexico, Nevada, Utah, and Arizona, in return for a payment covering the costs of the war. The land represented half of Mexico's original territory, and was worth far more than the amount of the US payment. It also completed the Americans' dream of expanding their borders to the Pacific Ocean.

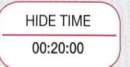
1 The word expansion in the passage is closest in meaning to

- (A) invasion
- (B) protection
- (C) growth
- (D) definition

2 According to the passage, the territory of Louisiana was gained

- (A) through non-violent means
- (B) after the defeat of the French army
- (C) after it was annexed by the United States
- (D) when it was bought from Mexico

3 According to paragraph 2, how did the Mexican government first lose the territory of Texas?

- (A) The Americans invaded Texas.
- (B) The Americans annexed Texas.
- (C) The Texan citizens rebelled.
- (D) They made costly mistakes.

4 According to paragraphs 1 and 2, the term border can best be explained as

- (A) a river that is claimed by more than one country
- (B) a territory that is taken through force
- (C) the line that separates the territories of two nations
- (D) a war fought over disputed territories

5 The phrase this disagreement in the passage refers to the disagreement regarding

- (A) the independence of Texas
- (B) the location of the Texas border
- (C) the annexation of Texas by the US
- (D) the American troops stationed near the Rio Grande

6 According to the passage, what event started the Mexican American War?

- (A) The invasion of California by the Americans
- (B) The Mexican attack on a US guard post
- (C) The movement of American troops near the Rio Grande
- (D) The revolution in Texas

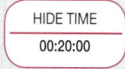

7 Which of the sentences below best expresses the essential information in the highlighted sentence in the passage? *Incorrect* choices change the meaning in important ways or leave out essential information.

(A) This proved that Mexico made costly mistakes when the Americans sent troops into Texas and invaded California, which was Mexican territory.

(B) As the Americans sent troops into Texas and California, which had been Mexican territories, their invasion proved to be a costly mistake.

(C) The costly mistakes of the Mexicans caused the Americans to send troops into Texas and invade California, which was Mexican territory.

(D) This proved to be a poor choice by the Mexicans, since the Americans not only sent troops into Texas, but also invaded the Mexican territory of California.

8 According to the passage, all of the following were results of the Mexican American War EXCEPT

(A) It greatly reduced the size of Mexico.

(B) It allowed America to expand to the Pacific Ocean.

(C) It allowed Texas to become a state.

(D) California became American territory.

Vocabulary Review

Choose the word from each group that does not have the same meaning.

1   (A) clear   (B) visible   (C) usual   (D) apparent

2   (A) massive   (B) enormous   (C) immense   (D) probable

3   (A) eventually   (B) altogether   (C) entirely   (D) completely

4   (A) correct   (B) precise   (C) deliberate   (D) accurate

5   (A) obvious   (B) capable   (C) noticeable   (D) perceptible

6   (A) distract   (B) divert   (C) distinguish   (D) sidetrack

7   (A) mouth-watering (B) tempting   (C) enticing   (D) attractive

8   (A) determined   (B) deadly   (C) lethal   (D) fatal

Fill in the blank with the correct word from the box.

massive	as long as	fatal	accurate
attract	entirely	widespread	distracted

9   Turn off the music while you study, or it will keep you _____.

10 I'm okay with the decision you made _____ you are happy with it.

11 If the map is _____, it won't be difficult to find the place.

12 The hospital is run _____ by women, and it is only for female patients;
    no men are allowed there.

13 Sometimes a dirty environment can put children at risk from severe and even
    _____ illnesses.

14 The industry is finally getting better due to _____ investments
    in the past few years.

15 I think the new MP3 player will _____ young users more than adults.

16 It is a(n) _____ rumor that she will get married to the famous actor soon.

Memo

Reading to Learn

This part of the test examines your overall reading comprehension skills. Summary completion and schematic table questions are given to test how well you can identify the main ideas of a passage and how efficiently you can classify important specific information.

PART

B

Part **B** +

Prose Summary

Schematic Table

Prose Summary

+ Introduction

Prose summary questions ask you to find and summarize major ideas within a passage. You will be given an introductory sentence together with six statements. Your task is to identify the three best statements to create a summary of a passage. The prose summary question appears as the last question in most reading passages and is worth 2 points.

+ Sample Question

TOEFL Reading

 REVIEW   HELP ?   BACK ◀   NEXT ▶ 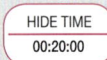 HIDE TIME 00:20:00

Directions: An introductory sentence for a brief summary of the passage is provided below. Complete the summary by selecting THREE answer choices that express the most important ideas in the passage. Some sentences do not belong in the summary because they express ideas that are not presented in the passage or are minor ideas in the passage. This question is worth 2 points.

On December 16, 1773 a group of American colonists threw 45 tons of British tea into Boston Harbor in what became known as the Boston Tea Party.

Ⓐ During the colonial period the colonies were under control of the British government.

Ⓑ The Boston Tea Party was held to protest British tax laws that the colonists felt were unfair.

Ⓒ The English Parliament passed the Tea Act in 1768.

Ⓓ The organizers of the Boston Tea Party went on to become some of the most important men in the American Revolution.

Ⓔ After the Boston Tea Party, King George punished the American colonists.

Ⓕ The Boston Tea Party was one of the most important events leading up to the American Revolution.

*In the actual TOEFL test, you are asked to drag three statements using the mouse and put them below the introductory sentence.

Strategies

❶ As you read, take notes on important facts and details.

❷ Find the clues hidden in the passage.

The introductory sentence usually contains the main idea of a passage. Remember that the three statements should be closely linked to the main idea.

❸ Skim the first few sentences of each paragraph for the main idea.

Major ideas can usually be found at the beginning of each paragraph.

❹ Eliminate any statements if they contain:

- only minor ideas
- information that is not mentioned in the passage

  OR

- information that contradicts details in the passage

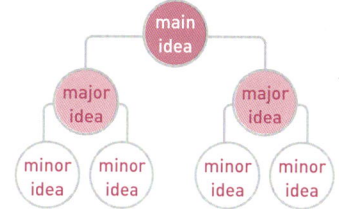

Recognizing the Questions

Directions: An introductory sentence for a brief summary of the passage is provided below. Complete the summary by selecting the THREE answer choices that express the most important ideas in the passage. Some sentences do not belong in the summary because they express ideas that are not presented in the passage or are minor ideas in the passage. ***This question is worth 2 points.***

Basic Drills (1)

Read the paragraphs below and underline the sentence which contains the main idea in each paragraph.

1 The first capital of the US was Philadelphia, which is about 100 miles north of Washington, D.C. in the state of Pennsylvania, but there were many disagreements about this. The new government asked George Washington to pick a place for the new capital, and the location he chose became known as Washington, D.C. Washington could not have made a worse choice. The land that he picked for the new capital was basically a huge swamp, and the workers had a difficult time building on the wet land. It took years to build the new capital, but in 1800 it was finally completed. Unfortunately, most of the city was burned by the British during the war of 1812 and had to be rebuilt.

- ☐ **disagreement:** expressions of different opinions
- ☐ **swamp:** very wet land

2 It's a well-known fact that nations in which guns are illegal are far safer than nations where they are legal. A simple comparison of nations like Japan and Korea, where guns are illegal, and the US and South Africa, where they are legal, shows this is true. South Africa and the US both have much higher murder rates. Despite this, some nations can offer powerful reasons for why they have not made guns illegal. One reason is that some nations feel that owning guns guarantees their citizens the ability to revolt if their government ever became a dictatorship. Thus, they claim guns help guarantee their freedom. Another powerful argument is that since most criminals already purchase their guns illegally, making guns illegal would not take guns out of the hands of criminals. Instead, it would simply make sure that regular citizens were unable to defend themselves from criminals.

- ☐ **comparison:** something with similar qualities
- ☐ **despite:** in spite of
- ☐ **revolt:** to take strong and violent action against the government
- ☐ **dictatorship:** government by a ruler with complete power
- ☐ **defend oneself:** to protect oneself from an attack

Basic Drills (2)

✉ **Read the paragraphs below and underline the main idea and major ideas in the paragraph. Do NOT underline supporting ideas.**

1 Many people travel to New Zealand to learn about the Maori culture. The Maori were the original inhabitants of New Zealand, arriving on the island around 1,500 to 1,000 years ago. Probably the best-known aspect of Maori culture is the haka, the Maori war dance. The main reason for this is that the New Zealand rugby team still dances this haka before all of their games. This, in addition to the fact that their rugby team is very good, has made New Zealand's rugby team one of the most famous teams in rugby. The intention of the haka is to intimidate the enemy. The dance seeks to intimidate people through stomping, loud shouts, and frightening facial expressions. Perhaps the most intimidating part of the haka is that it is done in perfect unison by all members.

☐ **inhabitant:** a person living in a particular place

☐ **intention:** purpose, desire

☐ **intimidate:** to frighten or threaten someone

☐ **stomping:** putting your foot down very hard

☐ **unison:** doing the same thing at the same time

2 One of the largest parts of the art business is the sale of ancient artifacts. Items from ancient cultures, such as pieces of pottery, armor, and statues, often sell for high prices. Both private collectors and museums show great interest in these objects. Many governments, however, want to completely stop, or at least tightly control, the sale of such ancient artifacts. One reason for this is that the demand for such artifacts has led to the destruction of many ancient archeology sites. People anxious to make money from the sale of artifacts take these items out of the site before they can be properly studied and documented. Another reason is that there has been a sharp increase in the number of forgeries. Many people are now making fake artifacts and trying to sell them as the real thing. This makes information about the past unreliable and wastes the money of museums.

☐ **artifact:** an ancient object such as a tool or a weapon

☐ **destruction:** destroying something

☐ **archeology:** the study of ancient societies

☐ **anxious:** wanting something very much

☐ **forgery:** copying official documents or money illegally

✉ **Read the paragraphs below and decide whether each answer choice is accurate, inaccurate or not contained.**

1   Bacteria are simple, single-celled organisms. They reproduce by simply splitting in two. Not all bacteria are harmful, but many bacteria can make you quite sick. Fortunately, most bacterial infections don't last long. The first reason for this is that the body is pretty good at fighting bacteria on its own. In addition, there are a whole range of medicines, called antibiotics, designed to kill bacteria. It is also relatively easy to prevent bacterial infections. Most bacterial infections are the result of a dirty environment. By washing your hands regularly and making sure that the food you eat has been prepared in a clean environment, you can avoid most bacterial infections.

☐ **organism:** any living thing

☐ **reproduce:** to produce young plants or animals

☐ **infection:** a disease that is caused by bacteria or a virus

(A) All bacteria can be harmful, but they do not always make you ill.   _____
(B) Bacteria divide their bodies in order to reproduce.   _____
(C) Medication is unnecessary to fight bacterial infections because most of them are the result of a dirty environment.   _____

2   Viruses cause many of the illnesses we suffer from. Viruses cannot reproduce on their own, which is an ability that every other living organism on Earth has. Viruses are collections of complex chemicals. They invade our cells, and once inside, they take over the cell to reproduce themselves. Viruses are hard to fight because there is no single medicine to fight them. Each virus requires a different medicine, and for many viruses, no medicine exists at all. We can prevent viral illnesses by getting vaccinations that prevent certain viruses. But again, we don't have a vaccine for every single virus.

☐ **invade:** to enter into an area in order to take control of it

(A) The complex chemicals in viruses give them abilities that no other organism on Earth has.   _____
(B) It is not always possible to prevent viral infections.   _____
(C) It is important to find medicines and vaccines for the viruses that we do not currently have them for.   _____

Read the short passage below and choose the correct answer choices.

1 Frogs are amphibians, meaning that they can live both in and out of water. All frogs lay their eggs in water, and a female frog will lay thousands of eggs at a time. When the eggs hatch, what come out are not frogs but rather tadpoles. Unlike frogs, tadpoles must spend all of their time in the water, being unable to breathe air at this point. Tadpoles also lack legs and have a tail which they lose as they develop into frogs. Tadpoles are herbivores, which means that they only eat plants. Specifically, tadpoles eat algae, a water plant which can be harmful if there is too much of it. Thus, tadpoles are important to keep most ponds healthy. As tadpoles develop into mature frogs, they develop the lungs which allow them to breathe air, and the legs which allow them to move across land. At this point the mature frogs leave the ponds, although some species stay near the water for their entire lives. Mature frogs are carnivores, eating insects and small fish. Most frogs hunt using their long, sticky tongue to catch their prey. Some species of frogs have developed extremely strong poisons to defend themselves from other animals.

□ **hatch:** to come out of an egg

□ **tadpole:** a small creature that has a long tail, lives in water, and grows into a frog or toad

Part B

4

Directions: An introductory sentence for a brief summary of the passage is provided below. Complete the summary by selecting TWO answer choices that express the most important ideas in the passage. Some sentences do not belong in the summary because they express ideas that are not presented in the passage or are minor ideas in the passage.

After hatching from their eggs, frogs have two separate stages of development: tadpoles and mature frogs.

(A) Tadpoles are unable to breathe air because they do not yet have lungs and must stay in the water.

(B) The bodies of tadpoles are different from those of mature frogs in many ways.

(C) The diet of tadpoles changes as they mature into fully developed frogs.

(D) Many frogs do not develop the poison they use for defense until they are mature frogs.

Biodiesel as Future Energy

The world's dependence on oil as a source of energy is quickly becoming its largest problem. Higher and higher prices for oil-based products like gasoline and diesel fuel are threatening to damage the world economy. Furthermore, the pollution that is caused by burning these fuels is damaging our environment. Researchers and car makers have been looking for alternative fuels for years. Ironically, while billions of dollars have been spent developing such technologies, one alternative fuel that could solve much of the problem has been around for almost 100 years.

Biodiesel is a fuel made from the fat and oils contained in plants. When mixed with alcohol and a few other chemicals, these oils produce a fuel that burns much like normal diesel fuel. Almost any plant can be used to produce biodiesel, but plants with plentiful oils and fats, like soybeans and peanuts, are better. Biodiesel was first produced in the early 1900s, but it was not a popular fuel choice because it was far more expensive than regular diesel fuel. Now, however, the high price of oil is quickly making biodiesel a more practical choice.

Biodiesel has a number of advantages over regular diesel fuel. First of all, it is a renewable energy source. We can always grow more crops, so there is no real danger of running out of biodiesel fuel. Biodiesel is also a much cleaner fuel. It only creates about half the air pollution that other fuels such as gasoline do. Given its many advantages and the rising cost of oil, it is likely that both you and your car could be eating more vegetables in the future!

1 **Directions:** An introductory sentence for a brief summary of the passage is provided below. Complete the summary by selecting THREE answer choices that express the most important ideas in the passage. Some sentences do not belong in the summary because they express ideas that are not presented in the passage or are minor ideas in the passage.

The rising cost of oil and the pollution it causes have prompted scientists to look at biodiesel as an alternative fuel.

(A) Biodiesel has been around for almost 100 years but was not used much because of its high price when compared to regular diesel.

(B) Biodiesel can be made from any plant that is high in oils and fats.

(C) Plants like soybeans and peanuts are the best plants for the production of biodiesel.

(D) As oil-based fuels become more expensive, the price of biodiesel is falling.

(E) Biodiesel has the advantages of being renewable and causing less pollution than regular diesel.

(F) In the future, people will no longer eat as many vegetables because we will use them to make biodiesel.

Find the right word from the passage!

❶ Able to be used instead of something original: _____

❷ In large enough amounts for people's wants or needs: _____

❸ A way in which one thing is better than another: _____

❹ Always available, like wind, water, and sunlight: _____

Problems with Injected Drugs

Many nations around the world are facing serious and growing drug problems. An increasing number of people around the world are addicted to illegal drugs, and one of the fastest-growing groups of drug users are those who inject drugs.

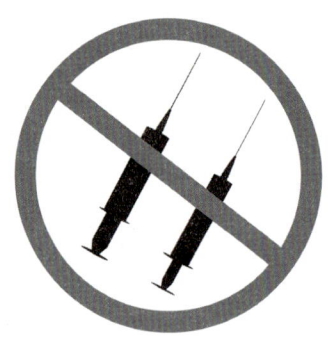

5 • While all illegal drugs are dangerous, injected drugs such as heroin are more dangerous than other drugs because they also carry the danger of spreading diseases such as AIDS.

This is true because many drug users share their needles with other drug users. Since they are using their needles for an illegal purpose, it is difficult for

10 • addicts to get new, clean needles. Instead, they simply use the same needle again and again, often sharing a needle between several people. Therefore, an addict infected with AIDS or another disease can easily spread that disease to other drug users. In fact, almost one third of all new AIDS cases in the world are a direct result of addicts sharing needles.

This is not only a problem for drug addicts, but for the rest of society as well. Most drug

15 • addicts do not have steady jobs, so when they get sick, society must pay their medical bills. In a country with a large number of drug addicts, this can amount to billions of dollars a year. To solve this problem, some cities have started needle exchange programs. In a needle exchange program, a person can exchange an old, dirty needle for a new, clean one. By giving addicts clean needles, the programs can help reduce the rates of infection of AIDS and other diseases. Needle exchange

20 • programs, however, are highly controversial. Many people oppose the programs because they think that by providing clean needles, the programs encourage drug use.

1 **Directions:** An introductory sentence for a brief summary of the passage is provided below. Complete the summary by selecting THREE answer choices that express the most important ideas in the passage. Some sentences do not belong in the summary because they express ideas that are not presented in the passage or are minor ideas in the passage.

Injected drugs pose an especially serious problem to society because they aid in spreading diseases as well as causing drug addiction.

(A) Injected drugs are among the quickest growing groups of illegal drugs.

(B) Injected drugs help spread disease because drug addicts often have to share needles, which are not easily available.

(C) AIDS is the most serious disease related to injected drugs, and nearly one third of all new AIDS cases are the result of the use of dirty needles.

(D) The infection of drug addicts with diseases like AIDS is a serious problem for society because society must help pay their medical bills.

(E) Although it has remained controversial, some people have suggested giving addicts clean needles in return for their old ones to reduce the spread of disease.

(F) Needle exchange programs are ineffective because they only encourage drug addiction by providing easy access to needles.

Find the right word from the passage!

❶ To put a drug into one's body using a needle: _____

❷ To cause people or animal to have a disease or illness: _____

❸ Being the subject of intense public argument, disagreement, or disapproval: _____

❹ To disagree with what others want to do and try to prevent them from doing it: _____

Pork Barrel Projects

The town of Ketchikan in northern Alaska (population 8,000) was supposed to get a new bridge. But there were two problems. At $315 million, the bridge was much too big and expensive.

5 • And it wasn't needed anyway! How did this plan happen? Blame pork. "Pork barrel projects" – often called just "pork" – are building projects which benefit only a few people but are paid for with public tax money. This means that all citizens pay for the projects, whether they benefit from the

10 • work or not. Here's how it works.

First, pork barrel projects need the support of powerful politicians. These politicians support pork barrel projects because in return, the citizens who benefit usually vote for the politicians in the next election. Next, the politicians have to secure money in the government's budget to pay for the project. This is often done at the last minute, so that people who disagree with the project

15 • do not have enough time to try to stop it. Once the government has approved the budget, then the pork barrel project is safely on its way. In the case of the Ketchikan bridge, the politicians were Alaska's congressmen. They backed the expensive bridge even though it would have served only 8,000 people and linked tiny Ketchikan with even smaller Gravina Island (population only 50). The bridge was never built. This time, the "pork barrel" got sealed! But many pork barrel

20 • projects go through. Then, everyone pays!

Pork barrel projects are not unique to American politics. You can find them in almost any society with a democratic government (one in which politicians must be elected). Japan is famous for pork barrel projects, most notably its bullet trains. Originally, Japan's bullet trains only linked its major cities. Now, however, bullet trains are being built to remote locations in the countryside

25 • with relatively small populations, at great expense to Japanese taxpayers. While this practice is more widespread in America and in Japan than in some other countries, if you look closely, you can probably find pork in your government too.

1 **Directions:** An introductory sentence for a brief summary of the passage is provided below. Complete the summary by selecting THREE answer choices that express the most important ideas in the passage. Some sentences do not belong in the summary because they express ideas that are not presented in the passage or are minor ideas in the passage.

Pork barrel projects are building projects with limited benefits which are carried out mainly for political reasons.

(A) The Ketchikan bridge, which would have cost $315 million but served only 8,000 people, was an example of a pork barrel project.

(B) Pork barrel projects exist because they are supported by powerful politicians to gain votes in the next election.

(C) To limit opposition to them, pork barrel projects are usually added to the government's budget just before the budget is approved.

(D) Many people dislike pork barrel projects because they feel they are an unfair and dishonest use of public money.

(E) Pork barrel projects are common in democratic governments around the world.

(F) Though useful when they were first built, Japan's bullet trains have now become pork barrel projects.

Find the right word from the passage!

❶ To formally agree to a plan or idea: _____

❷ Unusual and special: _____

❸ Far away from cities and places where most people live: _____

❹ If you do something _____ someone's _____, they provide the money for it.

*i*BT Practice 1

 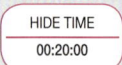
The Evolution of Submarines

Although they had existed since the American Civil War, submarines only came to be seen as major military weapons by many nations during World War II. They had also been used in World War I, but advances in technology made them much more effective in the Second World War. In this war, Germany had the largest submarine fleet by far. This was a natural consequence of the way the war developed. Germany's major enemy was Britain, an island nation. Britain was dependent on supplies brought by ship to supply its army. Therefore, it was natural for Germany to develop a large submarine fleet to stop British shipping.

At the start of the war, things looked bad for Britain. German subs were sinking British ships at an incredible rate, and Britain's supply line was in severe danger. However, the development of new technologies, namely sonar and aircraft that could find and attack submarines, eventually brought an end to the threat of the German subs. At the end of the war, German subs had sunk over 3,500 allied ships. However, this came at an incredible cost to the German fleet. Over 75% of the German sub fleet was lost during the war.

After the war it seemed that the usefulness of submarines was coming to an end. The two new superpowers, the US and the Soviet Union, were not as dependent on shipping as Britain had been, and the ease with which submarines could be found and destroyed limited their effectiveness. The development of nuclear technology, however, gave the submarine new life. Using nuclear power, submarines could stay at sea for much longer periods than older diesel powered subs. Furthermore, subs could now be loaded with nuclear missiles. This gave subs a new mission. Since they were at sea, nuclear subs would not be destroyed in a surprise nuclear attack. This eliminated all possibility of launching an effective surprise attack with nuclear weapons. Even if one nation managed to completely destroy the other, its subs would survive and then destroy the attacker. This idea that a nuclear war was guaranteed to destroy both nations was a key factor in preventing the use of nuclear weapons during the Cold War.

1 The word **they** in the passage refers to

(A) nations

(B) submarines

(C) weapons

(D) advances in technology

2 According to the passage, submarines only became major military weapons during the Second World War because

(A) submarines did not exist before the Second World War

(B) there were no supply ships for them to attack

(C) earlier subs were ineffective because of poor technology

(D) Germany was not yet at war with Britain

3 The word **consequence** in the passage is closest in meaning to

(A) requirement

(B) example

(C) evolution

(D) result

4 Which of the sentences below best expresses the essential information in the highlighted sentence in the passage? *Incorrect* choices change the meaning in important ways or leave out essential information.

(A) The fact that submarines were now easier targets limited their effectiveness, and besides, the Soviet Union and the United States were less reliant on sea transport than Britain.

(B) The fact that the Soviet Union and the United States did not depend on shipping made submarines easier to find and destroy, limiting their effectiveness.

(C) The Soviet Union and the United States limited the effectiveness of submarines by finding and destroying them easily and not relying on shipping.

(D) Submarines are only effective when they cannot be found and destroyed easily and a nation is dependent on shipping.

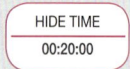
5 According to the passage, submarines became less effective during the Second World War because

- Ⓐ Britain became less dependent on shipping for supplies
- Ⓑ the development of new technology made them easier to find and destroy
- Ⓒ the development of nuclear weapons made them unnecessary
- Ⓓ the US and the Soviet Union were not island nations

6 The word eliminated in the passage is closest in meaning to

- Ⓐ questioned
- Ⓑ damaged
- Ⓒ removed
- Ⓓ decided

7 **Directions:** An introductory sentence for a brief summary of the passage is provided below. Complete the summary by selecting THREE answer choices that express the most important ideas in the passage. Some sentences do not belong in the summary because they express ideas that are not presented in the passage or are minor ideas in the passage.

Submarines first came to be seen as major military weapons in World War II.

- Ⓐ During World War II, the Germans used submarines to prevent supplies from reaching Britain.
- Ⓑ Germany had the largest and most effective submarine fleet during World War II.
- Ⓒ While they enjoyed early success during World War II, advances in technology made submarines less effective as World War II progressed.
- Ⓓ After World War II, no nations wanted to keep their submarine fleets because they were seen as useless.
- Ⓔ Submarines were important in the Cold War, but they could not be used effectively to launch surprise attacks.
- Ⓕ The development of nuclear submarines played an essential role in maintaining peace during the Cold War.

*i*BT Practice **2**

Crop Rotation

Intensive farming, growing more crops in an area than would naturally grow there, is an essential activity for human civilization. Without intensive farming, it would not be possible to produce enough food to support a large population in a small area. This fact can easily be seen in historical records, which clearly show that intensive farming and the first large-scale 5• civilizations developed around the same time. Before that, humans existed in small groups of hunter-gatherers.

Intensive farming also has a fundamental problem, however. Growing more crops than would grow naturally in an area takes the nutrients out of the ground faster than they are replaced, and eventually the soil is no longer good for farming. The first civilizations dealt 10• with this problem by living in river valleys which flooded on a regular basis. The floods would carry nutrients from farther up the river into the river valley, replacing the nutrients that were lost through intensive farming. But as human civilizations grew and spread to new areas, new solutions to this problem had to be found.

The solution was crop rotation. Crop rotation takes many different forms, but the basic 15• idea is always the same. Different crops take different nutrients out of the soil. By changing which crops they grow each year, farmers can use the same fields for a longer period. The most common crop rotation for much of history has been the three-year rotation. In the three-year rotation, farmers would grow one crop for one year, switch to another the next year, and not grow anything in that field the third year. Farmers would divide their land into three different 20• fields. In this way, they could farm two-thirds of their land continuously without damaging the soil. Crop rotation also has the added benefit of helping to control pests. Certain animals and insects only eat certain types of crops. By changing the crops they grow from year to year, farmers can make sure that these pests do not have a constant supply of food, forcing them to move from one area to another and limiting their population.

Part B
4

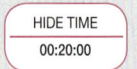
1 The author states that intensive farming has a fundamental problem in order to indicate that the problem

(A) has only one possible solution

(B) is a central fact of intensive farming

(C) makes intensive farming impossible

(D) can be avoided with planning

2 According to the passage, early civilizations were located in river valleys in order to

(A) avoid the dangerous floods farther up the river

(B) claim lands not taken by hunter-gatherers

(C) take advantage of the floods which renewed the soil

(D) avoid the need to farm the land intensively

3 The phrase this problem in the passage refers to the problem of

(A) frequently occurring floods in the river valleys

(B) not being able to grow enough food to support large populations

(C) living in areas where the soil is not good for farming

(D) the soil losing its nutrients through intensive farming

4 Based on the information in paragraph 3, the term crop rotation can best be explained as

(A) only growing crops which do not take nutrients out of the soil

(B) alternating crops in order to keep the land useful for farming

(C) changing from growing wheat to growing more productive crops

(D) farming on a continuous basis without damaging the soil

5 According to paragraph 3, all of the following are true of the three-year rotation EXCEPT

(A) it has been used for a long time

(B) it includes rest periods for fields

(C) it produces greater amounts of crops each year

(D) it requires the separation of land into different fields

REVIEW 目

HELP ?

BACK ◀

NEXT ▶

HIDE TIME
00:20:00

Part B

4

6 Which of the sentences below best expresses the essential information in the highlighted sentence in the passage? *Incorrect* choices change the meaning in important ways or leave out essential information.

(A) By changing the methods used to grow crops from year to year, farmers can make sure that pests do not have enough food to become a problem.

(B) By switching to different crops annually, farmers can control pests by interrupting their food supply, which both controls their populations and forces them to move to new areas.

(C) Farmers can force pests to move into new areas and limit their populations by changing their crops each year, but this limits the farmers' food supply.

(D) Farmers change the crops they grow each year because they can't limit the population of pests or force them to move into new areas if they do not.

7 **Directions:** An introductory sentence for a brief summary of the passage is provided below. Complete the summary by selecting THREE answer choices that express the most important ideas in the passage. Some sentences do not belong in the summary because they express ideas that are not presented in the passage or are minor ideas in the passage.

Intensive farming is an essential activity for human civilization, but it takes the nutrients out of the soil.

(A) We have learned that intensive farming allowed the development of large-scale civilizations by studying the records of early hunter-gatherers.

(B) While early civilizations dealt with the problems of intensive farming by only farming in river valleys, later civilizations used crop rotation.

(C) Crop rotation works because different crops need different nutrients, allowing the soil to refresh itself from year to year.

(D) Early farmers quickly learned that although there are many methods of crop rotation, the three-year rotation is the best system.

(E) The main disadvantage to the three-year system is that it requires a lot of land, because the fields must be divided into three parts.

(F) In addition to allowing farmers to farm the same land without damaging the soil, crop rotation also helps to control pests.

Vocabulary Review

Choose the word from each group that does not have the same meaning.

1   (A) be against   (B) oppose   (C) insist   (D) disagree

2   (A) permit   (B) approve   (C) agree to   (D) compare

3   (A) usual   (B) special   (C) unique   (D) exclusive

4   (A) distant   (B) direct   (C) far   (D) remote

5   (A) intimidate   (B) threaten   (C) frighten   (D) encourage

6   (A) controversial   (B) renewable   (C) disputed   (D) debatable

7   (A) definite   (B) alternative   (C) substitute   (D) other choice

8   (A) effectively   (B) as a result   (C) consequently   (D) therefore

Fill in the blank with the correct word from the box.

suffering from	aspects	advantages	plentiful
approve of	infected	alternative	disagreement

9   I think the movie tried to show different _____ of love.

10   Nancy's parents didn't _____ her decision to be a pilot.

11   There will be a(n) _____ supply of good food and drink at the party.

12   After having a big _____, we didn't talk to each other again.

13   One of the _____ of being a student is that you can get discounts on many things.

14   He's been _____ a bad headache for a long time.

15   Farmers must kill any chickens that are _____ with bird flu.

16   I was interested in _____ medicine and decided to study aromatherapy.

Part B +

Prose Summary

Schematic Table

Schematic Table

+ Introduction

In schematic table questions, you need to categorize specific facts in the passage. You will be given a chart with two or three categories, and be asked to place five or seven statements in the appropriate category. There are two unnecessary statements to distract you.

A schematic table question can be worth up to 3–4 points depending on the question type and number of correct answers.

+ Sample Question

TOEFL Reading

REVIEW   HELP   BACK   NEXT   HIDE TIME
                                00:20:00

Directions: Select the appropriate phrases from the answer choices and match them to the type of civilization to which they relate. TWO of the answer choices will NOT be used.

Answer Choices

- Small, independent kingdoms
- Large, well-organized army
- Relied on outer areas for food production
- Had more influence on later cultures
- Fought many wars against neighbors
- Developed only writing system in the Americas
- Destroyed by Spanish invaders

Mayan

- _____
- _____
- _____

Aztec

- _____
- _____

*In the real test, you are asked to drag each answer choice using your mouse and place it under the correct category.

+ Strategies

❶ As you read, check to see if a passage...

- compares or contrasts more than one idea
- splits a category into several small categories
- compares situations before and after a historical event

If it does any of the above, it is most likely to include a schematic table question.

❷ As you read, take notes on important details.

❸ As you answer, look for keywords in answer choices and scan the parts where these keywords appear.

❹ Eliminate answer choices if they…

- contain information not mentioned in the passage
- include details that contradict the passage

  OR

- do not belong in any of the categories

+ Recognizing the Questions

Directions: Select the appropriate phrases from the answer choices and match them to the source of fresh water to which they relate. TWO of the answer choices will NOT be used. ***This question is worth 3 (or 4) points.***

✉ **Read the paragraph about the differences between drones and worker bees.**

1   In any beehive, there are basically two kinds of bees: worker bees (females) and drones (males). Worker bees are by far the largest portion of the bee population, outnumbering the drones by over a hundred to one. As their name shows, worker bees do all the work in the beehive, from building the hive to finding and gathering food. Worker bees are also the soldiers of the beehive, defending it against any form of attack. In an attack the drones would be relatively useless, not only because of their small numbers, but also because they lack stingers. A drone's only function in the beehive is to fertilize the eggs of the queen.

☐ **beehive:** a structure that bees build to live in

☐ **outnumber:** to be more numerous than another group

☐ **drone:** a male bee that does no work

☐ **relatively:** fairly, comparatively

☐ **stinger:** a sharp needle of an insect

Q. Complete the table below, and then go back and underline the places in the paragraph where you found the information for each number.

	Drones	Worker Bees
(1) No role in defense of beehive		
(2) Responsible for food collection		
(3) Less than 1% of bee population		
(4) Have stingers		

Basic Drills (2)

Read the paragraphs below and write whether the answer choices contain accurate information, inaccurate information or information not mentioned in the passage.

1 One of the most famous gunfights in the history of the American West involved two families: the Earps and the Clantons. The Earps, led by their brother Wyatt, ran a bar in the town of Tombstone. But they also worked as lawmen, keeping order in the town. The Clantons lived outside of town, and were primarily cow thieves and highway robbers. When Wyatt Earp took a job protecting the stagecoaches that the Clantons had been robbing, the Clantons decided to get rid of the Earps. The gunfight at the OK Corral took place on Oct 26, 1881. The Clantons lost, and only a few of them survived. A few days later, they killed one of the Earp brothers, and Wyatt swore he would get revenge. Over the next year, he killed all of the Clantons.

☐ **lawman**: a police officer

☐ **stagecoach**: a vehicle pulled by horses

(A) The Clantons made their living through illegal activities. _____
(B) The gunfight at the OK Corral ended the fight between the Earps and the Clantons. _____
(C) The Clantons wanted the Earps dead because the Clantons wanted their business. _____

2 The earliest humans did not have the technology to mine or produce metals. Therefore, when making their tools, they had to rely on materials that they could find naturally. The two most important materials for early humans were stone and the bones of animals. Many animal bones can be carved into sharp points, and early humans used them to make small knives and other hunting tools like fish hooks. Stone was also used for many of the tools needed by early humans. Stone was heavier and made sharper points, so it was superior to bone for making many tools. For instance, a stone axe could be used to cut down a small tree, but bone tools were neither heavy enough nor strong enough for this.

☐ **superior**: better, more powerful, more effective

(A) Stone tools allowed early humans to later develop metal tools. _____
(B) Bone could only be carved into sharp, hooked points. _____
(C) Stone made better tools for hard work. _____

Select the appropriate phrases from the answer choices and match them to the type of colony to which they relate by checking the correct box. TWO of the answer choices will NOT be used.

1　　During the 9th and 10th centuries, the Vikings set up a number of colonies in the far north, most notably in Iceland and Greenland. Some of these colonies were successful, and others were not. The Greenland colony, for instance, disappeared after 450 years. The Iceland colony, however, survived centuries of poverty and is now a successful, independent nation. Both have poor soil, and are not good places to grow crops. But there are important differences that explain why the Greenland colony failed while the one on Iceland survived.

　　Both the Iceland and Greenland settlers switched from farming to raising sheep, which further destroyed the quality of the soil. The Iceland colonists, however, were quick to realize that their sheep were destroying the land, and took steps to limit the destruction. One such step was to switch from eating meat to eating fish. Fish made up a large part of the Icelandic diet, but the Greenlanders seem not to have eaten much fish at all. They continued to eat the traditional Viking diet of meat and dairy products, despite the large amount of seafood in Greenland. After 450 years the environmental destruction caused by their animals had already brought the Greenland colony near total collapse. The final push came when the Inuit, Native Americans commonly known as Eskimos, moved back into Greenland and attacked the Greenland settlers in large numbers. Already weakened by their poor environmental practices, the settlers were unable to resist, and were destroyed.

☐ **colony:** a country that is under the political control of a more powerful country

☐ **notably:** especially, in particular

	Iceland Colony	Greenland Colony
(1) Adjusted diet to match their environment		
(2) Unable to form a good relationship with natives		
(3) Stopped raising sheep and other destructive animals		
(4) Survived by becoming independent		
(5) Continued with environmentally destructive practices		

2   If you look at most plant eaters around the world, you will notice that most of them fall into two basic groups: those of a small size and those which are much larger. An example of a small plant eater would be a mouse, while an elephant would be a good example of a large one. Both small and large sizes are evolutionary solutions to the problems that plant eaters face danger from meat eaters.

By growing to a very large size, animals like elephants and rhinos are able to avoid the danger of predators, because there are no animals large enough to eat them. Once these animals grow past a few months old, they are no longer in danger of being eaten. This is always a danger for smaller plant eaters because there are always predators which are larger than they are, but their high populations mean that not all of them will be eaten. The main problem for small plant eaters is that they can only go out to find food at certain times because they must hide when predators are out hunting. Larger plant eaters also tend to have longer life spans than smaller animals. This, however, is a disadvantage in some ways. Large animals reach maturity more slowly, and have babies less often and in smaller numbers. This means that their populations recover from disease or drought far more slowly than those of smaller plant eaters, which have more babies more often. This leaves large plant eaters in greater danger of extinction.

☐ **evolutionary:** relating to the development of plants and animals

☐ **rhino:** a large heavy African or Asian animal with thick skin and either one or two horns on its nose

☐ **life span:** the length of time an animal lives

☐ **maturity:** the state when something is fully grown or developed

☐ **disadvantage:** a drawback, handicap, obstacle

☐ **extinction:** when a particular type of animal or plant stops existing

	Large Plant Eaters	Small Plant Eaters
(1) Able to look for food at any time		
(2) Able to hide from predators more easily		
(3) Primary danger comes from sudden drops in population		
(4) Less likely to die out as a species		
(5) Require more food to feed larger number of babies		

The American and French Revolutions

In 1776, the American colonists revolted against the power of King George III of Britain. For the Americans, the revolution was a huge success. Not only did they win their independence, they also went on to set up a political system that would be copied by nations around the world.

In 1789, perhaps inspired by the success of the Americans, the French revolted against Louis XVI, who was an absolute monarch. While the French Revolution was successful in some ways, and Louis XVI did lose his throne (as well as his head), it did not have the same long-range success as the American Revolution. The French Revolution led to ten years of chaos and murder in France, and years of dictatorship after that. In fact, France did not achieve a relatively stable democratic government until nearly 75 years after its revolution.

There are a number of reasons why the American Revolution was successful while the success of the French Revolution was questionable at best. First, while America was a British colony, the Americans had a separate culture in many ways. They saw the British as outsiders. Once they had won the war, the Americans no longer had to worry about the British. The French Revolution involved one united culture. Once their war was over, they had to find a way to heal the divisions in their society, which proved to be very difficult. French society was made up of the nobility and the common people, and the differences in their wealth and social status were huge. While America certainly had rich and poor people, they had no system of nobility. Besides, America was a growing country, and even the poor felt that they had a chance to prosper. This was not the case in France, where it remained extremely hard to move up in class. For these reasons, French society had a great deal of trouble in uniting to form a stable government.

1 **Directions:** Select the appropriate phrases from the answer choices and match them to the revolution to which they relate. TWO of the answer choices will NOT be used.

Answer Choices

- Resulted in the death of a king
- Provided inspiration for all later revolutions
- Did not fix the divisions in society
- Resulted in a stable government
- Involved separate cultures
- Brought about a more equal society
- Did not involve a noble class

American Revolution

- _____
- _____
- _____

French Revolution

- _____
- _____

Find the right word from the passage!

❶ To perform or carry out with success; accomplish: _____

❷ Not easily moved or changed: _____

❸ Not completely reasonable or acceptable: _____

❹ Social or professional position: _____

Training Camps

Before the start of their season, most sports teams, regardless of whether they are professional, college, or high school teams, hold a training camp. The training camps can last anywhere from two to three months. They serve several purposes. Obviously, they are intended to train the players and improve their skill, but they also help coaches make decisions about the
5 • team. As they watch their players in training camps, coaches can see which players they will keep on the team and which players will be dropped. They can also see what game strategies will work best for their team.

Training camp generally starts with about two weeks of conditioning. The intention of this phase of training camp is simply
10 • to get the players into good physical shape. It consists mostly of exercise, and players may not even play their actual sport. There are two types of conditioning: endurance conditioning and strength training. Endurance conditioning basically involves a lot of running and exercises to make the heart stronger. Strength training involves
15 • exercise to strengthen specific muscles. Most athletes agree that this is the most physically demanding part of training camp, and this is when the majority of training camp injuries occur.

While athletes may think conditioning is the hardest part physically, skills training is definitely the most stressful. Skills training takes up the rest of training camp and teaches players
20 • the specific skills of their positions. This involves much longer practices than conditioning, although the practices are less intense. It also means that players must study hours and hours of game tapes to learn the offensive and defersive strategies of other teams. Perhaps the most stressful part is the time when coaches make the major decisions about what players they will keep on the team.

1 **Directions:** Select the appropriate phrases from the answer choices and match them to the phase of training camp to which they relate. TWO of the answer choices will NOT be used.

Answer Choices

- Game strategy is developed
- Higher risk of injuries
- Longer practices
- Lasts for most of training camp
- Players are dropped from the team
- Practice against other teams
- Muscle development

Conditioning

- _____
- _____

Skills Training

- _____
- _____
- _____

Find the right word from the passage! 🖊

❶ A plan made in order to achieve something: _____

❷ A certain stage of development: _____

❸ Requiring a lot of time, energy, or attention: _____

❹ To use a particular amount of time, space, or effort: _____ _____

❺ Extreme in degree, strength, or size: _____

Moon Formation

Many of the moons in our solar system are captured moons, meaning that they were traveling freely through space, and the gravity of their planet captured them and held them in its orbit. This is normally easy to explain because most moons are very small or their planets are very large. In the case of our moon, however, it is hard to imagine a situation in which the Earth's gravity would have been strong

enough to capture an object the size of the moon. Another problem with the capture theory is that most captured moons orbit their planets in the opposite direction of their planet's spin, but the moon's orbit is the same as the spin of the Earth. Finally, since they formed separately, captured moons are usually chemically different from their planets.

But the US moon missions of the 1970s showed that the moon and the Earth are quite similar chemically. This gave rise to a new theory for moon formation, called impact theory. According to this theory, a planet about the size of Mars struck the Earth about 4.5 billion years ago. That planet was completely destroyed and large amounts of the Earth's surface were thrown into space. A huge ring of dust and tiny rocks began to orbit the Earth. That ring eventually formed into our moon. The impact theory explains a number of things. First, it helps explain why the orbits of the Earth and the moon are similar. More importantly, it helps explain why the Earth and the moon are so similar chemically. It also explains why the moon lacks heavy metals like iron. Those metals would have been too heavy to be thrown into space by the collision and would have stayed on Earth.

1   **Directions:** Select the appropriate phrases from the answer choices and match them to the type of moon to which they relate. TWO of the answer choices will NOT be used.

Answer Choices

- Much smaller than their planet
- Only orbit the Earth and Mars
- Lack heavy metals
- Majority of moons in the solar system
- Form outside of the solar system
- Similar orbit with their planet
- Differ from their planet chemically

Captured Moons

- _____
- _____
- _____

Impact Moons

- _____
- _____

Part B

5

Find the right word from the passage! ✏

❶ The force which causes things to drop to the ground: _____

❷ The act of forming something or of taking form: _____

❸ On the other side of a space from something: _____

❹ A _____ occurs when a moving object crashes into something.

The Cuban Missile Crisis

In 1962, the Soviet Union placed nuclear missiles on the island of Cuba, only 90 miles from the United States. At this distance, a missile would have a flight time of about three minutes, and the US would basically have no warning if the Soviets attacked them. This move completely upset the balance of power between the two nations. The Americans demanded that the Soviets remove the missiles, and the standoff that followed is known as the Cuban missile crisis. The Cuban missile crisis was one of the most significant events of the Cold War. Not only did it bring the US and the USSR close to nuclear war, it also illustrated exactly how bad the two nations were at dealing honestly with each other. It also led to greater opposition to nuclear weapons.

By the late 1950s the US knew it led the Soviets in both total numbers of missiles and missile range. At the end of Eisenhower's presidency, the US decided to place missiles in Turkey, less than 150 miles from the Soviet border. It was obvious that this would upset the balance of power, as the USSR had no missiles capable of hitting the continental United States at the time. The US knew it would upset the Soviets, and Eisenhower compared it to the USSR placing missiles in Mexico or Cuba. Declassified documents also reveal that the missiles in Turkey became operational almost one month before the Cuban missile crisis, adding to the sense that the Russian's placement of missiles in Cuba was largely a reaction to this.

Generals on both sides favored a military solution to the crisis, and Khrushev and Kennedy found it difficult to control their militaries. On the 13th day of the crisis, several military mistakes brought the world the closest it has ever been to nuclear war. A Russian commander shot down a U-2 spy plane over Cuba and another U-2 veered off course and flew into Soviet airspace. Both nations interpreted each other's actions as the opening steps to further military actions. On that day, Kennedy himself expressed a feeling which sums up all of the failures of the crisis. Upon learning of the flight over Soviet airspace, he said "There's always someone who doesn't get the message."

1 According to the passage, the Americans opposed the placement of Soviet missiles in Cuba because

- Ⓐ the Americans wished to protect Cuba
- Ⓑ this would allow the Soviets to launch a surprise attack
- Ⓒ this would allow the Soviets to launch more missiles at the US
- Ⓓ this would force the Americans to remove their missiles from Turkey

2 The phrase This move in the passage refers to

- Ⓐ The Soviet attack on the US
- Ⓑ The warning to the US
- Ⓒ The placement of missiles in Cuba
- Ⓓ The launch of Soviet missiles

3 According to the passage, all of the following are true of the Cuban missile crisis EXCEPT that

- Ⓐ it showed that the US and the USSR were unable to trust each other
- Ⓑ it led to the placement of missiles in Turkey as a reaction
- Ⓒ it heightened resistance to nuclear weapons
- Ⓓ it brought the world close to a nuclear war

4 According to paragraph 2, the placement of American missiles in Turkey upset the balance of power because

- Ⓐ it increased the range of the American missiles
- Ⓑ it gave the Soviets little warning in the event of an attack
- Ⓒ the missiles became operational before the Soviets were prepared
- Ⓓ the Soviets had no missiles within range of the US

5 Which of the sentences below best expresses the essential information in the highlighted sentence in the passage? *Incorrect* choices change the meaning in important ways or leave out essential information.

- Ⓐ Declassified documents also show that the missiles in Turkey were operational almost one month before the Cuban missile crisis, and that the placement of missiles in Cuba was a reaction to this.
- Ⓑ The idea that the placement of missiles in Cuba was a response to the American missiles in Turkey is suggested by documents which show the missiles became functional one month before the Cuban missile crisis.

Part B

5

C The presence of the missiles in Turkey was revealed in documents almost one month before the Cuban missile crisis, adding to the sense that placement of missiles in Cuba was a reaction to this.

D Declassified documents reveal that the missiles in Turkey were operational, adding to the sense that the Cuban missile crisis was a reaction to this.

6 The word interpreted in the passage is closest in meaning to

A translated

B viewed

C opposed

D feared

7 **Directions:** Select the appropriate phrases from the answer choices and match them to the nation to which they relate. TWO of the answer choices will NOT be used.

US

- _____
- _____
- _____

USSR

- _____
- _____

Answer Choices

- Intended to launch a surprise attack
- Plane flew into enemy airspace
- Leader wanted a military solution to the crisis
- Missiles incapable of reaching the other nation before the crisis
- More missiles with longer ranges
- Shot down enemy spy plane
- Took provocative moves before the crisis

iBT Practice 2

The Norman Invasion

Modern British culture, as well as the modern English language, stems from 1066 A.D., when Normans of northern France invaded and conquered England. Prior to this, England had been ruled by the Anglo-Saxons. Over time, these two cultures blended together to form what we know as the modern English culture and language.

The Normans were descended from the Vikings and had been invited to come and live in northern France by the French king in the 9th century in order to help protect the northern coasts of France. Thus, the Normans were separate from the culture of southern France. Their language had elements of French and Latin in it, but it also contained elements of the Germanic languages spoken by their Viking ancestors. The Normans were essentially a warrior society, and were always looking to expand their holdings. But until 1066, they had very little opportunity to do so, because they could not very well take land from the French, who were essentially their hosts, for fear of angering them.

The Anglo-Saxons had come to England in the 5th century, shortly after the end of Roman rule in England. Their ancestors were a mixture of Germanic tribes, and their language was purely Germanic in origin. By the 10th century, the Anglo-Saxons had gained control of all of England, and their main concern was defending themselves against invasions from the Vikings.

The Norman invasion started when the Anglo-Saxon king, Edward the Confessor, died in 1066 with no heir. The Normans saw this as their chance, and their king, William I, claimed the throne of England. He was not the only one, however, to do so. Harold Godwinson, an Anglo-Saxon noble, also claimed the throne for himself. So William invaded England, and on October 14th defeated and killed Godwinson at the Battle of Hastings. The Anglo-Saxons were not happy about being ruled by foreign invaders, but William's decision to replace all the Anglo-Saxon nobles with Norman ones meant there was little they could do about it. The first 100 years or so of Norman rule were indeed difficult, and the Normans kept control of England only through the use of force. Gradually, however, the two cultures began to mix together, until the Normans were no longer considered outsiders, and their rule was more acceptable to the people of England.

1 The word stems in the passage is closest in meaning to

- (A) branches
- (B) originates
- (C) develops
- (D) continues

2 According to the passage, what effect did the Norman invasion have?

- (A) It destroyed the original Anglo-Saxon culture.
- (B) It brought an end to Norman culture in France.
- (C) It resulted in the creation of a new, mixed culture.
- (D) It brought an end to the Viking invasions of England.

3 The word holdings in the passage is closest in meaning to

- (A) armies
- (B) wealth
- (C) culture
- (D) territory

4 According to paragraph 2, what prevented the Normans from gaining more land prior to 1066?

- (A) The English king had not yet died.
- (B) They were unable to invade England.
- (C) They could not anger their French hosts.
- (D) They were busy fighting off Viking invasions.

5 The word this in the passage refers to

- (A) the Norman invasion of England
- (B) the death of Edward the Confessor
- (C) King William's claim to the throne of England
- (D) the multiple claims to the throne of England

6 Which of the sentences below best expresses the essential information in the highlighted sentence in the passage? *Incorrect* choices change the meaning in important ways or leave out essential information.

- (A) While the Anglo-Saxons hated Norman rule, they could not really oppose it, since William replaced all the Anglo-Saxon nobles with Norman ones.
- (B) The Anglo-Saxons were not happy about being ruled by foreigners until William decided to replace all the Anglo-Saxon nobles with Norman ones.
- (C) William's decision to replace all the Anglo-Saxon nobles made them very unhappy, but since he was a foreign invader, there was little they could do about It.
- (D) The Anglo-Saxons were not happy, but since they were ruled by foreign invaders and William decided to replace all of their nobles, they could do nothing about it.

7 **Directions:** Select the appropriate phrases from the answer choices and match them to the culture to which they relate. TWO of the answer choices will NOT be used.

Normans

- _____
- _____
- _____

Anglo-Saxons

- _____
- _____

Answer Choices

- Primarily concerned with stopping Viking invasions
- Took land from the French through invasion
- Warrior society
- Language a mixture of other languages
- Society based on Roman laws
- Rulers of England after 1066
- Descended from Germanic tribes

Vocabulary Review

Choose the word from each group that does not have the same meaning.

1 (A) unprotected (B) sensitive (C) sensible (D) vulnerable

2 (A) extreme (B) enough (C) intense (D) great

3 (A) accompany (B) accomplish (C) achieve (D) fulfill

4 (A) comparatively (B) relatively (C) realistically (D) rather

5 (A) questionable (B) doubtful (C) understandable (D) controversial

6 (A) without doubt (B) immediately (C) clearly (D) obviously

7 (A) remaining (B) division (C) splitting up (D) separation

8 (A) eliminate (B) remove (C) get rid of (D) renovate

Fill in the blank with the correct word from the box.

endurance	conquered	gravity	status
survive	formation	phase	opposite

9 I stopped when I saw the car coming from the _____ direction.

10 The Normans _____ England in 1066.

11 The HIV virus cannot _____ in the mosquito's body.

12 People of higher _____ tend to be more careful about choosing a job.

13 Marathon runners must have a great deal of _____ .

14 I'm going through a(n) _____ where everything I used to believe doesn't seem to be true anymore.

15 My childhood experience had a great influence on the _____ of my personality.

16 A falling apple led Isaac Newton to his discovery of the law of _____ .

Memo

Making Inferences

This part of the test examines your skills to "read between the lines." You are asked to identify the author's underlying message and purpose, the organizational pattern of the passage, and the logical place of an additional sentence.

PART

Part **C** +

Inference

Rhetorical Purpose

Sentence Insertion

Inference

+ Introduction

When we read, we think one step further and make logical predictions from the information given in a passage. This process is called "inference." Inference questions test your ability to figure out information that is only implied, not directly mentioned in a passage. Basically, they require the ability to "read between the lines." There are 0–2 inference questions for each passage. These questions are worth 1 point each.

+ Sample Question

TOEFL Reading

REVIEW | HELP ? | BACK ◀ | NEXT ▶ | HIDE TIME 00:20:00

For many years, people taught their children not to hide under a tree during a thunderstorm because lightning strikes the tallest object in an area. However, the large number of lightning strikes that happen on golf courses and cattle ranches show this is not always the case.

Based on the information in the paragraph, it can be inferred that

  Ⓐ there are few trees on golf courses and cattle ranches

  Ⓑ lightning and its behavior are still poorly understood

  Ⓒ lightning does not actually strike the tallest object

  Ⓓ lightning is random

Answer & Explanation

The answer is (A). The author mentioned golf course and cattle ranges as an example to counter-argue the traditional theory, which implies that trees are prone to lightning strikes. Therefore, we can guess that the golf course and cattle ranches have few trees.

+ Strategies

❶ Try to have a complete understanding of the passage.

It is difficult to make correct inferences without fully comprehending the passage.
Take notes of important information as you read.

❷ Do not look for answer clues outside the passage.

Inferences must be made based on the information given in the passage.
Your personal experiences, ideas, or values should be excluded.

❸ Use different strategies depending on the question type.

If the question asks you ...

• to make an inference based on one or more statements
   → *Pay attention to specific details.*
• to find a correct conclusion based on the entire passage
   → *Skim the entire passage and take notes of the major ideas.*
• to predict a possible outcome or result
   → *Try to understand the basic principles.*

+ Recognizing the Questions

• Which of the following can be inferred about ...?
• The author of the passage implies that ...
• Which of the following can be inferred from paragraph 1 about ...?

Basic Drills (1)

✉ **Read the short paragraphs below and choose the correct inference.**

1 For 300 years, the Vikings terrorized much of Europe. Their small, swift boats allowed them to attack the coasts of Europe with little warning. The Vikings also knew of the existence of North America, but the Native Americans were saved from the Vikings' raids due to their inability of their small boats to cross the open ocean.

☐ **terrorize:** to frighten people with threat

☐ **raid:** an attack

(1) The Vikings did not have to cross the open ocean to attack European nations. ☐
(2) The Europeans learned of the existence of North America during the Viking raids. ☐

2 One way to spot poor mining practices is to watch the health of people near the mine. The appearance of increased rates of cancer and birth defects can show that a mine has been dumping its waste into the water. Mine waste carries many poisonous chemicals like cyanide and arsenic. These chemicals are expensive to dispose of properly, and many mines are tempted to simply dump their waste rather than pay the cost of waste disposal.

☐ **birth defects:** disabilities that babies have when they are born

☐ **dispose:** to get rid of

☐ **be tempted to:** to be attracted to doing something

(1) Mines do not make enough money to dispose of their waste properly. ☐
(2) Cyanide and arsenic can cause cancer and birth defects. ☐

3 One of the major causes of forest fires is the disappearance of slow-growth trees. They generally have a very thick bark that makes them resistant to fires. These are also the trees most valued by logging companies. Logging companies cut down slow-growth trees and replace them with faster growing trees, which the company can cut down for wood sooner. Unfortunately, this also allows forest fires to spread more easily.

☐ **bark:** the outer covering of a tree

☐ **resistant:** strong

☐ **replace:** to exchange something with another

(1) Logging companies are not concerned about trees as long as they can cut down trees quickly. ☐
(2) Fast growing trees have thinner bark and are less resistant to fire than slow growth trees. ☐

Basic Drills (2)

Read the short paragraphs below and decide if each inference is True (T) or False (F) according to the passage.

1 Predators may kill other animals for two basic reasons. The first is to eat that animal. But this is not always the reason, especially among large predators. They often compete for the same animals as prey. However, the numbers of prey animals are limited, and can only support small populations of predators. This can mean that while one predator eats, an other goes hungry. In order to ensure their own food supply in areas with limited resources, predators often resort to killing other predators that hunt the same prey. But hunting another large predator can be dangerous, and the resulting fight could seriously injure the animal even if it doesn't kill the other predator. This explains why lions often seek to kill cheetah cubs while the mother is away hunting.

- **predator:** an animal that kills and eats other animals
- **ensure:** to make sure that something happens
- **resort to:** to do something because there is no other option
- **cub:** a baby of a wild animal such as a lion or a bear

(1) Lions often hunt cheetahs as a source of food. ☐ T ☐ F
(2) Lions are unable to kill-full grown cheetahs. ☐ T ☐ F

2 In the mid-1800s, hundreds of thousands of Americans began to move west looking for new lands. Most of the Midwest lands belonged to Native American tribes. When the Americans first started to move west, the tribes were friendly. They thought that there was plenty of land for everyone and they were eager to trade with the new settlers. As more settlers moved west, they took more and more land, and more importantly, they started to kill large numbers of buffalo. When the Native Americans saw that an essential part of their food supply was in danger, they began to oppose the settlers. Over the years there were many sad battles between them, and the Native Americans were slowly forced to sign peace agreements that gave most of their lands to the settlers.

- **settlers:** new arrivals in a place
- **oppose:** to be against, to fight

(1) The American settlers always intended to steal the land from the Native Americans. ☐ T ☐ F
(2) Buffalo was an important food source for the Native Americans. ☐ T ☐ F

Basic Drills (3)

✉ **Read the passage below and answer the following questions.**

Animals have many different strategies for reproduction. One such strategy is called territoriality. In this strategy, each male animal has a selected territory from which he will chase away all other males. In this way, he can ensure that any females within his territory only mate with him. A good example of this would be the bluegill, a fish which can be found in much of eastern North America. Bluegills are school fish, meaning that they travel in groups. But during mating season, each male bluegill makes its own nest. Bluegills will fiercely defend their nests and chase any other males away. The largest males make their nests in the center of their pond or stream, and those on the outside have little chance of finding a mate.

Thus, smaller fish have to develop other reproductive strategies. One such method is called the "sneaker strategy." Smaller males cannot directly challenge the males at the center. Instead, they wait until the larger males are mating with a female and not paying attention. Then, they sneak into the nest and fertilize some of the eggs before the larger male notices them. This method is not entirely effective. Not only does the smaller male fertilize a smaller number of eggs, but larger males also have been seen selectively eating the young of the smaller males in their nests once the eggs have hatched.

□ **reproduction:** producing babies, young animals or plants

□ **mate:** to have sex to produce babies

□ **sneak into:** to move secretly into

□ **fertilize:** to make new animal or plant life develop

□ **effective:** successful

1 Based on the information in paragraph 1, it can be inferred that

(A) males in every animal species are territorial
(B) most female bluegills can be found in the center of a pond
(C) large male bluegills are the only males able to mate

2 Based on the information in paragraph 2, it can be inferred that

(A) large male bluegills are easily distracted
(B) smaller bluegills are faster than large bluegills
(C) male bluegills can tell their young from the young of other bluegills

Basic Drills (4)

📩 **Read the passage below and answer the following questions.**

For hundreds of years large companies, representing powerful nations, have been taking valuable resources out of poorer nations. In many cases, especially in modern times, these large companies have been welcomed by poor nations because they bring much needed jobs. That happiness often turns to rage in later years when the effects of those companies become visible.

Since many poor nations do not have strong laws protecting their environments or their workers, these companies can keep their costs down by using environmentally destructive methods or by exposing their workers to dangerous situations. Here is a quick example. In the 1980s, an American chemical company operated a factory in India. The company followed almost none of the safety procedures that would have been required in a richer nation. As a result, they had a terrible chemical accident in 1984, when a poison gas leaked out of the factory and killed nearly 4,000 people. Since then, the American Company, Union Carbide, has paid hundreds of millions of dollars to settle lawsuits in India. In addition, they face strong opposition from local populations whenever they try to open new factories in other countries. This has led to the idea of a social contract. According to this idea, companies should act in a socially and environmentally responsible way, even when the laws of a nation do not require them to or when it is more expensive. The logic is that this is cheaper in the long run because there will be fewer lawsuits.

□ **rage:** a strong feeling of anger

□ **safety procedures:** steps to follow to stay safe

□ **leak:** to flow through a small hole or crack

□ **settle a lawsuit:** to end a lawsuit, to reach an agreement between parties

Part C

6

1 It can be inferred from the passage that local people often become angry at large companies because

(A) they only provide low paying jobs to the local people
(B) these companies steal all the resources of their nation
(C) they cause damage to the local environment and people

2 What can be inferred from the passage about Union Carbide?

(A) They went bankrupt after the accident in India.
(B) They were very sorry that they caused so much damage in India.
(C) They chose not to follow safety procedures to save money.

The Geneva Conventions

By the late 1800s, the invention of machine guns and cannons was changing warfare in terrible ways. In 1859, a man named Henri Durant saw this for himself when he witnessed a particularly violent battle between French and Austrian soldiers. It was unlike any other battle he had seen before. After the battle, 38,000 soldiers lay dead or wounded on the battlefield, but for three days no one went to care for the wounded soldiers. The problem was that the two sides could not agree to stop the fighting long enough to go get the wounded. Horrified, Durant finally convinced the citizens of a nearby town to get the wounded and take care of them.

After the war, Durant remained deeply troubled by what he had seen. His efforts led to the first Geneva Convention of 1864. Basically, the first Geneva Convention said that during a war, armies had a responsibility to allow wounded soldiers to be taken off the battlefield, and that they had a responsibility to provide medical care for those wounded soldiers, regardless of what side they fought for. Originally, 47 countries signed the Geneva Convention, and for these countries, the Geneva Convention became the law. Over the next 100 years, there were three more Geneva Conventions creating rules for the fair treatment of prisoners of war and rules to protect citizens in a war zone. World War II showed that the Geneva Conventions needed to be revised to give them more power and make it easier to punish those who violated them. This was done in 1949.

The 1949 revisions also made it a war crime to use certain types of weapons, such as poison gas. Today, nearly every nation on Earth has signed the Geneva Conventions, and they are considered to be international law. War is still horrible, but the Geneva Conventions have helped to place at least some limits on that horror.

1   Based on the information in paragraph 1, it can be inferred that

(A)   machine guns wounded more people than they killed
(B)   Henri Durant was either a French or Austrian doctor
(C)   the citizens who helped Durant were not afraid of the soldiers
(D)   machine guns greatly increased the numbers of deaths and injuries in war

2   According to paragraph 2, what can be inferred about World War II?

(A)   The Geneva Conventions were violated during the war.
(B)   World War II did not actually end until 1949.
(C)   World War II was the most horrible war in history.
(D)   Not many countries had signed the Geneva Conventions before the war.

Part C

6

Find the right word from the passage!

❶ To see something happen: _____

❷ To persuade to do something: _____

❸ The people who live in a town or city: _____

❹ To change something in order to improve it: _____

The Sumerians

There is much debate between archeologists* about when and where the first civilizations developed. That is because the answer to that question depends on what one defines as a civilization. If a civilization is simply a small group of people with a similar culture and beliefs, then civilizations have existed in many parts of the world for thousands of years. If a civilization is defined as a larger, more complex society with a government and the construction of cities, then the first civilization was probably the Sumerian civilization in what is now Iraq. The Sumerians were descended from the Ubaid culture, which was made up of small villages of farmers who lived slightly farther north. Sometime around 4,000 B.C. these farmers moved down into the valley along the Tigris River.

This land received little rain, and was unsuitable for farming. Therefore, it was empty and the Sumerians had plenty of room and little competition from other peoples. What allowed the Sumerians to successfully farm in this dry land was their knowledge of irrigation, the practice of taking water from a river or lake and moving it to fields through the use of man-made canals. This allowed the Sumerians to farm here successfully despite the lack of rain. We know that the Sumerians had a great understanding of irrigation because their language is filled with words related to it. With their advanced farming technology and the absence of other cultures competing for the land, the Sumerian population grew and spread throughout the entire Tigris valley. Their villages grew into small city-states and they began to form more complex government and social systems. We owe many of the basic technologies of human civilization to the Sumerians. Not only did they perfect irrigation, they also developed the first writing system, which continued to be used by other civilizations after their downfall.

□ archeologist: someone who studies ancient societies by examining what remains of their buildings, graves, tools, etc.

1 According to paragraph 1, it can be inferred that

(A) most archeologists believe that Sumeria was the first civilization
(B) cities and governments can be found in earlier civilizations than Sumeria
(C) archeologists lack a common definition for the term "civilization"
(D) farming began sometime around 4,000 B.C.

2 Which of the following can be inferred from the passage about the Sumerian civilization?

(A) They moved into the Tigris valley to avoid attacks from other cultures.
(B) The Tigris River was their source of water for irrigation.
(C) They only grew crops that required little water to grow.
(D) Their downfall was caused by water shortages in the Tigris River.

3 Based on the information in paragraph 2, what can be inferred about the Sumerian language?

(A) It was developed to help irrigation only.
(B) It formed the basis for later languages.
(C) It has been successfully translated.
(D) It had a better writing system than other languages.

Find the right word from the passage! ✏️

❶ A discussion on a subject on which people have different views: _____

❷ A human society with its own social organization: _____

❸ Not having the right qualities for a certain purpose: _____

❹ A sudden failure or collapse: _____

European Museums

Europe is famous for its art museums. This is not only because Europe has produced a great number of artists, but also because over the centuries, European nations have acquired huge collections of art from other cultures. For example, some European museums hold larger collections of early Egyptian art than Egyptian museums. This is a consequence of centuries of European colonialism throughout the world.

Starting in the 15ᵗʰ century and lasting in some parts of the world until World War II, European nations operated colonies from which they took the valuable natural resources which they needed to run their empires. In addition to those natural resources, however, Europeans also stripped many of their colonies of their cultural treasures. The Europeans sent native art back to their homelands by the boatload from their colonies in South America, Africa, and other parts of the world. Some of this art remained in the hands of private collectors, but much of it eventually wound up in the museums of Europe. The case of the Benin bronzes is a fairly typical example.

Benin was an African kingdom with a rich artistic heritage. In the 1800s, it was also under increasing pressure from Britain to become a British colony. This resulted in a short war in 1897 which the British easily won. After their victory, the British took much of Benin's art back to England, including 1,000 bronze plaques which were one of Benin's greatest cultural treasures. About 200 of these plaques went to the British National Museum. The others were sold to private collectors. Since then, Nigeria, the nation which now stands on the former kingdom of Benin, has managed to buy 50 of these plaques from the Museum. But the Nigerians want all of the plaques returned to them, arguing that they were wrongfully stolen, and the British museum has no right to them. The case of the Benin bronzes is only one such case. All across the world, former colonies are calling for the return of their cultural treasures.

1 Which of the following can be inferred from paragraph 1?

(A) European museums would not be famous without art from other cultures.

(B) Egyptian art is more highly valued in Europe than in Egypt.

(C) Egypt was once colonized by a European nation.

(D) European museums have a lot of money to buy art.

2 According to the passage, what can be inferred about the art from other cultures in European museums?

(A) It will have to be returned to the former colonies.

(B) The majority of it comes from the kingdom of Benin.

(C) Most of it was acquired in wars.

(D) Much of it dates from before World War II.

Part C

6

Find the right word from the passage! 🖊

❶ To buy or obtain something: _____

❷ Something that happens as a result: _____

❸ A very valuable and important object: _____

❹ Traditional beliefs, values, and customs of a country or society: _____

Dating Archeological Sites

Archeologists are scientists who study past cultures. Much of what we know about these cultures comes from investigating the places where they lived. For example, an archeologist may examine the site of an ancient farm, or that of an old fort or city. As archeologists slowly and carefully dig through these sites, the things they find, such as old tools, can tell us a great
5 • deal about the people who lived or worked there. When archeologists find such an object, one of the most difficult and important jobs is to figure out how old it is, because this allows them to track the development of the culture the object belonged to.

Archeologists use layering to determine the age of the objects they find. According to this idea, the deeper underground an object is found, the older it is, because more time has passed
10 • to allow dirt to build up over it. This gives archeologists a basic point of comparison. As they dig, archeologists usually find objects in layers that stack one on top of another. Archeologists can then guess that the objects they find in a particular layer all come from the same basic time period. One of the problems with layering, however, is that it only tells us if an object is younger or older than other objects found at the same site. It does not tell us how old a particular
15 • object is.

For that, archeologists must use radiocarbon dating. Carbon exists in two basic forms: carbon-12, which is stable, and carbon-14, which is unstable and eventually turns into nitrogen. This happens at a steady pace. All living things have an equal percentage of carbon-12 and carbon-14 in their bodies. When they die, however, they stop taking carbon-14 into their bodies,
20 • and that percentage slowly changes as the carbon-14 turns into nitrogen. From measuring the amount of carbon-14 found in bones or in products that come from plants at a site, we can learn how old they are.

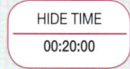
1 The word site in the passage is closest in meaning to

- (A) view
- (B) evidence
- (C) location
- (D) wreckage

2 According to paragraph 1, it is important to determine the age of objects found during an archeology dig because

- (A) this is the most difficult part of the archeology dig
- (B) this allows us to understand how the civilization progressed
- (C) this allows us to know which culture the object belonged to
- (D) this allows us to better understand how ancient farms worked

3 According to the passage, what can be inferred about a knife buried several inches below a shovel?

- (A) The knife came from a more advanced culture than the shovel.
- (B) The shovel was used to bury the knife.
- (C) The knife and the shovel came from two different cultures.
- (D) The knife was older than the shovel.

4 The phrase one on top of another in the passage refers to

- (A) objects
- (B) layers
- (C) archeologists
- (D) archeology sites

5 According to paragraph 3, all of the following are true of carbon-14 EXCEPT

- (A) it eventually is converted into nitrogen
- (B) it is present in all living things
- (C) it is essential to layer dating
- (D) it is used to determine the exact age of an object

6 According to the passage, it can be inferred that radiocarbon dating

- (A) is useless in dating metal tools
- (B) has allowed us to know the full history of ancient cultures
- (C) is a relatively new tool for archeologists
- (D) requires expensive equipment not available to all archeologists

Part C

6

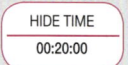
7   **Directions:** An introductory sentence for a brief summary of the passage is provided below. Complete the summary by selecting THREE answer choices that express the most important ideas in the passage. Some sentences do not belong in the summary because they express ideas that are not presented in the passage or are minor ideas in the passage.

One of the most important facts archeologists working at any site must learn is the age of the objects they find.

(A) Unfortunately, it is extremely difficult to find the age of objects, and sometimes it is impossible.

(B) Determining the age of an object gives archeologists the ability to determine how advanced a culture was at different points in its history.

(C) By studying the depths at which they find different objects, archeologists can determine their relative ages.

(D) It is important for archeologists to slowly and carefully count the number of layers that they find at a particular site.

(E) To find out the age of an object, archeologists must measure the amount of carbon-14 that it has in it.

(F) Without carbon-14 it would be impossible to determine the exact age of the objects that archeologists find.

*i*BT Practice 2

Cuteness

Most people will agree that puppies and kittens are cute, even if those people are not especially animal lovers. When asked to explain why they think a kitten or a puppy is cute, however, most people would probably have trouble providing a clear explanation. It turns out, however, that there is a clear scientific reason for why we find these animals to be cute. Cuteness apparently depends on a few factors, some of which are physical and some of which have to do with how these animals act. First, cuteness is most often associated with animals or people that have small bodies when compared to the size of their head and eyes, as is true with human babies and many baby animals. When looking at actions, playfulness is seen as being cute. This is again another characteristic of babies.

The reason for this is that some animals have evolved to be cute when they are babies. This makes sure that they are cared for by their parents. There is a significant amount of evidence for this theory. First of all, animals that cannot care for themselves when they are born are mostly mammals. Snakes, for example, do not need the care of their parents when they hatch. But then, a baby snake isn't exactly cute. A kitten, which certainly is cute, requires its mother's care for at least the first few months of its life. Without that care, the kitten will almost certainly die.

Further evidence comes from the reactions of animals to cute babies which are not theirs, or perhaps not even of the same species. There are many cases in which a cute animal has been adopted by a mother from a different species. The most famous case may be that of a female lab gorilla which adopted and cared for a small kitten. In humans, the same response has been documented. Humans routinely adopt and care for cute animals. Furthermore, psychological studies have shown that adults react more positively towards, and are more likely to show concern for, babies that are considered cuter. Thus, cuteness is not simply an opinion; it is an instinctive reaction that all of us share.

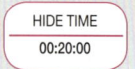
1 According to paragraph 1, all of the following are characteristics associated with cuteness EXCEPT

(A) loving animals

(B) being playful

(C) having a small body

(D) having large eyes

2 According to the passage, how does being cute help young animals?

(A) It ensures that their parents will play with them.

(B) It ensures that people will adopt them.

(C) It ensures that they will be cared for.

(D) It ensures that their parents want more babies.

3 According to the passage, what can be inferred about cute animals?

(A) They are mostly mammals.

(B) They are only cute as babies.

(C) They make good pets for people.

(D) Gorillas will always care for them.

4 The word reactions in the passage is closest in meaning to

(A) concerns

(B) responses

(C) emotions

(D) assistance

5 The word routinely in the passage is closest in meaning to

(A) happily

(B) easily

(C) apparently

(D) regularly

6 Which of the sentences below best expresses the essential information in the highlighted sentence in the passage? *Incorrect* choices change the meaning in important ways or leave out essential information.

(A) Additionally, psychological studies have shown that adults react more positively to the concern shown by cuter babies.

(B) Furthermore, it has been proven in psychological studies that adults respond better to and show more concern for cuter babies.

(C) Furthermore, cuter babies are better for psychological studies because adults are more likely to react positively to and show more concern for them.

(D) Furthermore, psychological studies have shown that adults prefer cuter babies because the babies are more likely to have positive reactions to them.

7 **Directions:** An introductory sentence for a brief summary of the passage is provided below. Complete the summary by selecting THREE answer choices that express the most important ideas in the passage. Some sentences do not belong in the summary because they express ideas that are not presented in the passage or are minor ideas in the passage.

Scientists now believe that cuteness is actually an evolutionary strategy.

(A) Even people who don't like animals agree that baby animals are cute, especially animals like kittens and puppies.

(B) Cuteness is defined by scientists as a particular set of characteristics that happen to be common in many young animals.

(C) Being cute ensures that young animals will be cared for when they cannot do it themselves.

(D) In studies, gorillas have reacted especially positively to cute animals and cared for them.

(E) Supporting evidence for the theory of cuteness comes from watching the behavior of both humans and animals.

(F) The theory of cuteness developed from psychology tests involving human babies, in which people preferred cuter babies.

Vocabulary Review

Choose the word from each group that does not have the same meaning.

1 (A) effective (B) successful (C) useful (D) careful

2 (A) conscience (B) consequence (C) result (D) effect

3 (A) civilization (B) society (C) communication (D) community

4 (A) discussion (B) organization (C) debate (D) argument

5 (A) stand for (B) serve as (C) represent (D) agree with

6 (A) make sense (B) make certain (C) make sure (D) ensure

7 (A) resistance (B) disapproval (C) indifference (D) opposition

8 (A) downfall (B) treatment (C) collapse (D) destruction

Fill in the blank with the correct word from the box.

citizens	represent	debates	exposed
defines	witnessed	unsuitable	Heritage

9 The police officer asked me if I had _____ the car accident the other day.

10 The palace is a part of the UNESCO World Cultural _____.

11 A friend of mine will _____ our country at the Miss World competition.

12 It is really dangerous to be _____ to nuclear radiation.

13 The subway is used by thousands of _____ and it should be kept safe at all times.

14 Small boats are _____ for traveling in the open ocean.

15 There have been a lot of _____ on that problem among the professors.

16 The dictionary _____ a miracle as "something lucky that you didn't expect to happen or didn't think was possible."

Part **C** +

Inference

Rhetorical Purpose

Sentence Insertion

Rhetorical Purpose

+ Introduction

Writers choose different rhetorical strategies to deliver their message effectively. These strategies include giving an explanation, listing examples, and making comparisons and contrasts.

The rhetorical purpose questions ask you to determine why the author states certain information in the passage. They may also ask you to identify which of the rhetorical strategies is applied. There are 0–2 rhetorical purpose questions for each passage. These questions are worth 1 point each.

+ Sample Question

TOEFL Reading   REVIEW   HELP ?   BACK ◀   NEXT ▶ 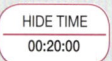 HIDE TIME 00:20:00

If you want to find the biggest machine on land, you'll have to go to a coal mine. There you will find the Caterpillar 797, the world's biggest truck. The 797 is built to carry huge amounts of rock away from the mines. It can carry 360 tons of rock. Each of its four tires is 13 feet tall and five feet wide and costs over $30,000. The engine of the 797 is enormous. It is more powerful than 30 average cars and uses 65 gallons of gasoline each hour. The truck is very complicated and is controlled by eight computers.

Why does the author mention the amount of gasoline used per hour by the Caterpillar 797?

(A) To stress the cost of operating it

(B) To better illustrate the size of its engine

(C) To further explain its design

(D) To suggest that it is bad for the environment

Answer & Explanation

The answer is (B). By stating that the engine of the 797 "is more powerful than 30 average cars and uses 65 gallons of gasoline each hour," the author emphasizes how huge it is.

+ Strategies

❶ Focus on how the specific information relates to the main idea.

Read the question and locate the relevant section in the passage. As you read, pay attention to the role of the information in supporting the main idea.

❷ Be familiar with how ideas are organized and what expressions are used.

Functions	Expressions		
Comparison & contrast	likewise	in the same way	similarly
	on the other hand	on the contrary	however
	despite	yet	whereas
Cause & effect	so	because	due to
	therefore	as a result	that is why
	consequently	for this reason	whereas
Classification	differences	features	characteristics
Example	for example	for instance	
Additional information	in addition	moreover	furthermore
	also	besides	

❸ Memorize expressions that are often used in answer choices.

to argue	to define	to illustrate	to prove
to describe	to introduce	to show	to persuade
to compare	to contrast	to explain	to give examples
to support	to summarize	to criticize	to suggest
to predict	to analyze	to present	to give a reason for

+ Recognizing the Questions

- The author discusses ... in paragraph 1 in order to ...
- Why does the author mention ... in paragraph 1?
- In paragraph 1, the author uses ... as an example of ...
- In paragraph 1, the author explains the concept of ... by

Basic Drills (1)

✉ **Choose the purpose of each paragraph.**

1 Deforestation, the cutting down of entire forests, is a problem for everyone, regardless of where they live. Deforestation produces a number of problems that affect the entire planet, such as global warming, more frequent droughts, and greater damage caused by storms. Therefore, deforestation in a country like Brazil affects not only the Brazilians, but people all over the world.

☐ **regardless of:** not affected by

(1)　To discuss the effects of deforestation ☐
(2)　To encourage Brazilians not to cut down their forests ☐

2 Most societies deal with crime by punishing criminals. While punishment is necessary, prevention is far more effective in dealing with crime. Most crimes are a result of social factors such as poverty and a lack of education. These social factors leave people with few chances to make an honest living, and make crime a more tempting option. By increasing the amount of money spent dealing with poverty and improving education, rather than spending that money on punishment, we could greatly reduce crime.

☐ **factor:** a cause, influence

☐ **poverty:** being poor

(1)　To describe different methods of dealing with crime and their benefits ☐
(2)　To argue that societies should focus on prevention of crime rather than punishment ☐

3 When learning an instrument, a good practice schedule is essential for development. Practice should be daily and at least thirty minutes in length, although a longer practice time is preferable. Practice should start with a short warm-up to loosen and relax the muscles. That should be followed by an intensive period focusing on one particular skill or technique. This should take up most of the practice time. Finally, some time should be given to playing for enjoyment to keep the student interested in the instrument.

☐ **preferable:** better, more suitable

☐ **loosen:** to make something less tight

☐ **intensive:** taking a lot of effort

(1)　To describe the elements of a good practice schedule ☐
(2)　To argue that good technique is most important in music ☐

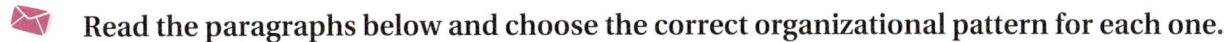

Read the paragraphs below and choose the correct organizational pattern for each one.

1 The Industrial Revolution took place in most countries during the late 19th century. One important impact of the Industrial Revolution was that it changed the relationship between workers and their bosses. Before then, workers had worked in small shops and had personal relationships with their bosses. In a factory of one or two hundred workers, however, the owner might not even know the names of all his workers. Furthermore, since workers were now simply running machines in the factories, they were more easily replaced than the skilled workers of earlier times. Both of these factors led to worsening conditions for many workers.

☐ **furthermore:** in addition

☐ **skilled:** trained

Q. What is the organizational pattern of this paragraph?

(A) Description / Explanation
(B) Comparison / Contrast
(C) Cause / Effect
(D) Sequence

2 Societies have two basic methods of decision making, called top-down and bottom-up decision making. In top-down decision making, decisions are made by a single leader or a small group of people. Those decisions are then made into laws which everyone must follow. In bottom-up decision making, decisions are only made after the entire group has discussed the issue and come to an agreement. Top-down decision making has the advantage of being fast and efficient. It is also good for large decisions, where most people may not have enough information to make a proper decision. The main drawback to top-down decision making is that at least some people will be unhappy with the decision. Since bottom-up decision making relies on agreement of all members of the group, it does not have that problem, but it may take much longer for a group to make a decision.

☐ **come to an agreement:** to agree, to reach an agreement

☐ **drawback:** a weak point, disadvantage

Q. What is the organizational pattern of this paragraph?

(A) Description / Explanation
(B) Comparison / Contrast
(C) Cause / Effect
(D) Sequence

Part C
7

✉ **Choose the correct answer for each question.**

1 When the Spanish first landed in South America, the Native American civilizations there were in awe of them. But as they realized that the Spanish were only interested in enslaving them and stealing their riches, they began to fight back. The Spanish only numbered in the few hundreds, and there were tens of thousands of Native American warriors. Yet, for the Spanish it was like fighting children because the stone weapons of the Native Americans were useless against the armor of the Spanish.

☐ **in awe of:** having admiration for someone

☐ **enslave:** to make someone into a slave

☐ **warrior:** a fighter, a soldier

☐ **armor:** metal or leather clothing that solders wear in battles

Q. Why does the author mention fighting children?

(A) To stress the cruelty of the Spanish soldiers in South America

(B) To illustrate the young age of Native American warriors

(C) To emphasize that the Native Americans had no chance of victory

2 One of the greatest challenges that many developing countries face is population growth. If the population of a country grows too quickly, or grows beyond a certain point, that country may not be able to grow enough food to feed its citizens. In many parts of Africa, Asia, and South America, this is a serious problem. Kenya, for example, has a growth rate of 4%. That means that the population of Kenya doubles every 17 years. To put that in perspective, let's apply that growth rate to an average American city. Washington, D.C. has a population of about 4 million people. If Washington, D.C. had a growth rate of 4% then it would have a population of 8 million by 2020, and a population of 16 million by 2040! Clearly such rapid growth would be a problem even for rich nations, so it should be easy to imagine the problems it causes for a poor nation like Kenya.

☐ **put something in perspective:** to think about something in a larger content

Q. The author mentions Washington, D.C. in order to

(A) show that rapid population growth is A especially problem atic for cities

(B) better illustrate how quickly Kenya's population is growing

(C) give an example of another area with high population growth

3 Some historians believe that history is determined by a small number of people whose actions change the world in some way. This theory, called the Great Man Theory, claims that without these people the great changes of the world would never have occurred. Isaac Newton's discovery of gravity formed the basis of modern astronomy and physics. Einstein's discovery of relativity led the way for nuclear power, and these are just two examples. Some people, however, question the Great Man Theory. They argue that the time in which a person lives is more important than the person himself. For instance, Einstein's work on relativity was based on the work of scientists in the late 1800s. In addition, Einstein was not the only scientist working on the theory of relativity. Many other scientists were working on the same problem. Einstein was simply the first one to solve it.

□ gravity: the power to cause things to drop to the ground

□ astronomy: the study of the stars and planets

□ theory of relativity: a theory related to space, time, and movement

Q. Why does the author discuss the other scientists who were working on relativity?

(A) To suggest that Einstein was not really a great scientist
(B) To call the Great Man Theory into question
(C) To suggest that Einstein may have stolen their work

4 Kings in early civilizations needed reasons to explain why people should follow them and serve them. In the earliest civilizations, most kings justified their rule by either claiming that they were gods, or that they were in direct contact with the gods. The reasoning was that the rest of the people should serve them because if they did not, the gods would punish them. Basically, there was a deal in which the people agreed to work for the king, and the king claimed to protect them from natural disasters, which were believed to be sent by the gods. Therefore, the greatest threat to a king's power was not from other politicians, but simple bad luck. Historical documents show that many ancient kings who lost their power did so at times when there were frequent floods, disease, or other natural disasters.

□ justify: to prove something is reasonable

Q. Why does the author discuss the frequency of natural disasters?

(A) To show that many kings failed to protect their people from the gods
(B) To provide an explanation of when and why kings lost their power
(C) To suggest that many kings simply used religion to keep themselves in power

Beaver Dams

Beavers are large rodents* that live in the streams of much of North America and Europe. Beavers are most widely known for the dams they build and their ability to cut down trees, which they use to build their

5 • dams. The main purpose of the beaver dam is defense. The dam and the pond that forms behind it ensure that predators like bears and wolves cannot reach the beaver. In order to build its dam, a beaver first cuts down trees on either side of the stream so that these trees fall into the stream. Those trees slow the speed of the stream, basically creating

10 • a traffic jam. Over time, small sticks, leaves, and other things build up and further slow the flow of the stream. The beaver then uses larger sticks to make its dam stronger, and the dam is then complete.

Beaver dams affect the environment in many a ways, which can be positive or negative. First and foremost, a beaver dam slows the speed of the stream above it. This does several

15 • important things. First, quick-moving streams dig away the soil on their sides, eventually taking away important soil and nutrients that plants need. By slowing the speed of the stream, a beaver dam lessens this effect. In addition, the slower speed of the stream allows the dirt that is in the stream to sink to the bottom, which it couldn't do if the stream were moving more quickly. This improves the quality of the water, both for animals and people who drink it. Beaver dams also

20 • change the types of plants that can be found near a stream. Since beavers cut down trees to make their dams, the forest becomes less thick, leaving open spaces where other plants like bushes and flowers can grow. Therefore, beaver dams also add to the variety of plant life in the forest.

☐ rodents: small mammals that have sharp front teeth. Rats, mice, and squirrels belong to this group

1 The author mentions a traffic jam in order to

(A) point out one possible negative effect beaver dams can have

(B) show that while beaver dams protect the beaver, they limit the speed at which it travels

(C) illustrate how material collects to form a beaver dam

(D) show that an effective beaver dam can totally stop a stream

2 The author uses the phrase First and foremost in order to

(A) indicate the following sentence discusses the most important effect of beaver dams

(B) begin listing the effects of a beaver dam in the order in which they happen

(C) show that the river must be slowed before a beaver dam can have positive effects

(D) show that the following sentence discusses only positive effects of beaver dams

Find the right word from the passage!

❶ Protecting someone or something from attack: _____

❷ Substances that help plants and animals to grow: _____

❸ To make something smaller in size, value, or importance: _____

❹ The _____ of something is how good or bad it is.

The Socratic Method of Teaching

Most students are used to a classroom where they ask questions and the teacher answers them. But what would you do if you found yourself in a classroom where the teacher asked all the questions, and you were expected to answer them? If this were the case, your teacher would be using the Socratic method of teaching. The Socratic method was developed by the great Greek philosopher Socrates in the 4th century B.C. The Socratic method is most often used to teach moral concepts like the meaning of justice. In the Socratic method, the teacher asks the student to answer a series of questions about a topic. The purpose of the questions is to reveal the weaknesses in the student's way of thinking, and lead the student to stronger, better ideas.

The Socratic method has been used by teachers for nearly 2,500 years, and it is still used today. It has both advantages and disadvantages. The major advantage is that it forces the student to think for himself or herself. Students must examine their own beliefs and often change them when their teacher's questions reveal problems in their way of thinking. This leads to much stronger beliefs than if the teacher simply told the student what is right and what is wrong. The disadvantage is that it takes a highly skilled teacher to properly use the Socratic method. The teacher must be able to ask questions that will show students the weaknesses in their reasoning. This is not always an easy thing to do. Furthermore, the Socratic method is not useful for teaching some kinds of concepts, especially scientific concepts. Scientific knowledge generally comes from careful experimentation and observation of the natural world. Simply asking questions of a student who has not done such experiments would do the student little good.

1 Why does the author mention how long the Socratic method has been used?

(A) To allow students to infer when Socrates was alive

(B) To suggest that newer, more modern methods are needed

(C) To show that the Socratic method is the best teaching method in history

(D) To show that the Socratic method is of proven effectiveness

2 Why does the author mention **experimentation and observation**?

(A) To suggest that these methods be added to the Socratic method

(B) To explain why the Socratic method is not good for teaching science

(C) To suggest that these are better teaching methods than the Socratic method

(D) To offer alternatives to the Socratic method of teaching

Find the right word from the passage!

❶ Relating to beliefs about what is right or wrong: _____

❷ An idea of how something is, or should be: _____

❸ Fairness in how people are treated: _____

❹ To _____ someone _____ means to benefit or improve them.

Stockholm Syndrome

Psychologists have long known that people in highly stressful situations can often display behavior which seems very difficult to explain. A good example of this would be Stockholm syndrome, which was named after a failed 1973 bank robbery. The workers and customers inside the bank were taken hostage by the robbers, who threatened to kill the hostages if the police did not let them go. After six days, the crisis ended peacefully and the bank robbers surrendered. To everyone's surprise, the hostages defended the bank robbers, and one hostage even formed a long-lasting friendship with one of them. This same phenomenon, in which hostages become emotionally close to their captors, has been documented in other hostage situations as well.

The causes of Stockholm syndrome are not well understood. It does not occur in every hostage situation, and in fact, most hostages never display any signs of it. Those who do, however, often have similar experiences as hostages. First, they are often the hostages most in fear of their lives. The Stockholm hostages had their lives repeatedly threatened by their captors. Furthermore, hostages

who suffer from Stockholm syndrome often say that they had little faith in the ability of the police to save them. Finally, the longer the period of their captivity, the more they seem to identify with their captors.

Occasionally, Stockholm syndrome has been used as a defense in criminal court cases. The most famous instance of this is that of Patty Hearst. She was kidnapped and held for ransom. After a while, however, she came to support her captors, and eventually took part in bank robberies and other crimes with them. When she was finally caught, she was put on trial for her part in the crimes. As a defense, she claimed that she had suffered from Stockholm syndrome. Her defense didn't work, as she was convicted and sent to jail. Later, however, she was released from prison by President Carter, who felt she was innocent.

1 Why does the author list the common experiences of hostages who have suffered from Stockholm syndrome?

(A) To give examples of the effects of Stockholm syndrome

(B) To explain why Stockholm syndrome is uncommon in hostages

(C) To suggest these experiences may be the causes of Stockholm syndrome

(D) To help the reader identify later cases of Stockholm syndrome

2 Why does the author mention the case of Patty Hearst?

(A) To suggest that bank robberies often cause Stockholm syndrome

(B) To show that Stockholm syndrome is never a good defense in a criminal case

(C) To point out that Patty Hearst did not actually suffer from Stockholm syndrome

(D) To provide an example of the use of Stockholm syndrome as a legal defense

Find the right word from the passage!

❶ To say you want to stop fighting because you know you can't win: _____

❷ The state of being kept in a prison: _____

❸ To think someone is the same as you or closely connected: _____ _____

❹ If someone is _____, they are found guilty of a crime in a law court.

*i*BT **P**ractice **1**

TOEFL Reading

REVIEW

HELP ?

BACK ◀

NEXT ▶

HIDE TIME 00:20:00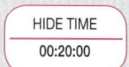

The Atacama Desert

The driest place on Earth is the Atacama Desert, which lies along the western coast of Peru and Chile. The Atacama is unique among the world's deserts because it contains essentially no life. Most deserts contain at least some life, such as scorpions, snakes, and some lizards. The Atacama, however, has none of these animals. In fact, scientists used the same instruments
5 • that they used to look for life in the soil of Mars to try to find life in the soil of the Atacama, with similar results. This is not surprising when you consider that the Atacama gets an average of 3 mm of rain per year, and sometimes goes as long as 40 years with no rain at all.

The Atacama is basically a coastal desert. Coastal deserts can be found along the western coasts of Africa and North and South America. Coastal deserts are caused by the cold water
10 • ocean currents that flow near their coasts. This cold water cools the air. Since the air's ability to hold water is a function of its temperature, the air blowing over these ocean currents becomes very dry. However, most coastal deserts get at least some rain. The coastal desert along the western coast of California, although very dry, gets 50 times more rain than the Atacama.

What makes the Atacama so much drier than other coastal deserts is that it is also a rain
15 • shadow desert. Rain shadow deserts are found below tall mountain ranges, like the Andes in Chile and Peru. Rain clouds usually form at around 2,000 to 10,000 feet. Mountains that are taller than this will block the rain clouds from passing to the other side. Again, this has a lot to do with air temperature. Anyone who has climbed a mountain knows that it gets colder the higher you climb. This also makes the air drier. In effect, rain is blocked from entering the Atacama on
20 • both sides. The cold water currents block rain from coming in off the Pacific Ocean to the west, and the Andes Mountains block any rain coming from the wetter regions to the east.

1 According to the passage, all of the following are true of coastal deserts EXCEPT

(A) they are the driest deserts in the world
(B) they can be found on the western coasts of continents
(C) most coastal deserts are wetter than the Atacama
(D) they form due to cold water currents

2 The author mentions the **soil of Mars** in order to

(A) suggest that it was also formed by coastal deserts
(B) show the complete lack of life in the Atacama
(C) illustrate the type of technology needed to work in the Atacama
(D) suggest that the Atacama is not as unique as scientists once thought

3 In stating that the air's ability to hold water is a **function of its temperature**, the author means that it is

(A) independent of its temperature
(B) directly related to its temperature
(C) partly influenced by its temperature
(D) not associated with its temperature

4 The author mentions The coastal desert along the western coast of California in order to

(A) give another example of an extremely dry desert
(B) illustrate the similarities in coastal deserts
(C) better emphasize the dryness of the Atacama
(D) give readers an example of where coastal deserts can be found

5 Based on the information in paragraph 3, it can be inferred that

(A) the Andes mountains are higher than 10,000 feet
(B) Chile and Peru are very dry countries
(C) there are deserts on both sides of the Andes
(D) the Andes are taller than the mountains in California

Part C

7

TOEFL Reading

REVIEW

HELP
?

BACK
◀

NEXT
▶

HIDE TIME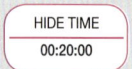
00:20:00

6 According to paragraph 3, the Atacama is the driest desert in the world because

(A) it is the world's only rain shadow desert

(B) its mountains are much taller than other mountains

(C) it has two effects that make it a desert

(D) it is one of the coldest places on Earth

7 **Directions:** Select the appropriate phrases from the answer choices and match them to the nation to which they relate. TWO of the answer choices will NOT be used.

The Atacama is the driest desert on Earth.

(A) The Atacama can go as long as 40 years without rain.

(B) The Atacama receives little rain from its ocean coast because of cold water ocean currents.

(C) Most other coastal deserts are much wetter than the Atacama.

(D) The Andes mountains block any rain coming from the east into the Atacama.

(E) The Atacama is both a coastal and a rain shadow desert.

(F) Dry air is most often a result of low air temperatures.

iBT Practice 2

Egyptian Obelisks

Ancient Egypt is famous for its pyramids, but the pyramids were not the only form of monument that the Egyptians built. Egyptians also built obelisks. Anyone who has seen a picture of the Washington Monument in Washington D.C. is already familiar with the form of the obelisk. These tall, thin monuments stand straight up, resembling a giant pencil stuck into the ground. The Egyptian obelisks were religious objects, and were placed at the entrance of temples as magical protection. The tops of obelisks were covered in a thin layer of gold so that they shone brightly, representing Ra, the Egyptian sun god who was believed to live inside them.

Construction of an obelisk was a difficult task. Obelisks were 100 feet tall on average, and were cut from a single piece of stone. That stone was then transported to the temple, which was sometimes many miles from where the stone was cut. The next step was to carve symbols into all four sides of the obelisk. These carvings represent the artistic and cultural value of the obelisks. Generally, the carvings are simply praise for the pharaoh who ordered the obelisk to be built. They told of his victories in war, his policies at home, and other great things he had done. Thus, obelisks form an important historic record from which we have taken much of our knowledge of ancient Egypt. Once the carving was complete, the Egyptians had to lift the giant stone, weighing hundreds of tons, into a standing position. Historians are still not exactly sure how they did this, but it must have been a long and difficult process.

Of the 27 obelisks that remain standing today, a large number are in Italy. In fact, Italy has more obelisks than Egypt itself. That is because the Romans took many Egyptian obelisks after they conquered Egypt. The Romans used obelisks to mark the midpoint at their racetracks. Thus, you can find Egyptian obelisks at the ruins of many Roman coliseums, as their sports arenas were called. In the 18th century, Napoleon further looted Egypt of its artistic and cultural treasures, so there are several obelisks in France as well. Moves are being made to return some of these stolen treasures to Egypt, but many have been heavily damaged by the polluted air in European cities.

TOEFL Reading

REVIEW

HELP

BACK

NEXT

HIDE TIME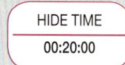
00:20:00

1 The author mentions the Washington Monument in order to

- (A) suggest it was built by the Egyptians
- (B) show how widespread the theft of Egyptian monuments was
- (C) give the reader a clearer idea of the shape of an obelisk
- (D) illustrate that many societies have copied the form of the obelisk

2 According to paragraph 1, what importance did obelisks have for the ancient Egyptians?

- (A) They were used to bury their pharaohs.
- (B) They were used as temples to the sun god.
- (C) They were used to guard temples.
- (D) The represented the home of the gods.

3 Which of the sentences below best expresses the essential information in the highlighted sentence in the passage? *Incorrect* choices change the meaning in important ways or leave out essential information.

- (A) The Egyptians believed their sun god, Ra, lived inside the obelisks, and they represented this by covering the top in bright, shining gold.
- (B) The Egyptians believed that they had to cover the top of the obelisk in gold so that their sun god, Ra, would live inside it.
- (C) The tops of the obelisks were covered in gold, which shone brightly in the sun, so that Egyptians would believe their sun god, Ra, lived inside them.
- (D) The tops of the obelisks shone brightly because they were supposed to represent the Egyptian sun god, Ra, who lived inside them.

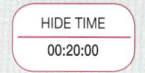
4 According to the passage, all of the following are true of obelisk construction EXCEPT

  Ⓐ each obelisk was made from a single stone

  Ⓑ the obelisk was completely covered in gold

  Ⓒ the obelisk was carved with symbols before it was raised

  Ⓓ Egyptian methods for raising obelisks remain unknown

5 According to the passage, the value of the carvings on obelisks in modern times is that

  Ⓐ they tell us of the religious beliefs of the ancient Egyptians

  Ⓑ European nations still pay high prices for Egyptian obelisks

  Ⓒ they provide much of what we know about Egyptian history

  Ⓓ they are used in Rome and France at race tracks and sports arenas

6 The word looted in the passage is closest in meaning to

  Ⓐ invaded

  Ⓑ robbed

  Ⓒ discovered

  Ⓓ destroyed

7 **Directions:** An introductory sentence for a brief summary of the passage is provided below. Complete the summary by selecting THREE answer choices that express the most important ideas in the passage. Some sentences do not belong in the summary because they express ideas that are not presented in the passage or are minor ideas in the passage.

Obelisks are tall, thin monuments which the ancient Egyptians used to protect their temples.

  Ⓐ The Egyptians built obelisks because Ra, their sun god, was their most important god.

  Ⓑ The construction method used to build the obelisks remains unknown, but building them must have been incredibly difficult.

  Ⓒ The carvings on obelisks dealt with the actions of Egyptian pharaohs and have taught us much about their history.

  Ⓓ Obelisks are made of a single piece of stone, which could weigh several hundred tons.

  Ⓔ Many obelisks have been damaged by the air in Europe and will be repaired before they are returned to Egypt.

  Ⓕ Many of the Egyptian obelisks were stolen by later invading European empires.

Part C

7

Vocabulary Review

Choose the word from each group that does not have the same meaning.

1 (A) at first   (B) initially   (C) in the beginning   (D) gradually

2 (A) downfall   (B) drawback   (C) disadvantage   (D) handicap

3 (A) concentrated (B) demanding   (C) effective   (D) intensive

4 (A) correct   (B) productive   (C) appropriate   (D) proper

5 (A) protect   (B) maintain   (C) take up   (D) preserve

6 (A) reduce   (B) decrease   (C) reject   (D) lessen

7 (A) above all   (B) partially   (C) incompletely   (D) in part

8 (A) replace   (B) take the place of   (C) take place   (D) take over from

Fill in the blank with the correct word from the box.

proper	identify with	do good	efficient
moral	justify	poverty	regardless of

9   He tried to _____ his actions but no one was on his side.

10 You can get a 10% discount _____ how much you buy in this shop.

11 E-mail is one of the most _____ ways of keeping in touch with people.

12 You need _____ equipment to hike Mt. Everest.

13 Do you think it will _____ me _____ if I start doing yoga every day?

14 The idea that stealing is wrong is a(n) _____ which almost every culture shares.

15 "Did you _____ the character you were playing?" the interviewer asked the actress.

16 They often say that _____ is the mother of crime.

Part C +

8

Inference

Rhetorical Purpose

Sentence Insertion

+ Introduction

Sentence insertion questions give you an extra sentence and ask you to find where it fits most logically in a passage. Four possible locations are marked with squares. Your task is to decide where the given sentence best fits. There is 1 sentence insertion question for each passage, and it is always the next-to-last question. The question is worth 1 point.

+ Sample Question

TOEFL Reading

 REVIEW HELP ? BACK ◀  NEXT ▶ HIDE TIME 00:20:00

Abraham Lincoln is perhaps the most famous president in American history. There are several reasons for this. **A** The first is that he was president during the Civil War, the only time Americans fought each other. **B** Another is that he made several historic decisions, including signing the Emancipation Proclamation, which freed the slaves. **C** Finally, Lincoln was the first American president to be assassinated. **D**

Look at the four squares [■] that indicate where the following sentence could be added to the passage.

He was killed by John Wilkes Booth shortly after the end of the Civil War.

Where would the sentence best fit? Circle a square [■] to add the sentence to the passage.

Answer & Explanation 📕

The answer is the fourth square. The given sentence contains additional information on how Lincoln died. Therefore, it connects best with "Finally, Lincoln was the first American president to be assassinated."

+ Strategies

❶ Remember the given sentence is additional relevant information.

TOEFL reading passages are written logically. The passages make sense, with or without the given sentence. Try to find a location where the extra sentence is connected most smoothly and closely.

❷ See if the given sentence has any transition words or phrases.

Transition words or phrases include "in addition," "however," and "therefore." Identifying their logical meaning will help you find out how the given sentence should be located within the context.

❸ See if the given sentence has any reference words or pronouns.

Reference words and pronouns tell you that nouns or ideas are already mentioned. Guess what the pronouns refer to and scan the passage for their logical location.

❹ Insert the sentence where you think it goes best, and double-check the passage to see if it reads logically.

+ Recognizing the Questions

- Look at the four squares [■] that indicate where the following sentence could be added to the passage.

    [You will see a sentence in bold]

    Where would the sentence best fit?

Basic Drills (1)

 Read the following groups of sentences and put them in the logical order.

1

(A) In studies, chimps have shown that they will not help other chimps, even when helping them causes no extra work.

(B) Scientists used to think that apes formed strong friendships in their communities, and that these friendships were based on helping each other.

(C) There is new evidence, however, that this is not true, or at least that the nature of chimp relationships has been misunderstood.

(D) Such unexpected findings have led many scientists to rethink what we believed to be true about group behavior in chimps.

(E) This belief came from watching chimps in the wild, where they spend a great deal of time grooming each other to remove ticks and fleas.

□ **chimp:** a chimpanzee

□ **community:** a group of animals that live in the same environment

□ **groom:** to clean and brush

□ **flea:** a very small insect that bites people to eat their blood

_____ → _____ → _____ → _____ → _____

2

(A) In recent years, evidence has been found suggesting that the ancient Chinese may have even traveled to the western coast of North America.

(B) Before the arrival of Marco Polo, the Chinese had the most advanced ships and the largest sailing fleets in the world.

(C) This lack of competition left the seas to the Europeans and opened the way for them to become the masters of the sea.

(D) Their ships traveled to India and the eastern coast of Africa, setting up trade with the local people there.

(E) For some reason, however, the Chinese gave up long-distance sea exploration and abandoned much of their trade with India and Africa.

□ **fleet:** a group of ships

□ **exploration:** an adventure, travelling to unknown places to search for something

□ **abandon:** to give up, to stop

_____ → _____ → _____ → _____ → _____

✉ **Read the following paragraphs and underline one sentence that doesn't belong to each paragraph.**

1 Beijing is famous for its yellow dust and air pollution. During the spring the problem is especially bad, and many Chinese wear masks over their faces to protect themselves. Part of the problem is, of course, the large number of cars and factories in and around Beijing. The other part of the problem is that the wind blows the loose soil in the countryside around Beijing into the air. To block this dust, the Chinese started a huge project called the green wall. Other large Chinese projects include the world's biggest dam and a huge canal system. The green wall is a large forest of trees that will be planted around the city to block the dust.

□ **yellow dust:** a harmful wind full of sandy dust

□ **soil:** ground

□ **block:** to stop

□ **canal:** a long tunnel filled with water where ships travel

Q. Which sentence doesn't belong in the paragraph?

2 In 1774 and 1775, the years before the American Revolution, there was a lot of anger between the American colonists and the British government. The Americans were angry about high taxes and what they saw as unfair treatment by the British. It was a violent year. Everyone expected war; the only question was when it would start. One of the American colonists working against the British at this time was Paul Revere, a jewelry maker. Paul Revere also worked as a dentist at times. During those tense years, he acted as a spy and messenger for the colonists. He is most famous for warning the colonists before the British attack on Concord and Lexington.

□ **unfair:** not right or fair

□ **at times:** sometimes, occasionally

□ **tense:** worried and nervous

Q. Which sentence doesn't belong in the paragraph?

Part C

8

1   In many cases, societies do things that are destructive to their environment and not in their best interests. **A** In the past, this has largely been because at the time, they lacked the knowledge to understand that they were damaging their environment. But in modern times, many societies are knowingly damaging their environments. **B** After the British started colonizing Australia in the late 1700s, they began to cut down the plants they found there in order to grow British crops and raise British animals like sheep. **C** The sheep had a devastating effect on the environment, but the colonists did not know this at the time. Today, raising sheep is still a basic part of the Australian economy, and it is still destructive to the environment. Modern Australians realize the damage that this does to their environment, but they continue to raise sheep for a number of reasons. **D** One such reason is that raising sheep is an important part of the Australian identity. For the Australians, giving up raising sheep would be like the French giving up the making of wine.

☐ **destructive:** causing damage

☐ **lack:** to not have something

☐ **colonize:** to rule over another country

☐ **devastating:** causing great damage

☐ **identity:** sense of self

Look at the four squares [■] that indicate where the following sentence could be added to the passage.

A good example of both of these situations would be Australia.

Where would the sentence best fit? Circle a square to add the sentence to the passage.

2 [A] During the Revolutionary War, the British fought many battles against the Continental Army, led by George Washington. But the British also suffered heavy losses from smaller groups of soldiers, called "minutemen." [B] Actually the minutemen were not regular soldiers; they were militia members. Militias are different from armies because their members are not full-time soldiers, but rather men from the local community who can be called to fight in times of need. [C] The minutemen had a long history of fighting the Native Americans, both to gain more land and to protect their colonies. [D] Fighting the Native Americans, the minutemen developed fighting techniques that proved very useful against the British. They would hide in the woods and wait for the British. Then they would attack, and before the British could fight back, they would move to a new position. There, they would wait for the British and repeat the whole process again. In this way they wore down the British without taking much damage themselves.

☐ militia: a group of people trained as soldiers

☐ in times of need: when needed

☐ wear down: to slowly make someone physically weaker

Look at the four squares [■] that indicate where the following sentence could be added to the passage.

The minutemen had existed in the American colonies long before the revolution.

Where would the sentence best fit? Circle a square to add the sentence to the passage.

Chipmunks

Chipmunks are small rodents which resemble small squirrels with shorter tails. Chipmunks can be found throughout much of the world, but are most common in North America, where there are twenty-

5 • five species of chipmunk. Chipmunks are solitary animals, with each one digging its own burrow in the ground. These holes can be up to four meters in length.

A Chipmunks are extremely territorial, and will defend their burrows aggressively from other chipmunks. **B**

10 • Like squirrels, chipmunks spend much of the fall collecting food to last them through the winter. **C** Depending on what particular species they belong to, chipmunks use two different methods of collecting food for the winter: larder hoarding and scatter hoarding. **A** In larder hoarding a chipmunk keeps all of its food for the winter in one location, usually in its burrow. **B** The disadvantage of larder hoarding is that the chipmunk's food collection is more open to theft.

15 • **C** Often, while a larder hoarder is out collecting more food, another chipmunk will steal some of the food it has already collected in its burrow. **D**

In scatter hoarding, a chipmunk hides food in tens or even hundreds of different locations around its burrow. **D** While this may seem like a lot of extra work, it forms a kind of insurance policy for the chipmunk. If one collection of nuts is found by another animal, the chipmunk still

20 • has many more left. One important effect of scatter hoarding is that the chipmunk will always forget about a few of its food stashes, and those uneaten nuts will grow to become new trees in the spring.

1 Look at the four squares [■] that indicate where the following sentence could be added to the passage.

The primary advantage of this method is that during the winter, the chipmunk does not have to leave the safety of its burrow to get food.

Where would the sentence best fit? Circle a square to add the sentence to the passage.

2 Look at the four circles [●] that indicate where the following sentence could be added to the passage.

This helps explain why chipmunks defend their burrows so aggressively.

Where would the sentence best fit? Circle a circle to add the sentence to the passage.

Find the right word from the passage!

❶ Spending a lot of time alone: _____

❷ _____ animals try to guard their land from others.

❸ In an angry, threatening way: _____

❹ The place where something is: _____

Ghettos

In any city you enter, you will most likely find that immigrants, especially immigrants from the same country or ethnic group, live in the same area. These areas are sometimes called ghettos. **A** Ghettos have existed as long as there have been cities with immigrants, but the actual term "ghetto" was first used in Venice during the 14th century. **B** At that time Venice, a mostly Catholic city, required that all Jews live in a certain part of the city, which was kept separate from the Catholic parts of the city. **C** Other cities in Italy and in Europe followed the example of Venice and created their own ghettos. The practice of forcing Jews to live in isolation was stopped in most of Europe by the 17th century, but it was started again under the Nazis in Germany during the 1940s. **D** Over time, the term "ghetto" came to be used for any neighborhood with a large immigrant population. But the word also kept many of its negative associations of discrimination and poverty.

There are, however, many ghettos which immigrants form voluntarily, regardless of their ethnic origin. Immigrants gain many advantages from living in the same area of a city. **A** One of the primary advantages is a continued connection to their mother culture. **B** Immigrants living in what is called a ghetto have easier access to restaurants that serve their own food, and theaters that show their own cultural events.  More importantly, living in the same area often provides immigrants with a social network that can provide them with help if they need it. **C** So while the term "ghetto" has taken many negative meanings, the function of a ghetto is often positive. **D**

1   Look at the four squares [■] that indicate where the following sentence could be added to the passage.

This Jewish part of the city was called the ghetto.

Where would the sentence best fit? Circle a square to add the sentence to the passage.

2   Look at the four circles [●] that indicate where the following sentence could be added to the passage.

There are more people who speak their language and can translate for them, and who understand their difficulties as immigrants.

Where would the sentence best fit? Circle a circle to add the sentence to the passage.

Find the right word from the passage!

❶ A person who comes from abroad to live in another country: _____

❷ The state of being separate from other people: _____

❸ An act of treating a certain group of people unfairly in society: _____

❹ Opposite of "positive": _____

The Intelligence of Cetaceans

Cetaceans* are a group of sea mammals that includes whales and dolphins. Cetaceans are well-known for their high intelligence, but exactly how intelligent they are is still open to debate. Cetaceans display many complex behaviors that seem to show intelligence. **A** For example, all cetaceans have a basic form of language, using different sounds to communicate with each other under water. **B** In addition, some cetaceans, most notably dolphins and killer whales, display highly developed forms of teamwork in their hunting methods. **C** Dolphins will work in a group to chase a school of fish into a narrow part of a river, where they can be more easily caught and eaten. **D**

Yet there are as many arguments for lower levels of cetacean intelligence as there are for high levels of intelligence. **A** Originally, many people thought that cetaceans must be very intelligent because they have large brains, even larger than human brains. **B** A dolphin's brain is about 20% larger than a human brain, and the brain of a sperm whale* is nearly 600% larger. **C** These numbers are a bit misleading, however, because the bodies of these animals are much larger than the body of a human. **D** Furthermore, the brain structure in cetaceans is much less developed than in humans. Finally, we know that human intelligence developed because the environment forced early humans to become smarter or die. Early humans had to learn to use tools, adjust to different environments, protect themselves from larger animals, and find new food sources. Cetaceans had no such reasons to develop high intelligence. Their environment remains basically the same, they use no tools, and since they are the largest sea animals, they have no natural predators.

☐ cetaceans: mammals that live in the sea, such as a whale
☐ sperm whale: a large whale sometimes hunted for its oil and fat

1   Look at the four squares [■] that indicate where the following sentence could be added to the passage.

This behavior greatly resembles the actions of humans herding cattle or sheep.

Where would the sentence best fit? Circle a square to add the sentence to the passage.

2   Look at the four circles [●] that indicate where the following sentence could be added to the passage.

The brain makes up 2% of the total body weight in a human, 0.9% in a dolphin, and 0.02% in a sperm whale.

Where would the sentence best fit? Circle a circle to add the sentence to the passage.

Part C

8

Find the right word from the passage!

❶ Opposite of "wide": _____

❷ Reasons that show something is true or untrue, right or wrong etc: _____

❸ To gradually become familiar with a new situation: _____

❹ To look like, or be similar to, something: _____

*i*BT Practice 1

 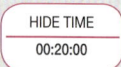
Human Brain Development

The brains of most animals are either fully developed or very nearly developed when they are born. Humans, however, are born with their brains only partially developed. In fact, a newborn baby's brain is only 45% developed, and our brains are not fully developed until the age of 12 or 13. This means that young children lack many of the thinking skills that adults have.

5 • The development of the human brain has four basic stages, each of which is identified through the development of new cognitive abilities in the child. **A** These stages are classified by ages at which they occur, but those ages can vary some from child to child. **B**

The first stage is called the sensory-motor stage, and lasts from birth to around the age of two. During this stage, most of the development in the brain is related to developing

10 • better muscle control and development of the five senses. **C** This is easily seen in the behavior of newborns, who spend much of their time touching things and putting things into their mouths. **D** The preoperational stage lasts from age 2 to 7. In this stage, children develop their language skills and the ability to concentrate for longer periods of time. Children also develop the ability to control their desires around this time. That means they begin to understand that

15 • they cannot always have everything they want. However, they lack the ability to understand most mathematical concepts at this stage. At age seven, children generally enter the concrete operational stage, which lasts until 12 or 13. This stage is marked by the development of more complex problem-solving abilities, increased understanding of mathematics, and the ability to organize things into different categories. The final stage of development is called the formal

20 • operation stage, when the child's brain has fully developed and the child begins to think in what we consider a more adult manner.

The discovery of these stages of brain development has had a huge impact on education. Obviously, there is no point in trying to teach a child a concept if the child's brain has not developed enough to allow the child to understand it. The understanding of brain development

25 • has basically shaped what classes we teach children at different ages, and greatly improved the quality of education.

REVIEW

HELP
?

BACK
◀

NEXT
▶

HIDE TIME
00:20:00

1 According to the passage, all of the following are true of human brain development EXCEPT

   (A) it occurs in four stages that are a function of age

   (B) it determines our ability to understand different ideas

   (C) it occurs at the same ages in every child

   (D) it is completed by the child's teenage years

2 The word cognitive in the passage is closest in meaning to

   (A) social

   (B) school

   (C) behavioral

   (D) thinking

3 According to paragraph 2, at what level of development do children learn to speak?

   (A) The sensory motor stage

   (B) The preoperational stage

   (C) The concrete operational stage

   (D) The formal operation stage

4 Which of the sentences below best expresses the essential information in the highlighted sentence in the passage? *Incorrect* choices change the meaning in important ways or leave out essential information.

   (A) The final stage of development operates when children begin thinking in what we consider an adult manner.

   (B) When children begin thinking in an adult manner, they have entered the last stage of development, called the formal operation stage.

   (C) Childhood is over when a person enters the formal operation stage and starts to think in what we consider an adult manner.

   (D) In the final stage of development the brain is fully developed by the child's ability to think in what we consider an adult manner.

Part C

8

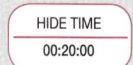
5 Based on the information in the paragraph 2, what can be inferred about mathematics?

- (A) It is easier to teach to adults than to teenagers.
- (B) It is generally not taught to children younger than 7.
- (C) It requires the most complex parts of our brains.
- (D) It was not taught before we understood brain development.

6 Look at the four squares [■] that indicate where the following sentence could be added to the passage.

This is a natural result of their developing senses of taste and touch.

Where would the sentence best fit? Circle a square to add the sentence to the passage.

7 **Directions:** An introductory sentence for a brief summary of the passage is provided below. Complete the summary by selecting THREE answer choices that express the most important ideas in the passage. Some sentences do not belong in the summary because they express ideas that are not presented in the passage or are minor ideas in the passage.

Unlike other animals, humans are not born with fully developed brains.

- (A) Humans go through four stages of brain development, which end at the start of their teenage years.
- (B) Each stage of brain development is marked by the development of increasingly complex thinking skills.
- (C) The preoperational stage is the most important stage in a child's development.
- (D) Children under the age of 7 are usually bad because they do not have the ability to control their desires yet.
- (E) Understanding brain development has brought about changes in educational policy.
- (F) Teachers never try to teach children concepts that their undeveloped brains will not allow them to understand.

iBT Practice 2

State Formation

The development of farming was without question the most significant development in early human history. It was the excess food produced by farming that allowed the growth of larger populations, which in turn allowed the growth of states. While we can date the time at which states arose, and we know that agriculture made this possible, we are still unsure of exactly why early states arose.

A One theory about the formation of the first states centers on irrigation. **B** Large-scale irrigation projects, in which canals were dug and dams were built to bring water to the fields, would have been far too much work for one person, or even one village. **C** They would have required the cooperation of large groups of people. Naturally, one person or a small group of people would have led such a project. This early form of cooperation may have led to the first states, and these project leaders may have become the first kings. There is some evidence to support this theory. All of the oldest city-states show evidence of large-scale irrigation projects, some of which appear to be older than the cities themselves. However, there is also evidence that suggests the irrigation theory may be incorrect. **D** Irrigation requires that farmers share water. If a farmer upstream took too much water, there wouldn't be any left for farmers further downstream. It seems unlikely that such sharing would have taken place if a government had not already existed to control water usage.

Another theory centers on the fact that all of the earliest states built large monuments. Even before states existed, the farming villages in a certain area shared the same religion and a common culture. It is possible that their holy men ordered them to build monuments to their gods. Again, this would have been too much work for just one village and would have required cooperation. Under this theory, these holy men would have become the first kings of the states that formed as a result of this cooperation. The fact that the earliest kings claimed to be gods, or that they represented the gods, seems to support this theory. Again, however, some people disagree, arguing that monument building was simply a tool used by the god-kings, who needed a way to justify their rule. Thus, monument building was a result of the creation of these states.

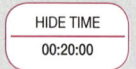
1 The word **agriculture** in the passage is closest in meaning to

- (A) government
- (B) civilization
- (C) farming
- (D) population

2 According to the passage, if either theory is correct, then state formation was the result of

- (A) cooperation on large construction projects
- (B) the shared culture of small farming villages
- (C) the need to produce more food for large populations
- (D) the desire of community leaders to become kings

3 The word **They** in the passage refers to

- (A) Early farmers
- (B) The first states
- (C) Irrigation projects
- (D) The fields of farmers

4 Based on the information in paragraph 2, what can be inferred about the first states?

- (A) They were all located in areas that lacked water.
- (B) They did not produce enough food to feed their citizens.
- (C) Irrigation was their most advanced technology.
- (D) They were downstream of other farmers.

5 Why does the author mention the need of the god-kings to justify their rule?

- (A) To illustrate the problems of the rulers of early states
- (B) To present a possible flaw in the monument theory
- (C) To explain the politics of early states
- (D) To offer further support for the monument theory

TOEFL Reading

REVIEW

HELP
?

BACK
◀

NEXT
▶

HIDE TIME
00:20:00

6 Look at the four squares [■] that indicate where the following sentence could be added to the passage.

Irrigation is the practice of bringing water into a dry area to make it better for farming.

Where would the sentence best fit? Circle a square to add the sentence to the passage.

7 **Directions:** Select the appropriate phrases from the answer choices and match them to the theory of state formation to which they relate. TWO of the answer choices will NOT be used.

Irrigation Theory

- _____
- _____
- _____

Monument Theory

- _____
- _____

Answer Choices

- Project leaders became kings
- Farming not essential to state formation
- States result from common culture in villages
- Some physical evidence to support theory
- Lack of existing government presents a problem in theory
- Priests became kings
- Favored by most archeologists

Part C

8

Vocabulary Review

Choose the word from each group that does not have the same meaning.

1   (A) offensive   (B) aggressive   (C) destructive   (D) intensive

2   (A) promise   (B) product   (C) certainty   (D) guarantee

3   (A) unfairness   (B) discrimination   (C) competition   (D) injustice

4   (A) result   (B) logic   (C) reason   (D) argument

5   (A) individuality   (B) identity   (C) cooperation   (D) personality

6   (A) isolated   (B) familiar   (C) unsociable   (D) solitary

7   (A) suburb   (B) community   (C) general public   (D) society

8   (A) take after   (B) resemble   (C) look alike   (D) look after

Fill in the blank with the correct word from the box.

in isolation	tense	voluntarily	association
access	misleading	adjust to	insurance

9   Henry's essay contained several _____ statements.

10   Fortunately, the _____ company will pay for the things I lost while I was traveling in Europe last summer.

11   To my surprise, he took the hardest part of the work _____.

12   It is impossible for anybody to live _____ complete _____.

13   There is a strong _____ between the time you spend studying and success you have later in life.

14   I always feel _____ before taking tests.

15   It was hard to _____ the new school system at first, but now I'm very happy with everything.

16   Nowadays you can get _____ to the Internet at any time and any place.

Memo

Actual Test
1-3

Reading Section Directions

This section measures your ability to understand academic passages in English.
The reading section is divided into 2 separately timed parts.

Most questions are worth 1 point, but the last question in each set is worth more than 1 point. The directions indicate how many points you may receive.

Some passages include a word or phrase that is underlined in blue. Click on the word or phrase to see a definition or an explanation.

Within each part, you can go to the next question by clicking **Next**. You may skip questions and go back to them later. If you want to return to previous questions, click on **Back**. You can click on **Review** at any time, and the review screen will show you which questions you have answered and which you have not answered. From this review screen, you may go directly to any question you have already seen in the Reading section.

Click on **Continue** to go on.

The Rise and Fall of Carthage

➡ One of the most powerful city-states of the ancient world was Carthage. Carthage was primarily a city of traders and merchants. The city was founded in 814 B.C. by the Phoenicians, who were also merchants and one of the world's earliest civilizations. Carthage was ruled by an oligarchy, a collection of powerful families, and the few elected leaders that it had held little real power. The Carthaginians worshiped a number of gods, and in times of trouble they practiced child sacrifice. In this practice, powerful families would kill their youngest child in order to gain protection and aid from their gods.

➡ By the 6th century B.C. the power of Carthage was on the rise, and the city quickly came into conflict with the Greek city-states over the control of trade in the Mediterranean Sea. **A** The Carthaginians were excellent sailors and had a powerful navy, and from the 5th to the 3rd centuries B.C. these two civilizations fought numerous wars. Most of these wars, however, were minor and relatively short-lived. But in the middle of the 3rd century, a new enemy would appear, with whom Carthage would fight much bloodier wars.

This new enemy was Rome. **B** Rome and Carthage fought three major wars from 264 B.C. to 146 B.C. **C** The first war severely weakened both kingdoms. In the end, however, Rome won the first war and forced Carthage to agree to heavy penalties in the peace treaty that followed.

After thirty years, however, Carthage had regained enough of its power that Rome felt threatened once again. **D** Rome declared war on Carthage, but before Rome had a chance to act, the Carthaginians invaded Italy. The attack by Carthage was so successful that it almost destroyed the Roman Empire. The Romans recovered, however, and Carthage was once again defeated. After this defeat, the power of Carthage was so greatly reduced that it no longer had the power to challenge Rome. But the Romans remembered how close they had come to total defeat in the second war and held a deep hatred for the Carthaginians. They attacked the weakened city. Afterwards, they completely destroyed Carthage, burning the city to the ground, destroying its harbor, and mixing salt into the ground so nothing would grow there again. The surviving Carthaginians were sold into slavery and their society ceased to exist.

TOEFL Reading

Question 1 of 29

REVIEW

HELP ?

BACK ◀

NEXT ▶

HIDE TIME
01:00:00
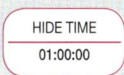

1 The word **founded** in the passage is closest in meaning to

(A) discovered

(B) started

(C) invaded

(D) defeated

2 According to paragraph 1, the government of Carthage was

(A) basically democratic in nature

(B) controlled by its elected officials

(C) organized like a family

(D) controlled by a small group of elite people

Paragraph 1 is marked with an arrow [➡].

3 The phrase **this practice** in the passage refers to

(A) the worship of many gods

(B) the sacrifice of children

(C) worship in times of trouble

(D) gaining protection from one's gods

4 Which of the sentences below best expresses the essential information in the highlighted sentence in the passage? *Incorrect* choices change the meaning in important ways or leave out essential information.

(A) After conflicts with the Greek city-states over the control of trade in the 6th century B.C., the city of Carthage began to rise in power.

(B) By the 6th century B.C., Carthage wanted to increase its power, so it quickly entered into conflicts with the Greek city-states over trade.

(C) The conflicts between Carthage and the Greek city-states over trade in the Mediterranean were a result of Carthage's increasing power in the 6th century B.C.

(D) Trade in the Mediterranean led to Carthage's rise to power and its conflicts with the Greek city-states in the 6th century B.C.

Actual Test

TOEFL Reading

Question 5 of 29

REVIEW

HELP ?

BACK ◀

NEXT ▶

HIDE TIME 01:00:00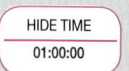

5   Based on the information in paragraph 2, what can be inferred about the Greek city-states?

    (A) They were the winners in their wars against Carthage.

    (B) They were merchants and sailors.

    (C) They were not as powerful as the Carthaginians.

    (D) They wished to destroy the Carthaginian society.

    Paragraph 2 is marked with an arrow [➡].

6   In stating that the wars with the Greek city-states were short-lived, the author means that

    (A) soldiers did not survive long during these wars

    (B) these wars resulted in many deaths

    (C) these wars were quickly forgotten

    (D) these wars were over quickly

7   According to the passage, why did the Romans wish to completely destroy Carthage?

    (A) They were fearful of Carthage's growing power.

    (B) They wanted revenge for the destruction Carthage caused in the second war.

    (C) They no longer wished to compete for control of trade in the Mediterranean.

    (D) They felt that they could no longer trust Carthage to honor its agreements.

8   According to the passage, all of the following were part of the effort by Rome to destroy Carthage EXCEPT

    (A) forcing Carthage to pay heavy fines

    (B) poisoning the land around Carthage

    (C) enslaving Carthaginian citizens

    (D) destroying the city's ports

TOEFL Reading

Question 9 of 29

REVIEW

HELP
?

BACK
◀

NEXT
▶

HIDE TIME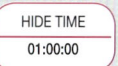
01:00:00

9 Look at the four squares [■] that indicate where the following sentence could be added to the passage.

As Rome began to expand, it entered almost immediately into a series of conflicts with Carthage.

Where would the sentence best fit? Circle a square to add the sentence to the passage.

10 **Directions:** An introductory sentence for a brief summary of the passage is provided below. Complete the summary by selecting THREE answer choices that express the most important ideas in the passage. Some sentences do not belong in the summary because they express ideas that are not presented in the passage or are minor ideas in the passage.

Carthage was one of the most powerful merchant cities of the ancient world.

- (A) The Carthaginians were descended from the Phoenicians, one of the oldest civilizations in the world.
- (B) Carthage came into frequent conflicts with other trading nations during much of its history.
- (C) The Carthaginians had a powerful navy, which they used to attack and destroy merchant ships from other nations.
- (D) The chief enemies of the Carthaginians were the Romans, against whom they fought three wars.
- (E) The Carthaginians nearly destroyed the Roman civilization by attacking the Romans before they were ready.
- (F) The wars against the Romans ultimately led to the destruction of Carthage.

Actual Test

Black Holes

➡ When stars larger than our sun die, they go out with a bang. These stars die in a supernova, a huge explosion which is more powerful than any other event in the universe. If the sun (over one million km wide) exploded in a supernova, the incredible power of the explosion would crush the sun to a size of only 3 km! At this point, something very important would happen. As objects get closer, the power of gravity increases. In a supernova, the atoms of the star get pushed so closely together and their gravity becomes so strong that nothing can escape them, not even light. At this point, the star has become a black hole.

A black hole is an object with incredibly strong gravity. It basically acts like a giant drain in space, sucking up anything that happens to be near it. Scientists suspected the existence of black holes for a long time. But since not even light can escape them, they are basically invisible, and their existence is very hard to prove. Scientists have proven their existence in two ways. Sometimes scientists will find a star that has a very strange movement. It will appear to be orbiting another object, but that object can't be seen. In this case, scientists can guess that the invisible object is a black hole. **A**

The other way in which scientists can prove the existence of black holes is a bit more complicated. As matter gets sucked into a black hole, it starts to spin in a circle, just as water does when it goes down the drain in your bathroom. As the matter gets closer and closer to the black hole, it spins faster and faster, and begins to heat up as a result. Thus, when scientists find spinning circles of extremely hot matter, they can again guess that a black hole is at the center of this. **B**

While black holes suck in and destroy anything that gets too close to them, they play a very important role in the universe. Scientists believe that giant black holes are at the center of every galaxy in the universe. **C** Each galaxy is held together by the intense gravity of the giant black hole at its center. Without these black holes, galaxies would not form, and life as we know it would not exist. **D**

TOEFL Reading

Question 11 of 29

REVIEW

HELP ?

BACK ◀

NEXT ▶

HIDE TIME 01:00:00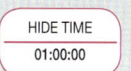

11   Based on the information in paragraph 1, the term supernova can best be explained as

    Ⓐ the act of crushing a star to a very small size

    Ⓑ a star that is several times larger than our sun

    Ⓒ a huge explosion at the end of a star's life

    Ⓓ an object whose gravity is incredibly strong

Paragraph 1 is marked with an arrow [➡].

12   According to paragraph 1, in order to form a black hole, the atoms in a star must

    Ⓐ reach extremely high temperatures

    Ⓑ spin in a circular motion

    Ⓒ be unable to put out light

    Ⓓ be packed extremely close together

Paragraph 1 is marked with an arrow [➡].

13   Which of the sentences below best expresses the essential information in the highlighted sentence in the passage? *Incorrect* choices change the meaning in important ways or leave out essential information.

    Ⓐ Supornovas happen when the atoms of a star get pushed so closely together that not even light can escape.

    Ⓑ In a star, atoms can get pushed so closely together by gravity that not even light can escape the star.

    Ⓒ In a supernova, gravity can become so strong that not even light can escape.

    Ⓓ During a supernova, atoms are tightly packed together, intensifying their gravity to the point where not even light can escape.

14   The word suspected in the passage is closest in meaning to

    Ⓐ feared

    Ⓑ guessed

    Ⓒ discovered

    Ⓓ investigated

Actual Test

TOEFL Reading

Question 15 of 29

REVIEW

HELP ?

BACK ◀

NEXT ▶

HIDE TIME
01:00:00

15 The word **them** in the passage refers to

(A) black holes

(B) scientists

(C) drains

(D) existences

16 According to the passage, some stars can help scientists infer the existence of black holes because

(A) they appear to be orbiting an unseen object

(B) they explode in supernovas

(C) they have extremely strong gravity

(D) they emit no light

17 The author mentions the drain in your bathroom in order to

(A) compare the speeds of objects entering a black hole

(B) suggest that there are many similarities between drains and black holes

(C) show that black holes suck up much of the water in the universe

(D) illustrate the motion of matter entering a black hole

18 According to the passage, all of the following happen to matter entering a black hole EXCEPT

(A) It moves in a circular motion.

(B) It is heated to high temperatures.

(C) It moves at a high speed.

(D) It emits all of its light.

TOEFL Reading

Question 19 of 29

REVIEW

HELP ?

BACK ◀

NEXT ▶

HIDE TIME 01:00:00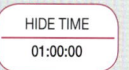

19 Look at the four squares [■] that indicate where the following sentence could be added to the passage.

These super-massive black holes are hugely important.

Where would the sentence best fit? Circle a square to add the sentence to the passage.

20 **Directions:** An introductory sentence for a brief summary of the passage is provided below. Complete the summary by selecting THREE answer choices that express the most important ideas in the passage. Some sentences do not belong in the summary because they express ideas that are not presented in the passage or are minor ideas in the passage.

Black holes are objects with gravity so intense that not even light can escape them.

- Ⓐ Black holes are formed in the death of stars that are several times larger than our sun.
- Ⓑ Black holes sometimes emit supernovas, which are the most powerful explosions in the universe.
- Ⓒ Black holes often make the orbits of stars seem strange and unnatural.
- Ⓓ While the existence of black holes cannot be proven directly, they can be found by observing other objects near them.
- Ⓔ Black holes absorb everything that comes near them and will eventually destroy the universe.
- Ⓕ Black holes are essential parts of the universe and central to the formation of galaxies.

Actual Test

Schizophrenia

➡ One of the most serious forms of mental illness is schizophrenia. Schizophrenia is a complex illness with many symptoms, and most people who suffer from schizophrenia do not display all of them. One common trait shared by almost every schizophrenic, however, is a basic inability to tell the difference between reality and fantasy. Every person has fantasies. Our imaginations create
5 • situations which are not real. In a healthy person, these fantasies are often called "daydreams," and the person is aware that they are not real. A schizophrenic, however, does not understand that his or her daydreams are not part of reality. **A** This can lead to powerful delusions in which a person may believe things that could not possibly be true. **B** For example, a schizophrenic may believe that he or she has been contacted by aliens, or some other situation which is just
10 • as unlikely. **C** Under extreme circumstances, these delusions may cause the schizophrenic to become violent and dangerous. **D**

The causes of schizophrenia are complex and not completely understood. We know that brain chemistry is somehow involved. We know this because certain drugs which help control a specific chemical in the brain are helpful in treating schizophrenia. We also know that people who
15 • come from a family in which schizophrenia is common are more likely to develop schizophrenia themselves. Furthermore, schizophrenia usually surfaces during or after a person's teenage years, right about the same time important chemical changes occur in the brain. All of these facts point to a biological cause for schizophrenia.

➡ At the same time, there is a great deal of evidence that shows that a person's environment
20 • and personal experiences are also important factors. For instance, one study showed that people living in a city are almost 70% more likely to develop schizophrenia, and minority groups show higher rates of the illness as well. This clearly shows that environment plays an important role alongside brain chemistry. Schizophrenia is an episodic illness, with periods of severe illness usually lasting several months. Severe schizophrenics experience these episodes more frequently than
25 • those with less severe forms of the illness. It is estimated that about 1% of the world population will experience a schizophrenic episode at some point in their lives. Treatment generally includes medication and, in severe cases, hospitalization.

TOEFL Reading

Question 21 of 29

REVIEW

HELP ?

BACK ◀

NEXT ▶

HIDE TIME 01:00:00

21 The word trait in the passage is closest in meaning to

   Ⓐ problem

   Ⓑ illness

   Ⓒ handicap

   Ⓓ characteristic

22 According to paragraph 1, the essential difference between the daydreams of a healthy person and those of a schizophrenic is that

   Ⓐ a schizophrenic does not know that his or her daydreams are imaginary

   Ⓑ the daydreams of schizophrenics make them violent and dangerous

   Ⓒ a healthy person's daydreams are more imaginative

   Ⓓ the daydreams of a healthy person occur far less frequently

Paragraph 1 is marked with an arrow [➡].

23 Based on the information in paragraph 1, the term delusions can best be explained as

   Ⓐ the belief in ideas that are untrue and highly unlikely

   Ⓑ serious forms of mental illness

   Ⓒ common symptoms among schizophrenics

   Ⓓ conditions which cause a person to become violent

Paragraph 1 is marked with an arrow [➡].

24 According to the passage, all of the following are proof that schizophrenia has biological causes EXCEPT

   Ⓐ drugs that control brain chemistry effectively treat schizophrenia

   Ⓑ schizophrenia causes important changes in the bodies of teenagers

   Ⓒ people with a family history of the illness are more likely to develop schizophrenia

   Ⓓ schizophrenia often occurs for the first time during adolescence

Actual Test

TOEFL Reading

Question 25 of 29

REVIEW

HELP ?

BACK ◀

NEXT ▶

HIDE TIME 01:00:00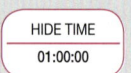

25 Based on the information in paragraph 3, what can be inferred about minority groups?

- (A) They have different brain chemistries.
- (B) They are often the most violent schizophrenics.
- (C) They often live in different environments than other people.
- (D) They are more likely to develop schizophrenia than people living in the city.

Paragraph 3 is marked with an arrow [⇨].

26 In stating that schizophrenia is an episodic illness, the author means that schizophrenia

- (A) is an illness which appears for a period of time and reappears later
- (B) is an illness which is only treatable for short periods of time
- (C) is an illness which can be overcome in a short period of time
- (D) affects people from every part of the world

27 The word those in the passage refers to

- (A) episodes
- (B) schizophrenics
- (C) periods of illness
- (D) experiences

28 Look at the four squares [■] that indicate where the following sentence could be added to the passage.

These delusions can be damaging to a person's professional and social life.

Where would the sentence best fit? Circle a square to add the sentence to the passage.

TOEFL Reading

Question 29 of 29

REVIEW

HELP ?

BACK ◀

NEXT ▶

HIDE TIME
01:00:00

29 **Directions:** An introductory sentence for a brief summary of the passage is provided below. Complete the summary by selecting THREE answer choices that express the most important ideas in the passage. Some sentences do not belong in the summary because they express ideas that are not presented in the passage or are minor ideas in the passage.

Schizophrenia is a serious mental illness.

Ⓐ Schizophrenia is characterized by the inability to tell reality from fantasy.

Ⓑ The delusions of schizophrenics can lead to violence in the most serious cases.

Ⓒ Medicines that control brain chemistry are effective in treating schizophrenia.

Ⓓ People living in cities and minorities show higher rates of schizophrenia.

Ⓔ Schizophrenia is believed to have both biological and environmental causes.

Ⓕ Schizophrenia is periodic in nature and is treated with medication or hospitalization.

Milgram's Experiments and the Power of Authority

After World War II, most Nazi leaders were caught and tried for crimes against humanity, but an important question remained unanswered. The leaders of Nazi Germany had not acted alone in their crimes. Thousands of German soldiers had worked at the concentration camps, where millions of innocent people had been killed. How could one explain the readiness of such large numbers of people to hurt and kill other people?

➥ In order to answer this question, a psychologist at Yale University named Stanley Milgram started an experiment in 1963. People were asked to participate in an experiment testing how memory worked (although this was not the true purpose of the experiment). The subjects were told to ask questions of a person in another room. **A** If the person gave an incorrect answer, the subjects were asked to push a button that would give the person an electric shock. At first, the electric shock was very weak, but it grew stronger with each wrong answer. (Actually, there was no real electric shock, and the person in the other room was an actor. But this was unknown to the subjects.) **B** Although the subjects could not see the actor, they could hear him scream in pain each time they pushed the button to shock him. **C** As the power of the shocks increased and these cries grew louder, many of the subjects started to get nervous and asked Milgram if they could stop the experiment. He assured them that it was OK, and that they must continue with the experiment. **D** Amazingly, about 65% of the test subjects continued to give the electric shocks, even when the power of the electric shocks was near lethal levels.

The experiment revealed that most people have an incredibly powerful wish to obey authority, even when that means doing something that they personally feel is wrong. In addition to changing the way psychologists think about morality and its power over our decisions, the experiment also changed the way psychology experiments are conducted. After the experiment was finished, Milgram explained the true purpose of the experiment to the subjects and told them that they had not really hurt anyone. Despite this, many of the subjects continued to feel deeply guilty about their actions and experienced severe emotion stress. Experiments like this are no longer performed because of the psychological damage they can cause.

TOEFL Reading

Question 1 of 29

REVIEW

HELP

BACK

NEXT

HIDE TIME 01:00:00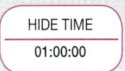

1   The phrase **this question** in the passage refers to the question of

  Ⓐ how German soldiers could be properly punished for their crimes

  Ⓑ how the actions of German soldiers in the concentration camps could be explained

  Ⓒ why Nazi leaders had chosen to kill millions of people in concentration camps

  Ⓓ how to teach the German soldiers that it was wrong to kill innocent people

2   Based on the information in paragraph 2, the term **subjects** can best be explained as

  Ⓐ experiments to test a person's willingness to hurt others

  Ⓑ people who have been given electric shocks

  Ⓒ people who are being tested in an experiment

  Ⓓ psychologists who conduct experiments

Paragraph 2 is marked with an arrow [➡].

3   According the passage, all of the following happened each time the actor gave an incorrect answer EXCEPT

  Ⓐ the person was told to give a stronger shock

  Ⓑ the actor experienced more pain

  Ⓒ the screams of the actor grew louder

  Ⓓ the subjects felt more uncomfortable

4   What can be inferred from the fact that the test subjects asked Milgram to stop the experiment?

  Ⓐ They realized the electric shocks were not real.

  Ⓑ They did not believe Milgram's experiment was effective.

  Ⓒ They did not wish to hurt the person in the other room.

  Ⓓ They feared that they were causing themselves psychological damage.

Actual Test

TOEFL Reading

Question 5 of 29

REVIEW

HELP

BACK

NEXT

HIDE TIME
01:00:00

5 The word lethal in the passage is closest in meaning to

- (A) inappropriate
- (B) painful
- (C) dangerous
- (D) deadly

6 Which of the sentences below best expresses the essential information in the highlighted sentence in the passage? *Incorrect* choices change the meaning in important ways or leave out essential information.

- (A) The experiment showed that the urge to follow orders is very powerful, even if those orders are considered immoral.
- (B) The experiment revealed that most people have a powerful wish to obey their superiors and do things they personally think are wrong.
- (C) The experiment showed that people only do things they feel are wrong in order to obey authority.
- (D) The experiment revealed that most people who obey authority have an incredibly powerful wish to do things they personally feel are wrong.

7 According to the passage, experiments like Milgram's are no longer performed because

- (A) we no longer need to put Nazi leaders on trial
- (B) the electric shocks injured too many people
- (C) they cause emotional suffering in the subjects
- (D) Milgram's experiments clearly proved the power of authority

8 The word conducted in the passage is closest in meaning to

- (A) justified
- (B) studied
- (C) funded
- (D) carried out

TOEFL Reading

Question 9 of 29

REVIEW

HELP ?

BACK ◀

NEXT ▶

HIDE TIME 01:00:00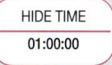

9   Look at the four squares [■] that indicate where the following sentence could be added to the passage.

Again, this person was an actor and was not really in pain.

Where would the sentence best fit? Circle a square to add the sentence to the passage.

10   **Directions:** An introductory sentence for a brief summary of the passage is provided below. Complete the summary by selecting THREE answer choices that express the most important ideas in the passage. Some sentences do not belong in the summary because they express ideas that are not presented in the passage or are minor ideas in the passage.

After World War II, Stanley Milgram ran an experiment to find out why so many German soldiers had followed the orders of their leaders to kill innocent people in the concentration camps.

(A)   The findings of Milgram's experiments were used to convict Nazi leaders of crimes against humanity.

(B)   In Milgram's experiment people were asked to give electric shocks to another person to see if they would follow Milgram's orders.

(C)   Large numbers of the test subjects gave the electric shocks, even though they believed doing so might seriously injure the other person.

(D)   The test subjects grew very nervous as the cries of pain grew louder, but Milgram told them it was OK because the other person was an actor.

(E)   The experiment proved that people's wish to follow authority is often stronger than their desire to do what they believe is right.

(F)   Experiments in which electric shocks are given to the test subject are no longer considered acceptable.

Actual Test

Apocalypse Myths

At first glance, many of the religions around the world would seem to have little in common. Hinduism and the religions of the Native Americans have many gods, while Christianity, Islam, and Judaism all express belief in a single god. The rules and customs of these religions are also very different. Christians go to church on Sundays and have basically no restrictions on what they can eat, while Muslims pray five times a day and are not allowed to drink alcohol or eat pork. As numerous as the differences between world religions are, there are also some interesting similarities.

➡ One of the most interesting similarities between many world religions is the startling likeness of their apocalypse myths. In almost every major religion, either past or present, the basic story is essentially the same. According to this story, the end of the world will be preceded by a time of wars and general lawlessness in which humanity will show its worst side. This will be followed by a great disaster which will destroy much or all of the world. The cause of this disaster varies from religion to religion, but the result is always the same: the world is destroyed and only a small part of humanity survives. Finally, either the head god or a messenger of the head god appears on Earth to restore order and remake the Earth. After the world has been destroyed and renewed, humanity lives in peace and perfection.

Of course, not every apocalypse myth is exactly the same. Christians believe that the end of the world will come once, while Hindus believe in a cycle of destruction and rebirth. But the similarities seem to far outweigh the differences, leading some researchers to conclude that perhaps the myths of many religions have a common origin. ◼A According to this theory, at some point thousands of years ago, there was a people with a common religion. ◼B As these people moved into new areas, they brought their religion with them. Over time, this religion began to change in different areas, eventually forming the religions we know today. ◼C The theory is far from perfect. There are a number of questions it does not answer, namely at what point in human history this common religion began to diverge. ◼D It does, however, present a new way for the people of the world to look at their differences.

TOEFL Reading

Question 11 of 29

REVIEW

HELP ?

BACK ◀

NEXT ▶

HIDE TIME
01:00:00

11 The word restrictions in the passage is closest in meaning to

Ⓐ beliefs

Ⓑ religions

Ⓒ ceremonies

Ⓓ limitations

12 Based on the information in the paragraph 2, the term apocalypse myths can best be explained as

Ⓐ religions which believe in the end of the world

Ⓑ religious stories about how the world will end

Ⓒ religious stories with common characteristics

Ⓓ similarities between seemingly different religions

13 According to paragraph 2, all of the following are common characteristics of apocalypse myths EXCEPT

Ⓐ a period of chaos on Earth before the apocalypse

Ⓑ widespread destruction and the death of much of humanity

Ⓒ the appearance of new gods to restore order to the world

Ⓓ the remaking of the world into a perfect and peaceful place

Paragraph 2 is marked with an arrow [➡].

14 According to the passage, the belief in a sequence of apocalypses and renewals is a characteristic of

Ⓐ Christianity

Ⓑ Judaism

Ⓒ Islam

Ⓓ Hinduism

Actual Test

TOEFL Reading

Question 15 of 29

REVIEW

HELP ?

BACK ◄

NEXT ►

HIDE TIME 01:00:00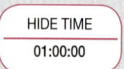

15 Which of the sentences below best expresses the essential information in the highlighted sentence in the passage? *Incorrect* choices change the meaning in important ways or leave out essential information.

(A) These similarities seem to outweigh the differences, leading some researchers to conclude that many religions are really myths with a common origin.

(B) When religions have more similarities than differences, researchers conclude that their myths must have a common origin.

(C) The similarities in the myths of many religions seem more significant than their differences, leading researchers to believe that these religions may have a common origin.

(D) These similarities seem too far to outweigh the differences, so researchers have concluded that they must have a common origin.

16 The word diverge in the passage is closest in meaning to

(A) disappear

(B) evolve

(C) separate

(D) spread

17 According to the passage, one flaw in the theory of a unified ancient religion is that

(A) there are too many differences in the myths of modern religions

(B) no one can accurately state when this ancient religion last existed

(C) the theory doesn't answer any of our questions regarding modern religions

(D) the theory does not provide a new way to view world religions

18 Look at the four squares [■] that indicate where the following sentence could be added to the passage.

Further support for this theory comes from the fact that we know that many world languages evolved from one common language, suggesting there was once a common culture as well.

Where would the sentence best fit? Circle a square to add the sentence to the passage.

TOEFL Reading

Question 19 of 29

REVIEW

HELP

BACK

NEXT

HIDE TIME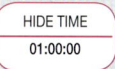
01:00:00

19   **Directions:** An introductory sentence for a brief summary of the passage is provided below. Complete the summary by selecting THREE answer choices that express the most important ideas in the passage. Some sentences do not belong in the summary because they express ideas that are not presented in the passage or are minor ideas in the passage.

Many religions around the world have similar apocalypse myths.

- (A) While world religions have similar myths, they have important differences in their rules and diets.
- (B) An apocalypse myth is a religion's story of how the world will end.
- (C) Unlike the Christian apocalypse myth, the Hindu myth involves a cycle of apocalypse and rebirth.
- (D) Most apocalypse myths share three key features: a period of chaos, the destruction of the world, and the remaking of a perfect world.
- (E) The similarities in apocalypse myths have led researchers to speculate that there was once a common religion from which modern religions developed.
- (F) While the theory of an ancient religion leaves many questions unanswered, it does allow people to realize that the similarities in their religions are more important than their differences.

Plate Tectonics

In the 1960s, scientists discovered that the Earth's surface is not made of a single piece, but rather a number of pieces, or plates, that basically float on a sea of lava that lies deep in the Earth. This discovery was to geology what Darwin's discovery of evolution was to biology. The theory which arose from it, called plate tectonics, forms the basis of modern geology.

5 • According to plate tectonics, the Earth's surface is currently broken up into 14 major plates and many other minor ones. These plates can be classified as either continental or oceanic. As their names imply, these two kinds of plates make up the major continents and the floors of the ocean. Oceanic plates are lower because they are made up of heavier minerals, and therefore sink deeper into the molten lava below them. The central idea behind plate tectonics is that

10 • the Earth's plates are moving, although extremely slowly, and it is this movement that explains nearly every other geological event, from earthquakes to the formation of mountains.

➡ Plates can move in three basic ways. **A** Some plates slide against each other, as the western edge of the North American plate and the eastern edge of the Pacific Ocean plate do. This sliding, however, is not a smooth motion. **B** It is this motion that is responsible for the majority

15 • of earthquakes. Others are drifting apart from each other. As they move apart, lava rises up to fill the crack that they make, bringing up important minerals from the center of the Earth. **C**

The final form of movement is when two plates collide. **D** This is the most complex type of movement, as its effects depend on the type of plates that are colliding. When a continental plate and an oceanic plate collide, the oceanic plate is naturally pushed under the continental plate

20 • because oceanic plates are made of heavier materials. This creates a line of mountains along the coast of the continental plate which has a large number of volcanoes. When two oceanic plates collide, one is again pushed under the other and volcanoes form. These underwater volcanoes eventually form island chains like Japan and Hawaii. Finally, when two continental plates collide, they both rise up, creating tall inland mountain chains like the Himalayas.

TOEFL Reading

Question 20 of 29

REVIEW

HELP ?

BACK ◄

NEXT ►

HIDE TIME 01:00:00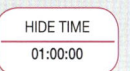

20 The author mentions Darwin's discovery of evolution in order to

- (A) suggest a connection between evolution and tectonic plate movement
- (B) show that the discovery of tectonic plates would not have been possible before Darwin's time
- (C) illustrate how important the discovery of tectonic plates was to the advance of geology
- (D) better explain the movements of tectonic plates and the effects on human development

21 According to the passage, the term plate tectonics can best be explained as

- (A) the major pieces of the Earth's surface that float on a sea of lava
- (B) a theory which explains the movements of the Earth's plates and their effects
- (C) the important differences between the continents and the ocean floor
- (D) a sideways motion of the Earth's plates which causes earthquake

22 The word imply in the passage is closest in meaning to

- (A) illustrate
- (B) investigate
- (C) suggest
- (D) explain

23 Which of the sentences below best expresses the essential information in the highlighted sentence in the passage? *Incorrect* choices change the meaning in important ways or leave out essential information.

- (A) One of the basic ideas of plate tectonics is that the Earth's plates are in motion and are very slowly forming mountains and causing earthquakes.
- (B) One of the basic concepts of plate tectonics is that major geological events can be explained by the slow movement of the Earth's plates.
- (C) The Earth's plates are moving slowly, and this is one of the central ideas used to explain earthquakes and mountain formation.
- (D) Plate tectonics can be used to explain how the slow movements of the Earth's plates are caused by geological events like earthquakes and mountain formation.

Actual Test

TOEFL Reading

Question 24 of 29

REVIEW

HELP ?

BACK ◀

NEXT ▶

HIDE TIME 01:00:00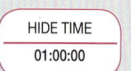

24 According to the information in the passage, all of the following are true of the Earth EXCEPT

   Ⓐ its surface is broken into a number of different pieces

   Ⓑ its geological features are set and unchanging

   Ⓒ its structure was not accurately understood until the 1960s

   Ⓓ its heaviest minerals are distributed unevenly on its surface

25 According to paragraph 3, it can be inferred that

   Ⓐ earthquakes occur anywhere that two tectonic plates meet

   Ⓑ the Pacific Ocean plate is much larger than the North American plate

   Ⓒ western North America experiences many earthquakes

   Ⓓ the strength of an earthquake is dependent on the size of the tectonic plates involved

Paragraph 3 is marked with an arrow [➡].

26 The word Others in the passage refers to

   Ⓐ Earthquakes

   Ⓑ Continents

   Ⓒ Edges

   Ⓓ Tectonic plates

27 According to the passage, why are plate collisions the most complex type of plate movement?

   Ⓐ They always occur underwater and therefore cannot be observed.

   Ⓑ Their results are more variable than other types of plate movements.

   Ⓒ It is impossible to know if they will cause volcanoes or not.

   Ⓓ Oceanic and continental plates collide at different speeds.

TOEFL Reading

Question 28 of 29

REVIEW

HELP
?

BACK
◀

NEXT
▶

HIDE TIME
01:00:00

28 **Directions:** Look at the four squares [■] that indicate where the following sentence could be added to the passage.

The two plates rub against each other, building pressure until they move suddenly in a quick jerk.

Where would the sentence best fit? Circle a square to add the sentence to the passage.

29 **Directions:** Select the appropriate phrases from the answer choices and match them to the type of tectonic plate to which they relate. TWO of the answer choices will NOT be used.

Answer Choices

- Located only in North America
- Commonly associated with volcanoes
- Made of lighter materials
- Involved in island formation
- Rise up to form mountain chains
- Usually pushed under in plate collisions
- Responsible for most earthquakes

Continental Plates

- _____
- _____

Oceanic Plates

- _____
- _____
- _____

Actual Test 3

TOEFL Reading

Reading 1

NEXT ▶

HIDE TIME
01:00:00

The Discovery of Pluto

➡ The first six planets have been known to mankind for all of our recorded history. **A** But the final three planets, Uranus, Neptune, and Pluto, are not visible in the night sky without the help of a telescope. **B** Their discovery had to wait until the invention of telescopes. Uranus, the seventh planet, was the first to be discovered in 1781 by William Herschel. **C** This proved to be an important breakthrough, because by studying unexpected changes in the planet's orbit, scientists could infer that it was being affected by the gravity of another, unknown planet. That unknown planet proved to be Neptune. It was found in 1846 with the help of calculations based on the abnormalities in Uranus' orbit, which told scientists where in the sky to look for Neptune. The discovery of these two planets proved to be relatively easy because both Uranus and Neptune are gas giants, huge planets many times the size of the Earth. This made them relatively easy to find, even with the telescopes of the 18th and 19th centuries. **D**

➡ Finding the ninth planet, Pluto, proved to be a much harder task because it is not even as large as our moon, and it is over a thousand times more distant. Again, the first clues to the planet's existence came from the orbits of other planets. It was determined that Neptune could not explain all the changes in the orbit of Uranus. Scientists guessed there was another planet out there, but they could not find it. They labeled the missing planet "Planet X." The first serious attempt to find Planet X came in 1915, when astronomer Percival Lowell made it his mission to find the planet. Lowell spent over a year studying the night sky. He discovered many other objects, including over 700 new stars. But he did not find the missing planet and died a disappointed man.

Success came in 1930, when Clyde Tombaugh used a new method to search for the planet. He took thousands of pictures of the night sky. Then he searched for any unknown objects that were moving against the background of the stars, which remain in the same place in the night sky. Using this method, he found a small point of light, which turned out to be Pluto.

TOEFL Reading

Question 1 of 29

REVIEW

HELP ?

BACK ◀

NEXT ▶

HIDE TIME 01:00:00

1   The word **This** in the passage refers to

Ⓐ The invention of the telescope

Ⓑ The discovery of Uranus

Ⓒ The visibility of the final three planets

Ⓓ The discovery of gravity

2   According to paragraph 1, why was the discovery of Uranus important?

Ⓐ It made scientists want to look for other planets.

Ⓑ It indirectly led to the discovery of Neptune and Pluto.

Ⓒ It helped scientists understand how orbits are affected by gravity.

Ⓓ It led to improvements in the quality of telescopes.

Paragraph 1 is marked with an arrow [➡].

3   The word **breakthrough** in the passage is closest in meaning to

Ⓐ advance

Ⓑ accident

Ⓒ experiment

Ⓓ task

4   The word **abnormalities** in the passage is closest in meaning to

Ⓐ typical characteristics

Ⓑ unusual qualities

Ⓒ known facts

Ⓓ important information

Actual Test

TOEFL Reading

Question 5 of 29

REVIEW

HELP
?

BACK
◀

NEXT
▶

HIDE TIME
01:00:00

5 Which of the sentences below best expresses the essential information in the highlighted sentence in the passage? *Incorrect* choices change the meaning in important ways or leave out essential information.

(A) The discovery of Neptune and Uranus was only possible because they are such huge planets.

(B) The fact that Uranus and Neptune are such enormous planets made finding them a relatively simple task.

(C) Huge gas giants like Uranus and Neptune are much easier to find than planets as small as the Earth.

(D) It is easier to prove the existence of gas giants like Neptune and Uranus because they are so much larger than the Earth.

6 According to the passage, what can be inferred about telescopes?

(A) The first telescopes were invented by William Herschel.

(B) They are required in order to view most of the planets in the night sky.

(C) The telescopes of the 18th and 19th centuries were not very powerful.

(D) They are less useful than gravity in finding new planets.

7 Why does the author discuss the Earth's moon in paragraph 2?

(A) To better explain the orbit of Pluto

(B) To give an example of an object that is easily visible

(C) To suggest there are many similarities between the moon and Pluto

(D) To better illustrate why Pluto was so hard to find

Paragraph 2 is marked with an arrow [⇨].

8 According to the passage, all of the following are true of Pluto EXCEPT

(A) it was discovered accidentally

(B) it was the last planet to be discovered

(C) it was discovered by tracking its motion

(D) it was discovered using new methods of searching for planets

TOEFL Reading

Question 9 of 29

REVIEW

HELP ?

BACK ◀

NEXT ▶

HIDE TIME
01:00:00

9   Look at the four squares [▇] that indicate where the following sentence could be added to the passage.

While early civilizations may not have understood that these objects were planets, they were clearly visible in the sky.

Where would the sentence best fit? Circle a square to add the sentence to the passage.

10   **Directions:** Select the appropriate phrases from the answer choices and match them to the planet to which they relate. TWO of the answer choices will NOT be used.

Answer Choices

- Irregular orbit
- Easily seen with telescope
- Most distant planet
- Extremely strong gravity
- First discovered through direct observation
- Can only be seen when moving
- Existence inferred before actual discovery

Pluto

- _____
- _____

Uranus

- _____
- _____
- _____

World Population and Climate Change

➡ In many ways, the increasingly rapid pace of climate change is a direct result of the growth of the human population. **A** In the last 100 years, the world population has more than tripled, from just under 2 billion at the beginning of the century to nearly 7 billion today. **B** In addition, the average person uses more energy and natural resources than the average person one hundred years ago, meaning that the rates of consumption are actually much higher than just the increase in population would imply. **C** For example, it took the world 125 years to use the first one trillion barrels of oil. The next trillion barrels will be used in less than 30 years, which is almost 5 times as fast, not three. **D**

All of these activities: food production, energy usage, and the use of natural resources, contribute to climate change in some way. The greater amounts of oil and other fuels burned to create energy release chemicals which add to global warming. In order to produce more food, farmers cut down trees to gain more land for their fields. In addition, we cut down trees to build the houses needed for a larger population. Those trees are an essential part of controlling global warming. These are just two examples of the impacts that the growing population has on global warming; others are too numerous to mention.

In addition to a growing population, the world also has a population that desires a higher standard of living than in the past, and a higher standard of living requires the use of even more natural resources. A look at one country will provide a clear example of this fact. China is the world's most populous nation, with 1.3 billion people. Currently, the standard of living for most of those people is far below that of people in first world nations. Therefore, the average Chinese citizen uses far fewer natural resources and less energy than the average citizen of the US or Japan. But China is growing in power, and more and more of its citizens are beginning to expect a first-world lifestyle. If every Chinese person attains a first-world lifestyle, the amount of energy and natural resources needed in the world will double, even if the standard of living in every other nation on Earth remains the same as it is today.

TOEFL Reading

Question 11 of 29

REVIEW

HELP ?

BACK ◀

NEXT ▶

HIDE TIME
01:00:00

11 The word **pace** in the passage is closest in meaning to

Ⓐ growth

Ⓑ speed

Ⓒ problem

Ⓓ pollution

12 The word **consumption** in the passage is closest in meaning to

Ⓐ development

Ⓑ usage

Ⓒ population

Ⓓ increase

13 According to the passage, how does food production contribute to global warming?

Ⓐ Producing more food leads to growth in the world population.

Ⓑ Food production uses many chemicals which add to global warming.

Ⓒ Food production requires that the forests be cleared to create farmland.

Ⓓ Food production decreases the ability of the air to release heat.

14 Why does the author mention the rate at which oil is being used in paragraph 1?

Ⓐ To illustrate that we are using resources faster than the speed at which the population is growing

Ⓑ To suggest that most of the problems of global warming are associated with our rapid use of oil

Ⓒ To suggest that our oil is likely to run out sometime in the next thirty years

Ⓓ To contrast the differences in lifestyle between people living a 100 years ago and people living today

Paragraph 1 is marked with an arrow [➡].

TOEFL Reading

Question 15 of 29

REVIEW

HELP

BACK

NEXT

HIDE TIME
01:00:00

15 The word others in the passage refers to

(A) problems of global warming in the modern world

(B) examples of the environmental consequences of population growth

(C) ways in which our usage of oil will effect the world climate

(D) the reasons why trees are essential in controlling global warming

16 According to the passage, how does the standard of living affect global warming?

(A) Higher standards of living are better for the environment.

(B) First world nations create less pollution than developing nations.

(C) The use of natural resources is directly related to the standard of living.

(D) High standards of living lead to increases in world population.

17 Which of the sentences below best expresses the essential information in the highlighted sentence in the passage? *Incorrect* choices change the meaning in important ways or leave out essential information.

(A) If China becomes a first-world nation and all other nations keep their current standard of living, the usage of energy and natural resources will double.

(B) If China doubles its usage of natural resources, it will attain a better standard of living, but other nations will have to remain as they are today.

(C) Even if the standard of living in every other nation on Earth remains as it is today, China will still try to attain a first world standard of living.

(D) When China attains a first world lifestyle, the amount of energy and natural resources used by other nations to keep their current standard of living will double.

18 Why does the author discuss China, Japan, and the United States?

(A) To compare the standards of living of their citizens

(B) To explain why China will not be able to become a first world nation

(C) To better illustrate the effects of an increase in standards of living

(D) To explain why the world's use of energy will need to double soon

TOEFL Reading

Question 19 of 29

REVIEW

HELP ?

BACK ◀

NEXT ▶

HIDE TIME 01:00:00

19 Look at the four squares [■] that indicate where the following sentence could be added to the passage.

Obviously, this has meant that the world has needed to produce three times as much food, energy, and other natural resources.

Where would the sentence best fit? Circle a square to add the sentence to the passage.

20 **Directions:** An introductory sentence for a brief summary of the passage is provided below. Complete the summary by selecting THREE answer choices that express the most important ideas in the passage. Some sentences do not belong in the summary because they express ideas that are not presented in the passage or are minor ideas in the passage.

Climate change is directly related to population growth and increases in the standard of living.

(A) The rate of population growth has dramatically increased in the last one hundred years.

(B) Population growth requires the use of greater amounts of natural resources, which causes global warming.

(C) If we are to reduce global warming, we will have to use less oil, and people will need to eat less food.

(D) On average, modern people use more natural resources than people in the past, and this increases the effects of global warming.

(E) First world nations are most responsible for global warming because they use the largest percentage of natural resources.

(F) As more people attempt to gain first world lifestyles, the amount of natural resources used increases.

Termites

➡ Termites are small, ant-like insects that rely on wood as a food source. While they are sometimes called "white ants" or "flying ants," termites are not actually ants. **A** They do, however, share many of the characteristics common to all social insects. **B** Like ants and bees, a termite colony has a queen, who lays all the eggs in the colony; workers, who do most of the work in the colony; and soldiers, who protect the colony from other insects. **C** Depending on the type of termite, there can be anywhere from several thousand to several million termites in a single colony. **D** When a termite colony starts to get overcrowded some of the termites will develop wings and fly off to create a new colony. Termites eat dead wood because it is easier to consume than live wood. While this is good news for logging companies, it is definitely bad news for home owners, because the wood used to build their homes makes a tasty meal for termites. For this reason, termites are generally seen as pests. The two most troublesome types of termites are drywood termites and subterranean termites.

Drywood termites are named for their ability to take all their water from the wood they eat. Therefore, they can live in very dry climates. They make their colonies directly in the wood that they eat, and as a result their colonies are generally smaller than those of subterranean termites, which have more room to build their colonies. Like most termites, drywood termites only leave their colony when it has become overcrowded. Since they do not leave their colony, drywood termites must constantly remove waste from it. Little piles of light, sandy material below a wooden structure are a sure sign of these pests.

Subterranean termites live in the ground and dig tunnels into the wood that they eat. Since they actually do leave their colony to reach the wood, they do not have to remove any waste from their colony and therefore, are much harder to spot. In fact, these termites are usually only discovered by the damage they have caused. Subterranean termites are not found in dry climates because they require a source of fresh water. Since they are located in the ground, subterranean termite colonies are much more likely to be attacked by ants or other insects, and therefore have large numbers of soldiers.

21   The word characteristics in the passage is closest in meaning to

   (A) behaviors   (B) colonies

   (C) traits   (D) wjobs

22   According to paragraph 1, all of the following are true of termites EXCEPT

   (A) they are social insects

   (B) they kill many trees

   (C) their colonies vary widely in size

   (D) they have the ability to fly

   Paragraph 1 is marked with an arrow [➡].

23   The word consume in the passage is closest in meaning to

   (A) kill

   (B) damage

   (C) locate

   (D) cat

24   The author mentions home owners in order to

   (A) warn them about the risks of termites

   (B) introduce harmful effects of termites

   (C) contrast them with logging companies

   (D) illustrate the type of wood that termites prefer

25   The phrase this reason refers to the fact that

   (A) termites only eat dead wood

   (B) termites commonly eat the wood in homes

   (C) termites do not damage logging companies

   (D) termites can fly to create new colonies

Actual Test

TOEFL Reading

Question 25 of 29

REVIEW

HELP

BACK

NEXT

HIDE TIME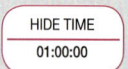
01:00:00

26 According to the passage, when do drywood termites leave their colonies?

(A) When they remove waste from their colony

(B) When they have eaten all the wood in the colony

(C) When the population of a colony becomes too large

(D) When they are attacked by ants or other insects

27 According to the passage, it can be inferred that termite waste

(A) has a light, sandy appearance

(B) is removed from colonies in large amounts

(C) is a problem for all kinds of termites

(D) can make termites sick if it is not removed

28 Look at the four squares [■] that indicate where the following sentence could be added to the passage.

Termites have different body shapes and sizes depending on their jobs within the colony.

Where would the sentence best fit? Circle a square to add the sentence to the passage

29 **Directions:** Select the appropriate phrases from the answer choices and match them to the type of termite to which they relate. TWO of the answer choices will NOT be used.

Answer Choices

- Cause greater levels of damage
- Colonies harder to locate
- Fewer soldiers
- Cannot live in desert environments
- Must travel to food source
- Smaller colonies
- More likely to create new colonies

Drywood Termites

- _____
- _____

Subterranean Termites

- _____
- _____
- _____

Orientation

I. TOEFL iBT / Next Generation TOEFL

2005년 9월을 기점으로 1998년 미국에서부터 시행된 TOEFL CBT은 인터넷을 기반으로 하는 TOEFL iBT 체제로 바뀌었다. 일부에서는 새롭게 시행되는 토플에 한국인들이 특히 강한 문법이 없어지고 한국인들이 상대적으로 약한 Speaking이 추가되어 이제 토플로 고득점을 획득하기는 어려울 것이라 생각하는 경우가 있는 것 같다. 하지만 새로운 토플을 면밀히 분석하여 그에 맞는 공부 방법으로 철저히 대비한다면 iBT에서도 고득점을 얻는 것이 충분히 가능하다.

1 TOEFL이란?

TOEFL(Test of English as a Foreign Language)은 영어가 모국어가 아닌 사람(EFL학습자 또는 non-native speakers of English)이 미국, 캐나다 등 영어 사용권 국가의 대학이나 대학원에 입학할 경우 치러야 하는 영어 사용 능력 검정시험이다. TOEFL시험은 미국 New Jersey주의 Princeton에 본부를 둔 ETS(Educational Testing Service)의 주관으로 전세계적으로 시행되고 있으며 5,000여 대학이나 교육기관에서 공인시험으로 인정하고 있다.

* What is ETS?

ETS는 Educational Testing Service의 약자다. ETS는 1947년에 설립된 미국 북동부의 New Jersey에 위치한 국가공인 시험 전문 비영리기관(Nonprofit Institution)이다. ETS는 TOEFL 등 영어에 대한 시험뿐만 아니라 미국의 고등학교, 대학교, 대학원 입학에 관련된 영어, 수학, 논리, 전공에 대한 시험을 주관한다. ETS에서 주관하는 대표적인 시험으로는 SAT(미국 대학 입학 능력 평가), GRE(미국 대학원 입학 능력 평가), GMAT(미국 경영대학원 입학 능력 평가), LSAT(미국 법대 입학 능력 평가) 등이 있다. 합격 또는 불합격에 대한 판정은 하지 않으며 단지 해당 시험 분야에 대한 능력만을 평가한다.

2 TOEFL iBT란?

2006년부터 전세계적으로 새롭게 시행되고 있는 인터넷 기반의 새로운 토플 시험을 Next Generation TOEFL(차세대 토플) 또는 TOEFL iBT(Internet-based Test)라고 한다.

* TOEFL iBT는 2005년부터 순차적으로 전세계적으로 시행되었다.

  2005년 9월 – 미국에서 시행

  2005년 10월 – 캐나다, 독일, 프랑스, 이탈리아 등 4개국에서 시행

  2006년 – 한국을 포함, 전세계적으로 시행 (한국에서는 2006년 9월 시행)

* TOEFL iBT는 인터넷을 기반으로 ETS에서 지정한 날짜(주로 금요일과 토요일)에 연중 30~40회 정도 시행이 되며, 시험장소가 대폭 확대되어 가까운 곳에서 편리하게 시험을 볼 수 있다.

* TOEFL iBT의 시험 등록은 인터넷, 메일, 전화 등 다양한 매체를 통해 가능하며, 비용은 $140~$170이다.

3 TOEFL *i*BT의 주요 변화

● **문법(Structure)이 없어지고 Speaking이 추가**

새로운 토플에서는 기존의 structure 평가영역이 사라지고 실제 의사소통 기능을 갖는 통합형 평가 방식 위주의 speaking이 보강되었다.

* 이는 문법이나 영어구조에 대한 학습은 중요하지 않고 speaking이 더 중요하다는 의미는 아니다. 우리와 같이 제한된 시간에만 영어에 노출되어 있는 EFL환경에서는 문법과 어휘 등 언어구조에 대한 학습이 필수적이라는 인식에는 이견이 없다. 따라서 새로운 토플체제하에서도 문법학습은 여전히 중요하다고 할 수 있다.

● **통합형 문제(Integrated Tasks)의 도입**

영어를 사용하는 실제 환경의 구현을 위해 [읽고+듣고+쓰기]와 같은 실제 의사소통 기능을 갖는 통합형 평가 방식(Integrated-Skills Approach)의 문제가 출제된다. 새롭게 도입된 통합형 문제 유형은 다음과 같다.

Read / Listen / Speak
Listen / Speak
Read / Listen / Write

● **Core Academic Skills Assessment 강화**

기존의 영어시험이 제시된 영어문장의 이해도를 주로 평가하는 것이라면 새로운 토플은 note taking, paraphrasing, synthesizing, summarizing 등과 같은 영어로 수업을 진행하는데 필요한 실질적인 능력(Core Academic Skills)을 요구하고 있다.

● **Reading과 Listening의 난이도는 종전 CBT와 같은 수준**

외형상 새로운 토플에 많은 변화가 있기는 하지만 Reading과 Listening은 대부분 기존에 익숙한 CBT 문제 유형을 그대로 사용하고 있다. 또한 새로운 토플에 등장하는 문장의 구조나 어휘범위, 토픽범위, Writing Topics 등이 CBT와 동일한 수준이다.

4 TOEFL iBT의 각 영역별 개요

	Reading (독해)	Listening (청해)	Speaking (말하기)	Writing (작문)
구성	• 총 지문 수: 3-5개 • 총 문제 수: 36-70개 • 각 지문 당 문제 수: 12-14개 • 각 지문 당 단락 수: 4-8개 • 각 지문 당 어휘 수: 약 700 단어	• Conversation: 2-3개 • Lecture: 4-6개(Interactive Lecture 2-3개; Academic Lecture 2-3개) • Conversation은 2-3분 정도 (400-500 단어의 길이), Lecture는 4-5분 정도 (600-800 단어의 길이) • 2-3개의 Conversation (각 5문제씩)과 4-6개의 Lecture(각 6문제씩)에서 총 34-51문제 출제	• Independent Speaking (개별 말하기): 2문제 • Integrated Speaking (통합형 말하기 시험): 4문제; (읽고 듣고 말하기): 2문제 • Integrated Speaking의 독해 지문은 75-100 단어 수준으로 45초의 읽기 시간이 주어진다. • Integrated Speaking의 듣기 지문은 150-280 단어 수준으로 1-2분 정도의 길이다. • 총 6문제 출제	• Integrated Writing (통합형 작문): 1문제(20분 동안 150-225 단어 정도 작성) – Integrated Writing의 독해 지문은 230-300 단어 수준으로 3분의 읽기시간이 주어진다. – Integrated Writing의 듣기 지문은 230-300 단어 수준으로 2분 정도의 길이다. • Independent Writing (개별 작문): 1문제(30분 동안 최소한 300 단어 이상 작성) • 총 2문제 출제
시간	총 60-100분 (각 지문당 20분씩)	대략 60-90분 정도 (듣는 시간을 제외하고 실제 문제를 푸는데 걸리는 시간은 20-30분)	대략 20분	대략 50분 (Integrated Writing: 20분; Independent Writing: 30분)
문제 유형	(1) Vocabulary Questions (2) Reference Questions (3) Sentence Simplification Questions (4) Factual Information Questions (5) Negative Fact Questions (6) Inference Questions (7) Rhetorical Purpose Questions (8) Insert Text Questions (9) Prose Summary Questions (10) Classifying, Categorizing, and Organizing Information Questions	(1) Main Idea Questions (2) Supporting Detail Questions (3) Organization Questions (4) Organization-Rhetorical Connection Questions (5) Content-Identifying Relationship Questions (6) Content-Linking Questions (7) Stance / Attitude Questions (8) Function-Purpose Questions	(1) Independent Speaking Personal Preference (2) Independent Speaking Paired Choice (3) Reading / Listening / Speaking Campus Situation Topic (4) Reading / Listening / Speaking Academic Course Topic (5) Listening / Speaking Campus Situation Topic (6) Listening / Speaking Academic Course Topic	(1) Reading / Listening / Writing Academic Course Topic (2) Independent Writing based on Experience & Knowledge
특징	• Glossary(어휘사전) 제공: 단어를 클릭하면 해당 단어의 설명이 나타난다. • Review(복습) 기능: 체크한 답과 그렇지 않은 답의 상태를 알 수 있어 그냥 지나간 문제를 확인할 수 있다. • 각 지문의 제목이 제시된다. • 문제는 보통 지문의 순서대로 주어지며, 문제가 왼쪽에, 지문이 오른쪽에 제시된다.	• Note Taking(받아적기) 가능: 듣는 동안에 요점을 종이에 쓸 수 있다. • 강의의 핵심 구문을 모니터 상에 제시한다. • 들은 내용을 그대로 다시 들려주고 푸는 Replay Item을 도입했다.	• Note Taking을 이용해 효율적으로 Speaking Task의 답변을 준비할 수 있다. • Independent Speaking은 일상 생활의 경험에 관한 질문 등 매우 익숙한 토픽에 대한 질문이다. • Integrated Speaking은 읽고 들은 내용을 바탕으로 Speaking Task가 주어진다. • 각 문제당 15-30초 정도의 답변 준비 시간이 주어지고 실제 답변 시간은 45초 또는 60초다.	• Note Taking을 이용해 효율적으로 Writing Task의 답변을 준비할 수 있다. • Independent Writing의 주제는 기존의 CBT TOEFL의 185 Writing Topics와 거의 동일하다. • Integrated Writing은 읽고 들은 내용을 바탕으로 Writing Task가 주어진다.

5 TOEFL *i*BT의 점수체계

● Next Generation TOEFL Scores

Four skill scores

Reading: 0 – 30

Listening: 0 – 30

Speaking: 0 – 30

Writing: 0 – 30

Total score: 0 – 120

* 각 영역별(Reading, Listening, Speaking, and Writing)로 0-30의 scale로 할당되며 total 120 scale이 만점이다.
또한 성적 통지표에는 4개의 영역 점수(four skill scores)와 더불어 total score난이 별도로 표기된다.

* Score Report는 테스트 후 15일 이후에 온라인에서 확인하거나 우편으로 받아볼 수 있다.

● 각 영역별 배점체계

	Reading (독해)	Listening (청해)	Speaking (말하기)	Writing (작문)
구 성	● 보통 문제당 1점의 원점수가 주어진다. ● Prose Summary Questions나 Classifying, Categorizing, and Organizing Information Questions 문제 유형은 부분 점수가 부여되는 Partial-Credit Item으로 0-4점 사이의 원점수가 부여된다. ● 모든 원점수를 합히여 30점 만점으로 환산한다.	● 보통 문제당 1점의 원점수가 주어진다. ● 일부 Supporting Detail Questions 문제의 경우 2점의 원점수가 주어질 수 있다. 이 경우, 해당 문제에 점수기준이 명시되어 있다. ● 모든 원점수를 합하여 30점 만점으로 환산한다.	● Scoring Rubrics를 바탕으로 각 문제당 0-4점 사이의 원점수가 주어진다. ● 6명의 human raters에 의해 채점된다. ● 모든 원점수를 합하여 30점 만점으로 환산한다.	● Scoring Rubrics를 바탕으로 각 문제당 0-5점 사이의 원점수가 주어진다. ● 2명의 human raters에 의해 채점된다. ● 모든 원점수를 합하여 30점 만점으로 환산한다.
문제 수	36-70	34-51	6	2
환산 점수	0-30	0-30	0-30	0-30

* 한국인의 토플 평균 점수는 200-210점(CBT기준)으로 추산된다. 이는 링구아 토플시리즈의 i-TOEFL단계에 해당하는 수준으로 약 5,000-6,000단어 정도의 어휘력을 갖는 것으로 추정하며, 이를 링구아 토플 중고급학습자로 분류한다.

* 보통 미국 대학에서 요구하던 토플 점수는 213점(CBT기준)으로 TOEFL *i*BT 80점에 해당하는 점수이다.

II. 점수 환산 기준

TOEFL Total Score Comparison

Internet-based Total	Computer-based Total	Paper-based Total
120	300	677
120	297	673
119	293	670
118	290	667
117	287	660–663
116	283	657
114-115	280	650–653
113	277	647
111–112	273	640–643
110	270	637
109	267	630–633
106-108	263	623–627
105	260	617–620
103-104	257	613
101-102	253	607–610
100	250	600–603
98-99	247	597
96-97	243	590–593
94-95	240	587
92-93	237	580–583
90-91	233	577
88-89	230	570–573
86-87	227	567
84-85	223	563
83	220	557–560
81-82	217	553
79-80	213	550
77-78	210	547
76	207	540–543
74-75	203	537
72-73	200	533
71	197	527–530
69-70	193	523
68	190	520
66-67	187	517
65	183	513
64	180	507–510
62-63	177	503
61	173	500
59-60	170	497
58	167	493
57	163	487–490
56	160	483
54-55	157	480
53	153	477
52	150	470–473
51	147	467
49-50	143	463
48	140	460
47	137	457
45-46	133	450–453
44	130	447
43	127	443
41-42	123	437–440
40	120	433
39	117	430
38	113	423–427
36-37	110	420
35	107	417
34	103	410–413
33	100	407
32	97	400–403
30-31	93	397
29	90	390–393
28	87	387
26-27	83	380–383
25	80	377
24	77	370–373
23	73	363–367
22	70	357–360
21	67	353
19-20	63	347–350
18	60	340–343
17	57	333–337
16	53	330
15	50	323–327
14	47	317–320
13	43	313
12	40	310
11	37	310
9	33	310
8	30	310
7	27	310
6	23	310
5	20	310
4	17	310
3	13	310
2	10	310
1	7	310
0	3	310
0	0	310

Range Comparison

Internet-based Total	Computer-based Total	Paper-based Total
111–120	273–300	640–677
96–110	243–270	590–637
79–95	213–240	550–587
65–78	183–210	513–547
53–64	153–180	477–510
41–52	123–150	437–473
30–40	93–120	397–433
19–29	63–90	347–393
9–18	33–60	310–343
0–8	0–30	310

TOEFL Score Comparison for Reading

Internet-based Total	Computer-based Total	Paper-based Total
30	30	67
29	29	66
28	28	64–65
28	27	63
27	26	61–62
26	25	59–60
24	24	58
23	23	57
21	22	56
20	21	54–55
19	20	53
17	19	52
16	18	51
15	17	50
14	16	48–49
13	15	47
12	14	46
11	13	44–45
10	12	43
9	11	41–42
8	10	40
7	9	38–39
6	8	36 37
5	7	34–35
4	6	32–33
3	5	31
1	4	31
0	3	31
0	2	31
0	1	31
0	0	31

Range Comparison for Reading

Internet-based Total	Computer-based Total	Paper-based Total
28–30	28–30	64–67
26–28	25–27	59–63
21–24	22–24	56–58
17–20	19–21	52–55
14–16	16–18	48–51
11–13	13–15	44–47
8–10	10–12	40–43
5–7	7–9	34–39
1–4	4–6	31–33
0	0–3	31

Memo

Final iBT

http://www.finalibt.co.kr

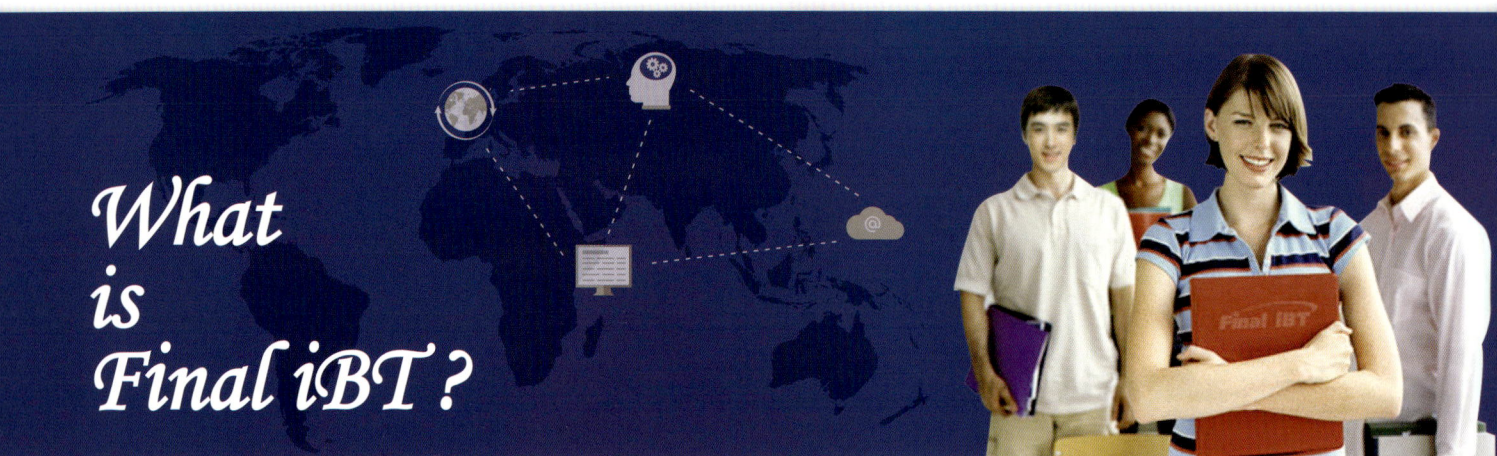

What is Final iBT ?

1 Final iBT는 TOEFL 시험을 준비하는 학습자를 위한 완벽한 준비 도구로서 실제 IBT시험을 치르는 것과 같은 full-length의 연습테스트를 제공합니다. 지난 시험들을 통해 철저히 분석된 문제들을 연습하게 되며 48시간 이내에 점수를 받아볼 수 있습니다.

2 시험을 마친 후 상세한 그래프와 함께 자신의 점수를 분석할 수 있습니다. 또한 자신이 풀었던 문제와 답뿐만 아니라 Reading, Listening, Speaking, Writing의 스크립트를 제공받아 철저한 복습이 가능합니다.
Final iBT는 토플 모의 시험으로써 토플 준비를 위한 완벽한 학습 자료가 될 것입니다.

시험 구성

: 시험 구성은 다음과 같습니다.

Level	Test Version	Questions (문항)			
		Reading	Listening	Speaking	Writing
고급	Full	39~42	34	6	2
	Short	14~28	17	3	1
	Half (R/L)	39~42	34	X	X
	Half (S/W)	X	X	6	2
초급	Short	21~24	13	2	1

* 총 40회분의 시험이 제공됩니다.

 http://www.finalibt.co.kr

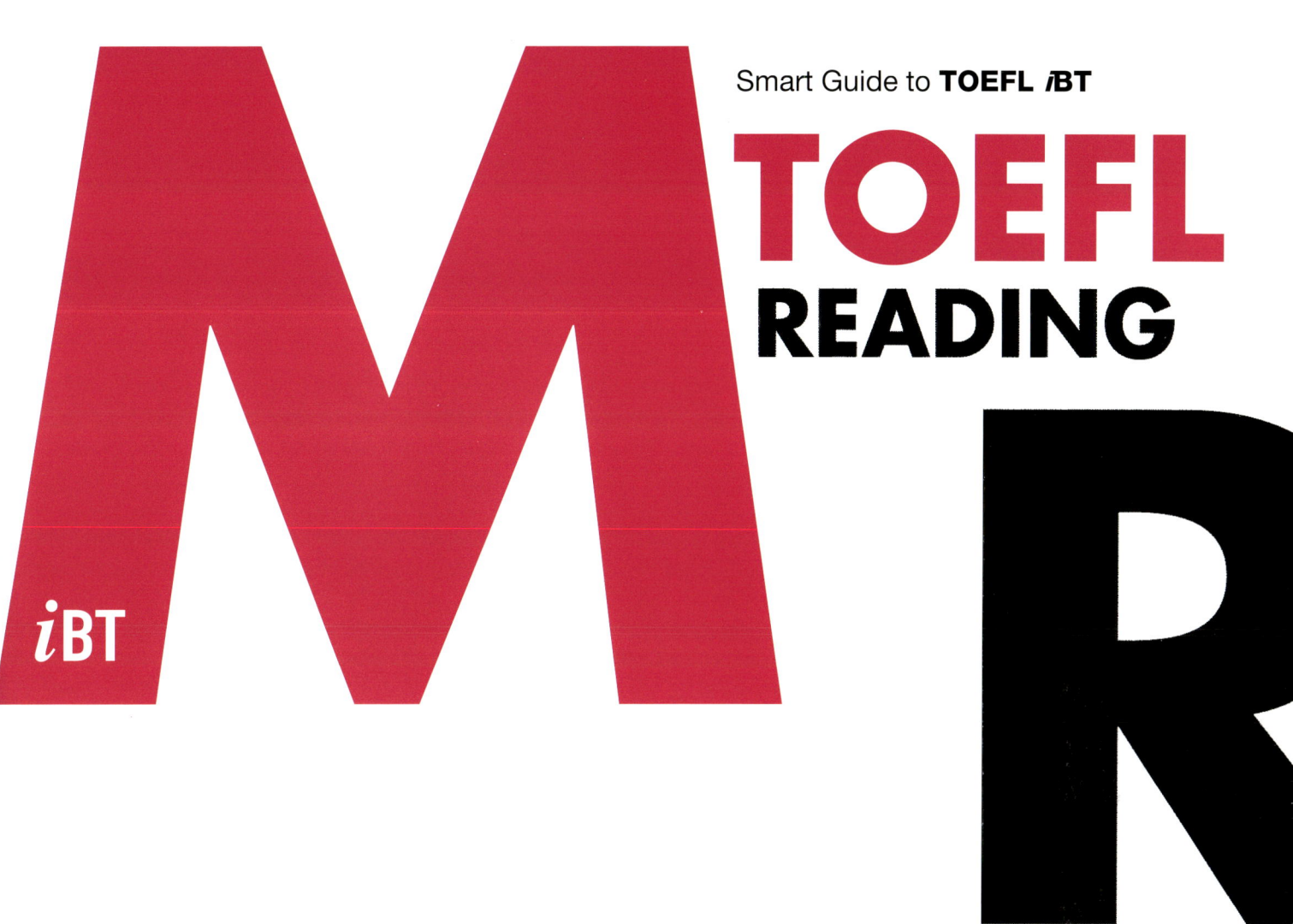

Smart Guide to **TOEFL iBT**

TOEFL
READING

Answer Key

LinguaForum

Answer Key

LinguaForum

1

Vocabulary & Reference

Basic Drills (1)   p.12

1. (C)   2. (C)   3. (C)   4. (D)   5. (B)
6. (B)

1. 많은 사람들은 비행기 타기를 두려워한다. 왜냐하면 비행기가 추락하는 경우에는 큰 뉴스 거리가 되기 때문이다. 사람들은 추락한 비행기 사진을 TV에서 보고 매우 두려워한다. 그러나 사실, 매일 얼마나 많은 사람들이 비행기를 타는지를 볼 때 항공 추락 사고를 당하는 사람들은 아주 적은 수에 불과하다. 비행기 추락 사고를 당할 확률은 번개에 맞을 확률 정도이다.

2. 많은 사람들은 선의의 거짓말을 한다. 선의의 거짓말이란 대개 사람들의 기분을 해치지 않기 위해서 하는 거짓말이다. 예를 들어, 친구가 당신이 보기에 아주 안 어울리는 옷을 샀을 때, 당신은 친구의 기분을 나쁘게 하는 대신에 옷이 잘 어울린다고 이야기할 수 있다. 이런 것이 선의의 거짓말일 것이다. 많은 사람들은 선의의 거짓말이 완전히 용납될 수 있다고 느끼지만, 나는 대부분의 상황에서 정직을 선호한다.

3. 자동차들은 오래될수록 더 많은 대기 오염을 유발한다. 그것은 일반적으로 오래된 자동차는 특히 관리 상태가 좋지 않을 경우에, 새 차보다 더 많은 연료를 태우기 때문이다. 사실, 차령이 5년 된 자동차의 경우 관리 상태가 좋지 않을 때 새 차에 비해 10배의 대기 오염을 발생시킨다. 이런 이유 때문에 대부분의 정부에서는 오래된 자동차 소유자들에게 매년 배기 검사를 받도록 요구한다. 자동차가 너무 많은 대기 오염을 유발하여 배기 검사를 통과하지 못할 경우에 소유자들은 그 자동차를 고쳐서 연료 소비량을 줄이도록 해야 한다.

4. 교도소 조직에서 가장 중요한 것 중 하나가 가석방 위원회이다. 가석방 위원회는 대부분 다섯 명에서 일곱 명으로 이루어지며 그들은 어려운 책무를 맡는다. 그들은 각 수감자들의 행동을 검토하고 계속 수감할지 아니면 석방할지를 결정한다. 그런 결정은 아주 중요하다. 일반 시민들을 위험하게 할 수 있기 때문에 가석방 위원회는 위험스러운 범죄자들은 석방시킬 수 없다.

5. 당신은 극도로 수줍어하는 사람들을 알고 있는가? 그들을 대화에 끌어들이기 어려운가? 그들은 그저 짧게만 대답하고, 대화를 빨리 끝내려고만 하는가? 그렇다면 당신이 아는 그 사람은 사회 불안 장애를 갖고 있는지 모른다. 사회 불안 장애란 정신 장애의 일종으로 주위의 사람들 사이에서 매우 불편해 하는 경우에 해당된다. 일반적으로 큰 문제는 아니고 심리학자를 통해 쉽게 치료될 수 있다.

6. 요즘에는 많은 회사들이 몇몇 도시에, 심지어는 몇몇 나라에 여러 사무실을 갖고 있다. 이것은 회사가 회의를 해야 할 경우 문제를 일으킨다. 곳곳의 여러 사무실 사람들이 한 곳에 모여야 할 수도 있겠지만 그 모든 사람들을 모으기 위한 비행기 표 값은 너무 비쌀 것이다. 그 대신에 그들은 전화 회의를 한다. 전화회의는 전화회사로부터 특별한 전화회선을 필요로 한다. 이는 비행기 표를 구입하는 것보다 훨씬 저렴하고, 서로 다른 사무실의 사람들이 실제로 한 방에 모이지 않고 그룹으로 대화 할 수 있게 해준다.

•• 해 설 ••

1. "But actually"로 시작되는 것으로 보아 많은 사람들이 비행을 두려워한다는 앞의 내용과 상반되는 뜻임을 알 수 있으며, 또한 뒷 문장에서 "chances of being hit by lightning"에 비유함으로써 의미가 명확히 드러나고 있다.

2. "but"으로 시작되는 문맥상, 글쓴이는 "To tell white lies is acceptable."의 반대 입장임을 알 수 있다.

3. 마지막 문장의 '너무 많은 오염을 일으키면 "emission test"를 통과하지 못한다'는 말에서 이 단어의 뜻을 유추해볼 수 있다.

4. "They have to review the behavior ... released from prison."의 문장에서 "parole board"의 역할을 설명해 주고 있다.

5. 다음 문장의 "give short answers,... the conversation quickly"에 해당하는 사람들이 어려워하는 것이라는 것을 고려해 볼 때 대화에 '참여하다'라는 뜻이 알맞다.

6. 마지막 두 문장이 이 단어에 대한 부연 설명이다. 특별한 전화선을 필요로 하고, 다른 사무실의 사람들이 그룹으로 회의를 할 수 있게 해주는 전화이다.

Basic Drills (2)   p.17

1. (1) there are only about three hours of darkness during the summer and only about three hours of daylight during the winter
   (2) the northern part of the world
2. (1) people (in Pakistan and Afghanistan)
   (2) The pieces of glass
   (3) to cut the string of the other person's kite

1. 노르웨이에서는 여름에는 밤이 겨우 세 시간 정도이고, 겨울에는 낮이 겨우 세 시간 정도이다. 이것은 지구가 기울어지는 방향 때문이다. 여름에는 지구의 북쪽이 태양에 가장 가까워지고 겨울에는 그 쪽이 가장 멀어진다. 그것은 여기에 도달하는 빛의 양이 일년 동안에 걸쳐 매우 많이 달라짐을 뜻한다.

2. 파키스탄과 아프가니스탄 사람들은 흥미로운 운동 경기를 한다. 그들은 연 싸움을 한다. 연 싸움에서 사람들은 아주 작은 유리 파편들이 달라붙어 있는 특별한 종류의 실로 연을 날린다. 유리 파편들은 모래알 정도의 크기지

만 꽤 날카롭다. 연 싸움에서 목적은 다른 사람의 연줄을 끊는 것이다. 이것은 자신의 연을 다른 사람의 연 주위로 둥글게 날림으로써 할 수 있다. 자신의 연줄로 다른 사람 것을 감싸면 붙어 있는 유리 파편이 줄을 끊어 낼 것이다. 연 싸움의 최종 승자는 마지막까지도 공중에 연을 날리고 있는 사람이다.

•• 해 설 ••

1. (1) 지구가 기울어져 있기 때문에 나타나는 현상 전체를 가리킨다.
   (2) 여름에 해에 가장 가까운 부분이며, 겨울에 가장 먼 곳이 되는 부분이다.
2. (1) 앞 문장에서 등장한 사람을 받고 있는 대명사이다.
   (2) 날카로운(quite sharp) 대상을 묻고 있다. "the pieces of sand"로 착각할 수도 있으나 이것은 가리키는 대상이 작다는 것을 강조하기 위한 비교대상일 뿐이다.
   (3) 앞 문장에서 나온 이 경기 목적이 되는 행동을 가리킨다.

Basic Drills (3) p.18

1. (B)   2. (C)   3. (C)   4. (D)

1. 1901년에 에어컨이 발명되기 전까지 사람들은 여름 동안의 더위를 다루기 위해서 다른 방법을 찾아야만 했다. 그 중에 하나는 여름에는 단순히 일을 적게 하는 것이었다. 사실, 이것이 학교에 여름 방학이 있는 이유이다. 그 시절에는, 수업을 하기에 여름은 단지 너무 더웠다.

2. 지난 20년 동안, 감시 카메라는 일상 생활 한 부분이 되어 왔다. 그것들은 엘리베이터 안에, 차고에, 심지어는 거리에도 있다. 물론 감시 카메라는 그것을 지켜보고 있는 경비원이 있을 때에만 유용하고, 세상에는 경비원의 수보다 훨씬 많은 수의 감시 카메라가 존재한다. 이것이 당신이 보는 감시 카메라 중 많은 것들이 가짜인 이유이다. 그것들은 카메라처럼 보이지만 실제로는 작동되지 않는다. 사람들이 감시당하고 있다고 생각하게 하기 위해서 있을 뿐이다. 범죄자들은 어떤 카메라가 진짜고 어떤 것들이 가짜인지를 모르기 때문에, 가짜 카메라들 역시 진짜인 것처럼 작용하고 있는 것이다!

3. 그가 항상 늦는다는 사실에도 불구하고 내가 아는 대부분의 사람들은 Tony를 매우 좋아한다. 내 생각에는 그가 항상 왜 늦는지에 대해 재미있는 이유를 갖고 있기 때문인 것 같다. Tony와는 어렸을 때부터 친구였기 때문에 나는 그 중에 많은 것들을 들었다. 나는 지각하는 이유가 무엇인지 듣기 위해서 그가 지각하기를 거의 바라기까지 할 정도였다. 이런 이유들 중에 최고는 작년에 그에게서 들었다. 우리는 크리스마스 파티에 참석하기로 했었고 물론 그는 지각했다. 그는 정말 미안하다며 그의 아버지를 굴뚝에서 꺼내 주려고 하다가 그랬다는 것이다. 실제는 그의 아버지가 Tony의 남동생을 놀라게 해주기 위해 산타 복장을 하고 벽난로로 내려오다가 굴뚝에 끼었다는 것이다!

4. Jack이 절도죄로 체포되었을 때, 우리는 충격을 받았다. Jack은 오랫동안 우리의 친구였고 언제나 확실하고 믿을 만한 사람이었다. 나는 곧, 우리가 땅에 떨어져 있는 지갑을 주웠을 때 Jack이 주인을 찾아 돌려주자고 우겼던 때를 생각했다. 경찰은 그에 대한 확실한 증거를 갖고 있다고 했지만 우리는 그래도 그가 결백하다고 생각했다. 우리는 단지 그가 그런 사람일 수 있다고 믿지 않았다.

•• 해 설 ••

1. 뒷 부분의 내용상 "those days"는 '너무 더워 수업을 할 수 없던 때'를 가리킨다는 것을 참조하자.
2. "the real ones"는 문장 앞쪽의 "the fake cameras"와 대조되는 대상이므로, "ones"가 가리키는 것을 쉽게 알아낼 수 있다.
3. "these reasons"와 "amusing reasons why he's late", "his excuse"는 모두 같은 대상을 가리킨다.
4. 글쓴이는 Jack이 무죄임을 확신하면서 그가 '그런 사람(such a person)'일리 없다고 했다. 그러므로 가리키는 것이 무죄와 반대되는 내용임을 짐작할 수 있다.

Reading Practice 1 p.20

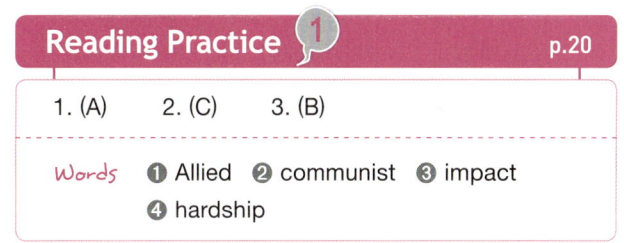

1. (A)   2. (C)   3. (B)

Words ❶ Allied ❷ communist ❸ impact ❹ hardship

베를린 장벽

제2차 세계대전의 종전 후 독일이 항복하자 연합국(영국, 프랑스, 미국, 소련)이 수도 베를린의 지배권을 차지했다. 처음에는 공동으로 시를 운영하기로 합의했지만, 냉전이 펼쳐지기 시작하며 그 협정은 빠르게 와해되었다. 소련은 도시의 동부를 지배하였고 미국, 프랑스, 영국은 도시의 서부를 지배하였다. 동베를린에 살던 많은 독일인들은 공산 정부가 아닌 민주 정부가 있는 서베를린으로 가기 위해 떠났다. 이에 대응해서 동독 정부는 도시의 양측을 갈라놓는 장벽을 세웠다.

베를린 장벽이라고 알려진 이 장벽은 베를린시의 주민들의 삶에 상당한 충격을 주었다. 장벽 때문에 베를린의 양측간 이동은 거의 불가능해졌다. 양측 정부의 허가가 없을 경우에는 아무도 장벽을 통과하지 못했다. 이런 허가서 없이 건너는 사람들은 24시간 장벽을 감시하는 군인들에 의해서 총격을 받기 쉬웠다. 장벽은 많은 가족을 갈라놓았고, 장벽 건너편에 직장을 가졌던 사람들은 일자리를 잃고 새로운 직업을 구해야만 했다. 장벽 양측의 독일인들에게 가져다 준 고난에도 불구하고 베를린 장벽은 거의 삼십 년 동안 서 있었다. 많은 사람들에게 베를린 장벽은 냉전과 미소간의 불신의 가장 명백한 상징이 되었다. 1989년에 장벽이 허물어졌을 때, 냉전 또한 결국 끝난 것으로 보였다.

Words

- surrender 항복하다
- communist 공산주의자
- impact 충격
- guard 지키다
- visible 눈에 보이는
- allied 연합한
- significant 명백한
- permit 허락
- hardship 곤란, 고생
- distrust 불신

Words

- citizen 시민
- rebel 반역자, 반란자
- conflict 분쟁
- lack 결여되다. 없다
- poverty 빈곤
- brutal 잔인한
- innocent 죄 없는, 무고한

•• 해 설 ••

1. 미국과 소련이 합의한 "partnership"이 냉전이 시작되며 깨짐으로써, 미국은 서독을 소련은 동독을 나누어 맡았다는 것에서 "partnership"의 의미를 짐작해 보자.

2. 각각의 보기를 "significant"의 자리에 대입하여 가장 적절한 것을 고른다.

3. 벽을 건너는 데 양측 정부로부터의 허가가 요하다고 한 다음, '이 서류들(these papers)' 없이 건너는 사람들이 군인들에게 총격 받기 쉽다고 했다. 그러므로 "these papers"가 가리키는 것이 양측 정부의 허가(permits)임을 짐작할 수 있다.

•• 해 설 ••

1. 다음 문장에서 이 지역의 다이아몬드를 판 돈이 전쟁에 필요한 무기와 물자를 사기 위해 쓰였다고 했다. "fuel conflicts"가 (A)와 같은 뜻으로 사용되는 경우도 있으나, 이 문맥에서 "conflicts"는 언쟁(arguments)이 아니라 '무력 충돌'의 뜻으로 사용되었으므로 '전쟁(war)'의 의미에 더 가깝다.

2. "such"는 항상 앞에 나온 내용을 가리킨다. 앞에 "clean water and electricity are often lacking"이라고 한 다음 "without such basic services"라고 했으므로, "clean water and electricity"와 같은 맥락으로 이해 할 수 있는 "energy and public health"가 답이다.

3. 앞에서 다이아몬드를 팔아 생긴 돈이 전쟁을 돕는데 쓰인다고 한 사실을 염두에 두고 각각의 보기를 대입해 보아 가장 적절한 것을 찾는다.

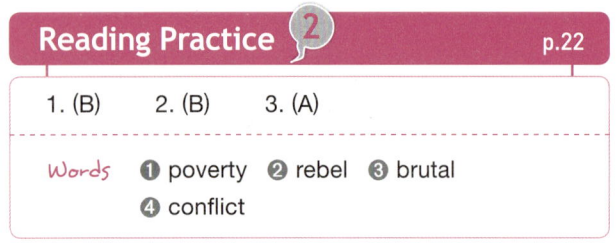

Reading Practice 2   p.22

1. (B)   2. (B)   3. (A)

Words ❶ poverty ❷ rebel ❸ brutal
❹ conflict

분쟁 다이아몬드

지구에서 가장 빈곤한 나라의 일부는 아프리카에 있다. 아이러니하게도 아프리카의 많은 빈곤한 나라들은 세계에서 가장 값진 지하자원을 갖고 있다. 시에라리온, 라이베리아, 앙골라, 콩고에는 모두 다이아몬드는 풍부하지만 그 주민들은 가난과 두려움 속에 살고 있다. 이것은 국가의 풍부한 지하자원이 잔인한 유형 분쟁을 부추기고 있기 때문이다. 이 국가들의 반역 단체들과 정부 모두 다이아몬드 판매에서 나온 수익을 그들의 군대에 물자를 공급하고 무기를 구입하는데 사용하며, 지금은 본질적으로 다이아몬드 무역을 장악하기 위한 싸움이 발생한다. 이런 상황에서, 이 국가들의 주민들은 희생자들이다. 전투에서 많은 무고한 사람들이 죽을 뿐만 아니라, 분쟁은 국가 발전도 가로막고 있다. 학교는 부서진 다음 다시 지어지지 않으며, 깨끗한 물과 전기는 자주 부족하다. 그런 기초 생활 서비스가 없어 질병과 굶주림은 국가 전체로 퍼진다.

직접 전투를 하는 정부와 반군들이 주민들의 고난에 큰 책임이 있지만, 선진국들 또한 비난받을 만도 하다. 종종 분쟁 다이아몬드라고 불리는 이런 국가들에서 온 다이아몬드는 유럽과 미국 전역의 보석상에서 팔린다. 이런 다이아몬드 판매로부터 나온 돈은 전쟁을 지속시키도록 보장할 따름이다. 이를 중단하기 위한 노력으로, 국제연합은 선진국들이 분쟁 지역으로부터 다이아몬드를 구입하지 않기로 한 합의를 통과시켰다. 이런 방법으로, 아마도 이런 끔찍한 전쟁들은 끝날 것이다.

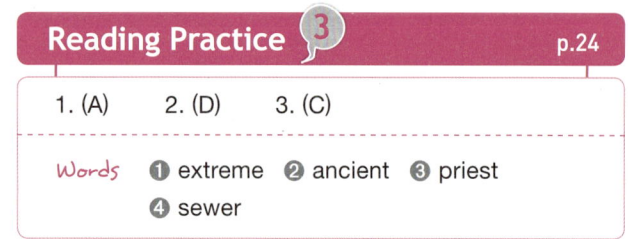

Reading Practice 3   p.24

1. (A)   2. (D)   3. (C)

Words ❶ extreme ❷ ancient ❸ priest
❹ sewer

카스트 제도

대부분의 현대 사회에서는 모든 남성과 여성이 같은 권리를 가진다고 믿지만, 항상 그런 것만은 아니었다. 많은 인류 역사에서, 인간 사회는 일부 집단이 다른 이들보다 더 많은 권력과 특권을 갖는 여러 집단으로 스스로를 나누었다. 가장 극단적인 형태로서 이런 집단 구분은 카스트 제도가 된다. 카스트는 한 사람이 태어나 속하는 사회 계급이다. 일단 특정 카스트에 속하게 되면, 그 사람은 다른 카스트로 이동할 수 없다. 많은 원시 사회에는 카스트 제도가 있었다. 그리스인과 로마인들에게는 단순한 카스트 제도가 있었다. 로마에서, 높은 계급은 원로원이라고 불리었고 낮은 계급은 평민이었다. 원로원 계급에 속한 이들만이 군대나 정부에서 일할 수 있었다. 평민들은 기본적으로 하인이었고 원로원 계급을 위해 일했다.

아마도 역사상 가장 복잡한 카스트 제도는 고대 인도에 존재하였다. 인도의 카스트 제도는 다섯 개의 서로 다른 카스트로 이루어졌다. 각각의 카스트는 각각 그들만이 가질 수 있는 특정한 직업이 있었다. 그들은 심지어는 서로 다른 종류의 음식을 먹었다. 사실, 한 사람의 카스트는 어디에 살 수 있는 지부터 누구와 결혼할 수 있는지까지 그 사람 삶의 거의 모든 부분을 지배하였다. 인도의 가장 높은 카스트는 성직자와 학자들이었다. 가장 낮은 카스트의 사람들은 불

가족천민이라고 불리었다. 불가촉천민들은 도로나 하수구를 청소하는 등의 인도 사회에서 가장 천한 직업을 가졌다. 그들의 직업이 더럽다고 여겨졌기 때문에 다른 카스트의 사람들과의 접촉은 금지되었다. 불가촉천민들은 마을 우물에서 물조차 마실 수 없었다. 이 카스트 제도는 아직도 인도 일부, 특히 전통적 믿음이 강한 시골 지방에 남아 있다. 그러나 현대 인도의 대부분 지방에서는 카스트 제도가 줄어들고 있으며 덜 중요해지고 있다.

📨 **Words**

☐ extreme 극도의, 극심한   ☐ servant 하인

☐ complex 복잡한   ☐ ancient 고대의

☐ priest 성직자   ☐ sewer 하수구

•• 해 설 ••

1. 본문에 따르면 많은 사회는 계급으로 나뉘었고, 특정 계급이 더 많은 힘과 "privileges"를 가질 수 있었다고 했다. 문맥 속에서 특별한 단서를 찾을 수 없으므로, 주어진 보기를 각각 "privileges"의 자리에 대입하여 글의 흐름에 맞는 가장 적절한 보기를 고른다.

2. 문제의 단어가 있는 문장은 '인도의 가장 높은 카스트 계급은 성직자와 "scholar"이다'의 뜻이다. 문맥 속에서 단서를 찾을 수 없는 문제이므로 각각의 보기를 "scholar"의 자리에 대입하여 가장 적절한 보기를 고른다.

3. 앞 문장에 "untouchables" 계급의 사람들이 갖는 직업이 제시되었다.

iBT Practice 1   p.26

1. (C)   2. (A)   3. (A)   4. (B)   5. (C)

6. (C)

올메크 모문화

아메리카 원주민 문화 중에서 가장 잘 알려진 것은 아마 1,500년에서 1,000년전 멕시코와 중앙 아메리카에 존재했던 아즈텍과 마야 문명일 것이다. 그러나 그 두 왕국의 모문화는 그보다 1,000년 전에 같은 지역을 차지하고 있던 올메크 사회였다. 올메크는 여러 면에서 아즈텍과 마야와 비슷했다. 이런 후기 문명처럼, 올메크 사람들은 뛰어난 건축가였고 공예가였다. 그들은 아메리카에서 최초로 피라미드를 만들었으며 가장 큰 도시들도 만들었다.

올메크 사회는 단단하게 조직되어 있었다. 그곳은 성직자와 귀족으로 이루어진 작은 계급이 다스린 반면, 사회의 다른 구성원들은 노예보다 약간 나은 수준이었고 이들 고위 계급에게 비참하게 억압받았다. 올메크에는 서로 다른 종류의 천연자원을 이용하기 위하여 위치한 세 군데의 큰 도시가 있었다. 각각은 종교와 사회 생활의 중심인 피라미드를 중심으로 둘러져 있었다. 연구자들이 발견한 제물 희생자 유골로부터 올메크에서 인신공희가 행해졌다는 것을 알 수 있다. 전사들을 제물로 바쳤던 아즈텍과는 다르게 대부분의 올메크 제물 희생자들은 노인이나 어린이였다. 왜 올메크인들이 이런 사람들을 희생자로 선택했는지는 모르지만, 그 대부분이 그들의 주신인 반인 반재규어 영령에 바쳐졌

고 알려져 있다.

비록 비참하고 억압적인 사회였지만, 올메크 사람들은 아메리카에 많은 발명을 가져다주었다. 서반구에서 최초로 피라미드를 만들었을 뿐만 아니라, 그들은 최초의 문자 체계와 달력을 창안하였다. 이 모든 발명들은 나중에 마야인과 아즈텍인에 의해서 모방된다. 비록 아즈텍과 마야에 비해 잘 알려지지는 않았지만, 올메크 문명이 고대 아메리카 문명 중 가장 위대한 것들 중의 하나임은 틀림없다.

📨 **Words**

☐ civilization 문명   ☐ occupy 차지하다, 장악하다

☐ artisan 공예가   ☐ priest 성직자

☐ noble 귀족   ☐ upper class 고위 계급

☐ oppress 억압하다   ☐ natural resources 천연자원

☐ sacrificial 제물로 바쳐진   ☐ hemisphere 반구

•• 해 설 ••

1. 첫 문단에 따르면 Aztec과 Maya 문명이 이 둘의 "mother culture"인 Olmec 문화와 많은 점에서 유사했고, Olmec 문명은 같은 지역에서 이 두 문화보다 훨씬 전에 존재했다. 따라서 Olmec 문명이 Aztec과 Maya 문명의 바탕이 되었음을 짐작 해 볼 수 있다.

2. Olmec 사람들은 뛰어난 건축가이며 "artisans"이고, 처음으로 피라미드와 큰 도시들을 지었다고 했다. 문맥상 피라미드와 큰 도시들을 지을 수 있는 자질을 가진 사람들임을 짐작할 수 있다.

3. 이 문장은 앞 문장으로부터 이어지며, Olmec의 큰 세 도시 각각이 지녔던 특성을 설명하고 있다.

4. 각각의 두시가 종교적, 사회적 생활의 "focus"인 피라미드를 중심으로 있었다고 했다. 각각의 보기를 대입해 보아 가장 적절한 것을 찾는다.

5. 연구자들이 희생자들의 해골을 발견함으로 피라미드에서 이 행위가 벌어졌다는 것을 알았다고 한 "because researchers have discovered the skeletons of the sacrificial victims"에서 구문의 뜻을 짐작 해 볼 수 있다.

6. 앞 문장에서 언급된 Olmec이 치르던 의식의 희생 제물로 쓰였던 대상을 지칭한다.

iBT Practice 2   p.28

1. (B)   2. (C)   3. (B)   4. (C)   5. (C)

6. (C)

어족

역사 학자들은 언제나 한 가지 특정한 어려움에 직면해왔다. 읽고 쓰기를 하는 인간사회는 약 5,000년 전쯤에 나타난 것으로 보인다. 사학자들은 쓰여

진 기록이 없는 그 이전의 사회에 대해서는 어떻게 알 수 있을까? 이 문제를 더욱 어렵게 만드는 것은, 이러한 오래 전 사회에 대해서는 주택이나 도구의 유물 같은, 학자들이 사회를 연구하는데 쓰는 대부분의 물리적 증거들도 더 이상 존재하지 않는다는 것이다. 그럼에도 학자들은 이런 고대 사회에 대해서 많은 것들을 알아내왔다. 이를 가능케 한 것은 언어 연구이다.

아마 알고 있겠지만, 많은 언어들은 서로 비교적 비슷한 단어들을 가지고 있다. 예를 들어, 영어의 police는 스페인어의 policia와 같다. 이런 유사성을 연구함으로써 우리는 어떤 언어들이 연관되어 있음을 알 수 있다. 즉, 그 모든 언어들은 원시의 공통 언어로부터 발생했다. 한 예로, 하나의 원시 언어인 라틴어로부터 발생한 스페인어, 프랑스어, 이탈리아어가 있다. 만약 서로 다른 집단의 사람들이 공통의 조상 언어를 갖고 있다면, 그들이 공통의 조상 또한 가졌을 것이라고 짐작할 수 있다. 이렇게 어족을 몇 천년 전으로 추적해감으로써 우리는 처음의 조상까지 추적해갈 수 있다.

인도-유럽어족은 가장 큰 어족 가운데 하나이다. 오늘날 인도-유럽어족은 431개의 언어로 구성되어 있다. 전세계에 걸쳐 퍼져 있는 30억 명 이상의 사람들이 이 언어를 사용한다. 그러나 7,000년 전의 그들은 같은 언어를 사용하는 하나의 공통의 조상을 가졌고 하나의 사회 속에 함께 살았다. 수년에 걸쳐서 그 사회는 분화되었고, 새로운 장소로 이동하였으며, 하나의 인도-유럽어는 서서히 현재 사용되는 수백 개의 언어로 바뀌게 되었다.

언어 연구는 단순히 어떤 집단의 사람들이 공통된 조상을 가졌는지 보다 더 많은 것을 알게 해준다. 그것을 통해 공통된 조상들의 삶이 어떠하였는지에 대해서도 알 수 있다. 한 어족 안의 여러 언어들에서 어떤 낱말들이 공통되는지를 연구함으로써 우리 조상들에 대해서 많은 것을 알 수 있다. 예를 들어, 인도-유럽인들은 말을 탔으며, 목동이자 양치기였으며(소와 양을 키웠다), 그들이 치른 전쟁에 대해서 시를 썼고, 하늘의 신을 숭배하였다는 것을 안다. 그리고 이 모든 것들은 단지 우리가 매일 쓰는 말을 연구함으로써 아는 것이다!

✉ Words

- □ particular 특정한
- □ physical evidence 물리적 증거
- □ related 연관이 있는
- □ trace 추적하다
- □ surface 나타나다,
- □ remains 유적, 유물
- □ ancestral 조상의
- □ herder 목동

•• 해 설 ••

1. 문맥상 단어의 뜻을 추측해 볼 수 있다. 뒷 문장에서 "one particular difficulty"가 무엇이었는지 구체적으로 설명해 주고 있다.

2. '문자를 읽고 쓰는 가장 이른 사회가 5,000년 정도 전에 surface 한 것으로 보인다'고 했다. (A)와 (D)는 문맥상 옳지 않다는 것을 쉽게 알 수 있다.

3. 문맥상, "ones"는 문자의 기록이 있기 이전의 '사회(societies)'를 가리킨다.

4. 세 번째, 네 번째 문단의 인도-유럽어족에 대한 설명이나. 어족을 연구함으로 알 수 있는 조상들의 생활 등의 내용에서, "language families"가 같은 고대 언어에 서 파생되어 나온 많은 공통점을 지니고 있는 언어들이라는 것을 알 수 있다.

5. 여기서 "they"는 앞 문장에 있는 "they"를 가리키며 그것은 다시 "Over three billion people (who) speak those languages"를 가리킨다.

6. 문맥상 단서가 주어지지 않은 문제이다. 고대 인도-유럽인들의 생활상에 대해 주어진 예의 하나로, "worship"이나 "deity"의 의미를 안다면 좀 더 쉽게 정답을 고를 수 있다.

Vocabulary Review   p.30

1. (C)   2. (C)   3. (A)   4. (D)   5. (C)
6. (B)   7. (B)   8. (C)
9. acceptable   10. outfit
11. extreme   12. visible
13. objective   14. trustworthy
15. conflict   16. innocent

Sentence Simplification

Basic Drills (1)   p.34

1. (D)   2. (A)   3. (C)

Basic Drills (2)   p.35

1. (D)   2. (B)   3. (B)   4. (C)   5. (C)
6. (B)

1-2. 동물들은 스스로를 방어하기 위한 여러 가지 방법을 갖고 있다. 어떤 동물들은 적으로부터 스스로를 숨기기 위해 즉시 색깔을 바꿀 수 있다. 가장 잘 알려진 예가 카멜레온이다. 카멜레온의 피부에는 피부색을 바꿀 수 있게 해주는 특별한 화학 물질이 들어 있다. 나뭇가지에 앉은 카멜레온의 피부색은 짙은 갈색일 것이다. 그러나 나뭇잎 위에 있을 때는 밝은 초록색일 것이다. 심해어들 역시 주위 환경에 따라 피부색을 바꿀 수 있는 능력을 갖고 있다. 이런 동물들은 두려움이나 분노를 연속적으로 재빠르게 바뀌는 색깔로 나타내는 등 색깔 변화를 의사 소통의 방법으로 사용할 수 있다.

3-4. 냉전 동안에, CIA는 러시아, 동독에 그 나라들의 군사 정보를 수집하는 일을 하는 간첩들을 많이 갖고 있었다. 정보를 빼내는 것도 어려웠지만, 그 정보를 가지고 출국해서 CIA로 가지고 가는 일은 더욱 어려웠다. 이런 일을 하기 위해서 그들은 마이크로도트라고 불리는 특수한 필름을 사용했다. 마이크로도트는 이 문장 끝에 찍힌 마침표 크기 정도로 아주 작다. 간첩은 그가 갖고 있는 어떤 정보이던지 사진을 찍어서 CIA로 보냈다. 간첩들은 편지 속의 마침표 같은 문자에 마이크로도트를 숨긴 다음 그 편지를 미국에 있는 다른 CIA 요원에게 보냈다. 이런 교묘한 발명품은 수많은 간첩들이 임무를 완수하는데 도움이 되었다.

5-6. 사람의 지능을 측정하기 위한 첫 번째 시도는, 한 사람의 지능을 패턴 인식과 문제 해결 능력을 통해 검증하는 검사인 지능지수 또는 IQ로부터 나왔다. IQ검사에는 역사나 과학에 대한 질문이 없으며, 특별한 정보를 필요로 하지도 않는다. 그러므로, 학교에 다니지 않은 사람들도 대학 졸업자들과 마찬가지로 쉽게 검사에 응할 수 있어야 한다. 그러나 지난 20년 동안, 좀 더 많은 학자들이 IQ 검사에 불만족하여, 지능을 측정하는 새로운 방법을 찾기 시작했다. IQ에 대한 가장 큰 불만은 특정 능력만을 검사한다는 것이다. 예를 들어, 수학을 잘 하는 사람은 IQ 검사에서도 아주 잘 할 수 있다. 그러나 한 사람이 똑똑하다는 것이 이런

방법뿐일까? 많은 학자들은 더 이상 그렇게 생각지 않는다.

•• 해설 ••

1. 어떤 동물들은 즉시 몸 색깔을 바꿀 수 있다/이것은 적으로부터 숨기 위한 능력이다.

2. 이 동물들은 의사소통의 방법으로 색깔변화를 사용할 수 있다/빠른 색깔변화를 통해 두려움이나 분노를 나타낸다.

3. 냉전기간에/CIA는 러시아나 동독에 많은 스파이를 가지고 있었다/그들의 임무는 그 나라 군대에 관한 정보를 가져오는 것이었다.

4. microdot를 편지 속 마침표 중 하나로 숨겨/그들은 그 편지를 보냈다/미국에 있는 다른 CIA요원에게.

5. 사람의 지능을 측정하는 첫 번째 시도는/IQ test의 도입이었다/이것은 패턴인식과 문제해결 능력의 평가로 사람의 지능을 결정했다.

6. 그러나/지난 20년 넘는 동안/좀 더 많은 과학자들은 IQ test에 불만을 가지게 되었다/그리고 지능을 평가할 새로운 방법을 찾기 시작했다.

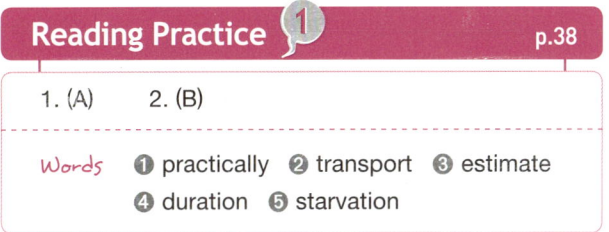

Reading Practice 1   p.38

1. (A)   2. (B)

Words ❶ practically ❷ transport ❸ estimate
❹ duration ❺ starvation

플랜테이션의 노예

1500년대 말부터 1900년대 초까지, 유럽 나라들은 신대륙에서 노예 노동력에 의지하는 많은 수의 플랜테이션과 농장을 운영했다. 거의 모든 유럽 식민지에서 이루어졌지만 특히 바하마 같은 카리브 해의 섬들에서는 아주 흔했다. 유럽인들이 사탕수수 농장을 운영했던 곳이 바로 이 섬들이다. 소유주들에게 고소득을 가져다주어 노예 경제의 주축이었던 사탕수수는 실제로 일을 해야 했던 노예들에게는 끔찍한 희생을 강요했다. 노예에게는 사탕수수 농장으로 보내지는 것이 거의 사형 선고와 다름없었다.

그들 노예의 사망률을 메우기 위해서 유럽인들은 아프리카로부터 새로운 노예들을 지속적으로 데려와야만 했다. 이것은 미국의 노예 역사상 가장 끔찍한 양상의 하나인 '중간 항로'로 이어졌다. 아프리카에서 팔리거나 잡힌 노예들은 아메리카로 선박을 통해 수송되어야 했다. 이 항로가 바로 중간 항로이다.

노예 수송선에서 나란히 채워져, 노예들은 날씨에 따라 한 달 내지 여섯 달의 얼마나 걸릴 지도 모르는 항해 내내 사슬에 묶여 있었다. 그들에게는 목숨을 유지할 만큼의 식량만이 제공되었다. 이에는 두 가지 목적이 있었다. 노예 무역꾼들의 비용을 낮출 뿐만 아니라, 거의 기아 상태에 이른 노예들이 중간 항로 내내 저항할 수 없도록 쇠약하게 유지된 것이다. 이토록 비참한 조건 아래서 중간 항로에서의 사망률이 농장 자체에서의 사망률보다 종종 높았다는 사실은 놀랍지 않다. 아프리카에서 데려온 2천만 명의 노예들 가운데 거의 절반 가량이 아메리카에 닿기도 전에 죽었다고 추정된다.

•• 해 설 ••

1. 주어진 문장은 다음과 같은 세 개의 의미 단위로 구성되어 있다. 이 의미들을 빠뜨리거나 왜곡하지 않고 전달하고 있는 문장을 찾아보자. "플랜테이션 소유자에게는 높은 이득을 가져다주어/사탕수수가 노예 경제의 기초였다/하지만, 실제 일을 했던 아프리카 노예들은 끔찍한 비용을 치러야 했다" "basis"가 "backbone"의 동의어이며, "took a terrible toll"이 많은 노예의 죽음을 의미한다는 것을 이해해야 한다.

2. 주어진 문장은 다음과 같은 세 개의 의미 단위로 구성되어 있다. "그것은 노예 무역업자들의 비용을 낮추게 해 주었을 뿐만 아니라/거의 기아 상태에 이른 노예들을 약하게 함으로/중간 항로 운반 도중 거의 저항할 수 없게 했다" "reduce their expenses"가 "keep their costs down"을, "resist"는 "rebellion"을 가리킨다는 것을 이해해야 한다. 노예를 굶긴 두 가지 이유를 빠뜨리지 않고 정확히 담고 있는 보기를 골라야 한다.

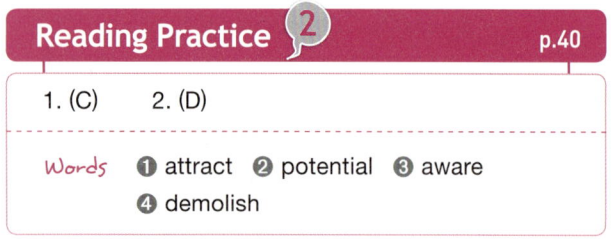

Reading Practice 2   p.40

1. (C)   2. (D)

Words   ❶ attract   ❷ potential   ❸ aware
      ❹ demolish

오래된 집의 잠재적 위험

많은 이유로, 사람들은 새 집을 사기보다 오래된 집을 산다. 헌 집의 낮은 가격에 끌렸을 수도 있고, 아니면 헌 집의 소유와 연관된 내력을 즐기는 것일 수도 있다. 하지만, 사람들이 헌 집을 살 때는 드러날 수 있는 잠재적 위험을 인식해야만 한다.

가장 큰 위험은 집안에 석면이 존재할 가능성이다. 석면은 불연성이 강한 물질이다. 이런 특징 때문에, 석면은 건설 자재로 많이 사용되어 왔다. 문제는 시간이 흐름에 따라 석면이 작은 날아다니는 입자로 부서져, 우리의 폐로 들어올 수 있다는 것이다. 일단 폐에 들어오면 석면은 암 같은 심각한 질병을 유발한다고 알려져 있다. 현재는 석면을 건설 자재로 이용하는 것이 대부분 나라에서 금지되어 있지만, 1980년대 이전에 지어진 대부분 건물에는 석면이 존재한다. 구식 건물에서 석면을 제거할 수는 있지만, 비용이 많이 드는 작업이다. 비록 그 효과는 건물이 일체로 보존될 때까지만 지속되지만, 대부분의 경우 건물 내에 석면이 존재하면 공기 중으로 날아가는 것을 방지하기 위해 다른 물질로 덮여 있다. 건물이 무너지거나 또는 대규모 공사를 했을 경우에, 석면은 또 다시 위험할 수 있다.

오래된 집의 흔한 건강 위험 요소 중 또 다른 하나는 납의 존재다. 납은 미국에서는 1978년까지, 다른 나라에서는 더 이후까지도 여러 페인트의 구성 성분이었다. 납을 함유하고 있는 페인트가 떨어져 나와 입 속으로 들어가면 위험하게 된다. 기본적으로 이것은 페인트 조각을 먹곤 하는 어린아이들에게 위험이 된다. 납을 먹게 되면 심각한 학습 장애가 유발된다. 석면처럼 납 페인트도 건물에서 제거될 수 있지만, 역시 이것도 비용이 많이 든다.

•• 해 설 ••

1. 주어진 문장은 다음 네 개의 의미 단위로 구성되어 있다. "문제는 / 시간이 흐름에 따라 / 석면이 작은 날아다니는 입자로 부서져, / 우리의 폐로 들어올 수 있다는 것이다." 각각의 의미 단위를 모두 왜곡하지 않고 바르게 전달하고 있는 보기를 골라야 한다. 정답에 가장 가까운 (B)에는 가장 중요한 정보인 석면에 대한 언급이 빠져 있다.

2. 주어진 문장은 다음 세 개의 의미 단위로 구성되어 있다. "비록 그 효과는 건물이 일체로 보존될 때까지만 지속되지만, / 대부분의 경우 건물 내에 석면이 존재하면 / 공기 중으로 날아가는 것을 방지하기 위해 다른 물질로 덮여 있다." "in most cases"는 "usually"와 같은 의미이며, "is only effective"와 "only works" 또한 같은 의미로 쓰였다.

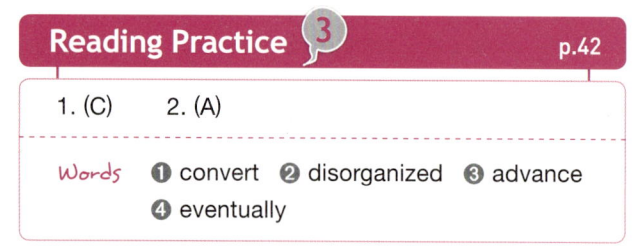

Reading Practice 3   p.42

1. (C)   2. (A)

Words   ❶ convert   ❷ disorganized   ❸ advance
      ❹ eventually

스페인의 무어족

16세기와 17세기 동안, 스페인은 여러 나라 중에서 가장 가톨릭적으로 알려져 있었다. 신교 개혁에 대한 저항이 가장 컸던 곳이 바로 스페인이었다. 신대륙에서, 원주민들을 기독교도로 개종시키는데 가장 적극적이었던 나라도 스페인이었다. 어떤 면에서 이것은 약간 아이러니한데, 왜냐하면 그 이전 한동안 스페인은 무슬림 지배하에 있었기 때문이다.

711년에, 서북 아프리카에 사는 무슬림인 무어인들은 유럽을 침략하였다. 북유럽의 크리스천 군대에 의해서 제지될 때까지 그들은 작고 조직적이지 못한 수많은 소 왕국의 지배를 받던 스페인 영토를 순식간에 삼켜 버리고는 프랑스까지 밀고 나갔다. 무어인들은 스페인 남부를 견고하게 장악하고 있었고, 그런 상태가 수백 년 동안 지속되었다. 무어인들의 지배하에서 스페인은 중동의 이슬람 왕국들과 느슨한 연관을 가진 우마이야 왕조의 지배를 받았다.

우마이야 왕조 지배하에서 스페인은 많은 진보를 했는데, 이것은 유럽 다른 지역에서는 잊혀졌던 고대 그리스와 로마의 지식을 무어인은 보존하고 있었기 때문이다. 따라서 그곳은 당연히 문화적으로나 예술적으로도 유럽에서 가장 진보된 지역이었다. 무어인들은 스페인에 지금도 많이 남아 있는 아름다운 모스크와 궁궐을 건설했다. 당시 그들의 예술 또한 높은 평가를 받고 있다. 스페인의 무어 문화의 최고점은 11세기였다. 그 이후 우마이야 왕조는 여러 개의 작은 왕국으로 분할되었고, 결국은 북부의 크리스챤 왕국들에 의해서 정복당했다. 그러나 스페인에서는 아직도 그들의 영향이 보인다. 스페인 남부의 어느 큰 도시 내 건축물들만 보아도 그렇다.

•• 해 설 ••

1. 주어진 문장은 다음 네 개의 의미 단위로 구성되어 있다. "북유럽의 크리스천 군대에 의해서 제지될 때까지 / 그들은 작고 조직적이지 못한 수많은 소 왕국의 지배를 받던 스페인 영토를 / 순식간에 삼켜 버리고는 / 프랑스까지 밀고 나갔었다." "had no large unified government"의 의미가 "was ruled by a number of small disorganized kingdoms"와 동일하다는 것, "easily conquered all of Spain"이 또한 "quickly swept through the territory of Spain"과 같은 내용이라는 것을 이해해야 한다.

2. 주어진 문장은 다음 네 개의 의미 단위로 구성되어 있다. "우마이야 왕조 지배하에서 / 스페인은 많은 진보를 했는데, / 이것은 유럽 다른 지역에서는 잊혀져 있던 고대 그리스와 로마의 지식을 / 무어인들은 보존하고 있었기 때문이다." 이 문제에서는 우선 우마미야 왕조가 무어인들의 왕국이라는 것을 이해해야 한다. 그러므로 이 두 단어가 한 문장에 중복될 필요가 없으며, "in control"이라는 표현이 '지배하에 있는'의 뜻임을 알아야 할 것이다.

iBT Practice 1　　　　　　p.44

1. (C)　　2. (D)　　3. (B)　　4. (A)　　5. (B)

6. (B)

기후 변화와 인류의 진화

과학자들은 예전부터 기온이 인간을 포함한 동물의 체구와 체형을 조절하는데 도움이 된다는 것을 알고 있었다. 이것은 세 가지 간단한 법칙으로 나타낼 수 있다. Allen의 법칙은 적도와 가까이 살고 있는 동종 동물의 팔과 다리가 더 길다는 것이다. Bergman의 법칙은 동종 동물들이 북쪽 기후 지방에 살 경우 일반적으로 몸집이 더 크고 무게도 많이 나간다는 것이다. 마지막으로 Gloger의 법칙은, 같은 종의 경우 적도와 가까이에 사는 동물들의 피부색이 극북이나 극남 기후 지방에 사는 동물들보다 더 어둡다는 것이다.

이 세 가지 법칙들은 꽤 논리적인데, 왜냐하면 그 세 가지의 신체적 특성은 모두 체온의 보존이나 방출과 직접적으로 관련되기 때문이다. 긴 팔과 다리를 가진 동물들은 짧은 팔다리를 가진 동물들보다 더 빨리 체온을 방출한다. 크고 무거운 동물들은 작은 동물들보다 체온을 더 많이 생성한다. 더 어두운 피부는 적도에 가까울수록 강해지는 태양 빛으로부터 더 잘 보호해 준다. 이 세 가지의 법칙은 오랫동안 사실인 것으로 인정되었는데, 이제 과학자들은 이전에 생각하던 것보다 기후와 기후의 변화는 진화, 특히 인간의 진화에 더 많은 영향을 준다고 생각하기 시작한다.

이제 과학자들은 더 복잡한 뇌의 진화 같은 인간의 진화에 있어서는 특히, 기후의 급격한 변화가 아주 중요한 역할을 했다고 믿는다. 가장 강력한 증거는 2백만 년도 더 전에 우리의 최초의 조상이 진화하기 시작했던 아프리카에 있다. 과학자들은 3백만 년 전부터 1백만 년 전 사이에 아프리카는 특히 강우량 등 기후의 급격하고 중요한 변화를 겪었다는 것을 알아냈다. 이 시기가 인류 진화의 중요한 단계와 긴밀하게 들어맞는 사실은 이런 단계를 재촉한 것이 바로 이러한 기후의 변화였다는 것을 암시한다.

특히, 과학자들은 기후의 변화가 매우 급격하고 심각하였기 때문에 우리 조상들 중에서 영리한 사람만이 적응하고 살아 남았을 것이라고 본다. 이런 이론에 따르면, 새로운 기후에서 살아남는 방법을 찾는 것에 대한 필요가 초기 인류의 뇌를 더 크고 복잡하게 발전하도록 촉진시켰다. 이에 대한 증거는 많이 있다. 이러한 급격한 기후 변화의 시기는, 즉 현대 인류를 정의하는 진보된 지능의 상징으로서 석기를 만들고, 큰 동물을 사냥하기 위해 집단을 조직하기 시작한 시기였다.

•• 해 설 ••

1. 앞 문단에서 언급한 세 법칙은 모두 동물 종의 신체적 특징에 관련한 것이다. 즉, 팔과 다리, 몸통 그리고 피부 색 이 세 가지를 지칭한다.

2. 뒤에 이어지는 "or loss"에서 이 단어가 '잃어버림'의 반대 의미일 것임을 추측해 볼 수 있다.

3. 주어진 문장은 다음 네 개의 의미 단위로 구성되어 있다. "이러한 법칙들이 오랫동안 사실로 인정되었는데 / 과학자들은 이제 생각하기 시작한다 / 기후와 기후의 변화가 진화, 특히 인류의 진화에 끼치는 영향이 훨씬 더 크다는 것을 / 전에 생각했던 것 보다" "changes in weather patterns"와 "climate change"가 같은 의미라는 것을 이해한다. 또한, "play a

larger part"는 '큰 영향을 끼친다'는 의미로 쓰일 수 있다.

4. 지문에 주어진 단서가 없으므로 내용상 가장 적절한 보기를 고른다.

5. 문장 앞부분의 "The timing of these changes closely matches important steps in human evolution, ..."에서 언급된 단계를 가리킨다.

6. 주어진 문장은 다음 네 개의 의미 단위로 구성되어 있다. "이런 빠른 기후 변화의 시기였다 / 인간이 도구를 만들기 시작하고 / 큰 동물의 사냥을 위해 조직화된 집단 사냥을 시작했을 때가 / 이 두 특징은 모두 현대 인류를 정의하는 진보하는 지식을 나타내 준다" "production of stone tools"와 "hunting in teams"는 각각 "making stone tools"와 "organized group hunts"를 가리킨다.

iBT Practice 2
p.47

| 1. (C) | 2. (D) | 3. (B) | 4. (B) | 5. (D) |
| 6. (B) | 7. (B) | 8. (D) | | |

체르노빌

1980년대에는 핵발전에 대해 전 세계적으로 강한 반대가 있었다. 이러한 반대는 1986년에 아직까지도 역사상 최악의 핵사고로 남아 있는 체르노빌 핵발전소의 폭발 이후 더 커졌다. 사고로 인해서 13만 5천명이 넘는 사람들이 고향을 떠나야 했으며, 아직도 발전소 주변 지역은 고도로 오염된 채로 남아 있다.

이 사고는 발전소 내 원자로의 잘못된 설계와 직원들이 올바른 안전 절차를 따르지 못한 것에 큰 원인이 있다. 4월 25일 발전소 직원들은 낮은 전력에서 어떻게 작동하는지를 실험하고 있었다. 이 실험을 하기 위해서 그들은 원자로 속의 핵반응 속도를 제어하고 제어되지 않은 반응을 막는 제어봉을 단 여덟 개만 남기고 모두 제거했다. 안전 절차는 한번에 최소한 30개의 제어봉을 사용할 것을 요구하고 있었지만, 무시되었다. 실험 도중에 원자로는 불안정해졌고 너무 많은 전력을 발전해 내기 시작했다. 부족한 제어봉 때문에 직원들은 반응을 늦출 수가 없었고, 원자로는 폭발하였다.

폭발은 방사성 기체와 그 밖의 유해 물질을 대기 속으로 퍼뜨렸다. 그로 인해서 생긴 방사능 구름은 러시아, 우크라이나, 벨로루시로 퍼져 나갔다. 아주 심각한 방사능 오염은 발전소 주변 10마일 이내였는데, 이곳은 아직도 너무나 많이 오염되어 사람이 살 수 없다. 사고 직후 56명이 사망했지만 방사능 오염으로 인한 영향은 종종 몇 년 후에야 나타나기 시작하기 때문에, 실제 사망자 수가 몇 명인지는 아마 알려지지 않을지 모른다. 연구에 따르면, 그 사고로 오염된 지역의 발암률은 다른 일반 지역보다 최고 10배 더 높이 나타났다.

이 같은 건강 문제 이외에도 소련은 물론 전세계에 중대한 정치적 결과를 가져왔다. 소련 내에서는 이 사고가 정부를 덜 비밀스러워 지도록 만들었고, 공산 정부 붕괴의 촉진을 도왔다. 세계적으로는 새로운 핵발전소 건설을 거의 중단시켰고, 기존의 많은 핵발전소들도 안전 문제 때문에 문을 닫도록 만들었다. 그러나 오늘날에는 고유가와 에너지의 필요 때문에 많은 나라들이 또 다시 핵발전을 시작하고 있다. 예를 들어 중국의 경우, 향후 십 년간 매년 최소한 두 군데

의 핵발전소를 건설할 것을 계획하고 있다. 핵발전이 다시 늘어남에 따라서, 체르노빌 같은 사고가 다시 일어나지 않기를 바랄 수밖에 없다.

✉ Words

☐ opposition 반대	☐ nuclear power plant 핵발전소
☐ to date 지금까지, 역사상	☐ contaminated 오염된
☐ reactor 원자로	☐ safety procedure 안전 절차
☐ control rod 제어봉	☐ radioactive 방사성의
☐ death toll 사망자수	☐ isolated 단 하나의, 유일한

•• 해 설 ••

1. 다음 문장에서 언급되고 있는 역사상 가장 끔찍하다고 보여지는 체르노빌의 핵폭발 사고로 인해 늘어난 전 세계적인 핵발전에 관한 반응이므로 부정적인 의미일 것임을 짐작할 수 있다.

2. 주어진 문장은 다음과 같은 두 개의 의미 단위로 구성되어 있다. "이러한 반대는 구 소련의 체르노빌 핵발전소의 폭발 이후인 1986년에 증가되었는데 / 이 사건은 아직도 역사상 가장 끔찍한 핵사고로 알려져 있다" 이 문장에서 말하는 증가된 것이 핵발전에 대한 반대임을 이해해야 한다. (A)는 정답에 가깝지만, 체르노빌이 오늘날 존재하고 있다고 하므로 틀린 답이며, (B)는 문장의 의미를 잘못 해석하고 있으며, (C)는 소련에 대한 반대가 증가했다고 했으므로 틀린 답이다.

3. 발전소 주변 지역이 "contaminated" 된 것은 체르노빌 핵발전소 폭발로 일어난 결과 중 하나이다.

4. 일꾼들이 '그것(it)'이 얼마나 저전력에서 작동할 수 있는지를 실험했다고 했다. 문맥상 '그것'은 발전소를 가리킨다.

5. 문제의 단어 "these"가 쓰인 문장에 따르면 안전 절차는 한번에 최소 30개의 제어봉을 사용할 것을 요구했지만, 이것들은 무시당했다고 했다. 따라서 '이것들'이 안전 절차를 가리킴을 알 수 있다.

6. 주어진 문장은 다음과 같이 세 개의 의미 단위로 구성되어 있다. "총 56명이 사고 후 즉시 사망했다 / 하지만 방사능 유해 물질의 효과는 수년 후에야 나타나는 경우가 많으므로 / 진정한 사망자 수는 결국 아마 알려지지 않을지도 모른다" "surface"와 "appear"는 유의어이다. 정답에 가장 가까운 (A)는 '아마 알려지지 않을지도 모른다'는 내용을 '아직 알려져 있지 않다'고 해석했으므로 틀리다.

7. 주어진 문장은 다음과 같은 두 개의 의미 단위로 구성되어 있다. "전세계적으로 그것(체르노빌 사건)은 거의 모든 핵발전소 건설을 막았고 / 또한 존재하고 있던 많은 발전소들도 안전 문제로 문을 닫도록 만들었다" (A)는 "all but stopped"의 의미를 '완전히 모두 멈추게 했다'로 해석하고 있지만, 이 표현의 올바른 의미는 '거의 모두 멈추게 했다'이다. (C)는 존재하고 있는 발전소들이 그들의 안전에 대한 생각을 없앴다고 했으므로 의미가 전혀 다르다. (D)는 두 의미 단위의 내용을 정확하게 담고 있지 않다.

8. 체르노빌 같은 사고가 다시 일어나지 않기를 바랄 수밖에 없다는 내용에서 이 단어의 뜻을 짐작해 볼 수 있다.

Vocabulary Review   p.50

1. (C)   2. (A)   3. (A)   4. (D)   5. (A)

6. (C)   7. (D)   8. (B)

9. attempt   10. estimate

11. duration   12. eventually

13. aware   14. dissatisfied with

15. countless   16. demolished

3

Factual Information & Negative Fact

Basic Drills (1)   p.54

1. (1) F   (2) T   (3) F
2. (1) F   (2) T   (3) T

1. 올림픽은 제우스신에게 경의를 표하기 위하여 고대 그리스의 도시국가들에서 창시되었다. 기원전 776년에 열린 첫 번째 대회에서는 그리스인들이 제우스가 살았다고 믿었던 올림포스산 아래에서의 도보 경주 한 종목만이 벌여졌다. 기원전 5세기에 이르러 올림픽은 그리스 축제 중에서 가장 중요한 것이 되었고 여러 가지 종목들도 추가되었다. 그리스인들을 4년마다 여름의 가장 더운 때에 대회를 개최하였고 특별한 규칙을 두었다. 가장 중요한 규칙은 대회 기간 동안에 그리스 도시들끼리의 전쟁은 중단되어야 한다는 것이었다.

2. 태양계 행성들의 영문 이름 가운데 많은 것들은 로마 신화에서 유래되었다. 태양으로부터 다섯 번째 행성인 목성(주피터, Jupiter)은 로마의 하늘의 신을 따라 이름 지어졌다. 고대 로마인들은 목성을 직접 볼 수 없었겠지만, 후대의 과학자들은 목성이 태양계 행성 중 가장 크기 때문에 이 신의 이름을 따와서 이렇게 이름 지었다. 고대 로마인들은 화성(마르스, Mars)을 직접 관측할 수 있었는데, 그 진한 붉은 색 때문에 선생의 신의 이름을 따와 그렇게 불렀다. 이런 식으로, 금성(비너스, Venus)이라는 이름의 기원인 사랑의 여신도 실제로 볼 수 있는 행성의 이름으로 사용된 것이다.

Basic Drills (2)   p.55

1. (C)   2. (A)   3. (B)   4. (B)

1. 갈색 은둔 거미는 물리면 가장 안 좋은 거미 중의 하나이다. 이 거미는 거미줄을 만들지 않는다. 크기는 약 반 인치 정도고, 북아메리카에서만 서식한다. 신발이나 상자 같이 좁고 어두운 곳을 좋아하기 때문에 대부분은 손이나 발에 물린다. 갈색 은둔 거미의 독은 치명적이지는 않지만, 건강에 심각한 문제를 일으킬 수 있다. 갈색 은둔 거미에 물린 상처는 매우 고통스럽다. 더 큰 문제는, 그 독액이 물린 상처 주변의 피부를 괴사시키는 것이다. 이런 상태가 최장 2주까지 지속되어 크기가 몇 인치에 이르는 검게 죽은 피부를 남길 수 있다. 또, 상처가 낫기까지는 6주에서 8주에 이르는 긴 시간이 걸리는데, 어떤 경우에는 수술이 필요할 수 있다.

2. 원시인들의 가장 큰 적은 거대한 동굴 곰이었다. 이 곰들은 정말로 무서웠

다. 뒷발로 서면 키가 20 피트에 이르기도 했다. 이는 현재의 가장 큰 곰의 두 배 정도이다. 게다가 이 곰들은 떼를 지어 살았다. 즉, 개들처럼 집단으로 이동했다. 인간들이 이들을 공격할 때면 한번에 최대 여섯 마리의 거대한 곰들과 싸워야 했다. 이렇게 강력한 놈들을 어떻게 인간이 이길 수 있었을까? 동굴 곰의 유골을 연구하면 이에 대한 답을 알 수 있다. 동굴 곰의 유골 대부분은 동굴 속에서 발견된다. 이것은 원시인들이 겨울에 동굴 곰이 잠들기까지 기다린 후 동굴에 들어가 동면 상태의 곰들을 죽였다는 것을 암시한다.

3. 큰흰상어는 주로 후각과 코 속의 특별한 전기 감각을 이용하여 먹이를 사냥한다. 이 상어들은 바닷속 수 마일 밖에서도 피 냄새도 맡을 수 있다. 살아 있는 모든 동물에 흐르는 전기까지도 느낄 수 있다. 먹잇감을 발견한 큰흰상어는, 보통 밑쪽에서부터 공격한다. 매우 빠르게 솟구쳐 먹잇감을 덮쳐서 큰 덩어리를 물어뜯는다. 보통 이 첫 번째 공격만으로도 그 불행한 동물을 죽이기에는 충분하다. 큰흰상어는 '포식 기계'로도 불리는데 이것은 기본적으로 사실이다. 가장 좋아하는 먹이는 바다표범이지만, 거의 아무거나 먹는다. 큰흰상어의 위 속에서는 고래의 일부, 거북이, 심지어는 자동차 배터리까지도 발견된다.

4. 1800년대 전에, 대부분의 유럽 나라들은 정부의 완전한 지배권을 가지고 있던 왕의 지배를 받았다. 이들 중 많은 왕들은 잔인하고 무관심한 통치자였다. 이런 나라의 백성들은 그런 상황을 좋아하지 않았지만, 그들이 이를 개선하기 위해 할 수 있는 것은 거의 없었다. 그러나 16세기와 17세기에, 상인과 실업가의 신흥 계급이 권력을 얻기 시작했다. 군주들은 이 부자 상인들이 내는 세금을 필요로 했기 때문에 그들을 완전히 무시할 수는 없었고, 그들의 권력을 잃기 시작했다.

•• 해 설 ••

1. keyword인 "the most severe effect"를 본문에서 찾으면, 마지막에서 세 번째 문장에 "A more serious effect"가 있다. 그로부터 세 문장을 참고하여 정답을 찾을 수 있다.

2. "kill the cave bears"를 keyword로 하여 찾으면, 마지막에서 네 번째 문장에 "beat such powerful creatures"가 나옴을 알 수 있다. 그 앞의 내용이 곰을 죽이기 어려웠던 이유이다.

3. keyword를 "eating machines"로 하여 본문에서 찾으면 끝에서 세 번째 문장에 그대로 "eating machines"가 있다. 그 다음 두 문장이 이렇게 불리는 이유를 명확히 설명해주고 있다.

4. keyword를 "hold on to absolute power"로 하여 찾으면 끝에서 두 번째 문장에 "however"가 나온다. 여기에서 앞 내용의 반대 상황이 나올 것이라는 것을 추측할 수 있다. 즉, 군주들은 상인들이 내는 세금이 필요해서 그들을 무시할 수 없었고, 그 때문에 상인들이 권력을 잡기 시작했다는 내용이다.

Basic Drills (3)   p.59

1. (1), (2)	2. (2), (3)
3. (1), (2)	4. (2), (3)

1. 금문교(Golden Gate Bridge)는 위험한 해역인 샌프란시스코만을 가로지른다. 옛날의 샌프란시스코에는 배만을 이용해 만을 건널 수 있었지만, 도시가 커짐에 따라 만을 건너는 더 빠른 수단이 필요해졌다. 그래서 1929년에 후버(Hoover) 대통령과 영(Young) 캘리포니아 주지사는 금문교 건설 계획을 시작했다. 다리는 1933년 착공되어 1937년에 준공되었다. 그 후로, 금문교는 샌프란시스코의 중요한 관광 명소 중의 하나가 되었다.

2. 인도네시아의 학자들은 놀라운 발견을 해냈다. 인도네시아 플로레스(Flores) 섬에서 소인종의 일종으로 보이는 화석을 발견한 것이다. 이 발견은 학자들 사이에서 논쟁을 불러일으켰다. 일부의 학자들은 이 화석들이 유럽의 네안데르탈인이 현생 인류와는 다른 종인 것처럼, 우리가 알고 있는 인류와는 완전히 다른 종이라고 생각한다. 그런데 또 다른 가능한 설명에는 섬의 왜소 발육화(island dwarfing)라고 불리는 것이 있다. 사람들이 섬에서 수천 년 간 고립되어 사는 경우에, 더 큰 체구에 필요한 식량이 부족하기 때문에 왜소한 쪽으로 진화하기 시작한다. 일부 학자들은 플로레스 섬의 화석들이 단지 섬의 왜소 발육화 현상의 극단적인 예일 뿐이라고 주장한다.

3. 미국인들은 1969년 7월 20일, 최초로 달에 착륙했다. 그 이후로 3년 동안 아폴로 계획으로 달에 다섯 번 더 다녀왔으며 800 파운드의 암석을 가지고 돌아왔지만 미국 시민들은 빠르게 흥미를 잃기 시작했다. 그들은 러시아를 제치고 달에 먼저 착륙하여 우주 경쟁에 있어서 가치 있는 일보를 내디뎠으나 아폴로 계획은 매우 돈이 많이 들고 위험한 계획이었다. 아폴로 1호기의 화재로 인해 사망한 세 명의 우주비행사 외에도 아폴로 13호기의 세 우주비행사들도 거의 죽을 뻔하였다. 그래서 1972년 아폴로 계획은 중단되었지만, 아직도 미국의 우주 역사상 가장 위대한 업적 중의 하나로 남아 있다.

4. 산불은 매우 파괴적이기는 하지만, 또한 필요하기도 하다. 산불은 여러 중요한 기능을 한다. 첫째로 산불은 숲 속의 늙고 병든 나무들을 제거한다. 그리고 여러 가지 방법으로 새로운 나무의 성장을 가능하게 한다. 산불이 태운 나무의 재는 영양분이 풍부하여 토양을 새로운 나무들에게 유익하게 만들어 준다. 더군다나 어떤 나무들은 씨앗이 자라기 위해서 실제로 불을 필요로 한다. 따라서 너무 커지거나 울창한 지대로 번지는 산불은 좋지 않지만, 어떤 산불들은 정말로 필요하다.

•• 해 설 ••

1. "as the city grew ... was needed"의 내용이, "in order to deal with the growth of the city"와 같다는 것을 이해해야 한다. "president"는 연방정부를, "governor"는 주정부를 대표하는 사람이며, 관광객의 관심을 끈 것은 다리 건설 후의 부수적인 효과일 뿐이지 목적이 아니다.

2. 많은 과학자들은 Flores에서 발견된 화석들이 네안데르탈인들처럼 완전히 다른 종이라고 생각했지, 그들과 연관이 있다고 말하지 않았다. "illness"는 "disease"의 동의어이다.

3. "They had beaten the Russians to the moon"과 "a victory over the Russians", "the risks or the cost"와 "expensive and dangerous"가 각각 paraphrase임을 이해해야 한다.

4. "The ash from the trees ... better for new trees."와 "enriching the soil in the forest"가 같은 의미이며, "get rid of old and diseased trees"와 "prevent the spread of disease" 또한 같은 내용임을 이해해야 한다.

Basic Drills (4) p.61

1. (C)   2. (A)

1. 자동차 회사들에게 오프로드(off-road) 경주는 중요하다. 이런 경주는, 자동차 회사들에게 그들의 차에 사용된 신기술을 시험해 보기 위해 이용된다. 예를 들어, 오프로드 경주에서 성공적이었던 새로운 엔진이나 제동장치는 곧 시판될 자동차에 장착될 수 있다. 또 오프로드 경주는 자동차 회사들에게 중요한 홍보 수단이다. 그 회사의 차가 경주에서 이길 경우, 자동차 판매를 늘리는데 도움이 된다. 유명한 오프로드 경주 중에는 파리-다카르 랠리(Paris-Dakar Rally)가 있다. 이 경주는 프랑스에서부터 아프리카까지에 이르며, 산에서부터 사막까지 상상할 수 있는 모든 종류의 지형을 통과한다. 이 경주는 자동차들에게 매우 힘들어서, 많은 차들이 완주조차도 하지 못한다. 도착하기도 전에 고장이 나는 것이다. 엄청난 난이도 때문에, 이 경주에서 우승하는 자동차 회사는 세계에서 정말 최고의 차를 만든다고 주장할 수 있다.

2. 화산의 종류에는 분석구 화산, 순상화산, 복합 화산 등 세 가지가 있다. 분석구 화산은 가장 흔한 화산이자 가장 작은 종류의 화산이다. 가파른 경사면과 꼭대기에 분화구라고 불리는 넓고 둥그런 공터를 가진다. 분석구 화산은 꽤 정확히 예보할 수 있다. 폭발하는 경우에 용암의 흐름은 느리고 일정하다. 순상화산은 여러 해에 걸친 폭발에 의해서 만들어졌다. 복합 화산은 가장 크고 가장 위험한 화산이다. 다양한 종류의 암석으로 이루어져 있고 무너지기도 쉽다. 많은 희생이 발생하는 화산 폭발은 보통 복합 화산의 경우이다.

•• 해 설 ••

1. "to test new technology"와 "to test new advances", "increase their sales"와 "promote their cars"가 각각 paraphrase라는 것을 이해해야 한다.

2. keyword인 "cinder cone volcanoes"에 해당하는 내용을 찾는다. "side"와 "slope"는 같은 뜻으로 쓰일 수 있다.

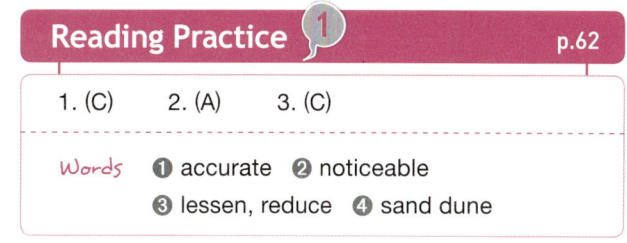

Reading Practice 1 p.62

1. (C)   2. (A)   3. (C)

Words ❶ accurate ❷ noticeable ❸ lessen, reduce ❹ sand dune

보초도

지난 몇 년간 세계 각지의 나라들은 허리케인과 태풍으로부터 점점 더 심각한 피해를 입어 왔다. 단순히 보면 이 폭풍들이 매년 더 강해지고 있는 것으로 보일 수 있다. 그러니 이는 엄밀하게는 정확한 표현은 아니다. 더 정확하게는, 그런 폭풍들에 대한 자연적인 보호 체계가 점점 사라지고 있기 때문에 더 큰 피해를 주고 있는 것이다.

폭풍에 대한 자연적인 보호 체계에서 가장 중요한 것은 보초도(堡礁島)이다. 보초도는 일반적으로 해안선으로부터 몇 마일밖에 떨어지지 않은 곳에 있는 길쭉하고 좁은 섬들이다. 보초도들은 세계 여러 해안 대부분에서 찾을 수 있지만 가장 크고 두드러진 것들은 미국의 동부 해안에 위치하고 있다. 보초도는 폭풍의 파도가 해안에 닿기 전에 약화시킴으로써 매우 중요한 보호막을 이룬다. 이것이 중요한 이유는 허리케인 피해의 대다수가 이런 대형 파도로 인한 범람이기 때문이다. 보초도가 사라지면서, 해안에 닿기 전까지 파도의 세력을 약화시키고 범람을 줄여 줄 수 있는 것도 없어져 버렸다.

보초도가 사라지고 있는 데에는 크게 두 가지 이유가 있다. 첫 번째는 이런 섬들의 개발 때문이다. 보초도는 종종 유명한 휴양지이기도 하다. 섬에 호텔이 건설되면서 파도의 세력을 약하게 해주는 사구(砂丘)가 줄어든다. 이러한 사구가 없으면, 다음 대형 폭풍 때는 섬 대부분이 휩쓸려 버린다. 다른 이유는 내륙 강의 댐 건설이다. 보통은 강을 통해 보초도까지 쓸려 가서 자연적으로 섬을 보강할 흙을 댐들이 가로막는다. 이런 흙이 없이는 섬들은 점차 없어지게 된다.

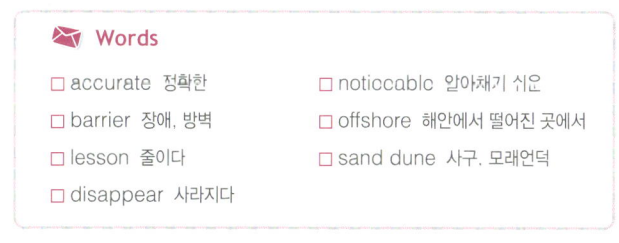

✉ Words

☐ accurate 정확한
☐ barrier 장애, 방벽
☐ lesson 줄이다
☐ disappear 사라지다
☐ noticcable 알아채기 쉬운
☐ offshore 해안에서 떨어진 곳에서
☐ sand dune 사구, 모래언덕

•• 해 설 ••

1. "small offshore islands"가 "barrier islands"와 같은 뜻임을 이해해야 한다. 첫째 문단의 마지막과 둘째 문단의 첫 부분에서 허리케인에 의해 늘어난 피해가 이런 섬들이 없어진 결과라고 설명하고 있다.

2. 9째 줄 "Barrier islands can be found off most coasts around the world"에서 보초도(방파제 역할을 하는 섬, barrier island)가 전 세계적으로 널려 있다고 했으므로 (A)는 잘못된 내용이다.

3. 셋째 문단에 따르면 이 섬들 위에 호텔을 지음으로 파도의 세력을 약하게 해주는 사구(모래 언덕)가 파괴되며, 사구가 없이는 섬의 많은 부분이 폭풍에 휩쓸려 버린다고 했다.

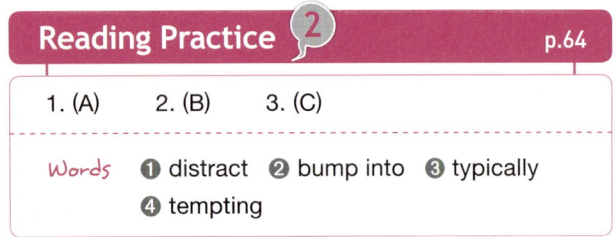

Reading Practice 2   p.64

1. (A)   2. (B)   3. (C)

Words   ❶ distract   ❷ bump into   ❸ typically
        ❹ tempting

소매치기

모든 휴양객들에게 물건을 사기 위해 돈을 내려고 주머니에 손을 넣을 때 지갑을 도둑맞았다는 것을 발견하는 일은 악몽이다. 그런 경우, 그 운이 없는 휴양객은 아마도 소매치기에게 당한 것이다. 소매치기는 당신이 알아채지 못하는 사이에 주머니에서 지갑이나 손가방을 훔쳐 가는 도둑이다.

뛰어난 소매치기의 기본 기술은 주의를 분산시키는 것이다. 소매치기는 피해자의 주의를 분산시켜서 그가 주머니에 손을 뻗고 있다는 사실을 알지 못하게 한다. 주의를 분산시키는 가장 기본적인 방법은 갑자기 우연하게 부딪치는 것이다. 소매치기는 지하철이나 거리에서 우연히 부딪친 척 할 것이다. 그 사람에게 부딪치는 사이에 소매치기는 피해자의 주머니에 손을 뻗을 것이다. 부딪치는 느낌이 주머니 속의 손의 느낌보다 더 세기 때문에 피해자는 도둑맞고 있다는 사실을 절대로 알지 못한다. 소매치기들은 종종 무리 지어 일한다. 한 소매치기가 어떤 사람의 지갑을 훔치고 있을 때 다른 소매치기는 그 사람에게 가서 부딪칠 것이다. 대부분의 소매치기는 숙련되었기 때문에 잡아내기가 매우 어렵다.

하지만 소매치기로부터 스스로를 보호할 수 있는 몇 가지 방법이 있다. 첫 번째는 모든 돈을 한 지갑에 넣고 다니지 않는 것이다. 최고의 소매치기들도 한 번에 한 개의 지갑만 훔칠 수 있다. 또 다른 방법은 지갑을 앞 주머니에 넣고 다니는 것이다. 일반적으로 앞 주머니는 지갑을 훔치기에 가장 어려운 주머니라서 대부분의 소매치기들이 시도하려 하지 않는다. 마지막으로, 관광객처럼 보이지 않도록 노력하라. 소매치기들은 사람들이 보통 때보다 휴가 때 더 많은 돈을 갖고 다닌다는 것을 알기 때문에 관광객들은 이들에게 탐나는 범죄 대상이다.

📧 **Words**

☐ purchase 구입   ☐ distract 주의를 흐트러뜨리다
☐ bump into 우연히 마주치다   ☐ typically 보통, 뻔하게
☐ tempting 유혹적인, 탐나는   ☐ target 목표

•• 해 설 ••

1. 보기 (A)의 "accidental contact"는 본문의 "bump into"와 같은 의미이다. 둘째 문단에서 소매치기들이 관광객들의 주의를 딴 데로 돌리기 위해서 쓰는 방법에 대한 설명을 찾을 수 있다.

2. 셋째 문단에 소매치기에게 당하지 않기 위한 세 가지 방법이 제시되어 있는데, 첫째는 주머니 하나에 모든 돈을 넣어 다니지 않는 것이고, 둘째는 앞 주머니에 지갑을 넣어 다니는 것이며, 셋째는 관광객처럼 보이지 않게 행동하는 것이다. (B)의 내용은 언급되지 않았다.

3. 마지막 문장에 소매치기들이 관광객을 표적으로 삼는 이유가 나온다. 즉,

휴가를 온 사람들은 보통 때보다 많은 돈을 가지고 다니기 때문에 탐나는 범죄 대상이 된다고 했다. 그러므로 관광객을 소매치기하는 것은 더 수익이 높다(more profitable)고 할 수 있다.

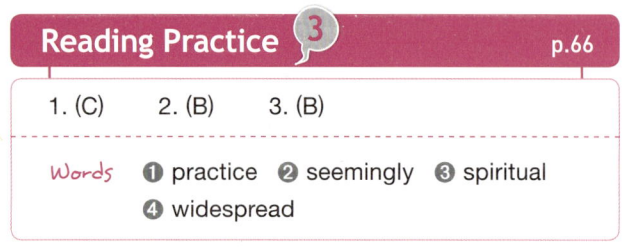

Reading Practice 3   p.66

1. (C)   2. (B)   3. (B)

Words   ❶ practice   ❷ seemingly   ❸ spiritual
        ❹ widespread

불 속을 맨발로 걷기

고대 문화에는 개인의 용기와 신념을 시험하기 위한 여러 훈련이 있었다. 거기에는 개인의 신념이 충분히 강하다면 위험하고 불가능해 보이는 일도 능히 해낼 수 있다는 생각이 있었다. 불 속을 맨발로 걷기는 그런 훈련 중의 하나였다. 불 속을 맨발로 걷기에서 사람들은 발에 화상을 입거나 어떤 식으로도 다치지 않고 뜨거운 숯이 널려 있는 곳을 걸어서 가로지른다.

맨발로 불 위 걷기는 아주 오래되고 널리 퍼져 있는 의식이다. 정확히 언제 또는 어디서 이것이 시작되었는지 아무도 모르지만, 맨발로 불 위 걷기에 대한 가장 오래된 문서 기록은 아직까지도 이러한 전통이 강하게 남아 있는 인도의 약 4천년 전의 것이다. 그러나 그것으로 맨발로 불 위 걷기가 거기에서 시작되었다고는 단언할 수 없다. 맨발로 불 위 걷기는 아메리카 원주민부터 일본인에 이르기까지 거의 모든 문화에 기록되어 있다.

고대 문화들은 불 속을 맨발로 걸을 수 있는 능력은 개인의 신념과 영혼의 순수성에서 비롯되었다고 믿었다. 그러나 오늘날, 불 속을 맨발로 걷는 것은 과학과 열이 물체 사이에서 이동하는 방식으로 쉽게 설명된다. 불 속 걷기에서 가장 먼저 알아야 할 것은, 실제로는 불을 가로질러 걷는 것은 아니라는 사실이다. 숯 위를 걸어가는 것이다. 숯은 나무가 타고 남은 것이다. 숯은 아주 뜨겁지만, 열기는 매우 천천히 방출된다. 게다가, 사람이 걸어가는 숯의 겉에는 재가 층을 이루어 덮고 있다. 열기는 재를 통해서는 쉽게 전달되지 않는다. 이런 두 가지 사실에 따라, 불 위를 걷는 사람이 다치지 않고 건널 수 있는 것이다. 한 곳에 너무 오래 서 있지 않는 한, 열기는 숯과 재를 지나서 그 사람의 발을 데이게 할 만큼 빨리 전달되지는 않는다.

📧 **Words**

☐ practice 실행, 실습, 의식   ☐ courage 용기
☐ seemingly 보기에   ☐ widespread 널리 퍼져 있는
☐ guarantee 보증   ☐ spiritual 정신적인
☐ purity 순수   ☐ layer 층, 레이어
☐ injury 상해, 손상   ☐ as long as~ ~하는 한은

•• 해 설 ••

1. 둘째 문단에 "fire walking"의 기원이 나온다. 인도에서 최초의 기록이 발견되었지만, 9째 줄에서 "That, however, is no guarantee that the practice started there."라고 분명히 나와 있다. 그러므로 (C)는 잘못

된 내용이다. "originate"는 "start"의 동의어이다.

2. 첫 문장에 이 의식을 행하는 이유가 제시되었다. "test a person's courage and faith"라고 했는데, 이는 "test the strength of their religious beliefs"와 같은 의미이다.

3. 마지막 문장에 따르면 사람이 한 곳에 오래 서 있지 않으면, 열기는 숯과 재를 지나서 그 사람의 발을 데이게 할만큼 빨리 전달되지 않는다고 했다.

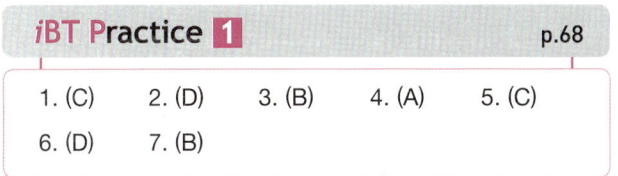

iBT Practice 1   p.68

1. (C)	2. (D)	3. (B)	4. (A)	5. (C)
6. (D)	7. (B)			

대멸종

대부분 사람들은 약 6천5백만 년 전에 공룡을 멸종시킨 대멸종이 있었다는 것을 알고 있다. (사실, 공룡만 멸종한 것이 아니라 지구상의 다른 종 가운데 85%도 멸종했다.) 대부분의 사람들은 일반적으로 이것이 지구에 충돌한 커다란 소행성 때문이었다고 받아들이고 있다. 많은 사람들이 모르고 있는 것은 이것이 단지 지구 역사상 가장 최근의 대멸종이었다는 사실이다. 지구 역사에는 이 외에도 대멸종이 있었으며, 그 중 어떤 것들은 공룡을 멸종시킨것보다 훨씬 강력했었다.

대멸종은 과학자들이 지구 생물의 종 중 상당한 비율이 상대적으로 짧은 시간(수 백만 년 사이의)에 멸종하는 경우를 지칭하는 용어이다. 우리가 아는 바에 따르면, 지난 6억년 사이에 이런 일이 최소한 여섯 번 있었다. 우리가 아는 최초의 것은 5억7천만 년 전에 일어났다. 이 대멸종에 대해서는 거의 알려진 정보가 없는데, 왜냐하면 당시 동물은 대부분 매우 원시적이었기 때문이다. 해파리나 민달팽이 같이 뼈가 없는 동물들이었기 때문에 우리가 연구할 수 있는 화석을 남기지 않았다. 그 이후의 대멸종에 대해서는 더 많이 알려졌다. 그러나 한가지 알 수 없는 것은 이런 대멸종의 원인이 무엇인지이다. 과학자들은 가장 최근의 대멸종이 소행성 때문에 일어났다는 것에 대해서는 상당히 확신하지만, 모든 대멸종이 이런 방식으로 발생하지는 않은 것으로 보인다.

대멸종을 일으켰을 만한 원인 중 대부분은 어떤 형태의 기후 변화와 관련이 있다. 예를 들어, 과학자들은 세계 여러 곳 해수면의 현저한 변화가 한 번 이상의 대멸종에 대한 원인이 되었을 거라고 추측하고 있다. 그 같은 해수면의 상승은 많은 양의 북극과 남극 지방 얼음이 녹으면서 유발되었을 것이다. 다른 가능성은 광범위하게 퍼진 가뭄이나 지구 평균 온도의 상당한 변화이다. 그러나 이 같은 변화가 애당초 무엇 때문에 발생했는지에 대해서는 일반적으로 알려져 있지 않다. 과학자들은 급격한 기후 변화가 멸종을 일으킬 수 있다는 것을 알고 있지만, 무엇이 처음 이러한 변화를 가져왔는지는 알지 못한다. 이것은 그러나 우리가 다음 번 대멸종에서 살아남기 위해서라면 풀어야 할 중요한 문제이다.

✉ Words

☐ extinction 멸종   ☐ species 종
☐ asteroid 소행성   ☐ crash 충돌하다
☐ portion 비율, 부분   ☐ primitive 원시적인
☐ jellyfish 해파리   ☐ slug 민달팽이
☐ widespread 광범위한, 널리 퍼진   ☐ initiate 유발하다

•• 해설 ••

1. 5-6째 줄에 따르면 지구의 역사에 여러 다른 대규모의 멸종이 있었고, 어떤 것들은 우리가 알고 있는 6천 5백만 년 전의 멸종보다 더 심각했다고 했다. 따라서 (A)가 답이 아니라는 것은 쉽게 알 수 있으며, 나머지 보기들을 "most recent" 자리에 대입해 문맥상 가장 적절한 보기를 고른다.

2. 주어진 문장은 다음과 같은 두 개의 의미 단위로 구성되어 있다. "대멸종은 과학자들이 사용하는 용어로 / 지구상의 많은 종들이 비교적 짧은 시간에 멸종하는 경우를 말한다" (A)는 과학자들이 생물들을 죽인다고 함으로 틀리며, (B)는 "significant portion"의 내용을 빠뜨리고 있다. (C)에서는 미래형을 사용했는데 이는 제시된 문장과 관련이 없다.

3. 앞 문장에서 대멸종의 정의를 내리고 나서, 이것이 적어도 6번 지구에서 일어났다고 했다.

4. 10째 줄 이하에 따르면, "We have very little information about this mass extinction because most of the animals at this time were very primitive."라고 하며, 그 때 존재했던 생물들은 뼈가 없어 화석이 존재하지 않는 것을 증거로 지적했다. 여기서 "primitive"는 "not advanced enough to leave behind evidence"와 같은 의미이다.

5. 3-4째 줄과 세 번째 문단에 대멸종의 가능한 원인들이 제시되어 있다. "periods without rain"은 "droughts"를 의미한다.

6. 마지막 부분 23-24째 줄에 따르면, 기후 변화가 멸종으로 이어질 수 있다는 건 알지만, 무엇 때문에 기후 변화가 일어나는지는 알려져 있지 않다고 했다.

7. 주어진 "initiates"의 자리에 각각의 보기를 대입해 보고 문맥상 가장 적절한 단어를 고른다.

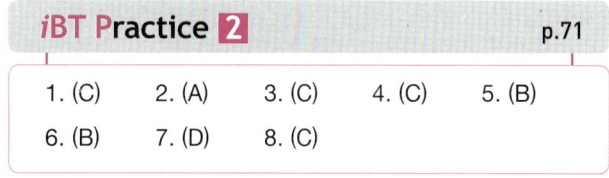

iBT Practice 2   p.71

1. (C)	2. (A)	3. (C)	4. (C)	5. (B)
6. (B)	7. (D)	8. (C)		

멕시코-미국 전쟁

미국 역사상 많은 부분은 국경의 확장과 연관이 있다. 사실, 초기의 많은 미국인들은 북아메리카 전체로 퍼져 나가는 것이 미국의 숙명이라고 믿었다. 이러한 사상은 영토확장론으로 불려졌는데, 많은 미국인들은 그것을 강력히 믿었다. 어떤 경우의 영토 확장은 다른 나라로부터 땅을 구입함으로써 평화적으로 이루어졌다. 미국이 1803년에 프랑스로부터 루이지애나 지방을 구입한 것이 좋은 예이다. 그러나 다른 많은 경우의 영토 확장에는 무력 사용이 따랐다.

1800년대 초에 텍사스는 멕시코 소속이었다. 미국인들은 이 지역에 눈독을 들였고 개척자들이 이주하기 시작했다. 이주민들은 처음엔 멕시코 시민으로 살았다. 그러나 시간이 흐르면서 그들은 멕시코로부터의 독립을 요구하기 시작했다. 1836년 테하노(Tajanos)라고 불리던 그 이주민들은 멕시코 정부에 대해 반란을 일으켰고 독립을 쟁취하였다. 이때까지만 해도 텍사스는 미국에 소속되지 않았었다. 독립된 공화국이었다. 그러나 1845년에 미국은 텍사스 영토를 병합하였다. 즉 텍사스 공화국이 미합중국에 참여하기를 동의했다는 뜻이다. 그러나 멕시코와 마찰이 있었다. 미국 정부는 텍사스 남쪽 국경선은 리오그란데강(Rio Grande River)이어야 한다고 생각했다. 멕시코인들은 훨씬 북쪽에 있는 누에세스 강(Neuces River)이어야 한다고 생각했다.

1846년, 이러한 의견 차이는 전쟁의 발발로 이어졌다. 미국은 영토에 대한 주장을 강화하기 위해서 리오그란데에 군대를 파견하기로 결정하였으나 이는 양국의 긴장만을 증대할 뿐이었다. 이에 대응하여 멕시코 군은 조그마한 미군 경비 초소 하나를 빼앗았고, 미국은 즉시 선전포고를 했다. 이것은 멕시코 정부에게는 크나큰 실수였는데, 왜냐하면 미국은 텍사스에만 군대를 파견한 것이 아니라 당시 멕시코 땅이었던 캘리포니아도 침공했기 때문이다. 전쟁은 비교적 금방 끝났고, 양국은 1848년 평화 조약을 체결했다. 이 평화 조약은 전쟁 비용을 보상해 주는 대가로 캘리포니아, 뉴멕시코, 네바다, 유타, 그리고 애리조나를 포함하는 엄청난 크기의 땅을 미국에 넘겨주어야 하는 것이었다. 멕시코 원래 영토의 절반에 해당하는 이 땅은 미국이 지불한 양보다도 훨씬 큰 가치가 있었다. 이는 또 태평양까지 국경을 확장하고자 했던 미국인들의 꿈도 이루어 주었다.

📨 Words

- □ expansion 확장
- □ settler 이주민
- □ annex 병합하다
- □ enforce 강화하다
- □ capture 빼앗다
- □ peace treaty 평화 조약
- □ manifest 분명한
- □ revolt 반란을 일으키다
- □ disagreement 의견 차이
- □ tension 긴장감
- □ declare 선전포고하다
- □ in return for ~을 대가로

•• 해 설 ••

1. 2-3째 줄에서 많은 초기 미국 사람들이 미국이 북아메리카 전체로 뻗어나가야 한다고 믿었다고 하며, 미국의 역사와 많은 관련이 있는 것이 국경의 "expansion"이라고 했다. 그러므로 "spread"와 "expansion"는 비슷한 의미일 것임을 추측해 볼 수 있다.

2. 첫째 문단에 미국이 평화적으로 영토 확장을 한 예로 Louisiana를 프랑스로부터 구입한 것을 제시하고 있다. "peaceful"은 "non-violent"와 같은 의미이다.

3. 11째 줄 이하에 주민들이 반역함으로써 맥시코 정부에서 독립하였다는 내용이 나온다. "revolt"는 "rebel"의 동의어이다.

4. 문단 전체를 통해, 그리고 특히 첫째 문장에서 "border"의 뜻을 짐작해 볼 수 있다. (A)와 (D)는 첫 문장에 언급된 '확장(expansion)'할 수 있는 대상이 아니다.

5. 이 단어의 앞부분의 내용에서, 미국과 멕시코가 텍사스의 경계선을 두고 서로 다른 의견을 가지고 있었다고 했으며, 이 이견이 전쟁으로 발전했다고 했다.

6. "started a war"는 "declared war"와 같은 의미로 볼 수 있다. 20째 줄 이하에 따르면 멕시코 군대가 작은 미군 경비 초소 하나를 빼앗았고 이를 계기로 미국이 전쟁을 선언했다.

7. 주어진 문장은 다음 세 개의 의미 단위로 구성되어 있다. "이것은 멕시코 정부에게는 크나큰 실수였는데, / 왜냐하면 미국은 텍사스에만 군대를 파견한 것이 아니라 / 당시 멕시코 땅이었던 캘리포니아도 침공했기 때문이다." 이 세 의미 단위의 내용이 모두 정확하게 포함된 보기를 찾는다.

8. 전쟁의 결과는 22째 줄의 평화 협정(peace treaty)을 맺었다는 내용에서부터 제시되어 있다. 텍사스가 미국의 한 주가 된 것은 전쟁 이전에 일어난 일이므로 (C)는 틀린 내용이다.

Vocabulary Review
p.74

1. (C)	2. (D)	3. (A)	4. (C)	5. (B)
6. (C)	7. (A)	8. (A)		
9. distracted		10. as long as		
11. accurate		12. entirely		
13. fatal		14. massive		
15. attract		16. widespread		

Prose Summary

Basic Drills (1)   p.80

1. The new government asked George Washington to pick a place for the new capital, and the location he chose became known as Washington, D.C.

2. Despite this, some nations can offer powerful reasons for why they have not made guns illegal.

1. 미국 최초의 수도는 워싱턴 D.C. (Washington, D.C.)로부터 약 100마일 정도 북쪽에 위치한 펜실베니아(Pennsylvania) 주의 필라델피아였지만, 여기에는 많은 의견 차이가 있었다. 새로운 정부는 조지 워싱턴(George Washington)에게 새로운 수도의 위치를 결정하도록 하였고, 그가 고른 위치는 워싱턴 D.C.로 알려지게 되었다. 워싱턴은 최악의 선택을 했다. 그가 새로운 수도의 위치로 고른 곳은 기본적으로 거대한 늪지대였고, 그래서 노동자들은 그 습지 위에서 건설하기가 매우 어려웠다. 새로운 수도를 건설하는데 수년이 걸렸지만, 1800년에 결국 완성되었다. 불행히도, 도시 대부분은 1812년 전쟁 와중에 영국에 의해 불타 버려서 재건되어야만 했다.

2. 총기가 불법으로 규정된 나라들이 합법인 나라보다 더 안전하다는 것은 널리 알려진 사실이다. 총기가 불법인 일본이나 대한민국 같은 나라들과 총기가 합법인 미국이나 남아프리카 공화국 같은 나라들의 단순 비교만으로도 이것이 사실임을 보일 수 있다. 남아프리카 공화국이나 미국은 훨씬 높은 살인률을 갖고 있다. 그럼에도 불구하고, 어떤 나라들은 총기를 불법으로 규정하지 않는 강력한 이유를 제공할 수 있다. 한 가지 이유는 어떤 나라들은 총기를 소지하는 것이 그들 정부가 독재 정권이 될 경우 시민들에게 그것에 대해 항거할 수 있는 능력을 보장해 준다고 생각한다는 것이다. 그렇게, 그들은 총기가 그들 자유를 보장해 준다고 주장한다. 또 다른 하나의 강력한 주장은, 이미 많은 범죄자들이 불법적으로 총기를 보유하고 있기 때문에, 총기 소지를 불법화하는 것으로는 범죄자들 손에서 총기를 빼앗아 오지 못하며, 대신에 그것은 보통 시민들이 스스로를 범죄자들로부터 지키지 못하도록 할뿐이라는 것이다.

•• 해 설 ••

1. 이 글은 Washington, D.C.가 미국의 수도가 된 과정에 대한 글이며, 첫 문장은 이 주제를 전개하기 위한 도입 문장일 뿐이다.

2. 이 글은 몇몇 나라들이 높은 범죄율을 감수하면서도 총기소지를 불법으로 정하지 않는다는 것과 그 이유를 두 가지로 제시하고 있다. 첫 부분은 본격적인 주제를 전개하기 위한 도입 부분일 뿐이다.

Basic Drills (2)   p.81

1. Main idea: Probably the best-known aspect of Maori culture is the haka, the Maori war dance.

   Major idea: The intention of the haka is to intimidate the enemy.

2. Main idea: Many governments, however, want to completely stop, or at least tightly control, the sale of such ancient artifacts.

   Major idea: ❶ One reason for this is that the demand for such artifacts has led to the destruction of many ancient archeology sites.

   ❷ Another reason is that there has been a sharp increase in the number of forgeries.

1. 많은 사람들이 마오리(Maori) 문화를 알기 위해 뉴질랜드(New Zealand)를 여행한다. 마오리족은 1,500년에서 1,000년 전에 뉴질랜드 섬에 들어가 살기 시작한 원주민들이다. 아마 마오리 문화의 가장 널리 알려진 일면은 마오리족 전사들의 춤인 하카(haka)일 것이다. 이에 대한 가장 큰 이유는, 뉴질랜드 럭비 팀이 아직도 모든 경기 전에 이 하카를 춘다는 것이다. 이것은, 그들 럭비 팀이 경기를 잘 한다는 사실에 더해서, 뉴질랜드 럭비 팀을 가장 유명한 럭비 팀 중 하나로 만들었다. 전쟁 축 하카의 의도는 상대를 위협하는 것이다. 그 춤은 발을 구르고 큰 소리를 지르고 무서운 얼굴을 함으로서 사람들을 겁먹게 만들고자 한다. 아마도 그 춤의 가장 위협적인 부분은, 그것이 모든 구성원들의 완벽한 조화로 행해진다는 것이다.

2. 미술 산업의 가장 큰 부분 중 하나는 고대 유물 판매이다. 도기류, 갑옷, 그리고 조각상 같은 오래된 유물들은 종종 비싼 가격에 팔린다. 개인 수집가들과 박물관 모두 이런 것들에 대해 매우 큰 관심을 보인다. 대부분 정부들은 그러나, 그런 고대 유물 판매를 완전히 중단시키거나, 또는 최소한 강력하게 통제하기를 원한다. 이런 이유 중의 하나는, 그런 오래된 유물의 판매가 많은 고고학적 고대 유적지의 파괴를 초래해 왔기 때문이다. 유물 판매를 통해 돈을 벌기 원하는 사람들은 유적지가 제대로 연구되고 기록되기 전에 이런 물품들을 꺼내어 간다. 또 다른 이유는 위조품 수가 급격하게 늘어났다는 것이다. 많은 사람들이 가짜 유물을 만들어서 진짜인 것처럼 팔려고 한다. 이것은 과거에 대한 정보를 신뢰할 수 없게 하고, 박물관 예산도 낭비하게 만든다.

1. Maori 족 문화 중 가장 잘 알려진 haka 춤과 그 춤을 추는 의도에 관한 글이다.

2. 많은 나라의 정부에서 고대 유물 매매를 금지하거나 통제하려 한다는 사실과 그 이유에 관한 글이다.

Basic Drills (3)　　p.82

1. (A) inaccurate　　(B) accurate
　(C) not contained

2. (A) inaccurate　　(B) accurate
　(C) not contained

1. 박테리아는 단순한 단세포 생물이다. 그들은 단순히 둘로 분열하는 것으로 번식한다. 모든 박테리아가 위험한 것은 아니지만, 많은 박테리아들이 당신을 병들게 할 수 있다. 다행히도 대부분 박테리아 감염은 오래 가지 않는다. 그 첫 번째 이유는, 우리 몸은 박테리아에 대한 저항력이 있기 때문이다. 게다가, 박테리아를 죽이기 위한, 항생제라고 불리는 약들도 있다. 박테리아 감염을 예방하는 것도 상대적으로 쉽다. 대부분 박테리아 감염은 더러운 환경으로 인한 것이다. 손을 정기적으로 씻고, 당신이 먹는 음식이 깨끗한 환경에서 조리되도록 하는 것으로, 대부분 박테리아 감염을 피할 수 있다.

2. 바이러스는 우리가 고통받는 많은 질병들을 유발한다. 바이러스는 지구상의 다른 모든 생명체들이 갖고 있는 기능인 자체 번식 능력이 없다. 바이러스는 복잡한 화학 물질의 집합체이다. 그들은 우리의 세포를 공격하고, 한 번 들어가면 번식을 위해 세포를 장악한다. 바이러스와는 맞서 싸울 수 있는 단독의 약이 존재하지 않기 때문에 싸우기가 어렵다. 각각의 바이러스는 서로 다른 약을 필요로 하고, 게다가 대부분 바이러스에는 약이 아예 존재하지 않는다. 우리는 특정 바이러스를 막는 백신을 접종함으로써 바이러스로 인한 질병을 예방할 수 있다. 그러나 역시, 모든 개별 바이러스에 대한 백신이 존재하지는 않는다.

•• 해 설 ••

1. 모든 박테리아가 해롭진 않다고 말한 사실에 유의하자. 우리 몸이 박테리아와 잘 싸울 수 있다고는 했지만, 약이 필요 없다는 말을 하진 않았다.

2. 지구상의 다른 모든 생명체가 가지고 있는 스스로 번식하는 능력이 바이러스는 없다고 했다. 우리가 가지고 있지 않은 바이러스 백신이나 약을 찾는 것이 중요하다는 것은 언급되지 않았다.

Basic Drills (4)　　p.83

1. (B), (C)

1. 개구리는 물 속과 밖에서 동시에 살 수 있는 양서류이다. 모든 개구리는 물 속에 알을 낳고, 한 마리의 암컷 개구리는 한 번에 수천 개의 알을 낳는다. 알이 부화하면 나오는 것은 개구리가 아니라 올챙이이다. 개구리와 달리 올챙이는 공기로 숨을 쉴 수 없는 상태이기 때문에 항상 물 속에서 지내야만 한다. 올챙이들은 다리가 없고, 개구리로 발육함에 따라서 없어지는 꼬리를 갖고 있다. 올챙이들은 초식동물로 식물만을 먹는다. 구체적으로, 올챙이들은 너무 많을 경우 유해할 수도 있는 수중 식물인 조류를 먹는다. 그러므로 올챙이들은 대부분의 연못을 건강히 보전하기 위해서 중요하다. 올챙이가 성숙한 개구리로 발육함에 따라서, 그들을 공기로 숨을 쉴 수 있게 해주는 폐와 땅에서 이동할 수 있게 해주는 앞다리와 뒷다리가 자란다. 이 때가 되면, 어떤 종들은 평생 물 가까이 살기도 하지만, 성장한 개구리들은 연못을 떠난다. 성장한 개구리는 육식동물로, 곤충과 작은 물고기를 먹는다. 대부분의 개구리는 먹이를 잡기 위해 그들의 긴고 끈적끈적한 혀를 이용한다. 어떤 종의 개구리들은 다른 동물들로부터 스스로를 보호하기 위해 매우 강한 독성을 띄게 되기도 한다.

•• 해 설 ••

1. (A), (B)와 같이 비슷한 내용의 두 보기가 있을 경우, 다른 하나를 포함하는 내용을 선택한다. 폐의 부재로 공기 중에서 숨쉴 수 없어 올챙이는 물속에 있어야 한다는 말은, 올챙이의 몸체가 개구리와 다르다는 서술 안에 포함된다. 본문은 어떤 단계에서 개구리가 유독성을 띄게 되는지에 관해 언급하고 있지 않다.

Reading Practice ①　　p.84

1. (A), (B), (E)

Words　❶ alternative　❷ plentiful　❸ advantage　❹ renewable

미래 에너지원 바이오디젤

에너지원으로서의 원유에 대한 세계의 의존은 매우 빠르게 가장 큰 문제가 되고 있다. 원유 기반 제품인 휘발유와 디젤유 등의 높아져만 가는 가격은 세계 경제를 위협하고 있다. 더구나, 이런 연료를 태워서 생기는 오염은 우리 환경을 해치고 있다. 연구자들과 자동차 회사들은 수년간 대체 연료를 찾아왔다. 아이러니하게도, 그런 기술 개발에 수십억 달러가 쓰여지는 동안, 문제의 많은 부분을 해결해 줄 수 있는 한가지 대체 연료는 거의 100여 년 전부터 있어 왔다.

바이오디젤(biodiesel)은 식물 속에 들어 있는 지방과 유지로부터 만들어지는 연료이다. 알코올과 다른 몇 가지 화학물과 섞일 경우, 이 유지는 마치 일반 디젤유처럼 타는 연료를 만들어 낸다. 거의 모든 식물이 바이오디젤을 생산하는데 사용될 수 있지만, 유지와 지방이 많은 콩이나 땅콩 같은 식물들이 더 좋다. 바이오디젤은 1900년대 초에 최초로 생산되었으나, 일반 디젤유보다 훨씬 비쌌기 때문에 인기 있는 연료로 선택되지 못했었다. 현재는 그러나, 원유의 높은 가격이 바이오디젤을 좀 더 실용적인 선택으로 만들고 있다.

바이오디젤은 일반적인 디젤유에 비해서 많은 장점을 갖는다. 첫째로, 그것은 재사용할 수 있는 에너지원이다. 우리는 항상 더 많은 곡류를 기를 수 있기 때문에 바이오디젤이 고갈될 것이라는 실제 위험은 없다. 바이오디젤은 또한 훨씬 깨끗한 연료이다. 휘발유 같은 다른 연료들이 유발하는 대기 오염의 약 절반 정도만을 발생시킨다. 이것이 가지는 많은 장점과 유가 상승을 고려할 때, 미래에는 당신과 당신 차 모두 더 많은 채소를 먹고 있게 될 확률이 크다!

•• 해 설 ••

1. 주어진 문제의 요약문 시작은 다음과 같다. "석유 값의 상승과 석유로 인한 오염 때문에 과학자들은 바이오디젤을 대체 에너지로 바라보게 되었다." (C)는 단지 바이오디젤 에너지의 공급원이 될 수 있는 원료의 예일 뿐이며, 석유 값이 오른다고 해서 바이오디젤의 값이 내리는 것은 아니므로 (D)는 본문과 일치하지 않는 내용이다. 또한, (F)는 전혀 관계없는 진술이다.

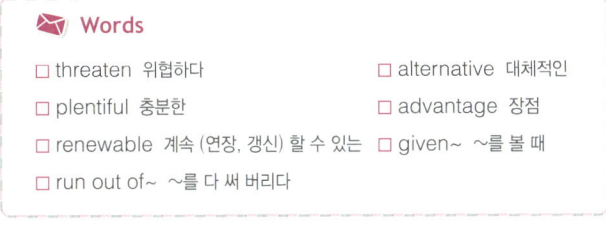

Reading Practice 2   p.86

1. (B), (D), (E)

Words ❶ inject ❷ infect ❸ controversial
❹ oppose

주사용 마약으로 인한 문제

세계 곳곳의 많은 나라들이 점점 거져 가는 심각한 마약 문제와 맞닥뜨리고 있다. 세계 여러 곳의 점점 많은 사람이 불법 마약에 중독되고 있고, 그 급속히 커지는 마약 사용자들 집단 중 하나는 주사용 마약을 사용하는 사람들이다. 모든 불법 마약이 위험하지만, 헤로인과 같은 주사용 마약은 에이즈와 같은 전염병을 퍼뜨릴 수 있는 위험을 갖고 있기 때문에 다른 마약보다 더 위험하다.

이 사실은 많은 마약 사용자들이 주사 바늘을 다른 마약 사용자들과 공유하기 때문이다. 중독자들은 주사 바늘을 불법적인 목적에 사용하기 때문에, 그들에게는 새로운 깨끗한 주사 바늘을 구하는 것이 어렵다. 대신에, 그들은 한 주사 바늘을 여러 번이고 계속 사용하고, 때로는 여러 명의 사람들과 주사 바늘을 공유한다. 그러므로, 에이즈나 다른 질병이 있는 중독자는 다른 마약 사용자들에게 그 질병을 쉽게 퍼뜨릴 수 있다. 사실, 에이즈 신규 발병의 가운데 거의 3분의 1은 중독자들이 주사 바늘을 공유하는 것의 직접적인 결과이다.

이것은 마약 중독자들 문제만이 아니라, 사회 전체 문제이기도 하다. 대부분 마약 중독자들이 안정된 직업을 갖고 있지 않기 때문에, 그들이 아플 경우, 사회에서 그들 의료비를 내주어야 한다. 마약 중독자들이 많은 나라의 경우, 의료 비용은 연간 수십억 달러에 이르기도 한다. 이를 해결하기 위해서, 어떤 도시들은 주사 바늘 교환 프로그램을 시작했다. 주사 바늘 교환 프로그램을 통해, 사람들은 오래된 오염된 주사 바늘을 새로운 깨끗한 것으로 교환할 수 있다. 이 프로그램은 중독자들에게 깨끗한 주사 바늘을 제공함으로써, 에이즈나 기타 질

병의 발병률을 감소시키는데 도움이 될 수 있다. 그러나 주사 바늘 교환 프로그램은 상당한 논쟁의 대상이다. 많은 사람들은 깨끗한 주사 바늘을 제공함으로써 그 프로그램이 마약 사용을 촉진한다고 생각하기 때문에 그런 프로그램에 반대한다.

•• 해 설 ••

1. 주어진 문제의 요약문 시작은 다음과 같다. "주사용 마약은 사회에서 특히 심각한 문제를 지닌다. 왜냐하면, 그것은 마약 중독을 일으킬 뿐만 아니라 질병의 전파도 돕기 때문이다." (A)에서 주사용 마약이 불법 마약 중 빠르게 늘어나고 있다는 말은 이 문제의 심각성을 강조하기 위한 부수적인 설명일 뿐이며, (C)에서 언급된 AIDS는 마약 삽입으로 감염되는 질병의 대표적인 예일 뿐이다. (F)는 지문의 내용과 일치하지 않는 내용이다. 많은 사람들이 주사 교환 프로그램을 반대하긴 하지만, 마약 중독을 부추기기만 하므로 비효과적이라고 하지는 않았다.

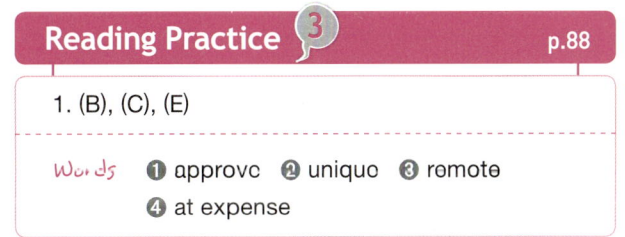

Reading Practice 3   p.88

1. (B), (C), (E)

Words ❶ approve ❷ unique ❸ remote
❹ at expense

포크 배럴 계획

알래스카 북부 케치칸(Ketchikan) 마을(인구 8,000명)은 새로운 다리를 갖기로 되어 있었다. 하지만 거기에는 두 가지 문제가 있었다. 3억1천5백만 달러에, 이 다리는 너무나도 크고 비쌌다. 그리고 그 것은 어찌되었든 필요하지가 않았다! 어떻게 이 계획이 생겼을까? pork를 탓하라. "폭 배럴 계획들(Pork barrel projects)"은-대부분 단순히 "폭(pork)"으로 불린다- 공공의 세금으로 지불되지만 적은 수의 사람이 혜택을 받는 건설 계획이다. 이 것은 혜택을 받던 말던 간에 모든 시민이 그 계획을 위해서 돈을 내야 한다는 뜻이다. 그 것은 이렇게 작동한다.

첫째로 포크 배럴 계획은 강력한 정치인의 지지를 필요로 한다. 이 정치인들이 포크 배럴 계획을 지지하는 이유는 다음 선거 때 해당 지역 주민들의 표를 얻을 수 있기 때문이다. 다음으로, 정치인들은 그 계획을 위한 자금을 정부예산에서 확보해야 한다. 이것은 그 계획에 반대하는 사람들이 그것을 막으려는 충분한 시간을 갖지 못하게 하기 위해 보통 마지막 순간에 벌어진다. 일단 정부가 예산안을 승인하면, 그 포크 배럴 계획은 안전하게 시행된다. 케치칸의 다리의 경우에는 그 정치인들은 알래스카의 하원 의원이었다. 그들은 오직 8,000명의

사람들에게 도움이 되었을 것이고 또한 작은 케치칸을 더욱 작은 가비나 섬(인구 단순히 50명)과 연결했을 것이었어도 이 비싼 다리를 지지하였다. 이 다리는 절대 지어지지 않았다. 이번에는 폭 배럴이 막아졌다! 그러나 많은 폭 배럴 계획들은 성사된다. 그러면, 모두가 돈을 낸다!

폭 배럴 계획은 미국 정치에서만 한정된 것이 아니다. (선거를 통해 정치인들을 선출하는) 민주 정부를 가진 거의 어떤 사회에서든 그것을 찾을 수 있다. 일본은 특히 초특급 열차 같은 포크 배럴 계획으로 유명하다. 원래 일본의 초특급 열차는 주용 도시들만을 연결했다. 그러나 지금은 일본의 납세자들이 내야 하는 거대한 비용으로 멀리 떨어져 있는 상대적으로 적은 인구의 시골 지역에까지도 초특급 열차가 건설되고 있다. 이런 경우는 다른 나라들보다 미국이나 일본에서 널리 퍼져 있지만, 자세히 살펴본다면 아마 당신의 정부에서도 포크를 찾을 수 있을 것이다.

✉ Words

- □ unfamiliar 친숙하지 않은
- □ approve 승인하다
- □ notably 두드러지게는
- □ remote 멀리 있는, 떨어진
- □ at expense to ~ ~의 비용으로
- □ benefit 이익을 주다
- □ unique 독특한
- □ bullet train 고속 열차
- □ location 위치, 장소

•• 해설 ••

1. 주어진 문제의 요약문의 시작은 다음과 같다. "포크 배럴 계획은 거의 정치적인 이유로 실행되는, 한정된 소수의 이익만을 위한 건설 계획이다."
   본문은 포크 배럴 계획에 대해 설명하는 글로, 이 계획이 실행되는 이유 (B), 그 방법 (C)와 실태 (E)에 관해 다루고 있다. (A)는 포크 배럴 계획의 하나의 예로 부수적인 내용이며, (D)의 내용은 본문에서 언급되지 않았다. (F)의 일본의 초특급 열차에 관한 내용도 포크 배럴 계획이 적용된 하나의 예일 뿐이다.

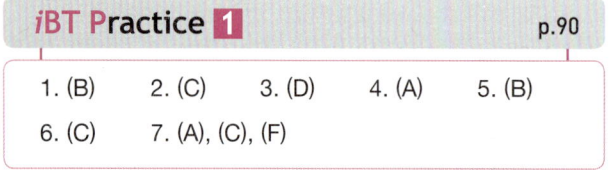

iBT Practice 1   p.90

1. (B)	2. (C)	3. (D)	4. (A)	5. (B)
6. (C)	7. (A), (C), (F)			

잠수함의 발전

잠수함은 미국 시민 전쟁 당시부터 존재해 왔지만, 많은 나라들에게 주요 전쟁 무기로서 인식되게 된 것은 제2차 세계 대전에서였다. 제1차 세계 대전에서도 사용되었지만, 기술의 발전은 제2차 세계 대전에서 잠수함을 더욱 효율적으로 만들었다. 이 전쟁에서, 독일은 가장 큰 잠수함 함대를 갖고 있었다. 이것은 전쟁이 발전해 나간 양상을 볼 때 자연스런 결과였다. 독일의 주적(主敵)은 섬나라인 영국이었다. 영국은 전쟁 수행 능력을 유지하기 위해서 배를 통해 들어오는 보급에 의존하고 있었다. 그러므로 독일은 대규모 잠수함 함대를 만들어 영국의 해상로를 통한 보급을 저지시킬 수 밖에 없었다.

전쟁 초기에, 상황은 영국에 불리해 보였다. 독일 잠수함은 영국 배를 엄청

난 속도로 침몰시키고 있었고, 영국 보급선은 심각한 위험에 처해 있었다. 그러나, 소나(수중 음파 탐지기, sonar)나 잠수함을 발견해 공격할 수 있는 항공기와 같은 새로운 기술은, 결국 독일 잠수함들을 무력화 시켰다. 종전에 이르러, 독일 잠수함은 3,500척이 넘는 연합군 선박을 침몰시켰지만, 독일 함대는 엄청난 대가를 치러야 했다. 독일은 잠수함 함대의 75% 이상을 전쟁 중에 잃었다.

전쟁 이후에 잠수함의 이용가치는 끝난 것처럼 보였다. 새로운 두 강대국인 미국과 소련은, 영국만큼 선박에 의존적이지 않았고, 또 잠수함을 발견하고 파괴하는 것이 용이해짐에 따라, 잠수함 사용은 제한되었다. 그러나 핵기술 발전은 잠수함에게 새로운 삶을 주었다. 원자력을 사용함으로써 잠수함들은 기존의 디젤 잠수함들보다 훨씬 오랫동안 바다 속에 머무를 수 있었다. 게다가, 잠수함들은 이제 핵미사일도 장착할 수 있게 되었다. 이는 잠수함들에게 새로운 임무를 부여했다. 바닷속에 있었으므로, 핵잠수함들은 기습 핵공격에도 파괴당하지 않을 수 있었다. 이것은 핵무기를 이용해서 실제의 기습적인 공격을 가할 모든 가능성을 없앴다. 만약 한 나라가 다른 나라를 완전히 파괴시키는 데 성공하더라도, 그 잠수함들은 살아 남아서 적국을 파괴할 수 있기 때문이다. 핵전쟁은 결국 양쪽 나라를 멸망시킬 수 있다는 이러한 개념은 냉전 동안 핵무기 사용을 막는데 있어서 중요한 요인이었다.

✉ Words

- □ effective 효율적인
- □ supplies 보급품
- □ sonar 수중 음파 탐지기
- □ superpower 초강대국
- □ consequence 결과
- □ incredible 엄청난
- □ come to an end 끝이 나다
- □ eliminate 없애다, 제거하다

•• 해설 ••

1. 대명사가 가리키는 지시 대상이 주절에 나오는 경우이다. 또한 이어지는 내용으로 보아도, "they"가 주절의 주어인 "submarines"를 의미하는 것을 알 수 있다.

2. 처음 부분에 의하면, 잠수함은 미국 남북전쟁 때부터 존재했고, 제1차 세계대전 때도 쓰였지만, 제2차 세계대전에 와서야 기술의 발전이 잠수함을 훨씬 효과적으로 만들었고 주요한 무기로 보여졌다고 했다.

3. 독일이 가장 큰 잠수함을 가지고 있었다(Germany had the largest submarine fleet by far)는 것이 전쟁이 발전해 가는 과정(the way the war developed)의 "consequence"라고 했다.

4. "두 새로운 강대국인 미국과 소련은, 영국이 그랬던 것만큼 선박에 의존적이지 않았고 / 잠수함을 발견하고 파괴하는 것이 쉬워져 잠수함의 효과를 한정적이게 만들었다"
   "easier targets"라는 말이 "the ease with which submarines could be found and destroyed"와 같은 의미로 쓰였음을 이해해야 한다. (B)는 소련과 미국이 선박에 의존적이지 않았던 이유로 잠수함이 발견되고 파괴되기 쉽게 된 것이 아니므로 틀리며, (C)도 마찬가지로 미국과 소련이 선박에 의존적이지 않음으로써 잠수함의 효과를 한정했다는 것은 틀린 설명이며, (D)는 전혀 다른 내용을 전개하고 있다.

5. 10째 줄 이하에 제2차 세계대전 당시 잠수함이 효과적이지 않게 된 이

유가 설명되어 있다. "the development of new technologies, … eventually brought an end to the threat of the German subs"의 내용을 참조한다.

6. 앞 문장의 '핵잠수함들은 바다에 있기 대문에 불시적인 핵공격에도 피해를 입지 않았다'는 사실이 '핵무기를 사용해 효과적으로 공격할 수 있는 가능성'을 "eliminated"했다고 말한 것에서 "eliminated"의 의미를 짐작해 보자.

7. "잠수함은 제2차 세계대전에서부터 주요 군사 무기로 간주되기 시작했다." 잠수함의 역사를 설명한 이 글을 이어서 간략하게 요약하면, 제2차 세계대전에서 독일은 영국을 저지하기 위해 잠수함을 이용했지만, 기술 발달로 잠수함 사용은 쇠퇴하였고, 그 후 핵잠수함 개발로 다시 상승세를 타며 냉전 시대 평화 유지에 큰 역할을 하였다는 내용이다. (A), (C). (F)는 이러한 내용을 요약해서 제시하고 있다. (B)는 세부 사항일 뿐이며, (D)는 언급되지 않았으며, (E)는 일치하지 않는 내용이다.

iBT Practice ❷ p.93

1. (B)   2. (C)   3. (D)   4. (B)   5. (C)
6. (B)   7. (B), (C), (F)

돌려짓기(윤작)

집약적인 농업, 즉 한 지역에 자연 상태에서 보다 더 많은 작물을 기르는 것은, 인간 문명에 있어서 중요한 활동이다. 집약적인 농업이 없이는 작은 지역에서 많은 인구를 부양하기에 충분한 양의 식량을 생산하는 것은 불가능했을 것이다. 이 사실은 집약적인 농업과 최초의 대규모 문명이 비슷한 시기에 생겨났다는 것을 명백히 보여주는 사료들에서 쉽게 찾을 수 있다. 그 이전의 인간들은 소규모의 수렵 채집민 집단으로 살았었다.

그러나 집약적인 농업은 근본적인 문제도 갖고 있었다. 더 많은 작물을 기름으로써 당연히 토양의 영양분이 대체되는 속도보다도 더 빨리 써 버리기 때문에 결과적으로 그 토양은 농사 짓기에 좋지 않은 땅이 되어 버린다. 최초의 문명들은 주기적으로 범람하는 강의 유역에서 삶으로서 이 문제에 대처했다. 범람은 강의 더 상류의 영양분을 강 유역으로 날라옴으로써 집약적인 농업으로 고갈된 영양분을 대체해 준다. 그러나 인류 문명이 자라고 새로운 지역으로 퍼져나감에 따라서, 이 문제를 해결한 새로운 방안을 찾아야야 했다.

그 해결책은 돌려짓기(윤작, crop rotation)이었다. 돌려짓기는 여러 형태를 띠지만, 그 기본 발상은 항상 같다. 매년 기르는 작물의 종류를 바꿈으로써, 농부들은 같은 땅을 더 오랜 기간 동안 사용할 수 있다. 역사상 가장 흔한 돌려짓기는 삼포식 돌려짓기이다. 삼포식 돌려짓기에서는 농부들은 1년간 어떤 작물을 기르면, 다음 한 해는 다른 작물을 기르고, 세 번째 해에는 그 땅에 아무 것도 기르지 않는다. 농부들은 그들의 땅을 세 구역으로 나눈다. 이렇게 함으로서 농부들은 토양을 해치지 않으면서 땅의 3분의 2만큼에서 지속적으로 농사를 지을 수 있다. 돌려짓기는 식물 기생충을 방지하는 데에도 도움이 되는 장점을 가진다. 경작하는 농작물을 매년 바꿈으로써, 해충들이 계속 옮겨 다니게 하고 그들의 수를 한정하며 농부들은 해충들이 지속적인 먹이 공급을 받을 수

없게 할 수 있다.

•• 해 설 ••

1. 앞 문단에서 "intensive farming"의 필요성을 설명하고서, 다음 문단에서 그것의 큰 문제점을 언급하고 있다는 것으로부터 "fundamental"의 뜻을 짐작해 보자.

2. keyword인 "river valleys"는 10째 줄에서 찾을 수 있다. 그 이하의 내용에서 초기 문명이 왜 강 협곡에서 성장했는지 알 수 있다. 11째 줄의 "replacing the nutrients that were lost through intensive farming"이 "renewed the soil"과 같은 의미임을 이해해야 한다.

3. 두 번째 단락은 초기의 문명사회들이 집약적 농업의 문제점을 해결하기 위해 강이 범람하는 지역에 거주했다는 이야기를 하고 있다. 그러나 문명이 발전하여 새로운 곳으로 영역을 넓혀야 했기 때문에 이 방법 외에 다른 방법을 찾아야 했다. 그러므로 여기서 "this problem"은 새로운 문제가 아니라 원래 있었던 집약적 농업의 문제점을 가리킨다.

4. '윤작(crop rotation)'의 내용은 15~16째 줄의 "Different crops take different nutrients... the same fields for a longer period"에서 설명되고 있다. "changing"은 "alternating"과 동의어이다. (D)는 윤작의 목적이지 윤작에 대한 설명은 아니다.

5. 본문에서 keyword인 "the three year rotation"을 찾으면, 19번째 줄부터 설명이 되어 있다. 오랜 역사 동안 사용되어 왔으며, 땅을 세 부분으로 나누어 매년 한 부분을 휴경지로 한다는 내용을 담고 있다. 매년 더 많은 농작물을 생산한다는 내용은 언급되어 있지 않다.

6. "경작하는 농작물을 매년 바꿈으로써 / 농부들은 해충들이 지속적인 먹이 공급을 받을 수 없게 할 수 있다 / 해충들이 계속 옮겨 다니게 하고 그들의 수를 한정함으로써" "change"는 "switch"와 동의어이며, "from year to year" 또한 "annually"의 동의어이다. (A)에는 세 번째 의미 단위의 내용이 빠져 있으며, (C)의 "but this limits the farmers' food supply"의 내용은 관계없는 내용이고, (D)는 둘째 의미 단위의 내용을 담고 있지 않으며 내용도 주어진 문장과 맞지 않다.

7. "집약 농업(intensive farming)은 인류 문명의 필수적 활동이나, 토양으로부터 모든 영양분을 앗아간다."
이어서 이 글을 간략하게 요약하면, ① 초기 문명은 강 주변에서 농사를 지음으로 토양 문제를 해결했고, 문명이 확장해감으로 윤작을 사용하게 되었다. ② 윤작이란 땅을 다른 부분으로 나눔으로써 휴경지를 놔두어 땅을 쉬게 하는 것이다. ③ 또한 윤작을 통해서, 해충을 통제할 수 있는 효과도 가질 수 있다. (B)는 ①의 내용을, (C)는 ②의 내용을, (F)는 ③의 내용을 각

각 요약하고 있다. (A), (D), (E)는 모두 본문에서 언급되지 않거나 일치하지 않는 설명이다.

<table>
<tr><td colspan="5">Vocabulary Review   p.96</td></tr>
</table>

1. (C)	2. (D)	3. (A)	4. (B)	5. (D)
6. (B)	7. (A)	8. (A)		
9. aspects		10. approve of		
11. plentiful		12. disagreement		
13. advantages		14. suffering from		
15. infected		16. alternative		

Part **B** +

Schematic Table

Basic Drills (1)   p.100

1. Drones: (1), (3)
   Worker Bees: (2), (4)

   (1) In an attack the drones would be relatively useless,

   (2) worker bees do all the work in the beehive, from building the hive to finding and gathering food

   (3) outnumbering the drones by over a hundred to one

   (4) because they lack stingers

1. 어떤 벌집이던, 기본적으로 일벌(암벌)과 수벌, 두 종류의 벌이 있다. 수벌보다 100배도 넘게 많은 수의 일벌은, 벌 개체 수의 가장 많은 부분을 차지한다. 이름에서처럼, 일벌들은 집을 짓고, 먹이를 구해 모으는 따위의 모든 일을 한다. 일벌은 또, 어떤 종류의 공격으로부터도 벌집을 보호하는 군대이기도 하다. 적은 수일뿐만 아니라, 수벌들에게는 침도 없기 때문에, 공격을 당했을 때 상대적으로 쓸모가 없다. 벌집에서 수벌의 유일한 기능은 여왕의 알을 수정시키는 것이다.

• • 해 설 • •

1. (1) '공격을 당했을 때 수벌들이 상대적으로 쓸모가 없다'라고 했다.
   (2) 일벌들이 벌집을 짓고 음식을 찾고 모으는 일까지 모두 한다고 했다.
   (3) 수벌 한 마리당 백 마리 이상의 일벌이 있다고 했다.
   (4) 수벌은 침이 없기 때문에, 적의 공격에 소용이 없다고 했다.

Basic Drills (2)   p.101

1. (B) inaccurate   (C) inaccurate
2. (A) not mentioned   (B) inaccurate

1. 미국의 서부 역사상 가장 유명한 총싸움 중의 하나는 어프가(Earp家)와 클랜튼가(Clanton家), 두 가문 사이에서 벌어졌다. 큰형인 와이어트(Wyatt)가 이끄는 어프가는 툼스톤(Tombstone) 마을에서 술집을 운영했다. 그러나 그들은 마을의 질서를 유지하는 보안관으로도 일했다. 클

랜튼가는 마을 밖에 살았고, 본래 소도둑이자 노상 강도들이었다. 와이어트 어트가 클랜튼가 일당이 약탈하던 역마차들을 보호하는 일을 맡자, 클랜튼가는 그들을 제거하기로 결심했다. OK목장의 결투는 1881년 10월 26일에 벌어졌다. 클랜튼가는 패배했고, 그들의 일부만 살아남았다. 며칠 후, 그들은 어프 형제들 중의 한 명을 죽였고, 와이어트는 복수를 하겠다고 다짐했다. 다음 해 동안, 그는 클랜튼가의 사람들을 모두 찾아 죽였다.

2. 최초의 인간들에게는 금속을 채굴하거나 생산하는 기술이 없었다. 그래서 도구를 만들 때, 그들은 자연에서 찾을 수 있는 재료에 의존해야만 했다. 고대의 사람들에게 가장 중요한 재료 중 두 가지는 돌과 동물의 뼈였다. 많은 동물 뼈들이 뾰족하게 깎아질 수 있었고, 고대 사람들은 그것을 작은 칼과 낚싯바늘 같은 다른 사냥 도구를 만드는데 사용했다. 돌 또한 고대 인간들이 필요로 하는 많은 도구를 만드는 데에 사용되었다. 돌은 더 무거웠고, 더 날카로운 끝을 만들 수 있었기에 여러 도구를 만드는데 있어 뼈보다 우세했다. 예를 들어, 돌도끼는 작은 나무를 베어 내리는데 사용될 수 있었지만, 뼈로 된 도구들은 이러기에는 충분히 무겁지도, 강하지도 못했다.

•• 해 설 ••

1. (A)는 4-6째 줄에서 찾아볼 수 있다. OK 목장의 결투는 두 집안간의 또 다른 유형극을 불러 일으켰으며, Clanton가는 자신들이 약탈해오던 역마차들을 Earp가가 지키게 되자 Earp가를 없애기로 결정했다.

2. (C)는 6-8째 줄의 내용을 참조한다. 석기가 후세에 철기의 발전을 가져왔다는 내용은 본문에 언급되지 않았으며, 동물의 뼈는 뾰족하고 낚시 바늘 같은 모양뿐 아니라, 작은 칼로도 만들어 졌다.

Basic Drills (3)   p.102

1. Iceland Colony: (1), (3)
   Greenland Colony: (5)

2. Large Plant Eaters: (1), (3)
   Small Plant Eaters: (4)

1. 9세기와 10세기 동안, 바이킹들은 특히 아이슬란드(Iceland)나 그린란드(Greenland)같은 극북 지방에 여럿의 식민지를 건설했다. 몇몇 식민지들은 성공적이었으나, 나머지는 그렇지 못했다. 예를 들어, 그린란드 식민지는 450년 후에 사라졌다. 그러나 아이슬란드 식민지는, 수세기 동안의 빈곤에서도 살아남아, 현재는 성공적인 독립 국가가 되었다. 그린란드와 아이슬란드 모두 나쁜 토양을 갖고 있어, 작물을 기르기에 좋은 곳이 되지 못한다. 그러나 왜 아이슬란드에서와는 달리 그린란드 식민지가 실패했는지를 설명해 주는 중요한 차이점들이 존재한다.
   아이슬란드와 그린란드의 정착민들은 농업에서 목양(牧羊)으로 전환했는데, 이는 토양 질을 더욱 망가뜨렸다. 아이슬란드 이주자들은 그러나, 곧 양들이 땅을 망가뜨린다는 것을 인식하고, 파괴를 제한하기 위한 조치를 취했다. 그런 조치 중 하나는 생선을 더 많이 먹는 것이었다. 아이슬란드인 식단에서 생선은 매우 큰 부분을 차지했지만, 그린란드인들은 생선을 아예 먹지 않았던 것으로 보인다. 그들은 그린란드의 많은 해산물에도 불구하고,

고기와 유제품으로 된 전통적인 바이킹(Viking)식 식단을 유지했다. 450년이 지난 뒤, 동물들로 유발된 환경 파괴로 그린란드 식민지는 거의 완전히 붕괴되기에 이르렀다. 마지막 위기는, 에스키모(Eskimo)로 잘 알려진 알래스카(Alaska)의 아메리카 원주민 이누잇족(Inuit)들이 그린란드로 돌아와 대규모로 그린란드 이주민들을 공격하던 때에 찾아왔다. 열악한 환경 상태로 이미 약해져 있던 이주민들은 대항할 수 없었고, 결국은 섬멸되었다.

2. 세계 곳곳의 초식동물을 보면, 그들 대부분이 작은 크기의 것들과 아주 큰 크기의 것들, 두 집단으로 나누어진다는 것을 알 수 있다. 작은 크기의 초식동물의 예에는 생쥐가 있고, 코끼리는 큰 초식동물의 좋은 예가 된다. 작은 크기나 큰 크기 모두 초식동물들이 직면하는 문제점, 즉 육식동물들로부터의 위험에 대한 진화론적인 해결책이다.
   매우 큰 크기로 커짐에 따라, 코끼리나 코뿔소 같은 동물들은, 그들을 잡아 먹을 만큼 큰 동물이 없기 때문에, 천적으로부터의 위험을 피할 수가 있다. 태어난 지 몇 달 이상이 되면서, 이들은 더 이상 잡혀 먹힐 위험은 없게 된다. 같은 이유로 그들보다 훨씬 큰 크기의 천적이 있기 때문에 작은 초식동물들은 언제나 위험에 처해 있지만, 그들의 엄청난 개체 수는 그들이 전부 잡아먹히지는 않을 거라는 것을 의미한다. 작은 초식동물들에게 있어서 가장 큰 문제점은, 천적들이 나와서 사냥을 하고 있을 때는 숨어야 하기 때문에, 어느 특정한 시간에만 먹이를 찾아 나설 수 있다는 것이다. 또한, 큰 초식동물들은 작은 초식동물보다 더 긴 수명을 갖는 경향이 있다. 그러나 이것은 어떤 면에서는 단점이다. 큰 동물들은 성숙하는데 더 오래 걸리고, 새끼도 더 가끔 적은 수로 낳는다. 이것은 작은 초식동물들보다 질병이나 가뭄에 대해서 개체 수를 회복하는데 더 오래 걸린다는 뜻이다. 이것은 큰 초식동물들을 더 큰 멸종 위기에 처하게 한다.

•• 해 설 ••

1. (1) 11-13째 줄에 따르면 Iceland 이주자들이 환경 파괴를 막기 위한 방법으로 식단을 생선 위주로 바꾸었다고 했다.
   (2) 이미 살고 있던 원주민들과의 관계에 대한 언급은 없다.
   (3) 9-10째 줄을 참조하자.
   (4) 독립을 함으로써 살아남게 되었다는 내용은 본문에 나와 있지 않다.
   (5) 9-17째 줄을 참조하자.

2. (1) 13-15째 줄에 나오는 자기보다 큰 천적에게 들키지 않으려면 특정한 시간대에만 먹이를 찾으러 갈 수 있는 작은 초식동물의 경우와 반대 입장에 있는 동물임을 알 수 있다.
   (2) 작은 초식동물들이 천적들로부터 항상 숨어 다녀야 한다는 내용은 있지만, 더 쉽게 숨을 수 있는 대상에 대한 언급은 없다.
   (3) 18-20째 줄을 참조한다. "disease or drought"가 "sudden drops in population"의 원인임을 이해해야 한다. 또한 "greater danger of extinction"도 참조한다.
   (4) 9-10째 줄에 나와있다. "die out"은 '서서히 소멸하다'의 뜻이다.
   (5) 더 많은 수의 새끼를 먹이기 위해 더 많은 먹이가 필요한 대상에 대한 언급은 되어있지 않다.

Reading Practice 1

p.104

1. **American Revolution**
   - Resulted in a stable government
   - Involved separate cultures
   - Did not involve a noble class

   French Revolution
   - Resulted in the death of a king
   - Did not fix the divisions in society

Words ❶ achieve ❷ stable ❸ questionable
      ❹ status

미국 혁명과 프랑스 혁명

1776년, 미국 식민지 개척자들은, 영국의 조지 3세(King George III)의 권위에 대항해 반란을 일으켰다. 미국인들에게 이 반란은 커다란 성공이었다. 그들의 독립을 쟁취했을 뿐만 아니라, 세계 곳곳의 나라들에서 모방될 정치 체제를 건설해 나가게 되었다.

1789년, 아마도 미국인들의 성공으로 고무되어, 프랑스인들도 절대적 군주인 루이16세(Louis XVI)에 대해 반란을 일으켰다. 루이16세가 그 왕위(와 그의 머리 역시)를 잃는 등, 프랑스 혁명은 어떤 면에서는 성공적이었지만, 그것은 미국 독립 전쟁만큼 장기적인 성공을 거두지는 못했다. 프랑스 혁명은 10년간의 프랑스 내 혼돈과 학살, 그리고 그 후 수년간의 독재로 이어졌다. 사실, 프랑스는 혁명 후 75년이 지날 때까지 상대적으로 안정적인 민주 정부를 이룩하지 못했다.

프랑스 혁명의 성공이 좋게 보아도 의심스러운 반면, 미국의 독립 전쟁이 성공적이었던 이유에는 여러 가지가 있다. 첫째로, 미국인들은 영국의 식민지 주민이었지만, 실제로는 서로 여러 면으로 다른 문화를 가지고 있었다. 그들은 영국인들을 외부인으로 바라보았다. 일단 전쟁에서 승리하자, 그들은 더 이상 영국인들에 대해서 걱정할 필요가 없어졌다. 프랑스 혁명은 통합된 문화 위에서 발생했다. 전쟁이 끝나자, 그들은 사회의 분열을 치유하기 위한 방법을 찾아야 했으나, 그것은 매우 어려웠다. 프랑스 사회는 귀족과 평민으로 이루어져 있었는데, 그들의 부와 사회적 지위의 차이는 매우 컸다. 미국에도 부자와 가난한 사람이 분명히 있었지만, 그들에게는 귀족 체계가 없었다. 또한, 미국은 성장하고 있는 나라로, 가난한 사람들 역시도 성공의 기회가 있다고 느꼈다. 이것은 계급 상승이 엄청나게 어려웠던 프랑스의 경우와는 달랐다. 이런 이유들로, 프랑스 사회는 안정적인 정부를 구성하기 위해 통합하는 데에 있어 큰 어려움을 겪었다.

✉ **Words**

□ revolt (against) 반란을 일으키다   □ throne 왕관, 왕위

□ chaos 카오스, 혼란, 혼돈   □ dictatorship 독재 정권

□ achieve 성취하다   □ stable 안정된

□ at best 기껏해야   □ division 분리

□ questionable 수상쩍은, 문제가 있는

□ nobility 귀족   □ prosper 번영하다

•• 해 설 ••

1. • Resulted in the death of a king: 8-9째 줄 참조
   • Provided inspiration for all later revolutions: 본문에 언급되지 않은 내용이다. 후세의 모든 혁명에 영향을 미친 혁명에 대해선 언급되어 있지 않다.
   • Did not fix the divisions in society: 18-20째 줄 참조
   • Resulted in a stable government: 3-5째 줄 참조
   • Involved separate cultures: 15-16째 줄 참조
   • Brought about a more equal society: 지문의 내용과 일치하지 않는다. 프랑스 혁명은 신분의 평등을 가져오는데 실패했고, 미국은 혁명 이전부터 신분 계급이 없었다. 따라서 둘 다 신분 계급의 변화는 가져오지 않았다.
   • Did not involve a noble class: 19-21째 줄 참조

Reading Practice 2

p.106

1. **Conditioning**
   - Higher risk of injuries
   - Muscle development

   Skills Training
   - Longer practices
   - Lasts for most of training camp
   - Players are dropped from the team

Words ❶ strategy ❷ phase ❸ demanding
      ❹ take up ❺ intense

훈련 캠프

시즌 시작 전에 대부분의 운동 경기 팀들은, 프로팀이던, 대학팀이던, 고등학교팀이던 간에 훈련 캠프를 연다. 훈련 캠프는 두 달에서 세 달 정도 동안 계속된다. 훈련 캠프에는 여러 가지 목적이 있다. 분명히, 선수들을 훈련시키고 기술을 발전시키기 위한 것이지만, 팀에 대한 감독의 의사 결정에도 도움이 된다. 훈련 캠프에서 선수들을 지켜보며, 감독들은 어떤 선수들이 팀에 남고 어떤 선수들이 탈락할 것인가를 생각할 수 있다. 어떤 경기 전략이 팀에게 가장 알맞을 지도 생각할 수 있다.

훈련 캠프는 일반적으로 두 주간의 컨디션 조절로 시작된다. 이 단계의 목적은 단순히 선수들의 몸을 좋은 상태로 만드는데 있다. 이는 대부분 훈련으로 구성되며, 선수들은 그들의 실제 종목을 경기하지도 못한다. 컨디션 조절에는 지구력 컨디션 조절과 근력 컨디션 조절의 두 가지가 있다. 지구력 컨디션 조절은 심장을 강하게 만들기 위해 기본적으로 많은 달리기와 훈련이 수반된다. 근력 훈련에는 특정한 근육들의 힘을 기르기 위한 훈련이 포함된다. 대부분 선수들은 이것이 훈련 캠프에서 가장 체력적으로 힘든 부분이라는 데에 동의하며,

훈련 캠프에서의 부상 가운데 다수가 이 때 일어난다.

운동 선수들이 컨디션 조절을 체력적으로 가장 힘든 부분이라고 생각할 수 있지만, 기술 훈련이 분명히 가장 스트레스를 주는 부분이다. 기술 훈련은 훈련 캠프 나머지를 이루며 선수들에게 그들 포지션에 맞는 기술을 가르친다. 비록 덜 격렬하긴 하지만, 이는 컨디션 조절보다 더 오랜 연습을 수반한다. 또한 선수들은 다른 팀들 공격과 수비에 대해서 알기 위해서 수 시간 분량의 경기 테이프를 연구해야 한다. 아마도, 가장 스트레스를 주는 부분은 감독이 어느 선수들이 팀에 계속 남아 있을 지에 대한 중대 결정을 내리는 순간일 것이다.

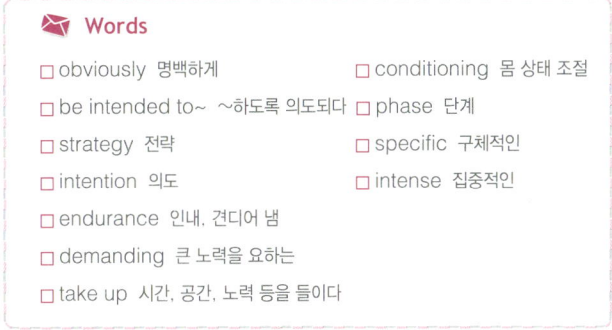

✉ **Words**

☐ obviously 명백하게
☐ be intended to~ ~하도록 의도되다
☐ strategy 전략
☐ intention 의도
☐ endurance 인내, 견디어 냄
☐ demanding 큰 노력을 요하는
☐ take up 시간, 공간, 노력 등을 들이다
☐ conditioning 몸 상태 조절
☐ phase 단계
☐ specific 구체적인
☐ intense 집중적인

•• 해 설 ••

1. • Game strategy is developed: 5-6째 줄에 언급되지만, 이는 전체적인 training camp에 관해서이지 conditioning이나 skills training에 해당하는 내용은 아니다.
   • Higher risk of injuries: 17째 줄 참조
   • Longer practices: 20-21째 줄 참조
   • Lasts for most of training camp: 20-21째 줄 참조
   • Players are dropped from the team: 23-24째 줄 참조
   • Practice against other teams: 정확하지 않은 내용이다. 훈련기간 동안 다른 팀의 플레이를 분석한다고 했지 다른 팀과 시합한다고 하지는 않았다.
   • Muscle development: 14-15째 줄 참조

Reading Practice 3   p.108

1. **Captured Moons**
   • Much smaller than their planet
   • Majority of moons in the solar system
   • Differ from their planet chemically
   Impact Moons
   • Lack heavy metals
   • Similar orbit with their planet

Words ❶ gravity ❷ formation ❸ opposite ❹ collision

달의 형성

태양계의 많은 위성들은 포획된 위성으로, 우주에서 자유롭게 이동하다가, 모행성의 중력이 그들을 포획하여 궤도 속에 가둔 것이다. 이것은 대부분 위성들이 매우 작거나 모행성이 매우 크기 때문에, 일반적으로 쉽게 설명된다. 그러나, 지구의 달의 경우에, 달 크기 정도의 개체를 포획할 만큼 지구의 중력이 클 것이라는 것은 상상하기 어렵다. 포획설에 있어서 또 다른 문제는, 대부분의 포획된 위성이 모행성의 자전 방향과 반대 방향으로 공전하는 것과 달리, 달의 공전 방향은 지구의 자전 방향과 같다는 것이다. 마지막으로, 각자 형성되었기 때문에, 일반적으로 포획된 위성은 모행성과 화학적으로 다르다.

미국의 1970년대 달 탐사 작전들은 달과 지구가 화학적으로 상당히 닮아 있다는 것을 보여주었다. 이것은 충돌설이라고 불리는 위성 형성에 관한 새로운 이론을 발생시켰다. 이 이론에 따르면, 화성 크기의 행성이 45억년 전 지구에 충돌했다. 그 행성은 완전히 파괴되었고, 지구 표면 중의 많은 양이 우주로 내던져졌다. 먼지와 작은 바위들로 이루어진 커다란 고리가 지구 둘레를 돌기 시작했다. 그 고리가 결국 우리의 달로 형성되었다. 충돌설은 여러 가지를 설명해 준다. 첫째로, 그것은 왜 지구와 달의 궤도가 비슷한지 설명해 준다. 더 중요하게, 그것은 지구와 달이 왜 그렇게 화학적으로 비슷한지 설명하는 데에도 도움이 된다. 또한, 왜 달에 철과 같은 중금속이 없는지도 설명해 준다. 그런 금속들은 충돌로 인해 우주로 던져지기에는 너무 무거워서 지구상에 잔존했을 것이다.

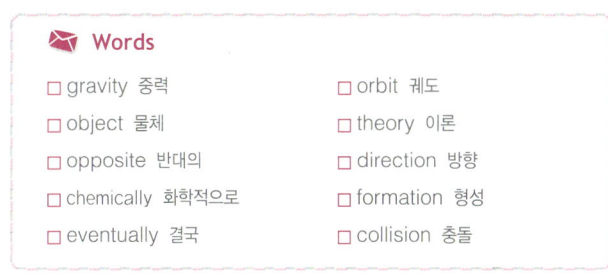

✉ **Words**

☐ gravity 중력
☐ object 물체
☐ opposite 반대의
☐ chemically 화학적으로
☐ eventually 결국
☐ orbit 궤도
☐ theory 이론
☐ direction 방향
☐ formation 형성
☐ collision 충돌

•• 해 설 ••

1. • Much smaller than their planet: 5-6째 줄 참조
   • Only orbit the Earth and Mars: 지구와 화성만을 도는 위성에 관해선 언급되지 않았다.
   • Lack heavy metals: 20째 줄 참조
   • Majority of moons in the solar system: 1-2째 줄 참조
   • Form outside of the solar system: 언급되지 않은 내용이다.
   • Similar orbit with their planet: 18-19째 줄 참조
   • Differ from their planet chemically: 11-12째 줄 참조

iBT Practice 1   p.110

1. (B)   2. (C)   3. (B)   4. (D)   5. (B)   6. (B)

7. US
   • Plane flew into enemy airspace
   • More missiles with longer ranges

- Took provocative moves before the crisis

USSR

- Missiles incapable of reaching the other nation before the crisis
- Shot down enemy spy plane

쿠바 미사일 위기(Cuban Missile Crisis)

1962년 소련은 미국에서부터 90마일밖에 떨어지지 않은 쿠바 섬에 핵미사일을 배치시켰다. 이런 거리에서, 미사일은 약 3분 정도의 비행 시간을 가지며, 따라서 기본적으로 미국은 소련이 공격하더라도 경고를 받을 수 없었다. 이런 조치는 양국의 세력 균형을 완전히 어지럽혔다. 미국은 소련에게 미사일을 철수할 것을 요구했고, 쿠바 미사일 위기로 알려진 교착 상태가 이어졌다. 쿠바 미사일 위기는 냉전의 가장 중요한 사건들 가운데 하나였다. 그것은 미국과 소련을 핵전쟁에 가까이 이르게 했을 뿐만 아니라, 양국이 서로를 얼마나 정직하지 못하게 대했는지를 명확히 보여주었다. 그것은 또 핵무기에 대한 격렬한 반대를 불러 일으켰다.

1950년대 말에 이르러 미국은 미사일의 총 개수와 사정 거리 모두에 있어서 그들이 소련을 능가한다는 사실을 알고 있었다. 아이젠하워(Eisenhower) 대통령의 임기 말에, 미국은 터키 내에 소련 국경으로부터 150마일도 안 되는 곳에 미사일을 배치하기로 결정했다. 이것은, 당시 소련에는 미국 대륙을 공격할 수 있는 능력이 되는 미사일이 없었기 때문에, 세력의 균형을 흐트러뜨릴 것이라는 것이 명백했다. 미국은 그것이 소련을 당황시킬 것이라는 것을 알고 있었고, 아이젠하워는 그것을 소련의 멕시코나 쿠바에의 미사일 배치와 비교하였다. 기밀 해제된 문서에 따라, 터키의 미사일들은 쿠바 미사일 위기가 발발하기 약 한 달 전부터 작전 운용이 가능해졌다는 것이 밝혀짐으로써, 러시아의 쿠바 미사일 배치가 거의 이에 대한 반응이었다는 의견이 더 힘을 얻었다.

양국의 장군들은 위기에 대해 군사적인 해결을 선호했고, 흐루시초프(Khrushev)와 케네디(Kennedy)는 그들의 군대를 통제하는데 어려움을 느꼈다. 위기의 13번째 날에, 여러 군사적 실수는 세계를 핵전쟁에 사상 가장 가까이까지 몰고 갔다. 러시아의 한 사령관이 쿠바 상공에서 U-2 정찰기를 격추시켰고, 이어서 또 다른 U-2기가 경로를 이탈해 소련 영공으로 날아갔다. 양국은 서로의 행동을 그 이상의 군사적 행동으로 이끄는 발판으로 해석했다. 그날, 케네디는 그 위기의 모든 실패를 요약하는 스스로의 감상을 표현했다. 소련 영공에서의 비행을 알고 난 후, 그는 "뜻을 이해 못하는 놈들이 꼭 있군"이라는 말을 했다.

📧 **Words**

□ upset 어지럽히다, 잘못되게 만들다 □ remove 철수하다, 제거하다
□ standoff 교착 상태 □ illustrate 분명히 보여주다
□ presidency 대통령 임기 □ declassified 기밀 해제된
□ veer 이탈하다, 방향을 바꾸다 □ airspace 영공

• • 해 설 • •

1. 두 번째 문장에 따르면 "the US would basically have no warning if the Soviets attacked them"이라고 했다. 이것이 "a surprise attack"을 의미함을 이해해야 한다.

2. 두 나라 관계의 균형에 영향을 미친 이 사건은 앞 부분에 언급된 소련이 쿠바에 미사일을 설치한 사건이다.

3. 둘째 문단에, 소련의 쿠바 미사일 설치가 미국이 터키에 미사일을 설치한 것에 대한 대응이었을 가능성을 제시하고 있다. (B)는 이와 반대되는 내용이다.

4. 12째 줄의 "It was obvious that this would upset the balance of power, as the USSR had no missiles capable of hitting the continental United States at the time."의 문장에서 미국의 터키의 미사일 배치에 대한 소련의 입장이 나와 있다. "capable of hitting the continental United States at the time"이 "within range of the US"와 같은 의미라는 것을 이해해야 한다.

5. "기밀 해제된 문서가 드러낸 바로는 / 터키의 미사일이 쿠바의 미사일 위기보다 거의 한달 전에 배치되었으며 / 러시아의 쿠바 미사일 설치는 거의 이것에 대한 대응이었다는 것을 알려주고 있다"
"suggested"가 "adding to the sense"와 같은 의미이다. 답에 가까워 보이는 (A)는 쿠바의 미사일이 미국의 터키 미사일 설치에 대한 대응이었다고 문서가 보여주었다고 했는데, 이는 문서에 쓰여진 내용이 아니고 문서를 보고 짐작할 수 있는 사실이기 때문에 답이 될 수 없다.

6. "interpret"에는 "translate"의 뜻도 있지만 문맥에 비추어 "interpreted"의 내용을 "두 나라가 서로의 행동을 군사적 행동의 발판으로 보았다(viewed)"고 해석하는 것이 타당하다.

7.
- Intended to launch a surprise attack: 정확하지 않은 내용이다. 본문에서 어떤 나라도 "surprise attack"을 의도하고 미사일을 설치한 것이라고는 말하지 않았다.
- Plane flew into enemy airspace: 20-21째 줄 참조
- Leaders wanted a military solution to the crisis: 본문에 맞지 않는 내용이다. 군사적 대응을 하려 했던 사람은 장군들이지 지도자들이 아니었다.(18째 줄 참조)
- More missiles with longer ranges: 10-11째 줄 참조. "it led the Soviets in both total numbers of missiles and missile range"가 "it had more missiles with longer ranges"와 같은 말이다.
- Missiles incapable of reaching the other nation before the crisis: 12-13째 줄 참조
- Shot down enemy spy plane: 20-21째 줄 참조
- Took provocative moves before the crisis: 12-15째 줄 참조. provocative는 '성나게 하는, 도발하는'의 뜻이며 처음 미사일 위기의 도화선이 된 나라를 묻고 있다. 쿠바 미사일 이전에 미국이 터키에 먼저 미사일 설치를 해 소련을 자극했다는 것을 이해해야 한다.

1. (B)　2. (C)　3. (D)　4. (C)　5. (B)　6. (A)

7. **Normans**
- Warrior society
- Language a mixture of other languages
- Rulers of England after 1066

Anglo-Saxons
- Primarily concerned with stopping Viking invasions
- Descended from Germanic tribes

노르만 정복

현대 영어와 함께 현대 영국 문화는, 서기 1066년 프랑스 북부의 노르만족이 영국을 침략해 정복한 때부터 유래되었다. 이 전에는, 영국은 앵글로-색슨족에 의해 통치되었다. 시간이 흐름에 따라 이 두 문화가 혼합되어 우리가 현대 영국의 문화와 언어로 알고 있는 것들을 형성했다.

노르만들은 바이킹의 후예로, 9세기에 프랑스 왕의 초대로 프랑스 북부 해안을 지키는데 도움을 주기 위해 북부 프랑스로 들어와 살게 되었다. 따라서, 노르만 문화는 남부 프랑스의 문화와는 달랐다. 그들의 언어에는 프랑스어와 라틴어의 요소가 들어 있었지만, 그들의 바이킹 조상이 쓰던 게르만어의 요소 역시 포함되어 있었다. 노르만족은 본래 전사들의 사회였고 언제나 그들은 소유지를 확장하려고 했다. 그러나 1066년까지 그렇게 할 수 있는 기회가 매우 적었는데, 그것은 실질적인 주인이었던 프랑스인들을 화나게 할 수 있다는 두려움에 프랑스로부터 땅을 쉽게 빼앗지 못했기 때문이다.

앵글로-색슨족은 로마의 영국 지배가 끝난 후 얼마 지나지 않은 5세기에 영국으로 들어왔다. 그들의 조상은 게르만 부족들의 혼혈이었고, 그들의 언어는 본래 순수한 게르만어였다. 10세기에 이르러 그들은 영국 전역의 통치권을 가지게 되었고, 그들의 주된 걱정은 바이킹으로부터의 침략으로부터 스스로를 보호하는 것이었다.

노르만족의 침략은, 앵글로-색슨 왕이던 참회왕 에드워드(Edward the Confessor)가 1066년에 후계자 없이 죽게 되자 시작되었다. 노르만족은 이를 기회로 여겼고, 그들의 왕, 윌리엄 1세가 영국의 왕위 계승권을 주장하였다. 그런 사람들이 그 외에도 있었다. 앵글로-색슨 귀족이었던 해롤드 고드윈슨(Harold Godwinson) 역시, 자기의 왕위 계승을 주장하였다. 그래서 윌리엄은 영국으로 쳐들어가, 10월 14일에 벌어진 헤이스팅 전투(Battle of Hastings)에서 고드윈슨을 죽이고 승리했다. 앵글로-색슨족은 외부의 침략자에 의해 지배를 받는 것이 불만스러웠지만, 모든 앵글로-색슨 귀족을 노르만 귀족으로 대체하기로 한 윌리엄의 결정은, 그들이 그것에 대해 할 수 있는 일이 거의 없었다는 것을 의미했다. 노르만족 지배의 첫 100여 년 동안은 정말 어려웠고, 노르만들은 무력의 사용을 통해서만 영국 통치를 유지했다. 그러나 점차적으로, 노르만들이 더 이상 외부인으로 여겨지지 않고, 영국 사람들에게 그들의 지배가 더 잘 받아들여질 정도로, 두 문화는 서로 융화되었다.

✉ Words

- stem from ~로부터 유래되다, ~에서 생겨나다
- blend 혼합되다
- holding 소유지, 자산
- throne 왕위 계승권
- gradually 점차적으로, 서서히
- nobility 귀족
- descend 내려오다
- heir 후계자
- indeed 정말,
- prosper 번영하다

•• 해 설 ••

1. 노르만의 침략으로 영국 문화가 새롭게 바뀌어 오늘날에 이르게 된 것이므로, '근대 영국 문화는 노르만이 영국을 지배했을 때부터 시작된 것이다'고 해석하는 것이 올바르다.

2. 첫 문단 마지막 문장에 "Over time, these two cultures blended together to form what we know as the modern English culture and language." 라고 한 것을 힌트로 답을 찾을 수 있다. 또한 이 문장은 전체 글의 중심 문장이기도 하다.

3. 노르만족이 본래 항상 그들의 "holdings"를 확장하려 했다는 본문 내용과 '그렇지만 그들이 프랑스로부터 땅(land)을 취할 수는 없었기 때문에, 1066년까지는 그럴 기회가 없었다'고 한 이어지는 문장의 내용에서 이 단어가 영토(territory)를 의미함을 짐작 할 수 있다.

4. 11째 줄 이하의 "because they could not very well take land from the French, who were essentially their hosts, for fear of angering them"에서 노르만족이 영토를 확장할 수 없었던 이유를 설명해 주고 있다.

5. "this"는 앞 문장에 제시된 앵글로 색슨족의 왕인 Edward the Confessor가 후계자 없이 죽은 사건을 가리키며, 이는 노르만족이 앵글로 색슨족을 침략하는 계기가 되었다.

6. "앵글로 색슨족은 외국인 침략자들에 의해 지배당하는 것을 좋아하지 않았지만 / 윌리엄에 의한 앵글로 색슨족의 모든 귀족을 노르만족으로 대치하기로 한 결정은 / 그들이 할 수 있는 일이 거의 없었다는 것을 의미했다"
"there was little they could do about it"이 "they could not really oppose it"과 같은 의미를 가진다는 것을 이해해야 한다. 외국 침략자들에 의해 지배되었기 때문이 아니라, 귀족들을 모두 노르만족으로 대치했기 때문에 앵글로 색슨족이 노르만족의 지배에 저항할 수 없었던 것이므로 (C)와 (D)는 답이 될 수 없으며, (B)는 전혀 다른 내용을 담고 있다.

7. • Primarily concerned with stopping Viking invasions: 16-17째 줄 참조
   • Took land from the French through invasion: 본문의 내용과 일치하지 않는 내용이다. 노르만은 침략을 통해 앵글로 색슨족의 땅을 빼앗았고, 프랑스로부터는 땅을 평화적으로 받은 것이었다.
   • Warrior society: 9-10째 줄 참조
   • Language a mixture of other languages: 7-9째 줄 참조

- Society based on Roman laws: 언급되지 않은 내용이다. 로마의 법에 바탕을 둔 사회에 관해서는 본문에 나와있지 않다.
- Rulers of England after 1066: 넷째 문단에 전반적으로 설명되어 있다.
- Descended from Germanic tribes: 14째 줄 참조

Vocabulary Review   p.116

1. (C)   2. (B)   3. (A)   4. (C)   5. (C)
6. (B)   7. (A)   8. (D)
9. opposite   10. conquered
11. survive   12. status
13. endurance   14. phase
15. formation   16. gravity

Inference

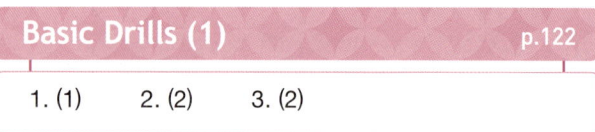

Basic Drills (1)   p.122

1. (1)   2. (2)   3. (2)

1. 바이킹은 유럽 대부분을 300년 동안 위협했었다. 그들의 작고, 날렵한 배는 거의 경고 없이 유럽 해안에 대한 급습을 가능하게 했다. 바이킹들은 또한 북아메리카의 존재를 알고 있었으나, 그들의 작은 보트가 대양을 건너지 못했기 때문에 아메리카 원주민들은 바이킹의 급습을 피할 수 있었다.

2. 잘못된 채광 형태를 발견하는 방법 중의 하나는 그 광산 주변 사람들의 건강을 관찰하는 것이다. 증가하는 암 발생률과 기형아 출산율의 등장은 광산이 폐기물을 물에다 아무렇게나 버려 왔다는 것을 보여준다. 광산 폐기물은 청산염이나 비소와 같은 많은 독성 물질을 함유하고 잇다. 이런 화학물질은 제대로 폐기 처리하기에 비용이 많이 들어서, 많은 광산들은 폐기물 처리에 대한 비용을 내는 대신에 폐기물을 그냥 아무렇게나 버리는 것에 이끌린다.

3. 산불의 주요 원인 중의 하나는 늦게 자라는 나무들의 사라짐이다. 일반적으로 그들은 불에 대해 더 잘 저항할 수 있게 해주는 매우 두꺼운 껍질을 갖고 있다. 이 나무들은 또 벌목 회사들이 가장 선호하는 나무들이기도 하다. 벌목 회사들은 늦게 자라는 나무를 베어 내고, 목재를 얻기 위해 더 빨리 벨 수 있는 빨리 자라는 나무를 심는다. 불행히도, 이것은 산불이 더 쉽게 번질 수 있게 한다.

•• 해 설 ••

1. 바이킹족은 그들의 배로는 넓은 대양을 건널 수 없어 북아메리카는 침략하지 못했으나, 유럽 나라들은 침략할 수 있었다. 따라서 유럽 침략 때는 그들이 북아메리카를 침략하지 못한 이유, 즉 넓은 대양을 건널 필요가 없었다는 것을 알 수 있다.

2. 광산 쓰레기에 청산염과 비소 같은 독성물질이 많고, 이런 쓰레기가 물에 버려진 주변에서 암과 선천적 기형의 비율이 높게 나타난다고 했으므로, 이 독성물질이 암과 기형의 원인이 됨을 알 수 있다.

3. 늦게 자라는 나무들은 화재에 저항하게 해주는 두꺼운 나무 껍질을 가지고 있는데, 이것들을 베어버리고 빨리 자라는 나무를 심음으로써 화재가 일어나고 퍼지기 쉽다고 하였다. 따라서 빨리 자라는 나무들은 이와 반대의 성질을 갖고 있음을 알 수 있다. 벌목회사가 나무를 빨리 벨 수 있다면 산불은 신경 쓰지 않는다는 것은 너무 비약적 추론이다.

1. (1) F　　(2) F
2. (1) F　　(2) T

1. 포식 동물들은 기본적으로 두 가지 이유로 다른 동물들을 죽일 수 있다. 첫 번째는 그 동물을 먹기 위해서이다. 그러나 특히 커다란 포식 동물들 사이에서는, 항상 이런 것은 아니다. 그들은 같은 동물을 놓고 먹잇감을 위해 경쟁하기도 한다. 그러나, 희생되는 동물의 수는 한정돼 있으므로, 적은 수의 포식 동물만을 부양할 수 있다. 이것은 어느 포식 동물이 먹이를 먹을 동안, 다른 포식 동물은 굶을 수도 있다는 뜻이다. 한정된 자원만을 가진 지역에서 그들 스스로의 식량 공급원을 확실히 하기 위해서는 같은 먹이를 놓고 싸우는 포식 동물들끼리 종종 서로를 죽이는 것에 의지할 수도 있다. 그러나 다른 큰 포식 동물을 사냥하는 것은 매우 위험할 수 있고, 그로 인한 싸움은 서로를 죽이지는 않더라도 매우 심각한 부상을 입힐 수가 있다. 이것은 왜 사자들이 종종 어미가 사냥하러 가서 없는 사이에 새끼 치타들을 죽이는지를 설명해 준다.

2. 1800년대 중반에, 수십만 명의 미국인들은 새로운 땅을 찾아서 서부로 이동하기 시작했다. 대부분의 중서부 땅들은 아메리카 원주민 부족들에게 속해 있었다. 미국인들이 처음 서부로 이동하기 시작했을 때, 그 부족들은 우호적이었다. 그들은 땅이 모두를 위해 충분히 많다고 생각했고, 새로운 이주자들과 거래하기를 열망했다. 점점 많은 이주자들이 서부로 이동하면서, 그들은 점점 더 많은 땅을 차지했고, 좀 더 결정적으로 그들은 많은 수의 버펄로들을 죽이기 시작했다. 그들의 식량 공급원의 중요한 부분이 위험에 처한 것을 보게 되자, 아메리카 원주민들은 이주자들과 대립하기 시작했다. 수년이 흐르는 동안, 그들 사이에 여러 슬픈 전투가 있었고, 아메리카 원주민들은 영토 대부분을 이주자들에게 내어 주는 평화조약에 서명하도록 서서히 강요당했다.

•• 해설 ••

1. (1) 포식동물들은 먹이를 위해서이기도 하지만, 같은 먹이를 먹는(경쟁관계에 있는) 동물들을 제어하기 위해 죽인다고도 했다. 치타는 사자의 먹이 감이 아니므로 두 번째 이유로 치타를 죽이는 것이다.

(2) 같은 큰 동물들끼리 싸우는 것은 매우 위험하기 때문에 사자가 아직 자라지 않은 약한 새끼 치타를 죽이는 것이다.

2. (1) 처음 미국 이주자들은 원주민들에게서 평화적으로 땅을 얻어냈으나 버펄로를 죽임으로써 원주민들과 대립하게 되었다.

(2) 원주민들은 버펄로를 죽이는 것을 자기들의 주된 음식 공급원이 위험에 처한 것으로 보았다.

1. (B)　　2. (C)

1-2. 동물들은 번식을 위한 여러 다른 전략들을 가지고 있다. 그런 전략 중의

하나는 텃세권이라고 불린다. 이 전략에서, 각각의 수컷 동물들은 다른 수컷들을 쫓아낼 수 있는 각자의 선택된 영역을 갖는다. 이런 방식으로, 그 수컷은 그의 영역 안에 있는 암컷들이 그하고만 짝짓기 하도록 할 수 있다. 이것의 좋은 예는 북아메리카의 동부 지방 대부분에서 발견되는 블루길이라는 물고기들일 것이다. 블루길은 무리를 지어 다니는, 집단 생활을 하는 물고기이다. 그러나 산란기 동안에는 각각의 블루길 수컷은 각자의 둥지를 만든다. 블루길은 각자의 둥지를 사납게 방어하며 다른 수컷들을 쫓아낸다. 커다란 수컷들은 연못이나 개울의 중심에 그들의 둥지를 만들며, 바깥쪽의 수컷들은 짝을 찾을 확률이 거의 없다.

그러므로, 작은 물고기들은 다른 번식 전략을 개발해야 한다. 그런 방법 중의 하나는 탁란(托卵)이다. 작은 수컷들은 중심의 수컷들에게 직접적으로 도전할 수 없다. 대신, 그들은 큰 수컷들이 암컷과 짝짓기를 하느라 주의를 잃을 때까지 기다린다. 그리고는, 그 둥지로 숨어 들어가 큰 수컷이 눈치채기 전에 일부의 알을 수정시킨다. 이런 방법은 완전히 효율적이지는 않다. 작은 수컷들이 적은 수의 알만을 수정시킬 뿐만 아니라, 알이 부화하면 큰 수컷들이 작은 수컷들의 새끼만을 선택적으로 잡아먹는 것이 목격된 바가 있기 때문이다.

•• 해설 ••

1. 가장 큰 수컷 물고기만 연못이나 냇가의 중심에 둥지를 만들 수 있고, 이밖에 있어야 하는 수컷들은 짝을 찾기가 힘들다고 했으므로 암컷들이 대부분 중심에 있음을 알 수 있다.

2. 다른 물고기가 자신의 둥지에 와서 낳고 간 알은 부화하면 먹어 버린다고 했다. 이로부터 이들이 자신의 새끼와 다른 새끼를 구분할 수 있다는 것을 알 수 있다.

1. (C)　　2. (C)

1-2. 강대국들을 대표하는 대형 기업들은 수 백 년간 가난한 나라의 값진 자원들을 빼내 왔다. 많은 경우에, 특히 현대에 들어, 이런 대형 기업들은 필요한 일자리를 많이 가져오기 때문에, 가난한 나라들에게서 환영을 받아 왔다. 이러한 만족은 세월이 흘러 그런 회사들의 영향이 가시화되면서부터 분노로 바뀌게 된다.

많은 가난한 나라들에는 환경과 근로자를 보호하기 위한 강력한 법이 없기 때문에, 이런 회사들은 환경 파괴적인 방법을 사용하거나 근로자들을 위험한 상황에 노출시키는 등으로 비용을 절감할 수 있다. 간단한 예가 있다. 1980년대에 미국의 화학 회사가 인도에 공장을 운영했다. 그 회사는 부유한 나라에서는 필요했을 안전 수칙을 하나도 이행하지 않았다. 그 결과, 독성 기체가 공장 밖으로 흘러 나와 거의 4,000명이 사망한 끔찍한 화학 사고가 1984년에 발생했다. 그 후로, 그 미국 기업 유니온 카바이드(Union Carbide) 사는 인도에서의 소송을 해결하기 위해 수억 달러를 지불했다. 게다가, 그들은 다른 나라에 새로운 공장을 개설하려고 할 때마다 지역 주민의 강력한 반대를 받아 오고 있다. 이는

사회적 계약 개념을 이끌어 냈다. 이 개념에 따르면, 기업들은 비록 법으로 요구되지 않거나 비용이 더 들더라도, 사회적, 환경적으로 책임감 있는 방식으로 행동해야 한다. 이 논리는 장기적으로 볼 때, 소송이 적어질 것이므로 비용이 더 싸다는 것이다.

•• 해설 ••

1. 첫 문단에서, 대기업이 미치는 영향이 드러날 때 가난한 나라 사람들이 대기업에 대해 분노를 느낀다고 했고, 두 번째 문단에서 그 영향이 환경과 사람들에게 주는 피해임이 설명되어 있다. 이 두 정보를 연결하여 답을 찾아보자.

2. 두 번째 문단을 보면 대기업이 환경을 파괴하고 근로자들을 위험에 처하게 하는 방식으로 비용을 절감한다고 되어 있다(these companies can keep costs down...). Union Carbide는 그러한 대기업의 예로 언급되었다.

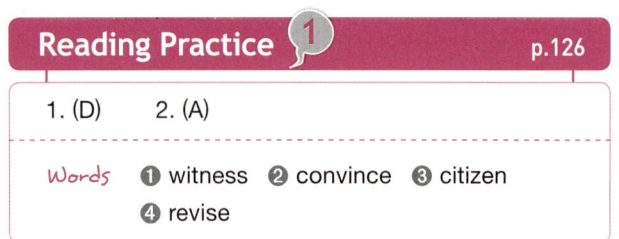

Reading Practice 1
p.126

1. (D)　　2. (A)

Words ❶ witness ❷ convince ❸ citizen
❹ revise

제네바 협정

1800년대 말, 기관총과 대포의 발명은 전쟁을 끔찍한 방식으로 바꾸고 있었다. 1859년, 헨리 듀란트(Henri Durant)라는 이름의 남자는 프랑스와 오스트리아 군대간의 특히 격렬했던 전투를 목격하며 이를 직접 확인했다. 그것은 그가 그전까지 보았던 다른 전투와는 완전히 달랐다. 그 전투 후, 38,000명의 군인이 전장에서 죽거나 다쳐서 누워 있었으나, 사흘 동안 아무도 다친 병사들을 보살피기 위해 가지 않았다. 문제는 양측이 부상자들을 데려오기 위해 충분히 휴전하는 데에 동의하지 못했다는 것이었다. 충격을 받은 듀란트는 결국 근처 마을 주민들에게 부상자들을 데려와 보살피도록 납득시켰다.

전쟁 후, 듀란트는 그가 본 것 때문에 계속 매우 당혹해 있었다. 그의 노력은 1864년 최초의 제네바 협정을 이끌어 냈다. 기본적으로, 그 첫 제네바 협정에 따르면, 전쟁 도중 군은 부상자들을 전장 밖으로 이동시킬 수 있게 허락할 의무가 있으며, 또 어느 편이던 간에 부상자들에게 의료 보호를 제공할 의무가 있다는 것이었다. 처음에, 제네바 협정에 47개국이 서명했고, 그 나라들에게 제네바 협정은 법이 되었다. 그 후 100년간, 전쟁 포로에 대한 정당한 대우를 위한 규칙과 전쟁 지역에서 민간인들을 보호하는 규칙을 만드는 등 세 번의 제네바 협정이 더 있었다. 제2차 세계대전은, 제네바 협정이 개정되어야 하며 거기에 더 많은 권한을 부여하고, 그것을 어긴 사람들을 더 쉽게 처벌할 수 있도록 해야 될 필요를 보여주었다. 그것은 1949년에 이루어졌다.

1949년의 개정은 또 독가스와 같은 특정 종류의 무기를 사용하는 것을 전쟁 범죄로 규정하였다. 오늘날, 지구상의 거의 모든 나라들이 제네바 협정에 조인하였고 그 협정은 국제법으로 취급된다. 전쟁은 그래도 끔찍하지만, 제네바 협정은 최소한 그런 공포에 어떤 한계를 두도록 도왔다.

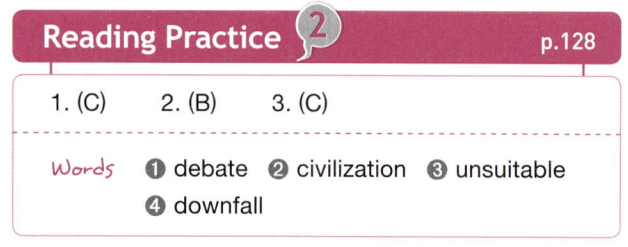

✉ Words

□ witness 목격하다
□ convince ~하도록 설득하다
□ treatment 대우
□ revise 개정하다, 교정하다
□ particularly 특히
□ regardless of~ ~에 관계없이
□ citizen 시민

•• 해설 ••

1. 첫째 문장에서 기관총과 대포 같은 무기의 발명이 전쟁을 끔찍하게 변화시키고 있었다고 했다. 전쟁에서 일어나는 끔찍한 일이 사람들을 죽거나 다치게 하는 것이며, 또한 첫째 문단에서 많은 군인들이 죽거나 다친 전투를 이것의 예로 들고 있는 것으로 보아, 이런 무기들이 전쟁에서 사망자와 사상자 수를 늘이는 역할을 했을 것이라는 것을 추론할 수 있다.

2. 19-20째 줄에 따르면 제 2차 세계대전이 제네바 협정이 개정될 필요성을 보여주었다고 했다. 이는 제네바 협정을 더 효력 있게 만들고 이를 어긴 사람들을 더 쉽게 벌주기 하기 위한 것이라고 했으므로, 제2차 세계대전 동안 이를 어긴 사람들이 있었고, 벌이 무겁지 않은 것이 그 원인이었을 것임을 추론해 볼 수 있다.

Reading Practice 2
p.128

1. (C)　　2. (B)　　3. (C)

Words ❶ debate ❷ civilization ❸ unsuitable
❹ downfall

수메르인

최초의 문명이 언제, 어디서 발상 했는지에 대해서, 고고학자들간에는 많은 논쟁이 있다. 그것은 그 질문에 대한 답이 사람마다 문명을 어떻게 정의하느냐에 달려 있기 때문이다. 만약, 문명이 단순히 비슷한 문화와 신앙을 가진 사람들의 작은 집단을 뜻한다면, 문명은 세계의 여러 곳에서 수천 년 전부터 존재해 왔다. 만약, 문명이 정치 체계와 도시의 건설을 갖는 더 크고 복잡한 사회로 정의된다면, 현재의 이라크(Iraq) 지역에 위치했던 수메르(Sumerian) 문명이 아마 최초의 문명이었을 것이다. 수메르인들은 약간 더 북쪽에 위치하던 작은 농촌 마을들로 이루어진 우바이드(Ubaid) 문화의 계통을 이었다. 기원전 4000년경, 이들 농민들은 티그리스(Tigris) 강 유역으로 내려왔다.

이 땅은 강수량이 적어, 농업에는 적절하지 못했다. 그래서, 그곳은 비어 있었으므로 수메르인들은 넓은 영역을 얻었고, 다른 민족들과의 경쟁이 거의 없었다. 수메르인들이 이 메마른 땅에 성공적으로 농사를 지을 수 있게 한 것은, 강이나 호수로부터 인공으로 낸 물길의 사용을 통해 농경지로 물을 대는 기술인, 관개(灌漑)에 대한 지식 덕분이었다. 이것은 비의 부족에도 불구하고 수메르인들이 여기에 성공적으로 농사를 지을 수 있게 했다. 그들의 언어가 관개농업과 관련된 낱말들로 채워져 있기 때문에, 우리는 수메르인들이 관개농업에 대해서 깊은 이해를 하고 있었다는 것을 알 수 있다. 그들의 진보된 농업 기술과 토지를 놓고 경쟁할 다른 민족의 부재로 인해, 수메르의 인구는 늘어나 티그리스 강 유역 전체로 퍼져 나갔다. 그들의 마을은 작은 도시국가로 커지게 되었고 그들은 더 복잡한 정치와 사회 체계를 구성하기 시작했다. 우리 인류 문명의 많은 기본 기술들은 수메르인들의 덕분이다. 관개술을 완성시킨 것 외에도, 그들은 그들의 멸망 이후에도 다른 문명들에 의해서 계속 사용된, 글자라는 것도 최초로 발명했다.

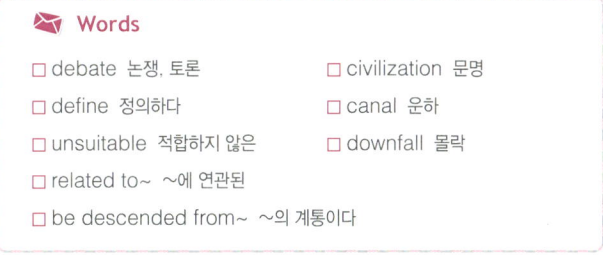

Words

□ debate 논쟁, 토론 □ civilization 문명
□ define 정의하다 □ canal 운하
□ unsuitable 적합하지 않은 □ downfall 몰락
□ related to~ ~에 연관된
□ be descended from~ ~의 계통이다

● ● 해 설 ● ●

1. 처음 문명이 발전한 때와 장소에 대해서 많은 논쟁이 있다고 하면서, 이것은 문명이라는 말을 어떻게 정의하는 지에 달려 있다고 했으므로, 아직 '문명'이라는 말의 정의가 확실히 정해지지 않았다는 것을 추론할 수 있다. 두 개의 문명의 정의 중 둘째 정의에 의해서만이 수메르 문명이 첫째 문명이므로, 대부분의 학자들이 그렇게 믿는다고 한 (A)는 옳지 않다. 도시와 정부를 문명으로 친다면 수메르 문명이 처음 문명이므로 (B)도 틀린 답이며, 기원전 4000년경에 농부들이 이주를 했다면, 농사는 그 이전부터 지어졌을 것임으로 (D) 또한 옳지 않다.

2. 두 번째 문단에 따르면 이주해 온 티그리스 강 유역이 강수량이 적어 농사에 적합하지 않자 강의 물을 끌어와 성공적으로 농사지을 수 있었다고 했으므로, 이 강이 그들의 물의 원천임을 알 수 있다.

3. 수메르인들이 관개에 능했다는 것을 그들의 언어가 이와 관계된 단어로 채워져 있는 것으로부터 알 수 있다고 했는데, 이것은 그들의 언어가 후세 사람들에 의해 해석될 수 있었기 때문에 알 수 있는 사실일 것이다. 이 본문에서 언어에 관한 내용은 수메르이의 관개술의 발달을 증명하기 위해 언급된 것일 뿐, 다른 설명은 되어 있지 않다.

Reading Practice ③　　　p.130

1. (C)　　2. (D)

Words ❶ acquire ❷ consequence ❸ treasure
❹ heritage

유럽의 박물관

유럽은 미술관으로 유명하다. 이것은 유럽이 많은 수의 예술가를 배출했을 뿐만 아니라, 수 세기 동안, 유럽의 나라들이 다른 문화들로부터 엄청난 수의 예술품들을 가져왔기 때문이다. 예를 들어, 어떤 유럽 미술관들은 이집트 미술관보다도 초기 이집트 예술품들을 더 많이 소장하고 있다. 이것은 유럽의 전 세계에 걸친 수 세기간의 식민지정책에 따른 결과이다.

유럽 국가들은 그들 제국을 유지하는데 필요한 값진 천연 자원을 가져오기 위해 15세기에 시작해서 제2차 세계 대전에 이르기까지도 세계 일부에 식민지를 운영했다. 그러나 그런 천연 자원에 더해서, 유럽인들은 그들 식민지의 문화재들 또한 빼앗았다. 유럽인들은 남아메리카, 아프리카, 그리고 세계의 그 밖의 지역에서 토착 예술품들을 배로 가득히 실어 자기들의 나라로 보냈다. 일부의 예술품들은 개인 수집가들의 손에 남겨졌지만, 대부분은 유럽의 미술관에 소장되는 처지가 되었다. 베닌(Benin) 청동 조각의 경우가 꽤 전형적인 예다.

베닌은 풍부한 예술적 전통을 가진 아프리카의 왕국이었다. 1800년대, 그 나라 역시 영국 식민지로 만들려는 영국의 압력이 커져갔다. 결국 영국은 1897년 짧은 전쟁을 일으켜서 쉽게 승리했다. 승리 후, 영국인들은 베닌의 가장 위대한 문화재였던 1,000개도 넘는 청동 장식판들을 포함해, 엄청난 양의 베닌 예술품을 영국으로 실어 보냈다. 이 조각들 중 약 200개는 대영 박물관으로 보내졌고 다른 것들은 개인 수집가들에게 팔렸다. 그 이후로, 현재 베닌 왕국의 자리에 위치하고 있는 나이지리아는 그 장식판들 중 50개를 박물관으로부터 구입할 수 있었다. 그러나 나이지리아인들은 그것들이 불법적으로 도난되었고 대영 박물관에게는 권리가 없다는 것을 이유로, 모든 장식판을 되돌려 받기를 바라고 있다. 베닌 청동 장식판의 경우는 그런 경우 중 하나일 뿐이다. 세계 곳곳에서, 옛 식민지들은 그들의 문화재를 되돌려줄 것을 요구하고 있다.

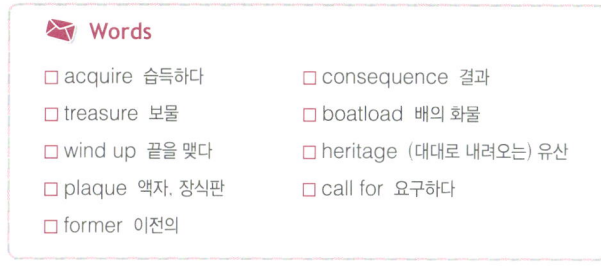

Words

□ acquire 습득하다 □ consequence 결과
□ treasure 보물 □ boatload 배의 화물
□ wind up 끝을 맺다 □ heritage (대대로 내려오는) 유산
□ plaque 액자, 장식판 □ call for 요구하다
□ former 이전의

● ● 해 설 ● ●

1. 첫 문단에 따르면, 유럽 국가들이 다른 나라들로부터 많은 예술품들을 가져왔으며 이는 이 국가들이 전세계적으로 식민지를 가졌던 시대의 결과라고 했다. 그런데 이 예로 이집트를 들었으므로, 이집트 또한 유럽 국가의 식민지였으며, 그 유럽 국가가 이집트에서 많은 예술품들을 가져갔을 것임을 알 수 있다.

2. 8-12째 줄을 읽어보면 15세기부터 제 2차 세계대전 때까지 지속된 식민 지배를 통해서, 유럽 국가들이 식민지로부터 많은 천연 자원과 예술품들을 가져왔다고 했으므로 (D)가 맞는 추론이다. (A)는 이전에 식민 지배를 받던 국가들이 주장하는 내용일 뿐이며, (B)의 Benin은 하나의 예일 뿐이다. 예술품들은 전쟁이 아니라 식민 지배를 통해 습득되었으므로 (C) 또한 옳지 않다.

iBT Practice 1　　　p.132

1. (C)　　2. (B)　　3. (D)　　4. (B)　　5. (C)
6. (A)　　7. (B), (C), (E)

고고학 유적지의 연대 측정

고고학자들은 과거의 문화를 연구하는 과학자들이다. 이런 문화들에 대해서 우리가 알고 있는 대부분의 것들은 그들이 살았던 곳을 조사 해봄으로써 나온다. 예를 들어, 고고학자는 고대의 농장 또는 요새나 도시 유적지를 조사해 볼 수 있다. 고고학자가 서서히 조심스럽게 유적지를 발굴해 가면서 그가 발견하는 옛 도구 같은 것들은, 우리에게 거기에서 살거나 일했던 사람들에 대해 많은 것들을 알려준다. 고고학자들이 그런 유물을 발견하는데 있어 가장 어렵고 중요한 작업 중하나는, 이로써 그 유물이 속해 있던 문화의 발전을 추적할 수 있게 해주기 때문에, 얼마나 오래 되었는지를 알아내는 것이다.

고고학자들은 그들이 발견한 물건의 연대를 알아내기 위해 층서법(層序法, layering, stratigraphy)을 이용한다. 이 이론에 따르면, 흙이 그 위로 더 많이 쌓일 수 있는 시간이 지났기 때문에, 더 깊은 땅에서 발견될수록 그 유물은 더 오래된 것이다. 이것은 고고학자들에게 비교를 위한 기본적인 관점을 제공한다. 고고학자들은 발굴해 가면서, 유물들을 기본적으로 한 층이 다른 층 위에 쌓여 있는 겹 구조로 있는 유물들을 발견한다. 그러면 고고학자들은 특정한 층에서 발견된 유물들은 같은 기본 연대에 속해 있다고 추측할 수 있다. 그러나, 층서법의 문제점 가운데 하나는, 그 방법은 어떤 유물이 같은 유적지에서 발견된 다른 유물들에 비해 더 오래되었는지, 덜 오래되었는지 만을 알려준다는 것이다. 그것은 특정한 유물이 정확히 얼마나 오래되었는지는 알려주지 못한다.

그렇기 때문에, 고고학자들은 방사성탄소연대측정법(radiocarbon dating, C14 dating)을 사용해야 한다. 탄소는 안정적인 탄소12와, 불안정하며 질소로 바뀌게 되는 탄소14의 두 종류의 기본 형태로 존재한다. 이 변화는 일정한 속도로 진행된다. 모든 생물은 몸 속에 같은 비율의 탄소12와 탄소14를 가지고 있다. 그러나 죽게 되면, 탄소14는 몸 속으로 더 이상 들어오지 않게 되고, 탄소14가 질소로 변하게 됨에 따라 그 비율도 천천히 바뀌게 된다. 유적지에서 발굴된 뼈나 식물의 생성물 속의 탄소14의 양을 측정함으로써, 우리는 정확히 그것들이 얼마나 오래 되었는지 알 수 있다.

✉ Words

- archeologist 고고학자
- layering 층서법
- stack 쌓이다
- radiocarbon dating 방사성탄소연대측정법
- eventually 결국
- investigate 조사하다
- determine 알아내다, 밝히다
- steady 일정한, 꾸준한

•• 해 설 ••

1. 앞 문장에서 우리가 아는 과거의 문화는 과거 사람들이 살았던 장소를 조사함으로써 알 수 있다고 한 다음 들어준 예에서 고대 농장의 "site"를 조사할 수 있다고 했으므로, 이것이 위치를 뜻하는 단어임을 알 수 있다.

2. 6-7째 줄 "because this allows them to track the development of the culture the object belonged to"에서 그 이유가 명확하게 진술되어 있다. "the development of the culture"가 "how the civilization progressed"와 같은 의미임을 이해해야 한다.

3. 9째 줄 이하의 "the deeper underground an object is found,

the older it is, because more time has passed to allow dirt to build up over it"의 내용에 따르면, 깊은 곳에서 찾은 것일수록 보통 더 오래된 것이라고 했으므로 삽 밑에서 발견된 칼이 더 오래되었음을 알 수 있다.

4. 문제의 단어가 있는 문장에서, 그들이 땅을 팔 때 보통 "one on top of another"에 쌓여 만들어진 층에서 물체들을 발견한다고 했다. 한 층 위에 다른 한 층이 쌓이는 것이므로, 이것이 "layers(층)"를 가리키는 것임을 알 수 있다.

5. 나이를 측정하는 두 가지의 방법, 즉, layer dating과 radiocarbon dating 중에서 carbon-14는 radiocarbon dating에서의 필수적인 요소이지 layer dating의 필수 요소가 아니다. "convert into"는 "turn into"와 같은 의미이다.

6. 셋째 문단에 나온 radiocarbon dating의 설명에 따르면, carbon-14는 살아 있는 생명만 취할 수 있으며 이 생명이 죽으면 이것이 질소로 바뀌기 때문에, 남아 있는 carbon-14를 측정하는 방법으로 나이를 알 수 있다고 했다. 그러므로 생명이 없는 금속 도구는 이 방법으로 나이를 측정할 수 없다.

7. 이 글의 요약은 주어진 문장인 "어느 곳에서 일하던지 고고학자들이 반드시 알아야 하는 가장 중요한 사실 하나는 그들이 찾는 물체의 나이이다."로 시작하며 물체의 나이를 결정하는 것이 왜 중요한 지와 두 가지의 나이 측정 방법을 제시하는 요약문을 골라야 한다. 그러므로 (B), (C), (E)가 올바른 요약문을 만들며, (A), (D), (F)는 모두 본문의 내용과 맞지 않거나 언급되지 않은 내용이다.

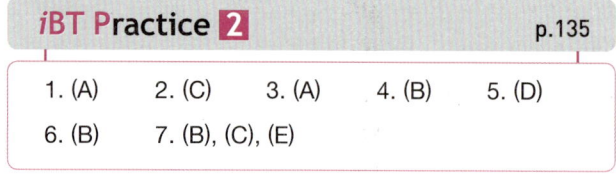

iBT Practice 2   p.135

1. (A)	2. (C)	3. (A)	4. (B)	5. (D)
6. (B)	7. (B), (C), (E)			

귀여움

특별히 동물을 좋아하는 사람이 아닐지라도, 대부분 사람들은 강아지나 새끼 고양이가 귀엽다는 것에 동의할 것이다. 그러나 왜 새끼 고양이나 강아지가 귀여우냐고 묻는다면 대부분의 사람들은 명확한 설명을 하기가 어려울 것이다. 그렇지만, 우리가 이런 동물들을 귀엽다고 여기는 데는 명확한 과학적 이유가 있음이 드러났다. 귀여움은 외적 요인과 이 동물들이 어떻게 행동하는가에 관련있는 요인에 좌우된다. 첫째로, 귀여움은 매우 자주 사람 아기나 많은 새끼 동물이 그런 것처럼, 머리나 눈의 크기에 비해서 작은 몸을 가진 사람이나 동물과 연관이 된다. 행동을 볼 때는, 장난기 많음이 귀여움으로 간주된다. 이것 역시도 새끼들의 특징이다.

이것의 이유는 어떤 동물들은 새끼일 시절에는 귀엽도록 진화해 왔기 때문이다. 이것은 그들이 부모에게 보호를 받을 수 있도록 해 준다. 이런 이론에 대해서는 상당한 양의 증거가 있다. 먼저, 태어난 후 스스로를 보호하지 못하는 동물들은 대부분 포유류이다. 예를 들어서 뱀은 부화한 후 부모의 보호를 필요

로 하지 않는다. 그렇지만, 새끼 뱀은 엄밀하게는 귀엽지가 않다. 확실히 귀여운 새끼 고양이는 그의 일생 중 최소한 첫 몇 달간은 어미의 보살핌을 필요로 한다. 그 보살핌 없이는 새끼 고양이는 거의 분명히 죽을 것이다.

그 이상의 증거는, 그들의 새끼가 아닌, 혹은 심지어 같은 종도 아닌 귀여운 새끼들에 대한 동물들의 반응들로부터 얻을 수 있다. 귀여운 새끼 동물이 다른 종의 어미 동물에게 입양되어 보살핌을 받는 경우가 많이 있다. 가장 널리 알려진 경우는 작은 새끼 고양이를 데려다 키운 실험실 암컷 고릴라의 경우이다. 사람들 속에서도, 그와 같은 반응이 기록된 바가 있다. 인간들은 일상적으로 귀여운 동물들을 데려다 키우며 보살핀다. 더욱이, 심리학 연구에 따르면, 어른 동물들은 귀엽다고 여겨지는 새끼들에게 더 긍정적으로 반응하며, 또 관심을 보일 가능성도 높다. 즉, 귀여움은 단순히 견해가 아니라, 그것은 우리 모두가 갖고 있는 본능적인 반응이다.

✉ Words

- ☐ factor 요인
- ☐ evolve 진화하다
- ☐ be associated with 연관이 있는
- ☐ response 반응
- ☐ playfulness 장난기 많음
- ☐ instinctive 본능적인
- ☐ reaction 반응
- ☐ routinely 일상적으로

•• 해 설 ••

1. 5째 줄 이하의 "Cuteness apparently depends on a few factors... This is again another characteristic of babies." 내용에 따르면, 귀여움이란 사이즈와 행동과 관련되어 있다고 했다. 즉, 눈과 머리에 비해 작은 몸집과 장난기 많음이다.

2. 10-11째 줄의 "This makes sure that they are cared for by their parents."에서 알 수 있다.

3. 2번째 문단의 내용에 따르면, 귀여움은 보살핌을 받기 위한 중요한 요소이며, 스스로 돌볼 능력이 없는 동물들이 대부분 포유류 새끼들인데 이들이 귀엽다고 예를 들어 설명했다. 정답으로 오인하기 쉬운 (C)는 사람들이 귀여운 동물을 많이 데려와 키운다는 언급은 있으나, 이것들이 좋은 애완동물인지에 대해선 말하지 않았으므로 답이 될 수 없다.

4. 이 문단에서 설명하고 있는 내용은 모두 귀여운 새끼들에게 대하는 다른 동물들의 행동이다. 그러므로, 이 단어가 '~에 대한 행동' 즉, '반응'을 의미함을 짐작해 볼 수 있다.

5. 지문에 주어진 단서가 없으므로, 보기 중 문맥에 대입해 보았을 때 가장 적합한 단어를 고르도록 한다.

6. 주어진 문장은 다음 네 개의 의미 단위로 이루어져 있다. "게다가 심리학 연구들이 보여준다 / 어른들은 좀더 긍정적으로 반응하며 / 더 많은 관심을 보인다는 것을 / 귀엽다고 생각되는 새끼들에게" (B)만이 모든 의미 단위의 내용을 정확하게 담고 있으며, "react positively"와 "respond better"가 같은 의미임을 이해해야 한다.

7. "과학자들은 이제 귀여움이 사실상 진화적 전략이라고 믿게 되었다." 이에 이어지는 요약문은, 귀여움이란 뜻의 정의와 귀여움이 가져다주는 혜

택, 그리고 이에 관한 증거들이 제시되어야 한다. 따라서 (B), (C), (E)가 옳은 답이며, (A)는 부연 설명일 뿐이고, (D)는 고릴라가 언급되긴 했지만 보기와 같은 내용은 없으며, (F)는 언급되지 않은 내용이다.

Vocabulary Review   p.138

1. (D)   2. (A)   3. (C)   4. (B)   5. (D)

6. (A)   7. (C)   8. (B)

9. witnessed   10. Heritage

11. represent   12. exposed

13. citizens   14. unsuitable

15. debates   16. defines

7

Rhetorical Purpose

Basic Drills (1)　　　　p.142

> 1. (1)　　2. (2)　　3. (1)

1. 숲 전체를 베어 없애는 삼림 벌채는 어디에 살던 간에 모든 사람들의 문제이다. 삼림 벌채는 지구 온난화, 더 잦은 가뭄, 폭우로 인한 극심한 피해 같은 지구 전체에 영향을 주는 많은 문제를 발생시킨다. 그러므로, 브라질 같은 나라에서의 삼림 벌채는 브라질 사람들뿐만 아니라, 세계 모든 곳의 사람들에게 영향을 준다.

2. 대부분 사회는 범죄자들을 처벌함으로써 범죄에 대처한다. 처벌도 필요하지만, 범죄를 다루는 데에는 예방이 훨씬 더 효과적이다. 대부분 범죄는 빈곤 또는 교육의 결여와 같은 사회적 요인들로 인한 결과이다. 이러한 사회적 요인들은 사람들에게 정직한 삶을 살 수 있는 기회를 거의 주지 않고, 범죄를 더 유혹적인 대안으로 만든다. 범죄 처벌에 돈을 쓰는 대신에, 그 돈을 빈곤과 교육 개선에 더 많이 사용한다면, 범죄를 상당히 줄일 수 있을 것이다.

3. 악기를 배울 때, 제대로 된 연습 스케줄은 발전을 위해 매우 중요하다. 연습은 매일 해야 하고, 더 긴 시간 동안이라면 좋겠지만, 최소한 30분은 해야 한다. 연습은 근육을 이완시키고 긴장을 풀어 주는 짧은 워밍업으로 시작해야 한다. 그 뒤는 특정한 하나의 기술이나 기법에 집중하는 시간이 따라야 한다. 이것이 연습 시간 대부분을 차지해야 한다. 마지막으로, 학생이 악기에 대한 관심을 유지할 수 있도록, 즐기기 위한 연주를 할 시간도 주어져야 한다.

• • 해 설 • •

1. 산림벌채가 전 세계적으로 일으키고 있는 현상과 문제점에 관해 설명하는 글이다.

2. 범죄를 징벌로써 다스리는 것과 예방하는 것, 두 방법을 제시하며 자신이 주장하는 의견을 뒷받침하고 있다.

3. 악기를 배우는 바람직한 연습 스케줄 절차와 내용을 나열하고 있다.

Basic Drills (2)　　　　p.143

> 1. (C)　　2. (B)

1. 산업 혁명은 19세기말 동안 대부분 나라에서 일어났다. 산업혁명의 한가지 큰 영향은 그것이 근로자와 고용자간의 관계를 변화시킨 것이다. 이전까지 근로자들은 작은 상점에서 일했고 고용자와는 개인적인 관계를 맺었었다. 그러나 일이백 명이 되는 근로자가 있는 공장에서는 소유주가 근로자들의 이름조차도 모를 수 있다. 게다가, 근로자들은 그저 기계만을 운용하면 되었기 때문에, 그들은 이전 시대의 숙련된 근로자들보다도 쉽게 교체될 수 있었다. 이 두 가지 요인들은 많은 근로자들의 조건을 악화되도록 이끌었다.

2. 사회들에는 하향식(top-down)과 상향식(bottom-up)으로 불리는 두 가지의 기본적인 의사 결정 방법이 존재한다. 하향식 의사 결정에서는, 결정은 한 사람의 지도자나 소규모 사람들로 이루어진다. 이런 결정들은 그 후 모두가 따라야 하는 법으로 만들어진다. 상향식 의사 결정에서는, 전체 집단이 문제에 대해 토론하고, 동의에 이르렀을 경우에만 의사 결정이 내려진다. 하향식 의사 결정은 빠르고 효율적이라는 장점이 있다. 이것은 모든 사람들이 적절한 결정을 내기 위해서 충분한 정보를 갖지 못할 수도 있는 큰 규모의 의사 결정에 좋다. 하향식 의사 결정의 주된 결점은, 최소한 누군가는 그 결정에 만족하지 못할 것이라는 점이다. 집단의 모든 구성원들의 동의를 바탕으로 하는 상향식 의사 결정에서는, 그 같은 문제점은 없지만, 상향식으로 의사 결정을 할 경우에는 집단이 결정을 도출해 내기까지 훨씬 오래 걸릴 것이다.

• • 해 설 • •

1. 19세기 산업 혁명으로 인한 변화로 일꾼들이 더욱 악화된 환경에서 일하게 되었다는 내용이다.

2. 두 개의 의견 결정 방법을 제시한 후, 그 둘을 대조하며 글을 전개하고 있다.

Basic Drills (3)　　　　p.144

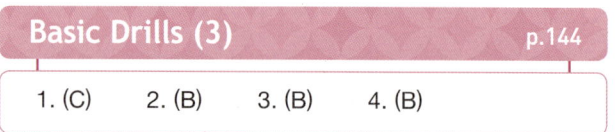

> 1. (C)　　2. (B)　　3. (B)　　4. (B)

1. 스페인 사람들이 처음 남아메리카에 상륙했을 때, 아메리카 원주민 문명들은 그들을 경외했다. 그러나 스페인 사람들이 그들을 노예로 만들거나 부를 훔쳐 가는 데에만 관심이 있다는 것을 알게 되자, 원주민들은 맞서 싸우기 시작했다. 스페인 사람들은 몇 백 명에 불과했고, 아메리카 원주민 전사들 수는 수만이었다. 그러나, 아메리카 원주민들의 돌로 된 무기는 스페인의 갑옷에는 아무 쓸모가 없었기 때문에 스페인 사람들에게 그것은 마치 어린아이들과 싸우는 것 같았다.

2. 개발도상국들이 직면하는 가장 큰 문제들 가운데 하나는 인구 증가이다. 한 나라 인구가 너무 빨리 증가하거나, 또는 어느 특정한 한계 이상으로 증가할 경우, 그 나라는 시민들을 먹이기 위한 충분한 양의 식량을 기르지 못하게 될 수도 있다. 아프리카, 아시아, 그리고 남아메리카의 많은 곳에서 이것은 심각한 문제이다. 예를 들어, 케냐는 4%의 인구 증가율을 가지고 있다. 이는 케냐 인구가 매 17년마다 두 배로 증가한다는 것이다. 전체적인 시야로 보기 위해서, 그 증가율을 미국 도시에 적용해 보자. 워싱턴(Washington) D.C.는 4백만 명의 인구를 갖고 있다. 만약 워싱턴

D.C.가 4%의 인구 증가율을 갖는다면, 그 인구는 2020년에는 8백만 명, 2040년에는 1천6백만 명이 될 것이다! 그런 급격한 증가가 부유한 나라들의 경우에도 문제가 될 것임이 분명한 만큼, 케냐와 같은 가난한 나라에서 그로 인해 생길 문제점들을 상상하기는 쉬울 것이다.

3. 어떤 사학자들은 그들 행동이 어떤 식으로든 세계를 변화시키던, 적은 수의 사람들에 의해서 역사가 결정된다고 믿는다. 영웅 이론(Great Man Theory)이라고 불리는 이 이론은, 이런 사람들이 없더라면 세계의 큰 변화들도 일어나지 않았을 것이라고 주장한다. 아이작 뉴턴(Sir Issac Newton)의 중력의 발견은 현대 천문학과 물리학의 기반을 이루었다. 아인슈타인(Einstein)의 상대성 이론의 발견은 원자력으로의 길로 인도했고, 이는 단지 두 가지 예에 불과하다. 그러나, 어떤 사람들은 영웅 이론에 의문을 품는다. 그들은 한 사람이 사는 시대가 그 사람 자신보다 더 중요하다고 주장한다. 예를 들어, 아인슈타인의 상대성 이론에 대한 업적은 1800년대 말 과학자들의 업적을 기반으로 한 것이었다. 게다가 상대성 이론에 대해서 연구하던 과학자가 아인슈타인만이었던 것은 아니다. 그 문제에 대해서 다른 과학자들도 연구 중이었다. 아인슈타인은 그저 그것을 풀어낸 첫 사람일뿐이었다.

4. 고대 문명의 왕들은 왜 백성들이 그들을 따르고 섬겨야 하는지를 설명하기 위한 이유가 필요했다. 가장 오래된 문명들에서, 왕들은 스스로를 신이라고 주장하거나, 그들의 신과 직접적으로 연결되어 있다고 주장함으로써 그들의 지배를 정당화시켰다. 그 논리는, 백성들이 그들을 섬기지 않을 경우 신이 벌을 내릴 거라는 것이었다. 기본적으로, 백성들은 왕을 위해 일하고 왕은 신이 일으킨 것이라고 믿어진 자연 재해로부터 백성들을 보호해 주는 식의 거래가 있는 셈이었다. 그러므로, 왕권에 대한 가장 큰 위협은 다른 정치인들부터가 아니라 단순한 불운으로부터였다. 역사 자료들은 고대의 왕들이 권력을 잃었던 때가 홍수나, 질병 또는 다른 자연 재해가 잦았던 때임을 알려준다

• • 해 설 • •

1. 원주민들의 수가 훨씬 많았음에도 불구하고, 그들의 구식 석기 무기로 스페인 군과 싸워 이기는 것은 불가능했다는 것을 강조하기 위해. 이를 어린 아이들과 싸우는 것과 같다고 비유했다.

2. 케냐의 인구증가율을 워싱턴 D.C.의 인구수에 대입함으로써, 이 인구증가율이 얼마나 높은 것인지 보다 선명하게 보여주고 있다.

3. 몇몇 개인의 업적에 의해 역사가 만들어진다는 이론을 반박하기 위한 글이다. 아인슈타인 외에도 다른 많은 과학자들이 상대성 이론을 연구하고 있었다는 예는 이를 뒷받침하기 위한 근거이다.

4. 많은 왕이 권력을 잃은 때가 큰 자연재해가 있을 때였다는 설명으로, 옛날 왕들에게 가장 큰 위협은 다른 정치세력이 아닌 단순한 운에 달려있었다는 이론을 뒷받침하고 있다.

Reading Practice 1   p.146

1. (C)   2. (A)

Words ❶ defense ❷ nutrients ❸ lessen ❹ quality

비버 댐

비버는 큰 설치류 동물로서 북아메리카와 유럽 대부분의 하천에 산다. 비버는 그들이 만드는 댐이나, 그 댐을 만드는데 사용할 나무를 갉아 넘어뜨리는 능력으로 널리 알려져 있다. 비버 댐의 주목적은 방어이며, 댐과 그 위에 형성되는 못은 곰이나 늑대 같은 포식 동물이 비버에 접근할 수 없도록 보호해 준다. 댐을 만들기 위해 비버는 하천의 양쪽의 나무들이 하천으로 넘어질 수 있도록 갉아 넘어트린다. 그런 나무들은 기본적으로 하천에서 교통 체증이 일어나도록 함으로 유속을 늦춘다. 시간이 흐르면서, 작은 가지, 잎사귀와 다른 것들이 쌓여 하천의 유속을 더욱 늦춘다. 그러면 비버는 큰 나뭇가지들을 이용해 댐을 보강하고, 그렇게 댐은 완성된다.

비버 댐은 긍정적 또는 부정적으로 자연에 많은 영향을 끼친다. 첫째로 가장 중요하게, 비버 댐은 댐 상류 하천의 유속을 늦춘다. 이것은 여러 중요한 일을 한다. 첫째, 빠르게 흐르는 하천은 하천 양변의 흙을 쓸어 가는데, 이는 결국 식물들이 필요로 하는 중요한 흙과 영양분을 뺏어 가는 것이다. 하천의 유속을 늦춤으로써, 비버는 이런 영향을 줄여 준다. 게다가 하천의 느린 유속은 하천이 빨리 흐를 경우와는 달리 하천수 속에 들어 있는 흙이 바닥으로 가라앉을 수 있도록 해 준다. 이는 사람들과 동물들이 마시는 수질을 향상시킨다. 비버 댐은 하천 주위에서 발견되는 식물 종류도 변화시킨다. 비버들이 댐을 만들기 위해서 나무를 베어 없애기 때문에, 숲은 덜 울창해지고, 덤불이나 꽃이 자랄 수 있는 열린 공간을 남긴다. 그러므로, 비버 댐들은 숲에 더 많은 종류의 식물을 더해 준다.

✉ Words

□ rodent 설치 동물   □ defense 방어
□ ensure 확실히 하다   □ predator 포식 동물, 약탈자
□ dig away 계속해서 파 나가다   □ nutrient 영양분
□ lessen 줄이다   □ quality 질

• • 해 설 • •

1. 비버가 댐을 만들어 물을 막는 모양을 교통 체증을 유발하는 것과 같다고 비유함으로써. 나뭇가지나 줄기들 같은 물체로 어떤 모양으로 물을 막게 되는지 머리 속으로 그 모양을 그려볼 수 있게 해 준다.

2. 비버가 만드는 댐이 많은 면에서 환경을 변화시킨다고 하면서, '첫째로 가장 중요하게, 비버 댐은 댐 상류 하천의 유속을 늦춘다'고 했다. 그러고 나서 이로 인해 생기는 부수적인 효과들을 나열했으므로. 이 문장이 비버 댐으로 생기는 여러 효과의 설명에 앞서 그것의 원인이 되는 가장 중요한 점을 제시하는 문장이라는 것을 알 수 있다.

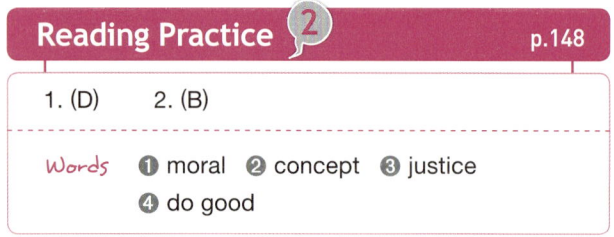

Reading Practice 2   p.148

1. (D)   2. (B)

Words   ❶ moral   ❷ concept   ❸ justice
           ❹ do good

소크라테스 교육법

대부분의 학생들은 그들이 질문을 하고, 선생님이 답을 하는 교실에 익숙해져 있다. 그런데, 만약 당신이 선생님이 모든 질문을 하고 당신이 답을 해야 하는 교실 안에 있다면 어떻게 하겠는가? 이런 경우라면, 당신 선생님은 소크라테스 교육법을 사용하고 있는 것이다. 소크라테스 교육법은 기원전 4세기, 고대 그리스의 위대한 철학자인 소크라테스에 의해서 개발되었다. 소크라테스 교육법은 정의의 의미와 같은 도덕적 개념을 가르치는데 사용된다. 소크라테스 교육법에서, 교사는 하나의 주제에 대한 일련의 질문에 답하도록 학생에게 묻는다. 질문의 목적은 학생의 사고 방식의 취약점을 지적하고, 더 견실하고 훌륭한 생각으로 이끌기 위함이다.

소크라테스 교육법은 교사들에 의해 2,500여 년 동안 사용되었고, 오늘날도 사용되고 있다. 그것은 장점과 단점을 모두 갖고 있다. 가장 중요한 장점은, 그 방법이 학생 스스로 생각하도록 강요한다는 것이다. 학생은 스스로의 생각을 점검해야 하고, 교사가 그의 사고방식의 문제점을 지적할 경우, 종종 그 생각을 바꾸기도 해야 한다. 이것은 교사가 학생에게 단순히 무엇이 옳고 무엇이 그른지를 알려주는 경우보다 훨씬 더 견실한 사고로 이끈다. 단점은, 소크라테스 교육법을 제대로 사용하기 위해서는 고도로 숙련된 교사가 필요하다는 것이다. 교사는 학생에게 그들의 사고의 취약점을 보여줄 수 있는 질문들을 할 수 있어야 한다. 이것은 언제나 쉬운 일인 것은 아니다. 더구나, 소크라테스 교육법은 특히 과학적인 개념과 같은 어떤 종류의 개념을 가르치는 데에는 유용하지 않다. 과학 지식은 보통 실험과 자연 세계에 대한 면밀한 관찰로부터 얻어진다. 그러한 실험을 한 적이 없는 학생에게 단지 질문을 하는 것은 별 도움이 되지 못할 것이다.

📩 Words

□ moral 도덕적인   □ concept 개념
□ justice 정의   □ properly 적절하게
□ experimentation 실험(법)   □ observation 관찰
□ do good 이익이 되다

•• 해 설 ••

1. 어떤 것이 오랫동안 많은 사람들에 의해 사용된다는 것은 보통 그것이 쓸모가 있기 때문이다. 따라서, Socratic method가 2,500년이라는 오랜 시간 동안, 그리고 현재에도 계속 사용되고 있다는 것은 이 방법이 효과적이라는 것을 증명해 주는 사실이라고 볼 수 있다.

2. '과학적인 지식의 습득은 보통 자연 세계에 대한 면밀한 실험과 관찰로부터 온다'고 언급함으로써, 이와는 다른 방법을 쓰는 교육 방법인 Socratic method가 과학적인 개념을 가르치는 데는 유용하지 않다는 것을 뒷받침

하고 있다.

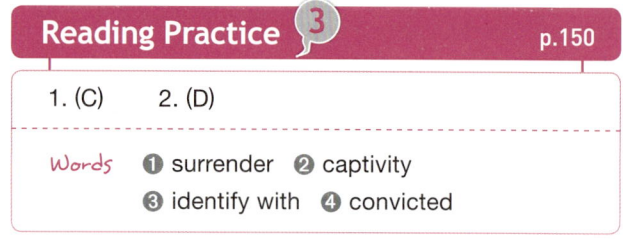

Reading Practice 3   p.150

1. (C)   2. (D)

Words   ❶ surrender   ❷ captivity
           ❸ identify with   ❹ convicted

스톡홀름 증후군

심리학자들은 사람들이 매우 긴장되는 상황에 놓이게 되면 종종 잘 설명하기 어려운 행동을 보일 수도 있다는 것을 오래 전부터 알고 있었다. 이것의 좋은 예는 1973년에 일어났던 실패한 은행 강도 사건의 이름을 딴 스톡홀름 증후군이 있다. 은행 직원들과 손님들은 경찰이 물러나지 않을 경우에는 죽여 버리겠다고 협박하는 강도들에게 인질로 붙잡혔다. 엿새 후, 위기는 평화적으로 해결되었고, 은행 강도들은 항복했다. 모두에게 놀라운 일은, 인질들이 은행 강도들을 옹호했다는 것과, 심지어 어떤 인질은 은행 강도 중 한 명과 오랫동안 친분을 유지했다는 것이다. 인질이 인질범에게 감정적으로 가까워지는 이와 같은 현상은, 다른 인질들의 기록에도 남아 있다.

스톡홀름 증후군의 원인은 잘 이해되지 않는다. 그런 현상은 모든 인질들에게서 나타나지 않으며, 사실 대부분 인질들은 전혀 그런 징조도 보이지 않는다. 증후군이 나타나는 사람들은 그러나 종종 인질로서 비슷한 경험을 가진다. 첫째, 그들은 대개 생명에 가장 위기를 느끼는 인질들이다. 스톡홀름 인질들은 인질범들로부터 계속적으로 생명의 위협을 받았었다. 더욱이, 스톡홀름 증후군을 보이는 인질들은 대개 경찰이 그들을 구출해 낼 것이라는 믿음이 거의 없었다고 얘기한다. 마지막으로, 더 오랫동안 잡혀 있을수록, 인질들은 스스로를 인질범들과 더욱 동일화하는 것으로 보인다.

때때로, 스톡홀름 증후군은 형사 소송 사건의 변호를 위해 사용되었다. 가장 유명한 예는 패티 허스트(Patty Hearst)의 경우이다. 그녀는 납치를 당해 몸값 때문에 붙잡혀 있었다. 그러나, 얼마가 지나서 그녀는 그 인질범들을 지지하게 되었고, 결국 은행 강도나 다른 범죄에도 그들과 함께 가담했다. 결국 그녀가 잡히자, 그녀는 그런 범죄에 가담한 죄 때문에 재판에 회부되었다. 변호를 위해, 그녀는 스톡홀름 증후군을 겪었다고 주장했다. 결국 유죄로 징역을 선고받게 됨으로써 그녀의 변호는 성공적이지 못했다. 그러나 나중에, 그녀는 그녀가 결백하다고 생각했던 카터(Carter) 대통령에 의해서 석방되었다.

📩 Words

□ surrender 항복하다   □ to one's surprise 놀랍게도
□ phenomenon 현상   □ captor 체포자
□ captivity 포로(의 상태)   □ identify with~ ~와 동일시하다
□ ransom 몸값   □ put on trial 재판에 부치다
□ convict 유죄를 입증하다

•• 해 설 ••

1. 모든 사람이 스톡홀름 증후군에 걸리기 쉬운 건 아니라고 했다. 두 번째 문

단에서 스톡홀름 증후군에 걸린 사람들이 가진 공통된 경험 즉, ①생명에 가장 위기를 느끼는 인질들이며, ②경찰이 그들이 구출할 것이라는 믿음이 부족했고, ③오랜 시간 동안 잡혀 있었다는 점을 제시함으로, 오히려 이 경험들이 스톡홀름 증후군의 원인일지도 모른다는 의견을 소개하고 있다.

2. 마지막 단락에서 스톡홀름 증후군이 때때로 법정에서 피고를 변호하기 위해서 쓰여 왔다는 것을 뒷받침하기 위해, Patty Hearst의 경우를 예로 들고 있다.

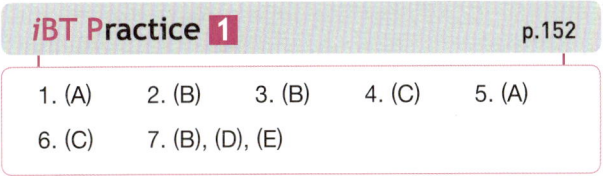

iBT Practice 1   p.152

1. (A)	2. (B)	3. (B)	4. (C)	5. (A)
6. (C)	7. (B), (D), (E)			

아타카마(Atacama) 사막

지구상에서 가장 메마른 지방은 페루(Peru)와 칠레(Chile)의 서해안을 따라 위치한 아타카마 사막이다. 아타카마 사막은 지구상의 사막 중 유일한데, 이 것은 기본적으로 아무런 생명체도 없기 때문이다. 대부분 사막에는 최소한 전갈, 뱀, 그리고 도마뱀 종류를 비롯한 몇몇 생명체가 살고 있다. 그러나 아타카마에는 이러한 동물도 없다. 사실, 과학자들은 생명체를 찾기 위해 화성의 흙을 조사하던 때 사용한 것과 똑같은 장비를 아타카마 사막 흙에서 생명체를 찾기 위해 사용했으며, 그 결과는 화성의 경우와 비슷했다. 아타카마 연 평균 강수량이 3 밀리미터이고, 가끔씩은 40년 동안이나 비가 오지 않는 경우도 있다는 것을 안다면, 이것은 전혀 놀라운 일이 아니다.

아타카마는 기본적으로 해안(coastal) 사막이다. 해안 사막은 아프리카와 남북 아메리카의 서해안에서 발견된다. 해안 사막은 해안 주변 한류 때문에 발생한다. 이 한류가 대기를 식힌다. 대기의 함수 능력은 기온의 기능이기 때문에, 이런 해류 위를 지나는 바람은 매우 건조해진다. 그러나, 대부분 해안 사막에는 최소한 어느 정도의 비는 내린다. 비록 매우 메마른 곳이기는 하지만 캘리포니아 서해안의 해안 사막에는, 아타카마의 50배만큼의 비가 내린다.

아타카마 사막을 다른 해안 사막보다 더욱 메마르게 만드는 이유는 그것이 또한 비 그늘(rain shadow) 사막이기 때문이다. 비 그늘 사막은 칠레와 페루의 안데스(Andes) 산맥 같은 높은 산맥 아래에서 찾을 수 있다. 비구름은 보통 2,000에서 10,000 피트 상공에서 형성된다. 이보다 높은 산들은 비구름이 반대쪽으로 이동하는 것을 막게 된다. 역시 이것은 대기 온도와 큰 관련이 있다. 등산을 해 본 사람이라면 누구나 높이 오를수록 더 추워진다는 것을 알고 있을 것이다. 이것 역시 대기를 건조하게 만든다. 그 결과, 비는 양쪽으로부터 아타카마로 들어가지 못하게 막힌다. 한류는 비가 서쪽의 태평양에서부터 오는 것을 막고, 안데스 산맥은 동쪽의 습윤한 지역으로부터 비가 오는 것을 막는다.

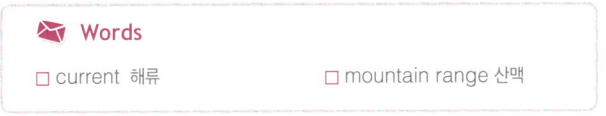

📧 **Words**
☐ current 해류   ☐ mountain range 산맥

1. 아타카마 사막이 세계에서 가장 건조한 사막이라고 했지, 해안 사막의 특성이 그렇다고 하지는 않았다. 또한 둘째 문단에 따르면 대부분 해안 사막에는 약간의 비가 내린다고 되어 있다.

2. 아타카마 사막을 전혀 생명체가 살 수 없다고 알려진 '화성의 토양'에 비교하여 설명하므로, 아타카마 사막이 얼마나 황량하고 생명이 살 수 없는지 강조하고 있음을 알 수 있다.

3. 공기가 수분을 포함할 수 있는 능력이 기온의 기능이라는 말은, 그것이 기온에 의해 조절되므로 기온과 직접적인 관련이 있음을 나타내는 것이다.

4. 아타카마 사막은 해안 사막에 속하지만 다른 어떤 해안 사막에 비해 훨씬 더 건조하다는 것을 강조하고 보여주기 위해, 같은 해안 사막이지만 50배가 더 넘는 강우량을 가지는 캘리포니아 서쪽 해안가에 있는 사막을 예를 들어 대조하며 설명하고 있다.

5. 보통 구름은 2,000에서 10,000 피트 사이에 형성되고, 산이 이보다 높아 구름을 막으면 비그늘 사막이 생기는데, 바로 안데스 산맥 주위에서 이런 비그늘 사막들이 발견되므로 안데스 산맥이 10,000 피트 이상으로 높을 것임을 추론 할 수 있다.

6. 마지막 문장인 "The cold water currents block rain from coming in off the Pacific Ocean to the west, and the Andes Mountains block any rain coming from the wetter regions to the east."에 따르면, 아타카마 사막을 형성하는 두 가지 요인, 해안 사막과 비그늘 사막의 두 특성이 합쳐져 이 사막이 다른 어떤 사막보다도 더 건조하다는 것을 알 수 있다.

7. 주어진 요약문의 첫 문장은 다음과 같다. "아타카마는 지구에서 가장 건조한 사막이다." 이 글은 아타카마 사막의 건조함과 그 두 원인을 설명하는 내용으로 이루어져 있는 글이다. 그러므로 그 두 원인인 (B), (D)와 글의 결론인 (E)를 고르도록 한다. (A)와 (C)는 아타카마의 건조함을 강조하기 위한 부연 설명이며, (F)는 본문의 내용과 일치하지 않는다.

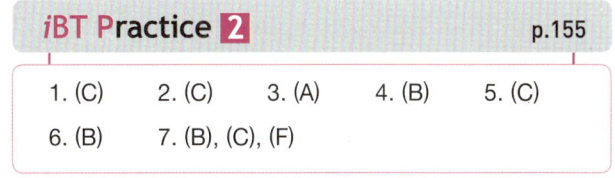

iBT Practice 2   p.155

1. (C)	2. (C)	3. (A)	4. (B)	5. (C)
6. (B)	7. (B), (C), (F)			

이집트의 오벨리스크(Obelisk)

고대 이집트는 피라미드로 유명하지만, 이집트인들이 건설한 기념물에는 피라미드만 있는 것이 아니다. 이집트인들은 오벨리스크도 만들었다. 워싱턴(Washington) D.C.에 위치한 워싱턴 기념비(Washington Monument)의 사진을 본 적이 있는 사람이라면, 이미 오벨리스크의 형태와 이미 익숙한 것이다. 이런 거대하고 늘씬한 기념비들은 땅 위에 꽂힌 거대한 연필을 닮은 형태로 곧추 서 있다. 이집트의 오벨리스크는 종교적인 대상물로, 사원의 입구에 마법의 방호물로써 세워졌다. 오벨리스크의 꼭대기는 그 속에 살

고 있다고 믿었던 이집트의 태양의 신인 라(Ra)를 나타내기 위해 얇은 황금 층을 입혀 밝게 빛나도록 되어 있었다.

오벨리스크 건설은 매우 어려운 작업이었다. 오벨리스크 높이는 평균적으로 100 피트 정도였고, 하나의 돌을 잘라 만들어졌다. 그 후, 이 돌은 돌이 절단된 곳에서부터 어떤 경우에는 수 마일씩 떨어져 있던 사원으로 이동되었다. 다음 단계는 오벨리스크 네 개의 모든 면에 기호를 새겨 넣는 것이었다. 이런 새김은 오벨리스크의 예술적, 문화적 가치를 나타냈다. 일반적으로, 그 새김문양은 단순히 오벨리스크의 건설을 지시했던 파라오에 대한 찬양이다. 그것들은 전쟁에서의 그의 승리, 국내에서의 정책, 그리고 그의 다른 업적들을 알려준다. 그러므로, 오벨리스크들은 고대 이집트에 대해서 우리가 알고 있는 많은 것들을 얻어내는 중요한 역사적 기록을 형성한다. 새김이 끝나면, 이집트인들은 무게가 수백 톤이나 나가는 거대한 돌을 들어서 세워야만 했다. 사학자들은 아직도 그들이 이것을 어떻게 했는지 확실하게는 모르지만, 그것은 분명히 길고 힘든 과정이었을 것이다.

현재까지도 남아 서 있는 27개 오벨리스크 중 많은 수는 이탈리아에 위치해 있다. 사실, 이탈리아에는 이집트보다도 더 많은 오벨리스크가 있다. 그것은 로마인들이 이집트를 점령한 후 많은 이집트 오벨리스크들을 가져갔기 때문이다. 로마인들은 오벨리스크를 경기장의 중앙을 표시하기 위해 사용했다. 그러므로, 콜로세움(coliseum)이라고 불린 로마의 경기장 유적 속에서 이집트의 오벨리스크를 찾을 수 있다. 18세기에는 나폴레옹(Napoleon)도 이집트의 예술적, 문화적 보물을 더욱 약탈해 가서, 프랑스에도 몇 개의 오벨리스크가 있다. 훔친 보물을 이집트로 돌려주려는 운동이 일어나고는 있지만, 유럽의 오염된 공기로 인해 다수가 상당한 손상을 입었다.

✉ Words

□ monument 기념물　　　　　□ carve 새기다, 조각하다
□ pharaoh 파라오　　　　　　□ conquer 점령하다, 정복하다
□ midpoint 중앙, 중심점　　　□ coliseum 콜로세움
□ loot 약탈하다

•• 해 설 ••

1. 오벨리스크 모양을 더 잘 설명하기 위해, 독자가 쉽게 연상할 수 있도록 그와 비슷하게 생긴 '워싱턴 기념비(Washington Monument)'의 예를 들었다.

2. 오벨리스크가 고대 이집트인들에게 어떠한 중요 기능으로 쓰였는지 묻는 문제이다. 5째 줄 이하 "The Egyptian obelisks were religious objects, and were placed at the entrance of temples as magical protection."의 내용에서 이것들은 신전 입구에 마법의 보호막으로써 놓였다고 했다.

3. 주어진 문장은 다음 세 개의 의미 단위로 이루어져 있다. "오벨리스크의 꼭대기는 얇은 금으로 덮여있었다 / 밝게 빛날 수 있도록 / 이것은 그들이 그 안에 살고 있다고 믿었던 이집트의 태양신 Ra를 나타내는 것이었다" 원래 문장의 의미를 왜곡하지 않고 모두 가지고 있는 것은 (A) 뿐이다. 태양신이 오벨리스크 안에 살고 있거나 살 수 있다고 생각했던 것은, 이집트인들이 믿었던 바일 뿐 사실은 아니므로 (B), (D)는 오답이며, 이집트인들

이 그들의 태양신이 그 안에 살고 있다고 믿게 하기 위해서 오벨리스크의 꼭대기를 금으로 씌운 것도 아니므로 (C) 또한 틀린 내용이다.

4. 6째 줄 이하 "The tops of obelisks were covered in a thin layer of gold…"에 따르면 오벨리스크의 꼭대기가 금으로 씌워져 있다고 했지, 오벨리스크 전체가 금으로 덮여 있다고 하지는 않았다.

5. 오벨리스크 표면의 새김들이 갖는 의미와 가치는 둘째 문단 12-16째 줄 "These carvings represent the artistic… we have taken much of our knowledge of ancient Egypt."에 진술되어 있다. 즉 이 새김들은 파라오의 업적을 찬양하는 내용이며, 이 내용으로 인해 우리가 현재 알고 있는 많은 이집트의 역사를 알 수 있다고 한 점을 유의하자.

6. 다음 문장 "Moves are being made to return some of these stolen treasures to Egypt,"의 "these stolen treasures(이 훔쳐진 보물들)"라는 표현에서 나폴레옹이 이집트로부터 이 보물들을 훔쳐 간 것임을 짐작해 볼 수 있다.

7. 주어진 요약문의 첫 문장은 다음과 같다. "오벨리스크는 고대 이집트인들이 그들의 신전을 보호하기 위해 사용했던 크고 얇은 유물이다." 이 글은 오벨리스크에 관해, 첫째 문단은 그것의 모양, 둘째 문단은 건축과 그 위에 새겨져 있는 문양의 의미와 가치, 그리고 셋째 문단은 오벨리스크의 역사에 대해 다루고 있다. 문제에 주어진 요약문의 첫 문장은 오벨리스크의 모양을 나타내므로 건축 방법을 진술하고 있는 (B), 새김에 대해 설명하는 (C), 역사의 요약인 (F)가 답이 된다. (A)와 (E)는 틀린 내용이며, (D)는 부연 설명이다.

Vocabulary Review ＿＿＿＿＿ p.158

1. (D)	2. (A)	3. (C)	4. (B)	5. (C)
6. (C)	7. (A)	8. (C)		
9. justify		10. regardless of		
11. efficient		12. proper		
13. do good		14. moral		
15. identify with		16. poverty		

Sentence Insertion

1. (B), (E), (C), (A), (D)
2. (B), (D), (A), (E), (C)

1. (1) 연구에 따르면, 침팬지들은 돕는데 추가의 노력이 들지 않더라도, 다른 침팬지들을 도우려 하지 않으려 한다.

(2) 학자들은 유인원들이 그들의 집단 속에서 강한 친교를 형성해 왔고, 이런 친교는 서로를 돕는 것에 기초한다고 생각해 왔다.

(3) 그러나, 이것이 거짓이라는, 또는 최소한 침팬지들간의 관계의 본질이 잘못 이해되어 왔다는 새로운 증거가 있다.

(4) 그 같은 의외의 발견은, 많은 학자들에게 침팬지들의 집단 행동에 대해 우리가 사실이라고 믿어 왔던 것들에 대해서 다시 생각하도록 만들었다.

(5) 이런 생각은 서로 진드기와 벼룩을 잡으며 털을 다듬어 주며 대부분의 시간을 보내는 야생의 침팬지들을 관찰함으로써 나왔다.

2. (1) 최근에, 중국인들이 북아메리카의 서해안까지도 진출했을 수 있다는 증거가 발견되었다.

(2) 마르코 폴로(Marco Polo)의 도착 이전까지, 중국인들은 세계에서 가장 진보된 배와 가장 큰 규모의 범선 한대를 갖고 있었다.

(3) 이러한 경쟁의 부재는 바다를 유럽인들에게 넘겨주었고 그들이 바다의 주인이 될 수 있는 길도 열어 주었다.

(4) 그들의 배는 인도와 아프리카 동해안까지 닿았고, 현지인들과의 통상을 시작했다.

(5) 그렇지만, 어떤 이유에선가, 중국인들은 장거리 바다 탐험을 그만두었고, 인도 및 아프리카와의 통상도 대부분 중단하였다.

•• 해 설 ••

1. 과학자들이 전에 생각했던 것이 새로운 연구에 따라 바뀐 과정과 그 이유에 대해 언급하고 있다.

2. 중국이 강력한 해상국가였다가 어떤 이유에선지 활동을 중단하고, 유럽이 그 역할을 차지하게 되었다는 글이다.

1. Other large Chinese projects include the world's biggest dam, and a huge canal system.

2. Paul Revere also worked as a dentist at times.

1. 북경은 황사와 대기 오염으로 유명하다. 봄철에는 문제가 특히 심각해, 많은 중국 사람들은 스스로 보호하기 위해 얼굴에 마스크를 쓴다. 문제의 일부는 물론 북경 안팎의 많은 수의 자동차와 공장들이다. 문제의 다른 부분은, 북경 근교 시골의 푸석푸석한 흙을 바람이 대기 중으로 불어 날린다는 것이다. 이 먼지를 막기 위해, 중국인들은 녹색 장벽이라고 불리는 거대한 계획을 시작했다. 중국의 다른 거대한 계획들에는 세계에서 가장 큰 댐과 거대한 운하가 있다. 녹색 장벽은 먼지를 막기 위해 도시 주변에 심어질 거대한 나무숲이다.

2. 미국 독립 전쟁 전인 1774년과 1775년에, 미국 식민지 이주자들과 영국 정부 사이에는 많은 분노가 있었다. 미국인들은 높은 세금과 영국인들에 의한 불공평한 대우라고 생각된 것들에 대해서 분노했다. 그 해는 매우 격렬했다. 모두가 전쟁을 원했고, 언제 시작되느냐가 유일한 문제였다. 당시 영국에 대항하는 활동을 하던 미국 식민지 이주자들 중의 한 명은 보석 세공사였던 폴 리비어(Paul Revere)였다. 폴 리비어는 때때로 치과의사로도 일했다. 그 긴박한 세월 동안, 그는 신민지 이주자들을 위해 간첩과 전령의 역할을 했다. 그는 콩코드(Concord)와 렉싱턴(Lexington)에 대한 영국의 공격을 사전에 경고한 것으로 가장 유명하다.

•• 해 설 ••

1. 중국의 황사현상과 그 원인, 이를 막기 위해 실행하고 있는 대책을 설명하고 있는 글이다. 관련 없는 소재가 언급된 문장을 고른다.

2. 미국 독립전쟁 전 긴장이 고조된 때의 상황을 설명하고 있는 글로, 글의 전체 주제와 관계없는 문장을 고른다.

1. **B**   2. **C**

1. 많은 경우에, 사회들은 환경 파괴적이고 그들에게 최선의 이익이 되지 못하는 일들을 벌이곤 한다. **A** 과거에는, 자신들이 환경을 파괴하고 있다는 것을 이해할 지식이 부족했기 때문에 이런 일들이 있었다. 그러나 현대에 와서는, 많은 사회들이 알면서도 환경을 파괴한다. **B** 영국이 오스트레일리아(Australia)를 처음 식민지화하기 시작한 1700년대 말에, 그들은 영국 작물과 양과 같은 영국 동물을 기르기 위해 그곳의 식물들을 베어 내기 시작했다. **C** 그 양들은 환경을 황폐화시키는 영향을 끼쳤는데, 당시 식민지 이주민들은 그것을 알지 못했다. 오늘날, 목양(牧羊)은 오스트레일리아 경제의 기본적인 부분이며, 아직도 환경에 해가 되고 있다. 현대의 오스트레일리아 사람들은 이것이 환경에 끼치는 손해를 인지하고 있지만, 많은 이유로 아직도 목양을 계속하고 있다. **D** 그런 이유 중의 하나는, 목양이 오스트레일리아의 정체성의 중요한 부분이라는 것이다. 오스트레일리아 사람들에게, 목양을 포기하는 것은 마치 프랑스 사람들이 와인 제조를 포기하는 것과 같을 것이다.

2. 🅐 미국 독립 전쟁 동안, 영국은 조지 워싱턴(George Washington)이 이끄는 미국 대륙군(Continental Army)과 많은 전투를 벌였다. 그러나 영국은 '긴급응소병(minutemen)'이라고 불리는 더 작은 단위의 군인들로부터도 많은 피해를 입었다. 🅑 사실 긴급응소병들은 정규군이 아니었고 민병대의 일원이었다. 민병은 전임 군인이 아니며, 어려울 때에 전투에 참가하기 위해 소집될 수 있는 지역 사회의 구성원이었다는 점에서 정규군과 달랐다. 🅒 긴급응소병은 영토를 넓히고 식민지 이주민을 보호하기 위한 아메리카 원주민들과의 싸움에 있어서 긴 역사를 갖고 있었다. 🅓 아메리카 원주민들과의 전투에서 긴급응소병은 영국에게 매우 효과적인 것으로 증명이 된 전투 기술들을 개발했다. 그들은 영국군을 기다리며 수풀 속에 숨어 있었다. 그리고 공격한 뒤, 영국군이 대항하기 전에 다른 위치로 이동한다. 거기서, 다시 영국군을 기다렸다가 이런 전체의 과정을 되풀이한다. 이런 방법으로 그들은 스스로는 큰 피해를 입지 않고도 영국군을 피곤하게 해 승리했다.

•• 해 설 ••

1. 주어진 문장은 앞서 제시되었을 두 가지 상황들의 예로, Australia의 경우를 설명하기 위한 도입 문장이다. 따라서 Australia에 대한 설명이 시작하기 전에 와야 함을 알 수 있다.

2. "minutemen"이 미국 독립혁명 오래 전부터 존재했다는 주어진 문장의 내용에 따라, 이 문장은 독립혁명이 있기 이전에 이들이 원주민들과 싸웠던 내용 앞에 위치해야 자연스럽다.

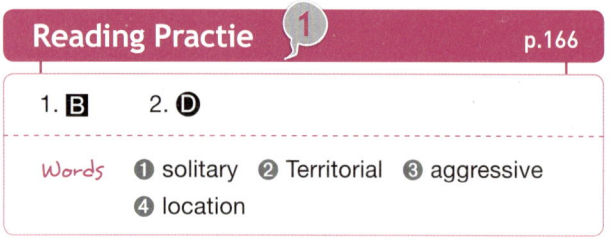

Reading Practie ① p.166

1. 🅑   2. 🅓

Words ❶ solitary ❷ Territorial ❸ aggressive ❹ location

칩멍크

칩멍크(Chipmunk)는 꼬리가 짧은 작은다람쥐처럼 생긴 소형 설치류 동물이다. 칩멍크는 세계 곳곳에서 찾을 수 있지만, 25종의 칩멍크가 있는 북아메리카 지역에서 가장 흔하다. 칩멍크는 각자의 땅굴을 파는, 독립 생활을 하는 동물이다. 이런 구멍은 길이가 4미터에 이를 수도 있다. 🅐 칩멍크들은 영역 의식이 강해서, 다른 칩멍크들로부터 공격적으로 땅굴을 방어한다. 🅑

다람쥐와 같이, 칩멍크들은 가을 대부분을 겨울을 나기 위한 먹이를 모으는데 쓴다. 🅒 어떤 특정한 종에 속해 있는지에 따라, 칩멍크들은 겨울 식량 수집을 위해, 저장 창고에 저장하거나 분산해 저장하는 두 가지의 방법을 쓴다. 저장 창고에 저장하는 방법에서 칩멍크는 보통 자신의 땅굴의 한 곳에다가 먹이를 저장한다. 🅐 저장 창고에 저장하는 방법의 단점은, 칩멍크가 모은 식량을 도둑맞을 가능성이 더욱 크다는 것이다. 🅐 종종, 칩멍크가 저장 창고에 저장할 더 많은 먹이를 모으기 위해 나간 사이, 땅굴에 이미 모아 둔 식량을 다른 칩멍크가 훔쳐 가기도 한다. 🅓

분산해 저장하는 방법에서, 칩멍크는 자신의 땅굴 주위 수십, 심지어는 수백 군데의 곳에다가 먹이를 숨겨 둔다. 🅓 이는 많은 추가적인 작업을 필요로 하는 것 같이 보이지만, 그것은 칩멍크에게 일종의 보험 정책이 된다. 한 군데의 도토리들이 다른 동물에게 발견되더라도, 칩멍크에게는 여러 군데가 남아 있다. 분산해 저장하는 방법의 중요한 효과 중 하나는, 칩멍크가 언제나 먹이를 숨겨 둔 곳 중 몇 군데는 잊어버릴 것이기 때문에, 그렇게 먹히지 않고 남은 도토리는 봄에 새로운 나무로 자랄 것이라는 것이다.

✉ **Words**

☐ species 종
☐ territorial 세력권을 가지려고 하는
☐ location 위치
☐ aggressively 공격적으로, 필사적으로
☐ solitary 고독한
☐ insurance 보험
☐ stash 저장고, 은둔처
☐ policy 정책

•• 해 설 ••

1. "이런 방법의 가장 큰 장점은, 겨울에 칩멍크가 먹이를 구하기 위해서 자신의 안전한 땅굴을 나가지 않아도 된다는 것이다."가 주어진 문장이다. 이 문장의 내용은 larder hoarding에 관한 내용이며, 장점을 언급하는 문장이므로, larder hoarding의 단점이 설명된 "The disadvantage of larder hoarding..."의 앞에 위치하거나, 단점에 대한 설명이 끝난 후에 위치해야 하는데, "primary"라는 표현이 사용되었으므로 앞에 오는 것이 더 자연스럽다.

2. "이것은 왜 칩멍크들이 땅굴을 그렇게 공격적으로 방어하는지를 설명해 준다."가 주어진 문장이다. 여기에 언급된 칩멍크가 그들의 땅굴을 공격적으로 방어해야 하는 이유가 "this"의 내용일 것이며, 그러므로 그 이유인 "Often, while a larder hoarder is out collecting more food, another chipmunk will steal some of the food it has already collected in its burrow."가 주어진 문장의 앞에 위치해야 글이 자연스럽게 이어질 수 있다.

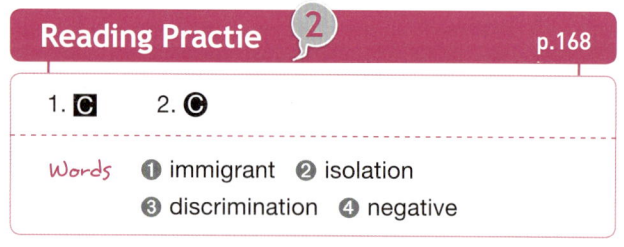

Reading Practie ② p.168

1. 🅒   2. 🅒

Words ❶ immigrant ❷ isolation ❸ discrimination ❹ negative

게토

어느 도시를 가던 간에 이민자들이, 특히 같은 나라에서 왔거나 같은 민족일 경우에는 더 많은 경우에, 같은 지역에 거주하는 것을 찾을 수 있을 것이다. 이런 지역은 종종 게토(ghetto)라고 불린다. 🅐 게토는 이민자들이 사는 도시가 있는 한 계속 존재해 왔지만, 게토라는 실제 용어는 14세기에 베니스(Venice)에서 처음 사용되었다. 🅑 당시에, 대부분이 카톨릭 신자였던 베니스에서, 모든 유대인들은 그들을 도시의 카톨릭 지역과 격리시키는 한 곳에 반드시 모여서 살아야 했다. 🅒 이탈리아와 유럽의 다른 도시들도 베니스의 예를 따라 각각의 게토를 만들었다. 유대인들을 격리시켜 살게 하는 정책은 대부분의 유럽에서 17세기에 중단되었으나, 1940년대 나치(Nazi) 치하의 독일에서 다시 시작되었다. **D** 시간이 흐름에 따라, 게토라는 용어는 많은 이민자수가 있는 어느 지역에 대해서도 사용되게 되었다. 그러나 그 낱말은 또한 차별과 빈곤과의 여러 부정적인 연관성을 지니고 있었다.

그러나, 이민자들이 출생 민족과 상관없이 자발적으로 형성하는 게토들도 많이 있다. 이민자들은 도시의 한 같은 지역에 거주함으로써 많은 장점을 얻는다. **A** 중요한 장점 중의 하나는 모국 문화와의 지속적인 관계이다. **B** 게토라고 불리는 곳에 사는 이민자들은 그들의 음식을 파는 식당이나 그들의 문화 행사가 열리는 극장으로의 더 쉬운 접근이 가능하다. 더 중요한 것은, 같은 곳에 삶으로서 대개 이민자들은 필요할 때 도움을 받을 수 있는 사회 조직을 얻을 수 있다는 것이다. **C** 그러므로, 게토라는 용어는 많은 부정적인 의미를 품고 있지만, 게토의 기능은 종종 긍정적이다. **D**

✉ Words

- ☐ immigrant 이주민
- ☐ term 용어
- ☐ voluntarily 자발적으로
- ☐ in isolation 고립되어
- ☐ association 관념, 연상
- ☐ access 접근 가능, 입구

•• 해 설 ••

1. "그 도시의 이 유대인 구역이 게토라고 불렸다."가 주어진 문장이다. '이 유대인 구역(This Jewish part of the city)'이 게토라고 불렸다고 했으므로, 이 문장 앞에 유대인 구역에 대해 언급하며 설명된 내용이 나와야 한다.

2. "그들의 언어를 사용하고, 통역을 해 줄 수 있으며, 이민자로서의 어려움을 이해해 주는 더 많은 사람들이 있다."가 주어진 문장이다. 이 내용은 게토에 사는 장점 중 하나이며, 내용상 사회적인 조직상에서 얻을 수 있는 장점의 실례에 속하므로 게토의 사회적 의미의 장점이 소개된 "More importantly, living in the same area often provides immigrants with a social network that can provide them with help if they need it."의 뒤에 위치해야 글의 흐름이 자연스럽다.

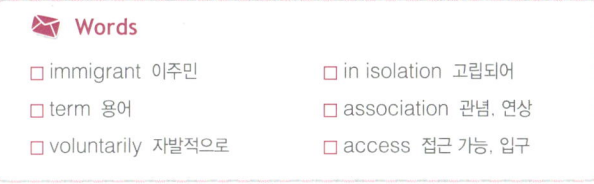

Reading Practie 3   p.170

1. **D**   2. **D**

Words ❶ narrow ❷ argument ❸ adjust ❹ aesemble

고래목 동물

고래목(cetacean)은 고래와 돌고래를 포함하는 바다 포유류의 무리다. 고래목 동물들은 높은 지능으로 유명하지만, 그들이 정확히 얼마나 똑똑한지는 아직 논의의 대상이다. 고래목 동물들은 그들의 지능을 나타내는 것으로 생각되는 여러 복잡한 행동을 보인다. **A** 예를 들어, 모든 고래목 동물들은 수중에서 여러 가지의 소리를 통해 서로 의사 소통을 하는 기본적인 언어의 형태를 갖

고 있다. **B** 게다가, 일부의 고래목 동물들, 특히 돌고래와 범고래들은, 먹이 사냥 방법에서 고도로 발전된 협동을 보여준다. **C** 돌고래들은 협동을 통해서, 더 쉽게 잡아먹을 수 있는 강폭이 좁은 부분으로 물고기 떼를 몰아 넣는다. **D**

그러나 높은 지능에 대한 주장이 있는 것처럼, 고래목 동물들의 낮은 지능에 대한 주장도 많이 있다. **A** 원래, 많은 사람들은, 고래목 동물들이 심지어 사람보다도 큰 두뇌를 갖고 있기 때문에, 분명히 그들의 지능이 높을 것이라고 생각했다. **B** 돌고래의 두뇌는 사람의 뇌보다 약 20%가 크고, 향유고래(sperm whale)의 경우에는 거의 600%가 크다. **C** 그러나, 고래의 몸이 인간의 몸보다 훨씬 크기 때문에 이 숫자들만으로는 오해의 소지가 있다. **D** 게다가, 고래목 동물들 뇌의 구조는 사람 보다 훨씬 덜 발달되었다. 마지막으로, 우리는 환경이 초기 인류에게 똑똑해지지 않으면 도태될 것을 강요했기 때문에 사람의 지능이 발전되었다는 것을 알고 있다. 초기의 인류는 도구를 사용하는 법을 배우고 다양한 환경에 적응하고 더 큰 동물들로부터 스스로를 지키며 새로운 식량 공급원을 찾아야 했다. 고래목 동물들에게는 높은 지능을 개발하기 위한 그러한 요인들이 없었다. 그들의 환경은 기본적으로 변함없고 도구를 사용하지도 않으며, 그들이 바다에서 가장 큰 동물이기 때문에 자연 상의 포식 동물도 없다.

✉ Words

- ☐ debate 논쟁하다, 논의하다
- ☐ argument 증명, 주장
- ☐ resemble 닮다
- ☐ misleading 오해의 소지가 있는
- ☐ a school of fish 한 떼의 물고기
- ☐ adjust to ~ ~에 적응하다
- ☐ herd (소나 양을) 몰다

•• 해 설 ••

1. "이런 행동은 소나 양을 모는 사람의 행동과 많이 닮았다."가 주어진 문장이므로 '사람이 소나 양을 모는 행동과 닮은 고래의 행동'이 제시된 문장 "Dolphins will work in a group to chase a school of fish into a narrow part of a river,..." 뒤에 위치해야 문맥이 자연스럽게 이어질 수 있다.

2. "두뇌는 사람의 전체 몸무게 중 2%를 차지하고, 돌고래는 0.9%, 향유고래는 0.02%를 차지한다."의 주어진 문장은 인간과 고래의 뇌와 몸체의 비율을 비교하고 있다. 본문에 따르면 과학자들은 원래 고래류의 뇌가 인간의 뇌보다 훨씬 크기 때문에 고래의 지능이 높을 것이라고 생각했었다. 하지만 그 뒤에서, 뇌의 단순한 크기 비교만으로는 고래의 몸체가 인간의 몸체보다 훨씬 크기 때문에 오해의 소지가 있다고 한 주장으로 이어진다. 이 문장은 바로 이 주장을 뒷받침하는 사실이므로 그 주장 뒤에 위치하여야 자연스럽게 글이 연결될 수 있다.

iBT Practice 1   p.172

1. (C)   2. (D)   3. (B)   4. (B)   5. (B)
6. **D**   7. (A), (B), (E)

인간 두뇌의 발달

대부분 동물의 두뇌는 태어날 때 이미 완전하게 발달되어 있거나, 거의 발달되어 있다. 그러나, 사람은 일부만 발달된 두뇌를 갖고 태어난다. 실제로, 갓난아기의 두뇌는 단 45%만 발달되었고, 우리 뇌는 12 또는 13살이 될 때까지 완전히 발달되지 않는다. 이는 어린아이들에게는 어른들에게 있는 많은 사고 기술들이 없다는 것을 의미한다. 인간 두뇌 발달에는 아이의 인지 능력 발달과 각각 연관된 네 가지의 기본 단계가 있다. **A** 이런 단계들은 그것이 일어나는 연령대로 구분되어 있는데, 그러나 이런 연령대는 아이에 따라 약간씩 변할 수 있다. **B**

첫 번째 단계는 감각운동기(sensory motor stage)로 불리며, 출생 시부터 대략 만 2살까지 지속된다. 이 시기 동안, 두뇌의 대부분의 발달은 근육의 더 나은 제어와 오감 발달과 연관된다. **C** 이는 많은 시간을 사물을 만지고, 입으로 가져가 넣는 것으로 보내는 갓난아이들의 행동에서 쉽게 볼 수 있다. **D** 전 조작기(preoperational stage)는 만 2살부터 7살까지 지속된다. 이 단계에서, 아이들은 언어 기술을 익히고, 더 오랫동안 집중할 수 있는 능력을 발달시킨다. 아이들은 또 이 시기 즈음, 욕구를 다스리는 능력도 개발한다. 그것은 그들이 원하는 것을 언제나 가질 수는 없다는 것을 이해하기 시작한다는 의미다. 그러나, 이 시기에 그들에게는 대부분의 수학적 개념을 이해할 수 있는 능력은 없다. 만 7살이 되면, 일반적으로 아이들은 12살에서 13살까지 지속되는 구체적 조작기(concrete operational stage)에 들어선다. 이 시기는 더 복잡한 문제 해결 능력의 발달, 수학에 대한 보다 깊은 이해, 그리고 사물을 여러 범주로 구분할 수 있는 능력으로 특징지어진다. 발달의 마지막 단계는 아이의 두뇌가 완전히 발달되고 우리가 더 어른스럽다고 여기는 방식으로 사고하기 시작하는 형식적 조작기(formal operational stage)이다.

이러한 두뇌 발달 단계의 발견은 교육에 엄청난 영향을 끼쳤다. 분명히, 아직 어떠한 개념을 이해할 수 있을 만큼 두뇌가 발달하지도 못한 어린아이에게 그것을 가르치는 것은 아무 의미가 없다. 두뇌 발달의 이해는 기본적으로 우리가 각 연령대의 아이들에게 어떤 수업을 가르쳐야 하는지 결정했고, 교육의 질또한 매우 향상시켰다.

📧 **Words**

□ partially 일부, 부분적으로
□ cognitive 인지의
□ sensory motor stage 감각운동기
□ preoperational stage 전 조작기
□ problem solving ability 문제해결능력
□ thinking skills 사고 기술
□ classify 구분하다, 분류하다

• • 해 설 • •

1. 6-7째 줄 "These stages are classified by the ages at which they occur, but those ages can vary some from child to child."에 따르면, 뇌 발달이 일어나는 나이는 아이들에 따라 다를 수 있다고 했다.

2. 문맥의 내용상 "cognitive abilities"는 뇌가 성장하면서 발전하는 능력이라는 것을 알 수 있다.

3. "begin to speak"과 "develop their language skills"가 같은 의미라는 것을 이해하면 12째 줄 이하 "The preoperational stage lasts from... ability to concentrate for longer periods of time."에서 쉽게 답을 고를 수 있다.

4. 주어진 문장은 다음의 세 의미 단위로 나뉠 수 있다. "발달의 마지막 단계는 형식적 조작의 단계(the formal operation stage)라고 불린다 / 이는 아이의 뇌가 완전히 발달하며 / 아이가 어른과 같은 방법으로 생각하기 시작할 때이다" 이 세 부분의 의미 단위가 모두 정확히 들어간 보기를 찾는다. "fully developed"가 "the last stage of development"와 같은 의미임을 이해해야 한다. (A)와 (C)는 두 번째 의미 단위의 내용이 빠져 있으며, (D)는 의미 단위의 연결이 잘못되었다.

5. keyword인 "mathematics"를 본문에서 찾으면 뇌의 발달의 세 번째 단계인 구체적 조작기(concrete operational stage)의 설명에서 찾을 수 있다. 이 단계는 보통 7살부터 12, 13살까지를 말하며, 또한 앞의 문장에서 7살 이전에는 수학적인 개념을 이해하는 능력이 결여되어 있다고 했다. 마지막 문단에 이 뇌의 발달 단계에 맞추어 학습 단계도 정해진다고 한 내용을 종합해 보면 7살 이후에 수학의 학습이 이루어져야 올바를 것임을 짐작할 수 있다.

6. "이것은 미각과 촉각의 발달로 인한 자연적 결과이다"라고 했으므로, 바로 이 결과의 내용 뒤에 위치하면 된다. 즉, "spend much of their time touching things and putting things into their mouths"가 아이들이 미각과 촉각의 발달로 인해 보여주는 행동이므로 이 뒤에 위치하는 것이 적절하다.

7. 이 글은 인간의 뇌가 발달하는 4단계의 설명과 함께, 이러한 발달이 교육에 미친 영향으로 끝을 맺는다. 따라서, 뇌 발달의 4단계를 제시한 (A)와 단계가 나누어지는 기준을 설명한 (B), 마지막으로 교육정책에 가져온 변화를 설명하는 (E)가 올바른 요약문을 이룬다고 할 수 있다. (C), (D), (F)는 모두 틀린 설명이거나, 언급되지 않은 내용이다.

---

*i*BT **P**ractice **2**   p.175

1. (C)   2. (A)   3. (C)   4. (A)   5. (B)   6. **B**

7. **Irrigation Theory**
   - Project leaders became kings
   - Some physical evidence to support theory
   - Lack of existing government presents a problem in theory

   Monument Theory
   - States result from common culture in villages
   - Priests became kings

국가의 형성

농업의 발달은 질문의 여지없이 인류 고대사의 가장 중요한 발전이었다.

인구의 증가를 가능케 하고 그 결과 국가의 성장을 가능하게 한 것은 농사로 생산된 잉여 식량이었다. 국가가 형성된 시기를 추정할 수 있고 농업이 이것을 가능하게 했다는 것도 알지만, 우리는 아직도 정확히 왜 이런 고대 국가들이 생겨나게 되었는지에 대해서는 모른다.

🄰 이런 고대 국가 형성에 대한 한 가지 이론은 관개(irrigation)에 중심을 둔다. 🄱 대지로 물을 대기 위해 운하를 파고 댐을 건설하는, 대규모의 관개 사업은 한 사람에게, 혹은 한 마을에게도 너무 큰 작업이었을 것이다. 🄲 그것들은 더 큰 집단의 사람들간의 협동을 필요로 하게 했을 것이다. 자연히, 한 사람이나 소집단의 사람들이 그런 사업을 이끌었을 것이며 이 같은 협동의 초기 형태는 초기 국가들로 이르게 했을 것이다. 그리고, 그 사업의 지도자들이 최초의 왕이 되었을 것이다. 이 이론을 뒷받침하는 몇 가지 증거가 있다. 가장 오래된 도시국가들 모두에서는 그 중의 일부는 도시 자체보다도 더 오래된 것으로 보이는 대규모 관개 사업의 흔적이 존재한다. 그러나, 관개 이론이 잘못된 것일지도 모른다는 것을 나타내는 증거도 있다. 🄳 관개 농업에서 농부들은 물을 공유해야 한다. 만약 상류 쪽의 농부가 너무 많은 물을 써 버릴 경우, 더 하류 쪽의 농부들에게는 쓸 수 있는 남은 물이 없을 것이다. 만약 물의 사용을 관리하기 위해 정부가 그 이전부터 존재하지 않았더라면 그런 물의 공유는 없었을 것으로 보인다.

또 다른 이론은 모든 초기 국가들은 대형 기념비를 건설했다는 사실에 중심을 두었다. 국가가 존재하기 전에도 특정 지역의 농촌에서는, 같은 종교와 공통의 문화를 공유했었다. 그들의 성직자들이 그들의 신을 위한 기념비를 건설하도록 명령했을 수 있다. 역시나 이것은 한 마을에게는 너무 큰 작업이었을 것이고, 협동을 필요로 했을 것이다. 이 이론 하에서, 이 성직자들이 협동으로 인해 형성된 그 나라들의 최초의 왕이 되었을 것이다. 최초의 왕들이 스스로를 신이라고 주장했거나, 또는 신을 상징했던 사실은 이 이론을 뒷받침하는 것으로 보인다. 그러나, 또 어떤 이들은 기념비 건설은 그들의 지배를 정당화하기 위한 방법이 필요했던 신격화된 군주들에게 도구로 사용된 것뿐이라고 주장하며 동의하지 않는다. 따라서, 기념비의 건설은 이들 국가들의 형성에 따른 결과였다는 것이다.

✉ Words

- ☐ without question 질문의 여지없이
- ☐ excess 잉여
- ☐ canal 운하
- ☐ downstream 하류로
- ☐ irrigation 관개
- ☐ upstream 상류로
- ☐ justify 뒷받침하다, 정당화하다

•• 해 설 ••

1. 앞 부분의 내용에서 농사를 지음으로 인구의 증가와 국가의 성장이 이루어졌다고 했다. 그러므로 다시 한번 언급된, 국가가 일어나는 것을 가능하게 했다고 한 "agriculture"가 '농사, 농업(farming)'과 유의어임을 알 수 있다.

2. 만약 관계설과 유적설 둘 중 하나의 이론이라도 맞는 다고 할 때, 국가 형성이 무엇의 결과이냐고 묻는 문제이다. 두 개의 이론에서 모두 많은 사람들의 협동 작업의 필요성으로 인해 국가가 형성되었다고 했다.

3. 이 문장의 주어는 앞 문장의 주어를 대명사로 받고 있다. 즉, 많은 사람

들의 협동이 요구되는 이것은 앞 문장의 주어인 운하나 댐의 건설과 같은 "(Large scale) irrigation projects"이다.

4. 관개설(irrigation theory)에 따른 초기 국가(the first states) 형성에 대한 알맞은 추론을 고르는 문제이다. 관개 공사를 위해 많은 사람들이 모여 협동하는 과정에서 국가가 설립되었고, 이는 농사에 필요한 물을 충당하기 위한 것이었으므로 그 지역에 물이 부족했음을 추론할 수 있다.

5. 유적 건설이 단지 자신의 통치를 정당화하기 위해 왕이 사용한 방법이라는 것은 유적설(monument theory)에 찬성하지 않는 사람들이 주장한 내용이므로, 이것은 유적설이 가지고 있는 오류의 가능성을 제시하기 위해 쓰였을 것이다.

6. "관개는 농사를 위해 건조한 지역에 물을 가져오는 행위이다"의 주어진 문장은 관개의 의미임으로, 관개(irrigation)라는 용어가 처음으로 소개된 후에 위치하는 것이 자연스럽다. 또한, "Large scale irrigation projects, … would have been far too much work for one person, or even one village."가 관개의 실제 예에 해당하므로 그 앞에 위치하는 것이 타당하다.

7. • Project leaders became kings: 11째 줄 참조
   • Farming not essential to state formation: 관개설에서 농업은 필수적 역할을 했으며 유적설과는 관계 없는 내용이다.
   • States result from common culture in villages: 19-20째 줄 참조
   • Some physical evidence to support theory: 11-13째 줄 참조
   • Lack of existing government presents a problem in theory: 16-17째 줄 참조
   • Priests became kings: 22-23째 줄 참조, "holy men"이 "priests"를 의미한다.
   • Favored by most archaeologists: 본문에 언급되지 않은 내용이다.

Vocabulary Review   p.178

1. (D)   2. (B)   3. (C)   4. (A)   5. (C)

6. (B)   7. (A)   8. (D)

9. misleading   10. insurance

11. voluntarily   12. in isolation

13. association   14. tense

15. adjust to   16. access

Actual Test ❶
p.182

1. (B)	2. (D)	3. (B)	4. (C)	5. (B)
6. (D)	7. (B)	8. (A)	9. **B**	
10. (B), (D), (F)	11. (C)	12. (D)	13. (D)	
14. (B)	15. (A)	16. (A)	17. (D)	18. (D)
19. **C**	20. (A), (D), (F)	21. (D)	22. (A)	
23. (A)	24. (B)	25. (C)	26. (A)	27. (B)
28. **C**	29. (A), (E), (F)			

Reading 1: 카르타고(Carthage)의 성쇠

고대 세계에서 가장 강력한 도시국가 중 하나는 카르타고였다. 카르타고는 원래 무역업자들과 상인들의 도시였다. 이 도시는 역시 상인들이자 세계에서 가장 오래된 문명 중 하나였던 페니키아(Phoenicia)인들에 의해 기원전 814년에 건국되었다. 카르타고는 과두 체제, 즉 강력한 가문들의 모임과 실제 권력은 거의 갖고 있지 않던 소수의 선출된 지도자들에 의해 통치되었다. 카르타고인들은 몇몇 신들을 숭배했으며, 어려운 시기에는 아이들을 제물로 바치는 관습이 있었다. 이런 관습에 있어서, 강력한 가문들은 신들로부터 보호와 도움을 받기 위해서 그들의 가장 어린아이를 죽였다.

기원전 6세기에, 카르타고의 세력이 커지고 있었으며, 그 도시는 곧 지중해 무역 지배권을 두고 그리스 도시국가들과 충돌하게 되었다. **A** 카르타고인들은 뛰어난 뱃사람들이었고, 그들에게는 강력한 해군이 있었으며, 기원전 5세기에서부터 3세기까지 이 두 문명은 수많은 전쟁을 벌였다. 그러나 대부분의 전쟁은 소규모였고 상대적으로 짧게 끝났다. 그러나 3세기 중반, 카르타고와 훨씬 더 잔학한 전쟁을 치러야 했던, 새로운 적이 나타나게 된다.

이 새로운 적은 로마였다. **B** 로마와 카르타고는 기원전 264년부터 146년 사이에 세 번의 전쟁을 했다. **C** 첫 번째의 전쟁은 양국을 심각하게 약화시켰다. 그러나 결국에는, 로마가 첫 전쟁에서 승리했고, 전쟁의 뒤를 이은 평화 조약에서의 막대한 불이익에 동의하도록 카르타고에 강요했다.

그러나 30년 후, 카르타고는 로마가 또 다시 위협을 느낄 정도로 그 세력을 다시 얻었다. **D** 로마는 카르타고에 선전포고를 했지만, 로마가 실제로 움직이기 전에, 카르타고인들은 이탈리아를 침략했다. 카르타고인들의 공격은 로마 제국 전체를 거의 파괴시킬 정도로 성공적이었다. 하지만 로마인들은 회복했고, 카르타고가 다시 한 번 패배했다. 이 패배 이후, 카르타고의 세력은 더 이상 로마에 도전할 수 없을 정도로 대단히 약해졌다. 그러나 로마인들은 자기들이 두 번째 전쟁에서 완전한 패배에 얼마나 가까웠는지를 기억했고, 카르타고인들에 대한 깊은 증오를 간직하고 있었다. 그들은 쇠약해진 도시를 공격했다. 그 뒤에, 그들은 도시를 잿더미로 불태워 버리고, 항만을 파괴하고, 아무 것도 자라지 못하도록 땅에 소금을 섞는 등으로 카르타고를 완전히 파괴시켰다. 살아남은 카르타고인들은 노예로 팔렸고, 그들의 사회는 멸망했다.

✉ Words
☐ primarily 원래, 주로
☐ elected 선출된
☐ conflict 충돌, 갈등
☐ weaken 약화시키다
☐ defeat 패배시키다, 물리치다
☐ short-live 짧게 끝나다, 오래가지 못하다
☐ burn something to the ground 잿더미로 불태우다, 초토화하다
☐ oligarchy 과두 체제
☐ aid 도움
☐ regain 다시 얻다, 회복하다
☐ hatred 증오
☐ afterwards 나중에, 그 뒤에

•• 해설 ••

1. 문맥에 드러난 힌트는 없지만 이 문장이 카르타고 역사의 시작을 설명하는 문장이라는 점을 참고하여, 가장 적절한 보기를 고른다.

2. 3째 줄에서 "Carthage was ruled by an oligarchy, a collection of powerful families"라고 했다. "elite"는 "powerful"과 같은 의미로 쓰였다.

3. "this"는 대부분 앞에 언급된 내용을 가리키는 대명사이므로, 앞 문장 "The Carthaginians worshiped a number of gods, and in times of trouble they practiced child sacrifice."내에서 "this practice"에 해당하는 것을 찾는다. 또한, 이 행위는 강력한 가문들이 신에게서 보호와 도움을 얻기 위해 그들의 가장 어린아이를 죽이는 것이었다는 내용이 이어지고 있다는 점을 참조하자.

4. 주어진 문장은 다음 두 의미 단위로 나누어 볼 수 있다. "기원전 6세기 경에 카르타고의 세력이 커지고 있었으며 / 이 도시는 곧 지중해 무역의 관할권을 놓고 그리스 도시국가들과 대립하기 시작했다" 이 문장에서 전하고 있는 요지가 카르타고가 그리스 도시국가들과 대립하게 되었으며, 그 이유가 다른 것이 아닌 카르타고의 세력이 커진 것 때문임을 이해한다면 어렵지 않게 오답들을 골라 낼 수 있다.

5. 이 문제에서 묻고 있는 대상인 그리스 도시 국가들이 지중해의 무역 문제를 놓고 카르타고와 싸웠다는 것에서, 이들이 카르타고인들과 마찬가지로 상인과 항해자들이었을 것임을 추론할 수 있다.

6. 대부분의 전쟁의 수명이 짧았다는 것은, 전쟁이 오래 끌지 않고 일찍 끝났다는 것을 의미한다.

7. keyword인 "completely destroy"를 본문에서 찾아보면 28째 줄에서 찾을 수 있으며, 22째 줄 이하 "But the Romans remembered how close they had come to total defeat in the second war and held a deep hatred for the Carthaginians."의 내용에서 그 이유를 찾을 수 있다.

8. 24째 줄 이하의 내용에서 로마가 마지막으로 카르타고를 파괴하면서 한 일들이 제시되고 있다. 많은 벌금 (heavy fines)을 부과한 것은 첫째 전쟁의 결과였지, 이 과정에서 일어난 일이 아니다.

9. 주어진 문장의 내용은 "로마가 확장하기 시작함에 따라, 거의 즉시 카르타고와 많은 분쟁을 일으키게 되었다." 이며 이 문장은 **B**의 자리에 들어

가야만, 로마와 카르타고 이 두 도시 국가 사이에 있었던 전쟁들을 구체적으로 설명한 다음 내용과 자연스럽게 이어질 수 있다.

10. 카르타고의 역사를 소개한 이 글은, 이 도시 국가가 겪어야 했던 전쟁에 초점을 두어 흥망의 이유와 역사를 설명하고 있다. (A)와 (E)는 사실이긴 하지만, 글의 요약에 들어갈 만큼 중요한 문장은 아니며, (C)는 본문에서 언급되지 않은 내용이다.

Reading 2:   블랙홀

우리의 태양보다 큰 별이 죽게 되면, 그들은 폭발을 일으키며 사라진다. 이런 별들은 우주의 어떤 다른 사건보다도 강력한 거대한 폭발인 초신성으로서 죽는다. 만약 태양(지름이 1백만 킬로미터가 넘는)이 초신성으로 폭발할 경우, 그 폭발의 엄청난 힘은 태양을 3 킬로미터의 크기로 압축시킬 것이다. 이 순간, 매우 중요한 일이 일어난다. 물체들이 가까워질수록, 중력은 커지게 된다. 초신성에서 그 별의 원자들이 매우 가깝게 압축되기 때문에, 그 중력은 빛조차도 빠져 나올 수 없는 엄청난 정도로 강해진다. 이 시점에서 별은 블랙홀이 된다.

블랙홀은 엄청나게 강한 중력을 가진 개체이다. 그것은 그 주위에 있는 모든 것들을 빨아들이며, 기본적으로 우주의 거대한 하수구 역할을 한다. 과학자들은 블랙홀의 존재를 오래 전부터 추측해 왔다. 그러나 빛조차도 빠져나올 수 없기 때문에, 그들은 기본적으로 보이지가 않으며, 그들의 존재도 증명하기 매우 어렵다. 과학자들은 그들의 존재를 두 가지 방법으로 증명했다. 가끔 과학자들은 매우 특이한 움직임을 갖는 별을 발견한다. 그것이 다른 개체의 둘레를 돌고 있는 것처럼 보이지만, 그 개체는 볼 수가 없다. 이런 경우, 과학자들은 그 보이지 않는 개체를 블랙홀이라고 추측할 수 있다. **A**

과학자들이 블랙홀의 존재를 증명할 수 있는 또 다른 방법은 약간 더 복잡하다. 물질이 블랙홀 안으로 빨려 들어갈 경우, 화장실의 하수구로 빨려 들어가는 물처럼 원을 그리며 돌게 된다. 물질이 블랙홀에 점점 더 다가갈수록, 더 빨리 회전하게 되고, 그 결과로 뜨거워지기 시작한다. 그러므로, 과학자들이 매우 뜨거운 물질의 원형 회전을 발견하게 되면, 그들은 역시 그 중심에 블랙홀이 존재한다고 추측할 수 있다. **B**

블랙홀은 그들 가까이 다가오는 모든 것들을 빨아들여 파괴하며, 우주에서 매우 중요한 역할을 한다. 과학자들은 거대한 블랙홀들이 우주의 모든 은하계들의 중심에 위치한다고 믿는다. **C** 각각의 은하계는 중심에 위치한 블랙홀의 집중된 중력에 의해 한데 유지되는 것이다. 블랙홀이 없었더라면, 은하계는 형성되지 않았을 것이고, 우리가 알고 있는 바와 같이 생명은 존재하지 않았을 것이다. **D**

✉ Words

□ supernova 초신성 □ atom 원자
□ suck 빨아들이다 □ orbit 둘레를 돌다, 궤도를 돌다
□ complicated 복잡한 □ spin 회전하다, 빙글빙글 돌다
□ intense 집중된, 강력한

•• 해 설 ••

11. punctuation clue를 찾을 수 있는 문제이다.

"a supernova, a huge explosion which is more powerful than any other event in the universe"와 이하 내용에서 이 단어의 뜻을 설명해 주고 있다.

12. 5째 줄에서 블랙홀이 형성될 때 발생하는 현상에서 "the atoms of the star get pushed so closely together"라고 설명해 주고 있다. 이와 같은 의미를 담고 있는 보기를 찾는다.

13. 문제의 문장은 다음과 같이 세 개의 의미 단위로 나누어 볼 수 있다. "supernova(초신성)에서는, 별의 원자들이 서로 아주 가까이 밀쳐져서 / 중력이 너무 강해 아무 것도 빠져나갈 수 없게 만든다 / 심지어 빛조차도" 모든 의미 단위가 정확하게 제시된 보기를 찾아야 한다. (A)는 중력에 대한 언급이 빠져 있으며, (B)는 가장 중요한 초신성에 대한 언급이 빠져 있고, (C)는 첫 번째 의미 단위의 내용이 완전하지 않다.

14. 주어진 문맥에서 명확한 힌트를 찾을 순 없지만, "the existence of black holes for a long time"이 과학자들이 추측했던 내용임을 참조하며, 주어진 보기들을 대입했을 때 가장 적절한 것을 고른다.

15. 빛조차 '그것들'을 빠져나갈 수 없기 때문에 블랙홀이 보이지 않아 그 존재를 증명하기 쉽지 않다고 한 문장의 의미에서 "them"이 가리키는 것이 블랙홀임을 알 수 있다.

16. 11째 줄부터 이어지는 "Scientists have proven their existence in two ways. ... It will appear to be orbiting another object, but that object can't be seen."에서 블랙홀의 존재를 증명할 수 있는 이유가 제시되어 있다.

17. 별들이 블랙홀로 빠져 들어가는 모습을 표현하기 위해 사용한 비유이다.

18. 셋째 문단에서 블랙홀로 들어가는 물체들에게 일어나는 현상들을 모두 설명해 주고 있으며, 빛을 방출한다는 내용은 언급되어 있지 않다.

19. **A**와 **B**는 거대한 블랙홀에 대한 언급이 있기 전이므로 답이 될 수 없다. 23째 줄 이하의 "Each galaxy is held together by the intense gravity of the giant black hole at its center."가 거대한 블랙홀이 중요한 이유를 말해주므로 주어진 문장은 그 앞인 **C**의 자리에 들어가는 것이 적절하다.

20. 이 글은 블랙홀의 의미와 이것이 생성되는 과정, 블랙홀의 존재를 증명할 수 있는 방법, 그리고 이것이 하는 역할을 설명하는 글이다. 그러므로 이 내용을 포함하고 있는 (A), (D), (F)가 답이며, (B)와 (E)는 부정확한 내용을 담고 있고, (C)는 세부 사항에 불과하다.

Reading 3:   정신분열증

정신분열증은 정신 질환 가운데 가장 심각한 형태의 하나이다. 정신분열증은 복잡한 질환으로 여러 가지 증상을 포함하며, 정신분열증을 앓는 대부분의 사람들이 모든 증상을 보이지는 않는다. 그러나 거의 대부분의 정신분열증 환자들이 공유하는 공통의 특징 중의 하나는 기본적으로 현실과 환상의 차이를 구별하지 못하는 것이다. 모든 사람은 환상을 갖고 있다. 우리의 상상은 실제가 아닌 상황을 만든다. 건강한 사람에게서 이런 환상은 "백일몽(daydreams)"

이라고 불리며, 그 사람은 그것이 현실이 아닌 것을 알고 있다. 그러나 정신분열증 환자들은 그것이 현실의 일부가 아니라는 것을 이해하지 못한다. **A** 이것은 현실일 수가 없는 것들을 믿게 되는 강력한 망상으로 이끈다. **B** 예를 들어, 정신분열증 환자는 그가 외계인과 만났었다고 믿거나, 아니면 그런 식의 비현실적인 상황을 믿게 된다. **C** 극단적인 상황에서, 이런 망상들을 정신분열증 환자를 폭력적이고 위험하게 만들 수 있다. **D**

정신분열증의 원인은 복잡하며 완벽하게 이해되지 않는다. 우리는 뇌 화학이 어떤 면에서 관련되어 있다는 것은 알고 있다. 이것은 뇌 속의 특정한 화학물질을 조절하는데 도움이 되는 약품이 정신분열증을 다루는 데에도 유용하기 때문이다. 또한 정신분열증이 흔한 가족에 속한 사람은 정신분열증에 걸리기 쉽다는 것도 알고 있다. 게다가, 정신분열증은 보통 뇌 속에서 중요한 화학적 변화가 생기는 시기인 십대 때나 그 이후에 겉으로 드러난다. 이런 모든 사실들이 정신분열증의 생물학적 원인으로 집중된다.

동시에, 한 사람의 환경과 경험 역시 중요한 요인이라는 증거도 많이 있다. 예를 들어, 도시에 사는 사람들은 정신분열증이 발병할 확률이 거의 70%가 높고, 소수 집단 역시 높은 발병을 보인다. 이것은 뇌 화학 외에도 환경이 중요한 역할을 한다는 것을 분명히 보여준다.

정신분열증은 심각한 병세가 보통 몇 달 정도 지속되는, 삽화성 질병이다. 심각한 정신분열증 환자에게는 덜 심각한 형태의 정신분열증 환자보다 이러한 삽화가 더 자주 나타난다. 전 세계 인구 중의 약 1%는 일생에서 언젠가 정신분열증 삽화를 겪을 것으로 예측된다. 치료는 보통 약물 치료를 포함하며, 심각한 경우에는 입원 치료가 필요하다.

✉ **Words**

□ schizophrenia 정신분열증　　□ symptom 증상
□ display 보이다, 드러내다　　　□ trait 특성
□ daydreams 백일몽　　　　　　□ delusion 망상
□ alien 외계인　　　　　　　　　□ point 보여주다, 시사하다
□ alongside ~와 함께, ~와 동시에　□ episodic 삽화

•• 해 설 ••

21. 이 문장에 따르면 정신분열증의 "trait"은 현실과 환상의 차이를 구분하지 못하는 것이라고 나왔다. 여기서 "trait"의 뜻을 짐작해 보도록 하자.

22. 5-7째 줄 "In a healthy person, these fantasies are often called "daydreams," and the person is aware that they are not real. A schizophrenic, however, does not understand that his or her daydreams are not part of reality."에서 설명되어 있다.

23. 이 문장의 뒷부분에서 structural clue를 찾을 수 있다. 즉 "delusions in which a person may believe things that could not possibly be true"에서 단어의 뜻을 추측해 볼 수 있다.

24. 정신분열증에 생물학적 원인이 있다는 증거는 둘째 문단에 설명되어 있다. 정신분열증이 십대들의 신체적 변화가 일어나는 시기에 함께 나타난다고 했지, 신체적 변화를 일으키는 원인이 된다고 하지 않았으므로 (B)는 틀린 내용이다.

25. 이 문단에서는 환경이 정신분열증에 미치는 영향을 설명하면서, 소수 그룹의 사람들이 (정상적인 환경에 사는 사람들 보다) 더 높은 발병 비율을 보인다고 했으므로, 이들이 정상적인 환경과 다른 환경에 살고 있음을 유추해 볼 수 있다.

26. 정신분열증이 "episodic illness"라는 내용이 소개된 이 문장의 뒷부분부터 다음 문장까지의 내용 "with periods of severe illness usually lasting several months. ... with less severe forms of the illness"에서 정신분열증 증상이 항상 꾸준히 나타나는 것이 아니라, 심하게 나타나는 시기와 약하게 나타나는 시기가 반복된다는 사실을 알 수 있다.

27. 본 문장에서는 "Severe schizophrenics experience these episodes more frequently than those with less severe forms of the illness."에서 두 대상, 즉 "Severe schizophrenics"와 "those with less severe forms of the illness"를 비교하고 있다. 그러므로 "those"는 "schizophrenics"를 가리킨다.

28. 주어진 문장은 "이런 망상은 개인의 직업적 혹은 사회적 생활을 파괴할 수 있다."의 뜻으로 망상이 야기할 수 있는 문제를 말하므로, 망상의 증상을 설명한 문장 "a schizophrenic may believe that... which is just as unlikely"와 그로 인해 생기는 극단적 피해의 경우를 제시한 문장 "Under extreme circumstances, ..."의 사이에 위치해야 한다. 그래야 망상에 대한 기본적인 설명으로부터 시작하여 극단적인 사례로 설명이 자연스럽게 마무리된다.

29. 이 글은 정신분열증의 증상인 (A), 생물학적, 환경적인 발병 원인인 (E)와 시기적 특성인 (F)에 대해 설명하고 있는 글이며, (B), (C), (D)는 모두 이러한 중심 내용을 뒷받침하는 부연 설명일 뿐이다.

Actual Test ❷

p.194

1. (B)	2. (C)	3. (B)	4. (C)	5. (D)
6. (A)	7. (C)	8. (D)	9. **C**	
10. (B), (C), (E)	11. (D)	12. (B)	13. (C)	
14. (D)	15. (C)	16. (C)	17. (B)	18. **C**
19. (B), (D), (E)	20. (C)	21. (B)	22. (C)	
23. (B)	24. (B)	25. (C)	26. (D)	27. (B)
28. **B**				

29. **Continental Plates**
   • Made of lighter materials
   • Rise up to form mountain chains

   Oceanic Plates
   • Commonly associated with volcanoes
   • Involved in island formation
   • Usually pushed under in plate collisions

Reading 1: 밀그램의 실험과 권위의 힘

제 2차 세계 대전 후, 대부분의 나치(Nazi) 지도자들은 반인류의 죄로 붙잡혀서 재판을 받았지만, 중요한 의문은 풀리지 않고 있었다. 나치 독일의 지도자들은 그들의 범죄에 있어서 홀로 행동하지 않았었다. 수천 명의 독일 군인들은 수백만 명의 죄 없는 사람들이 학살당했던 강제 수용소에서 근무했었다. 다른 사람들을 가해하고 죽일 수 있는 그렇게 많은 사람들의 준비성을 어떻게 설명할 수 있을까?

이 질문에 답하기 위해서, 예일(Yale) 대학교의 스탠리 밀그램(Stanley Milgram)이라는 심리학자는 1963년에 한 가지 실험을 시작했다. 사람들은 기억력이 어떻게 작동하는지(비록 이것이 실험의 진짜 목적은 아니었지만)에 대한 실험에 참가하도록 요구되었다. 피험자들은 다른 방에 있는 사람에게 질문을 하도록 되어 있었다. 만약 그 사람이 잘못된 대답을 할 경우, 피험자들은 그 사람에게 전기 충격을 가할 수 있는 단추를 누르도록 되어 있었다. 처음에는 전기 충격이 약했지만, 잘못된 답을 할 때마다 점점 강해졌다. (사실은, 전기 충격은 실제로는 없었고 다른 방의 사람은 연기자였다. 그러나 피험자들은 이것을 몰랐다.) 피험자들은 그 연기자를 볼 수 없었지만, 충격을 주기 위해 단추를 누르는 순간마다 고통으로 비명을 지르는 소리를 들을 수 있었다. 전기 충격이 커질 때마다 그럼 비명 소리가 커져 갔고, 많은 피험자들은 걱정하기 시작하며 밀그램에게 실험을 중단해도 되는지 물었다. 그는 그들에게 괜찮다고 확신하고, 실험을 계속해야 한다고 말했다. 놀랍게도, 피험자의 약 65%가 전기 충격이 강도가 치명적인 수준이 될 때까지도 계속해서 전기 충격 주었다.

실험은, 그것이 스스로는 잘못된 일을 하는 것이라고 느끼는 때에도, 대부분의 사람이 권력에 대해 대단히 강력하게 복종하기를 원한다는 사실을 밝혔다. 우리의 결정에 있어서의 도덕성과 그것의 지배력에 대한 심리학자들의 생각을

바꾸었고, 심리학 실험들이 행해지는 방식도 바꾸었다. 실험이 끝난 뒤, 밀그램은 피험자들에게 실험의 원래 목적과, 실제로는 아무도 해치지 않았다는 것을 이야기해 주었다. 이럼에도 불구하고, 많은 피험자들은 그들의 행동에 대해 깊은 죄책감을 계속 느꼈고, 심각한 정서적 압박을 경험했다. 이와 같은 실험은, 그것이 끼칠 수 있는 심리적인 손상 때문에, 더 이상 시행되지 않는다.

✉ Words

☐ be tried for ~혐의로 재판을 받다
☐ humanity 인간애, 인도적임
☐ concentration camp 강제 수용소
☐ readiness 준비성
☐ electric shock 전기충격
☐ incredibly 대단히, 믿을 수 없을 정도로
☐ subject 피험자
☐ lethal 치명적인
☐ conduct 행하다
☐ morality 도덕성

•• 해 설 ••

1. "this"는 대부분 앞서 언급된 내용을 가리키므로, 여기서의 "this question"은 바로 앞줄에 나온 질문인 "How could one explain the readiness of such large numbers of people to hurt and kill other people?"을 가리킨다.

2. 여기서의 "The subjects"가 앞서 언급된 사람들 즉, "People (who) were asked to participate in an experiment testing how memory worked"를 가리킨다는 것을 이해한다면, 이로부터 이 단어의 일반적 의미를 짐작해 볼 수 있다.

3. 지문에 여러 번 언급되어 있듯이, 실험 대상들의 질문을 받고 틀릴 때마다 더 강한 전기 충격을 받는다고 알려진 사람들은 연기자들이며 녹음된 비명 소리를 사용했을 뿐, 실제 충격이 가해지진 않았다.

4. 실험에 참가한 사람들이 Milgram에게 실험을 중단해도 되냐고 물은 것은, 그들이 상대편 사람들이 고통스러워 지른다고 생각했던 비명 소리를 들었을 때였으며, 이로부터 이들이 상대편 사람들을 다치게 하고 싶지 않아 했다는 것을 추론할 수 있다.

5. 주어진 문맥상 단서는 찾을 수 없지만, 내용으로 보아 전기 충격이 사람에게 줄 수 있는 최후의 단계임을 짐작할 수 있다. (C)는 (D)가 없으면 답이 될 수 있지만 "lethal"은 사람을 죽일 수 있을 정도로 대단히 위험한 상태를 가리키므로 "deadly"에 가까운 의미이다.

6. 본 문장은 다음의 세 의미 단위로 나뉘어 진다. "이 실험은 밝혀 주었다 / 대부분 사람들은 권위에 복종하고자 하는 대단히 강한 열망을 가지고 있다는 것을 / 그들이 하는 일이 개인적으로는 잘못된 것이라고 느껴질 때조차도" 이 모든 의미 단위의 내용을 누락하지 않고 정확히 담고 있는 보기를 고르면 된다. "wish to obey authority"가 "urge to follow orders"와 같은 의미라는 것, "immoral"이 '옳지 않다고 생각되는 것'을 의미한다는 것을 이해해야 한다.

7. 마지막 문장인 "Experiments like this are no longer performed because of the psychological damage they can cause."에

명확하게 제시되어 있다. "psychological damage"와 "emotional suffering"이 같은 의미를 내포한다는 것을 이해해야 한다.

8. 문맥의 내용상, 심리 실험이 '실행되는' 방법이 변했다고 보는 것이 타당하다. 가장 답에 가깝게 보이는 (B)의 "studied"는 실험이 연구되는 대상이 아니므로 답이 될 수 없다.

9. 주어진 문장은 "다시 말하지만, 이 사람은 연기자이며 실제로 고통을 당하진 않았다."이다. 다시 말한다고 했으므로 위의 내용이 전에 한번 언급된 후여야 한다. 하지만 **B**에 위치한다면, 앞 문장에서 말했던 내용을 곧바로 반복하는 것이 되기 때문에 자연스럽지 않으며, 반복될수록 더 높아가는 비명 소리가 언급된 후인 **C**에 위치하는 것이 적합하다.

10. 본문의 내용을 알맞게 요약하고 있는 것은 (B), (C), (E)이다. (A)는 실험의 결과가 비 인류적 범죄를 저지른 나치 지도자들의 판결을 내리기 위해 사용된 것은 아니었고, (D)는 실험에 참가한 사람들은 자신들이 고통을 주고 있다고 믿고 있던 사람들이 연기자들이라는 것을 몰랐기 때문에 틀린 내용이며, (F)는 전기 충격이 가해지는 실험이 없어지게 된 것이 아니라, 심리적인 고통을 줄 수 있는 실험을 없애는 결과를 가져온 것이기 때문에 각각 틀린 답이다.

Reading 2:   종말의 신화

언뜻 보면, 세계의 여러 많은 종교들은 공통점이 거의 없는 것처럼 보인다. 힌두교와 아메리카 원주민들의 종교에서는 신이 많은 반면, 크리스트교, 이슬람교, 유태교는 유일신에 대한 믿음을 표현한다. 이런 종교들의 규칙과 관습 역시 매우 다르다. 크리스트교인들은 매 일요일에 교회에 가고 먹는 것에 대해 기본적으로 제한이 없지만, 회교도들은 매일 다섯 번 기도하고, 알코올이나 돼지고기를 먹으면 안 된다. 세계 종교들의 차이점이 많은 것처럼, 몇 가지 흥미로운 유사점도 있다.

많은 종교들 사이의 가장 흥미로운 유사성 중의 하나는 놀랄 만큼 비슷한 종말의 신화이다. 과거 또는 현재의 거의 모든 큰 종교에서 기본 이야기는 본질적으로 같다. 이 이야기에 따르면, 세상의 종말 뒤에는 인류의 가장 최악인 면을 보여줄 전쟁의 시기와 전반적인 무법 상태가 따른다고 한다. 이 뒤에는 대부분 또는 전체의 세상을 파괴할 엄청난 재앙이 올 것이라고 한다. 이 재앙의 원인은 종교마다 다르지만, 세상이 멸망하고 인류의 작은 일부만이 살아남을 것이라는 결과는 언제나 같다. 마지막으로, 신의 우두머리나 그의 사자가 질서를 되살리고, 세상을 다시 만들기 위해 지상에 나타난다. 세상이 종말하고 다시 새롭게 된 후면, 인류는 평화와 완벽 속에 살 것이다.

물론 모든 종말 신화가 똑같지는 않다. 크리스트교인들은 세상의 종말이 한 번 있을 것이라고 믿는데 반해, 힌두교인들은 파괴와 재생의 순환을 믿는다. 그렇지만 일부 연구자들이 많은 종교의 신화가 사실은 하나의 뿌리를 갖고 있다고 결론짓게 할 정도로, 그 차이보다는 유사성이 훨씬 중대하다. 이 이론에 따르면, 수천 년 전 언젠가 공통의 종교를 갖는 사람들이 살았었다. 이 사람들이 새로운 곳으로 이주하면서 그들은 그들의 종교를 가지고 갔다. 시간이 흐름에 따라, 이 종교는 지역에 따라 서로 달라지기 시작했고, 결국 오늘날 우리가 알고 있는 종교들을 형성했다. 이 이론은 결코 완벽하지 않다. 인류 역사의 언제부터 이 공통의 종교가 분화되기 시작했는가와 같은, 그것이 답하지 못하는 여러 의문점들이 남아 있다. 그러나 이것은 세계의 사람들에게 서로의 차이를 바라보는 새로운 방식을 제공했다.

✉ Words

☐ glance 얼핏 봄
☐ Judaism 유태교
☐ numerous 많은
☐ likeness 유사성
☐ precede ~에 앞서다
☐ rebirth 재생
☐ outweigh ~보다 훨씬 중대하다. ~보다 더 크다

☐ Hinduism 힌두교
☐ restriction 제한
☐ startling 흥미로운, 아주 놀라운
☐ apocalypse myth 종말의 신화
☐ restore 되살리다, 회복하다
☐ diverge 분화하다, 갈라지다

•• 해 설 ••

11. Muslim을 Christian과 대조하여 설명하면서, Muslim이 할 수 없는 것들을 제시했으므로, 반대로 앞의 Christian들은 이런 '할 수 없는 것(제한)'들이 없다는 내용임을 짐작해 볼 수 있다.

12. 어떤 종교이던 간에 "apocalypse myths"가 놀랍도록 비슷하다고 제시하고서, 이 설에 따른 비슷한 여러 종교의 세계 종말 신화에 대해서 설명하고 있다는 것을 참조하여 알맞은 보기를 고른다.

13. 공통된 종말 신화의 특성이 아닌 것을 고르는 문제이다. 세상을 재건하기 위하여 "the head god" 혹은 "a messenger"가 재림한다고 했지, "new gods"가 나타난다고 하지 않았음을 유의하자.

14. 17째 줄 이하 "Christians believe that the end of the world will come once, while Hidus believe in a cycle of destruction and rebirth."에 제시되어 있다. "a sequence of apocalypses and renewals"가 "a cycle of destruction and rebirth"와 같은 의미라는 것을 이해해야 한다.

15. 주어진 문장은 다음과 같은 세 개의 의미 단위로 구성되어 있다. "그러나 유사점들이 차이점들을 훨씬 능가하는 것으로 보인다 / 이것은 몇몇 연구원들로 하여금 다음과 같이 결론 내리게 했는데 / 아마도 많은 종교의 전설은 공통의 기원을 가지고 있다고" 유사점이 차이점을 훨씬 능가한다는 말이 유사점이 차이점보다 훨씬 명백해 보인다는 말과 같은 뜻이라는 것을 이해해야 한다. 가장 답에 가까운 (A)는 많은 종교가 신화라고 결론 짓게 했다는 것이 틀린 해석이며, 따라서 답이 될 수 없다.

16. 앞에서 현재 많은 종교가 원래는 하나의 종교에서 갈라졌다(Over time, this religion began to change in different areas)고 하면서, 어느 시점에서 "diverge" 하였는지에 관해서는 대답할 수 없다고 하였다. 따라서 이 단어가 '갈라지다'의 의미임을 추측할 수 있다.

17. 현대의 여러 종교가 통합된 하나의 고대 종교에서 왔다고 주장한 이론의 결점을 묻는 문제이다. 23째 줄의 "The theory is far from perfect." 이하의 내용을 보면, 어느 시점에서 이 하나의 종교가 갈라지기 시작했는지에 대한 물음에는 답할 수 없다고 한 것을 확인 해 볼 수 있다.

18. 주어진 문장은 "이 이론을 더욱 뒷받침하는 것은 한때는 하나의 문화가

존재했으며, 많은 세계의 언어가 하나의 같은 언어로부터 진화해 왔다는 사실이다."이며 이는 어떤 이론을 뒷받침하는 설명임을 알 수 있다. 따라서 본문에 제시된 특정 이론 뒤에 와야 하며, "further support"라는 말에서 또 다른 증거가 앞서 제시되었어야 한다는 것을 알 수 있다. **C** 다음 문장은 이미 이 이론에 관한 평가를 내리고 있으므로, 이 뒤에 위치할 수는 없다.

19. 종말의 신화를 소개하고 있는 이 글은 (B)와 (D)에서의 이 신화의 정의와 내용에서 시작하여, 유사한 종말론으로부터 도출해 낼 수 있는 이론인 (E)로 전개하고 있다. 세계의 다른 종교에 다른 점도 있다는 것은 이에 따르는 부연 설명에 불과하기 때문에 (A)와 (C)는 답이 될 수 없으며 (F)의 고대 유일 종교 이론에는 답할 수 없는 많은 의문점이 있기 때문에, 사람들이 그들 종교의 차이점보다 유사점이 중요하다는 것을 깨닫게 해준다는 설명은 본문에 언급되어 있지 않다.

Reading 3:   판구조론

　　1960년대에, 과학자들은 지각이 하나의 조각으로 되어 있지 않고, 기본적으로 지구 깊이 있는 넓은 용암 위에 떠 있는 여러 개의 조각, 또는 판으로 이루어져 있다는 사실을 발견했다. 이것은 지질학에 있어서, 생물학에 있어서의 다윈(Darwin)의 진화에 대한 발견과 비견할 만한 것이었다. 판구조론이라고 불리는, 그로부터 발전한 이론은 현대 지질학의 기반을 형성한다.

　　판구조론에 따르면, 현재 지각은 14개의 주요 판과, 여러 다른 작은판으로 나뉘어 있다. 이런 판들은 대륙판과 해양판으로 구분될 수 있다. 그 이름이 암시하듯, 두 종류의 판은 주요 대륙과 해저를 이루고 있다. 해양판들은 더 무거운 광물들로 되어 있으므로 그 밑의 용암에 더 깊숙이 가라앉기 때문에 더 아래쪽에 존재한다. 판구조론을 뒷받침하는 중심 개념은 비록 대단히 느린 속도지만 이런 지각 판들이 이동하고 있으며, 이 움직임이 지진에서 산맥의 형성에 이르기까지 다른 거의 대부분의 지질학적 사건들을 설명해 준다는 것이다.

　　판들은 기본적으로 세 가지의 양상으로 움직인다. **A** 어떤 판들은 북아메리카 판의 시쪽 경계와 대평양판의 동쪽 경계가 그런 것과 같이, 서로에 대해서 미끄러진다. 이 미끄러짐은 그러나, 부드러운 움직임이 아니다. **B** 대부분의 지진에 대한 원인은 바로 이 움직임 때문이다. 다른 판들은 서로에게서 멀어진다. 서로 멀어지게 되면서, 그들이 만드는 틈을 메우기 위해 용암이 지구 중심의 중요한 광물들을 싣고 올라오게 된다. **C**

　　움직임의 마지막 형태는 두 판이 충돌할 때이다. **D** 이것은 가장 복잡한 움직임 종류인데, 그 영향은 충돌하는 판의 종류에 따라 달라진다. 대륙판과 해양판이 충돌할 경우, 해양판은 대륙판 아래로 자연스럽게 섭입되는데, 이것은 해양판이 더 무거운 광물로 되어 있기 때문이다. 이는 대륙판의 해변을 따라 여럿의 화산이 있는 산맥을 형성시킨다. 두 개의 해양판이 충돌할 경우, 하나의 판이 다른 판의 아래쪽으로 섭입되며 화산이 형성된다. 이런 해저 화산은 결국 일본과 하와이 같은 열도를 형성한다. 마지막으로, 두 대륙판이 충돌할 경우, 서로 융기되며 히말라야와 같은 내륙의 높은 산맥을 만든다.

✉ **Words**
- plate tectonics 판구조론
- geology 지질학
- molten 녹은
- collide 충돌하다
- lava 용암
- imply 암시하다
- drift 이동하다. 움직이다

•• 해 설 ••

20. 지질학에 있어 판구조론(plate tectonics)이 생물학에서 다윈의 진화론과 같다고 했다. 생물학에서 진화론이 매우 중요한 역할을 차지한다는 것을 이해하면, 쉽게 답을 찾을 수 있다. 또한 다음 문장 "The theory forms the basis of modern geology."에서 판구조론이 명확히 현대 지질학의 기초 역할을 한다고 진술되어 있다.

21. "plate tectonics"란 본문에 전반적으로 설명된 판구조론이며, 이 이론이 설명하는 현상과 이것이 미치는 영향을 모두 포괄하는 보기를 골라야 한다.

22. 이 단어가 있는 문장에 따르면 '대륙판과 해양판으로 분류되는 이 이름들이 "imply"하는 것처럼 이 판들은 주요 대륙과 대양을 구성한다'고 했으므로, 문맥의 내용상 이것이 '암시하다'의 "suggest"의 뜻에 가장 가까움을 짐작 할 수 있다.

23. 주어진 문장은 다음과 같은 세 개의 의미 단위로 나뉠 수 있다. "판구조론의 중심 개념은 / 비록 아주 느리기는 하지만, 지구의 판들이 움직이고 있고 / 이 움직임이 지진에서부터 산맥의 형성까지 거의 모든 지질학적 현상을 설명할 수 있다는 것이다" 따라서, 모든 의미 단위의 정확한 내용을 모두 담고 있는 것은 (B)뿐이다. "major geological events"가 "nearly every other geological event, from earthquakes to the formation of mountains"의 내용을 의미한다는 것을 이해해야 한다. 가장 답으로 착각하기 쉬운 (C)는 이 현상이 지진과 산의 형성만 설명한다고 했으므로 답이 될 수 없다.

24. 본문에서 설명하고 있는 판구조론의 중심 내용이 지구는 판으로 이루어져 있고, 이들은 계속해서 움직이고 있다는 것을 파악한다면, 지구의 지리학적 특성이 고정되어 변하지 않는다고 한 (B)는 쉽게 답이 아니라는 것을 알 수 있다.

25. 판이 기본적으로 세 방법으로 움직일 수 있다는 내용을 제시하고 있는 이 문단의 내용에 따르면, 북아메리카의 서쪽 끝과 태평양의 동쪽 끝이 충돌해 많은 지진을 일으킨다고 했다. (A)는 본 문단에서 충분한 근거를 찾을 수 없는 추론이며, (B)와 (D)는 이 문단에서 언급되지 않은 내용이다.

26. 일반적으로 others는 some과 짝을 이루어 사용된다. 12째 줄의 "Some plates"는 서로 같은 방향으로 충돌하며 일어나는 현상이며, 두 번째 이동 방법으로 "others"가 반대 방향으로 이동하는 것이므로 "others"가 "other (tectonic) plates"를 의미함을 알 수 있다.

27. 17째 줄 이하의 "This is the most complex type of movement, and its effects depend on the type of plates that are colliding. ..."의 내용에 따르면, 판의 충돌이 가장 복잡한 형태라고 하면서 이때 일어나는 현상의 여러 가지 예를 들었다. 어느 판이 어떤 경로로 충돌하느냐에 따라 여러 다양한 결과를 가져 올 수 있다는 점을 참조하여 정답을 고르자.

28. 주어진 문장은 "이 두 판이 서로 마찰을 일으키며, 압력을 쌓아 가다가 갑작스럽게 움직여 빠른 경련을 일으킨다."이다. 판이 움직이는 세 가지 방법 중, 위의 문장은 두 판이 서로를 향해 움직이는 첫 번째 방법에 해당하며, 이 설명이 지진이 일어나는 과정임을 이해한다면 지진에 대해 언급되기 전인 **B**의 자리에 들어가야 함을 알 수 있다. 또한, 이 현상이 "a smooth motion"이 아니라고 전제하고 있는 문장 뒤에 위치해야 자연스럽게 이어질 것이다.

29.
- Located only in North America: 본문에서 언급되지 않은 내용이다.
- Commonly associated with volcanoes: 20-22째 줄을 참조하면, 화산은 거의 대양 판이 충돌할 때 생김을 알 수 있다.
- Made of lighter materials: 18-20째 줄 참조. 해양 판이 더 무거운 물질로 구성되어 있다고 했으므로 대륙판이 더 가벼운 물질로 이루어져 있을 것임을 알 수 있다.
- Involved in island formation: 21-24째 줄 참조.
- Rise up to form mountain chains: 20-21째 줄 참조. 대륙판과 해양판이 충돌하면, 대륙판의 해안가가 산맥이 된다.
- Usually pushed under in plate collisions: 19째 줄 참조.
- Responsible for most earthquakes: 지진을 일으키는 판이 대륙판인지 해양판인지 구분되어 언급되지 않았다.

Actual Test ❸ p.206

1. (B)	2. (B)	3. (A)	4. (B)	5. (B)
6. (C)	7. (D)	8. (A)	9. **A**	

10. Pluto
- Most distant planet
- Existence inferred before actual discovery

Uranus
- Irregular orbit
- Easily seen with telescope
- First discovered through direct observation

11. (B)	12. (B)	13. (C)	14. (A)	15. (B)
16. (C)	17. (A)	18. (C)	19. **B**	
20. (B), (D), (F)	21. (C)	22. (B)	23. (D)	
24. (B)	25. (B)	26. (C)	27. (A)	28. **C**

29. Drywood Termites
- Fewer soldiers
- Smaller colonies

Subterranean Termites
- Colonies harder to locate
- Cannot live in desert environments
- Must travel to food source

Reading 1: 명왕성의 발견

첫 여섯 개의 행성들은 인류에게 유사 이래 알려져 있었다. **A** 그러나 천왕성, 해왕성, 그리고 명왕성의 마지막 세 행성은 망원경의 도움 없이는 밤하늘에서 볼 수가 없다. **B** 그들의 발견은 망원경이 발명될 때까지 기다려야 했었다. 일곱 번째 행성인 천왕성은 1781년 윌리엄 허셜(William Herschel)에 의해 처음으로 발견되었다. **C** 천왕성의 발견은 중요한 비약적 진보였는데, 천왕성 궤도의 돌발적인 변화에 대한 연구는 또 다른 미지의 행성이 천왕성의 궤도에 영향을 줄 것이라는 추측을 낳았기 때문이다. 그 미지의 행성은 해왕성임이 입증되었다. 그것은 1846년, 우주의 어디쯤 해왕성이 있는지는 천왕성 궤도의 비정상에 기반하여 계산한 결과 발견되었다. 이 두 행성의 발견은 천왕성과 해왕성 모두 가스로 된 지구 크기의 몇 배나 되는 거대한 행성이었기 때문에, 상대적으로 쉬웠다. 이것은 18세기와 19세기의 망원경만으로도 비교적 그들을 발견하기 쉽도록 만들었다.

아홉 번째 행성인 명왕성을 발견하는 것은, 그것이 우리의 달의 크기만큼도 되지 않고 또 수천 배나 멀리 떨어져 있기 때문에, 매우 어려운 작업이었다. 역시, 이 행성의 존재에 대한 첫 번째 단서는 다른 행성들의 궤도에서부터 나왔다. 해왕성의 연구 후, 그것이 천왕성의 모든 궤도 변화를 설명하는데 충분하지 않아 보였다. 과학자들은 그 바깥에 다른 행성이 있을 것이라고 예상했으나 찾을 수는 없었다. 그들은 그 미지의 행성을 "X 행성(planet X)"이라고 불렀다. X 행성을 발견하기 위한 첫 번째의 진지한 시도는, 1915년 퍼씨벌 로웰(Percival Lowell)이라는 천문학자가 그 행성을 찾는 것을 그의 사명으로 삼았을 때였다. 로웰은 일년이 넘도록 밤하늘을 연구했다. 그는 700개가 넘는 별들을 포함해, 많은 다른 것들을 발견했다. 그러나 그는 미지의 행성을 발견하지 못하고, 실망한 채로 사망했다.

성공은 1930년 클라이드 톰보(Clyde Tombaugh)가 그 행성을 찾기 위해 새로운 방법을 사용함으로써 왔다. 그는 수천 장의 밤하늘 사진을 찍었다. 그는 밤하늘에서 고정되어 있는 별들과 반대로 움직이고 있는 미지의 대상을 살폈다. 이런 방법을 통해 그는 작은 불빛 점을 발견했고, 그것이 명왕성임이 밝혀졌다.

✉ **Words**

☐ Pluto 명왕성   ☐ Uranus 천왕성
☐ Neptune 해왕성   ☐ telescope 망원경
☐ breakthrough 비약적 진보   ☐ infer 추론하다, 암시하다
☐ abnormality 비정상, 이상   ☐ label 부르다, 이름을 붙이다
☐ astronomer 천문학자

•• 해 설 ••

1. "this"는 대부분 바로 앞에 언급된 내용을 가리키는 대명사이다. 여기서는 바로 앞 문장에 언급된 천왕성의 발견을 말한다.

2. 5-7째 줄의 "because by studying unexpected changes in the planet's orbit, ...in Uranus' orbit, which told scientists where in the sky to look for Neptune"과 13째 줄 이하 "Again, the first clues to the planet's existence came from the orbits of other planets. ..."의 내용에 따르면, 해왕성과 명왕성이 존재는 모두 천왕성의 궤도 연구를 통해 알 수 있었다.

3. 천왕성의 발견이 중요한 "breakthrough"라고 한 이유가 '다른 행성들의 존재를 알아 낼 수 있었기 때문(because by studying unexpected changes in the planet's orbit, scientists could infer that it was being affected by the gravity of another, unknown planet)'이라는 것을 참조하여 가장 적절한 보기를 고른다.

4. "abnormalities"의 자리에 보기들을 대입해 보고 본문의 내용상 가장 적절하게 설명 할 수 있는 뜻을 고른다. 문맥상 천왕성 궤도의 변칙적인 행로에 대해 연구하다가 해왕성의 존재를 알 수 있었다는 것이 이 문장의 내용이라는 것을 참조하자.

5. 주어진 문장은 다음 두 개의 의미 단위로 나눌 수 있다. "이 두 행성의 발견은 상대적으로 쉬운 것이었다 / 왜냐하면 천왕성과 해왕성 모두 가스로 된 지구 보다 수 배가 더 큰 거대한 행성이기 때문이다" 이 두 의미 단위를 누락하거나 왜곡하지 않고 정확하게 담고 있는 보기를 고른다. (A)의 "only possible"은 문장의 의미를 왜곡시키며, (C)와 (D)는 모두 주어의 내용이 문장의 의미를 왜곡하고 있다.

6. 10-11째 줄의 "This made them relatively easy to find, even with the telescopes of the 18th and 19th centuries."에서, '심지어 18, 19세기의 망원경으로도 발견할 수 있었다'고 표현한 것으로부터 이때의 망원경 성능이 그다지 좋지 않음을 추론할 수 있다.

7. 12째 줄 이하의 "Finding the ninth planet, Pluto, proved to be a much harder task because it is not even as large as our moon,"에 따르면, 명왕성이 우리의 달보다도 작아서 더욱 발견하기 힘들었다고 했다.

8. 천왕성의 변칙 궤도로 인해 존재가 밝혀지고, 1915년 Percival Lowell이 처음 시도하고 1930년 Clyde Tombaugh에 의해 발견되기까지. 명왕성의 발견은 오랜 많은 연구 끝에 가능했다.

9. 주어진 문장은 "고대 문명은 이것들이 행성인지는 몰랐지만, 그것들은 하늘에서 육안으로 분명히 볼 수 있었다." 이다. 이는 육안으로 볼 수 있던(clearly visible) 행성에 관해 언급하고 있는 문장이므로, 이와는 반대로 망원경이 있어야 볼 수 있던(not visible in the night sky without the help of a telescope) 행성이 대조되어 설명되고 있는 문장인 "But the final three planets, Uranus, Neptune, and Pluto, ..." 앞에 와야 글이 자연스럽게 이어질 수 있다.

10. • Irregular orbit: 5-6째 줄 참조
    • Easily seen with telescope: 3-4, 10-11째 줄 참조
    • Most distant planet: 14째 줄 참조
    • Extremely strong gravity: 언급되지 않은 내용이다.
    • First discovered through direct observation: 3-4째 줄 참조
    • Can only be seen when moving: 언급되지 않은 내용이다.
    • Existence inferred before actual discovery: 15-16째 줄 참조

Reading 2:   세계 인구와 기후 변화

여러 면에서, 점점 더 급격해지는 기후 변화는 인구 증가의 직접적인 결과이다. Ⓐ 지난 100년간, 인구 변화는 세기초에 20억 명 이하에서 오늘날 70억 명에 이르도록 세 배가 넘도록 증가했다. Ⓑ 게다가, 100년전 1인당 평균 에너지 및 천연 자원의 소비량보다 현대의 1인당 평균 소비량이 훨씬 더 높다. 다시 말해, 실제 인구 증가율보다 에너지 소비 증가율이 훨씬 더 높다는 뜻이다. Ⓒ 예를 들어, 최초의 원유 1조 배럴을 사용하는데 125년이 걸렸다. 다음 1조 배럴을 사용하는 데에는, 3배가 아닌 5배가 빠른, 30년 미만이 걸릴 것이다. Ⓓ

식량 생산, 에너지 사용, 천연 자원의 이용 등의 모든 활동은 어떤 방법으로든 기후 변화를 야기한다. 에너지를 생성하기 위한 더 많은 양의 원유와 다른 연료의 연소는 지구 온난화를 악화시키는 화학 물질을 방출한다. 더 많은 식량을 생산하기 위해서, 농부들은 더 넓은 땅을 확보하려고 나무를 베어 낸다. 더군다나, 우리는 더 많은 인구를 위한 주택을 건설하기 위해서 나무를 베어 낸다. 그런 나무들은 지구 온난화를 통제하는 데에 있어 핵심적인 부분이다. 이것들은 증가하는 인구가 지구 온난화에 미치는 영향의 단순한 두 가지의 예일 뿐이고, 다른 예들은 너무 많아 일일이 언급할 수 없다.

인구 증가에 더해서, 세계에는 과거보다 더 높은 삶의 질을 열망하는 인구가 있으며 삶의 질을 높이기 위해서 더 많은 천연 자원의 소비를 필요로 한다. 한 나라를 살펴보면 이 사실에 대한 명확한 예를 줄 수 있다. 중국은 13억 인구

의, 세계에서 가장 인구가 많은 나라이다. 현재, 이 대부분 사람들의 삶의 수준은 제1세계 사람들보다 훨씬 아래에 있다. 그러므로, 평균적인 중국 시민은 평균적인 미국이나 일본 시민보다 훨씬 적은 천연자원과 에너지를 사용한다. 그러나 중국의 세력은 점점 커지고 있으며, 더욱 더 많은 중국인들이 제1세계의 생활양식을 기대하기 시작하고 있다. 만약 중국인들이 제1세계의 생활양식을 달성할 경우, 세계 다른 나라의 삶의 수준이 현재와 같은 정도를 유지하더라도, 전세계의 에너지와 천연 자원 요구량은 두 배가 될 것이다.

✉ **Words**

☐ triple 세배가 되다   ☐ consumption 소비

☐ trillion 1조   ☐ currently 현재

☐ standard of living 삶의 질, 생활수준   ☐ attain 달성하다, 이루다

☐ populous 인구가 많은

•• 해 설 ••

11. "pace"의 자리에 각각의 보기를 대입해 보고 가장 적절한 것을 찾는다. 이 문장이 이 글의 중심 문장이므로 전체 내용을 이해한다면 더욱 도움이 될 것이다.

12. 평균적으로 개인이 연료와 천연자원을 100년 전보다 더 많이 사용한다는 것이, 인구의 증가보다 "consumption" 비율이 더 높다는 것을 의미한다는 문장의 내용을 참고하여 가장 적절한 표현을 고른다.

13. 11-14째 줄 "In order to produce more food, farmers cut down trees to gain more land for their fields. ... Those trees are an essential part of controlling global warming."의 내용에서 확인할 수 있다.

14. 6-8째 줄 "For example, it took the world 125 years to use... which is almost five times as fast, not three."에서 3배로 증가하는 인구수에 비해 석유는 거의 5배의 빠른 비율로 사용된다는 사실을 제시하며, 자원이 인구 증가의 속도보다 훨씬 더 빠른 속도로 소비되고 있음을 나타내고 있다.

15. 이것들은 두 개의 "examples of the impacts that the growing population has on global warming"에 불과하며, '다른 것'들은 너무 많아 언급할 수 없다고 했으므로 이것이 '다른 예들'을 가리킴을 알 수 있다.

16. 16-18째 줄 "In addition to a growing population, the world also has a population... requires the use of even more natural resources."에서 더 높은 생활 수준이 더 많은 천연 자원의 사용을 요구한다고 선명하게 언급되어 있다.

17. 주어진 문장은 다음과 같은 세 개의 의미 단위로 구성되어 있다. "만약 모든 중국인들이 제1세계의 생활양식을 갖는다면 / 연료와 천연자원의 전세계적인 수요량은 두 배가 될 것이다 / 지구상의 다른 모든 나라의 생활 수준이 오늘날과 똑같이 유지된다 하더라도" 이 세 의미 단위의 내용을 모두 정확히 포함하고 있는 표현을 고른다. "the standard of living in

---

every other nation on Earth remains the same as it is today" 가 "all other nations keep their current standard of living"과 같은 의미임을 이해해야 한다.

18. 생활 수준이 연료 소비에 미치는 영향을 설명하기 위해, 글쓴이는 가장 인구가 많은 나라인 중국이 일본이나 미국과 같은 높은 생활 수준을 갖게 될 경우의 예를 들었다.

19. "명백히 이것은 세계가 세 배 더 많은 식량, 연료와 천연자원을 필요로 하게 되었다는 것을 의미한다."가 주어진 문장이다. 논리적으로 볼 때 인구가 세 배로 늘어남에 따라 인류가 소비하는 자원도 세 배가 더 필요할 것이므로, 이것의 내용이 인구가 세 배로 늘어난 것을 지칭한다는 것을 알 수 있으며, 주어진 문장은 이 내용이 나온 뒤에 위치하는 것이 알맞다.

20. 본문은 기후 변화에 많은 영향을 미치는 요인을 세 가지로 설명하고 있다. 즉, ①자원의 사용은 인구가 증가함과 함께 늘어났고, ②개인이 사용하는 연료의 양도 옛날보다 더 많아졌으며, 또한, ③생활 수준이 높아짐에 따라 더 많은 연료를 사용함으로 지구 온난화를 일으킨다고 했다. 따라서 각각의 내용을 포함하고 있는 (B), (D), (F)가 답이다. (A)는 부연 설명일 뿐이며, (C)와 (E)는 언급되지 않은 내용이다.

Reading 3:   흰개미

흰개미(termites)는, 나무를 먹이로 삼는 작고 개미처럼 생긴 작은 곤충이다. 그것들은 종종 "흰개미(white ants)" 또는 "날개미"로 불리기도 하지만, 실제로는 개미가 아니다. **A** 그러나 그들은 모든 군거성 곤충들과 많은 공통의 특징을 공유하고 있다. **B** 개미나 벌과 같이, 흰개미 군체에는 모든 알을 낳는 여왕개미, 군체의 대부분의 일을 하는 일개미, 그리고 다른 곤충들로부터 군체를 보호하는 병정개미들이 있다. **C** 흰개미의 종류에 따라, 한 군체에 수천에서 수백만 마리의 흰개미가 살 수 있다. **D** 흰개미 군체가 너무 과밀화되면, 일부의 흰개미들은 날개를 발달시켜 새로운 군체를 만들기 위해 날아간다. 흰개미들은 살아 있는 나무보다 소화시키기 좋기 때문에 죽은 나무를 먹는다. 이것은 벌목 업자들에게는 좋은 소식이지만, 집을 만드는데 사용하는 목재가 흰개미들에게 맛있는 먹이가 되기 때문에, 가구주들에게는 분명히 나쁜 소식이다. 이런 이유로 인해서, 흰개미는 보통 해충으로 여겨진다. 가장 문제를 많이 일으키는 흰개미는 건조목재흰개미(drywood termites)와 지중흰거미(subterranean termites)이다.

건조목재흰거미는 그들이 먹는 나무에서 모든 수분을 취하는 능력을 따라서 이름 붙여졌다. 그러므로, 그들은 매우 건조한 기후에서도 살 수 있다. 그들은 먹이인 나무 속에 직접 군체를 지으며, 따라서 그 결과, 그들의 군체는 군체의 건설을 위해 더 큰공간을 갖는 지중흰거미에 비해서 일반적으로 작다. 대부분의 흰개미처럼, 건조목재흰개미도 군체가 과밀화될 경우에만 군체를 떠난다. 군체를 떠나지 않기 때문에 건조목재흰개미들은 지속적으로 군체의 쓰레기를 내버려야 한다. 목재 구조물의 아래에 생기는 밝고, 모래 같은 물질의 더미는 이런 해충의 확실한 증거이다.

지중흰개미는 땅 속에 살며 먹이로 먹는 나무까지 굴을 뚫는다. 그들은 나무에 이르기 위해 군체를 떠나기 때문에, 군체에서 아무 쓰레기를 내 버릴 필요가 없고, 따라서 찾아내기 훨씬 힘들다. 실제로, 이런 흰개미들은 보통 그들이

끼친 피해를 통해서만 발견된다. 지중흰개미들은 신선한 물의 원천을 필요로 하기 때문에 건조한 기후 지역에서는 발견되지 않는다. 땅에 위치하기 때문에, 지중흰개미들은 개미나 다른 곤충들로부터 공격받기가 훨씬 쉽고 따라서 많은 수의 병정개미를 갖고 있다.

•• 해 설 ••

21. 흰개미는 실제로 개미는 아니지만 개미와 공통된 많은 "characteristics" 를 공유한다는 문맥을 참조하며 주어진 보기를 대입하여 가장 적절한 보기를 고른다.

22. 8-9째 줄 "Termites eat dead wood, because it is easier to consume than live wood."에서 흰개미는 살아 있는 나무가 아닌 이미 죽은 나무를 먹는다고 했으므로 흰개미가 나무를 죽인다는 것은 옳지 않다.

23. '산 나무보다 "consume"하기 쉽기 때문에, 죽은 나무를 먹는다'고 했으므로, 문맥상 '먹는다'의 뜻으로 쓰였음을 짐작 할 수 있다.

24. 자기들이 나무로 지은 집을 먹어 버릴 수 있기 때문에 흰개미들은 집주인들에게는 반가운 존재가 아니라고 했다. 이것은 흰개미가 죽은 나무를 먹기 때문에 일으키는 피해이다. 이로 인해 흰개미가 해충으로 여겨진다는 뒤의 내용을 참고하면, 흰개미의 폐해를 설명하기 위해 "home owners"를 언급하고 있음을 알 수 있다.

25. "this"가 가리키는 것은 보통 바로 앞에 언급되는 내용이며, 여기서는 문맥상 흰개미가 일반적으로 해충으로 보여지는 이유를 묻는 것임을 이해하자.

26. 16-17째 줄 "Like most termites, drywood termites only leave their colonies when it has become overcrowded."에 설명되어 있다. "overcrowded"가 "the population becomes too large"와 같은 뜻이라는 것을 이해해야 한다.

27. 17-19째 줄 "Since they do not leave their colony, drywood termites must constantly remove ... are a sure sign of these pests."의 내용에서 흰개미의 분비물의 특성에 대해 추론해 볼 수 있다.

28. 주어진 문장은 "흰개미들은 군체 내에서 각자의 직책에 따라 서로 다른 체형과 몸집을 갖는다."의 뜻이므로, 흰개미가 맡고 있는 여러 직책(jobs)이 나열된 문장 "Like ants and bees, a termite colony has a queen, ... who protect the colony from other insects." 뒤에 오는 것이 가장 자연스럽다.

29. • Cause greater levels of damage: 언급되지 않은 내용이다.

• Colonies harder to locate: 22-23째 줄 참조

• Fewer soldiers: 24-26째 줄 참조, subterranean termites가 침입을 받기 더 쉬워 많은 수의 군인을 가지고 있다고 했다.

• Cannot live in desert environments: 23-24째 줄 참조

• Must travel to food source: 20-21째 줄 참조

• Smaller colonies: 15-17째 줄 참조

• More likely to create new colonies: 언급되지 않은 내용이다.

🔍 시험 상세 : 시험 화면은 다음과 같이 구성되었습니다.

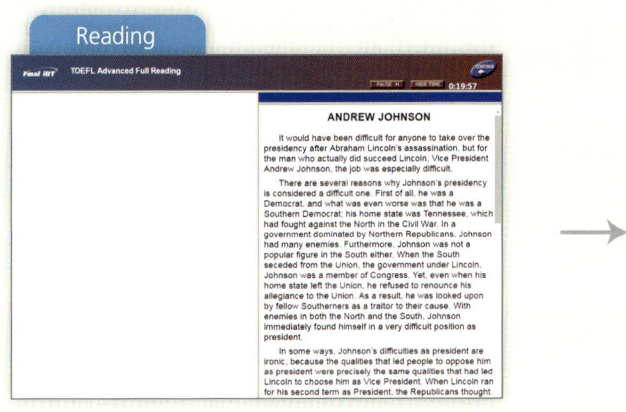

학술적인 내용의 지문을 이해하는 능력을
평가합니다.

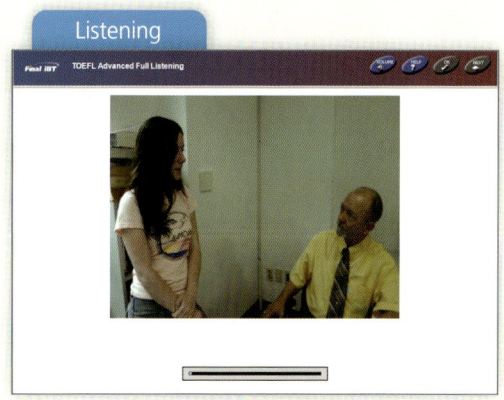

강의, 교실 토론 및 대화를 듣고 이해하는
능력을 평가합니다.

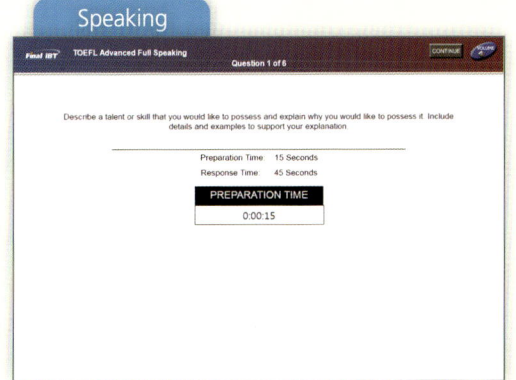

다양한 주제에 대해 말할 수 있는 능력을
평가합니다,

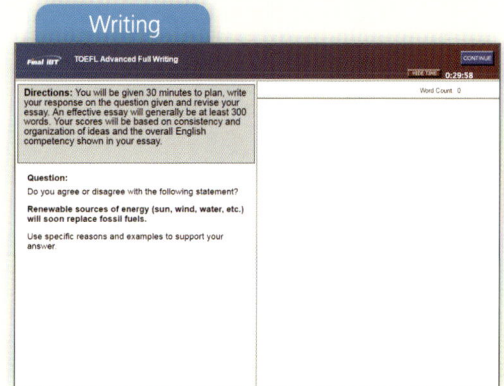

강의내용을 요약하고 자신의 의견을 정리하는
작문능력을 평가합니다.

각각의 모의 테스트를 마친 후 **예상점수를 확인**할 수
있습니다. SPEAKING과 WRITING 점수는 **채점 전문
인력**에 의해 매겨집니다.

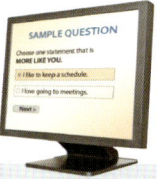

시험 준비 세팅

먼저, 마이크가 있는 헤드셋을 준비해주세요.
그리고 인터넷이 연결된 상태에서 크롬브라우저로 접속하여 시험에 응시하시면 됩니다.

 📞 시험 응시 및 문의 사항 Tel : 02-3483-2786

초급부터 실전까지 토플교재의 바이블

링구아포럼 TOEFL Series

- 아시아 최초로 2003년부터 미국은 물론 전 세계로 영어 교재와 판권 수출
- 온라인 서점 아마존닷컴 토플 판매 1위 (2003년, 2004년)
- 주니어 토플 개념 정의
- 최초 6단계별 토플 시리즈 개발

링구아포럼의 6단계별 토플 교재 eBASIC / e / b / m / i / Hooked on / Insider / Test Book

– eBasic 시리즈를 시작으로 e, b, m, i, Hooked On 순으로 단계가 올라갑니다. 영문 종합서 Insider 와 모의고사집 Test Book이 있습니다.

1 단계 — New Edition eBasic Series

중학교 1~2학년 수준으로 토플을 처음 접하는 학습자를 위한 입문 단계로, iBT의 주제와 형식, 문제유형에 입문 수준의 어휘와 문법으로 구성되었습니다.

〈개정판〉

2 단계 — New Edition e Series

중학교 2~3학년 수준의 토플 학습자를 위해 개발된 두번째 초급 단계이며, iBT의 주제와 형식, 문제유형에 입문 수준의 어휘와 문법으로 구성되었습니다.

〈개정판〉

3 단계 — b Series

중학교 3학년 이상의 영어능력을 가진 학습자를 대상으로 개발. 링구아포럼 eBasic, e 시리즈를 학습한 학습자에서부터, 토플을 처음 접하는 대학생/성인들 모두 토플에 적응하고 중급~고급 단계로 진입할 수 있도록 구성 되었습니다.

4 단계 — m Series

중급 수준(성인 입문)의 토플 학습자를 대상으로 개발. iBT에 등장하는 모든 주제와 문제유형 등을 모두 다루었으며, 실전보다 조금 쉬운 수준으로 연습할 수 있습니다.

〈개정판〉

5 단계 — New Edition i Series

실제 토플 시험을 준비하는 학습자를 대상으로 개발. 링구아포럼 토플 시리즈의 중/고급단계로, iBT에 등장하는 모든 주제와 문제유형 등을 모두 다루었으며, 실전과 거의 유사한 수준으로 연습할 수 있습니다.

6 단계 — New Edition Hooked On Series

실제 토플 시험을 준비하는 학습자를 대상으로 한 고급단계로, iBT에 등장하는 모든 주제와 문제유형등을 모두 다루어,실전과 동일한 수준으로 연습할 수 있습니다.